Communicable Crises

Prevention, Response, and Recovery in the Global Arena

A volume in
Research in Public Management

Series Editors:
L. R. Jones and Nancy C. Roberts
Naval Postgraduate School

Research in Public Management

L. R. Jones and Nancy C. Roberts, Series Editors

Communicable Crises

Prevention, Response, and Recovery in the Global Arena

edited by

Deborah E. Gibbons
Naval Postgraduate School

INFORMATION AGE
PUBLISHING

Charlotte, North Carolina • www.infoagepub.com

Library of Congress Cataloging-in-Publication Data

Communicable crises : prevention, response, and recovery in the global
arena / edited by Deborah E. Gibbons.
     p. cm. — (Research in public management)
  Includes bibliographical references.
  ISBN 978-1-59311-607-1 (pbk.) — ISBN 978-1-59311-608-8 (hardcover)
1. Emergency management. 2. Emergency communication systems. 3.
Emergency management--Case studies. I. Gibbons, Deborah E.

  HV551.2.C634 2007
  363.34--dc22   2006101886

ISBN 13: 978-1-59311-607-1 (pbk.)
         978-1-59311-608-8 (hardcover)
ISBN 10: 1-59311-607-1 (pbk.)
         1-59311-608-X (hardcover)

Printed in the United States of America

CONTENTS

FOREWORD

The International Public Management Network (IPMN) is a forum for sharing ideas, concepts, and research findings relevant to the practice of public management and the management of international organizations. To stimulate critical thinking about alternative approaches to problem solving in the public sector, IPMN convenes its members in annual conferences and workshops. Selected papers presented at these events are published in a book series, in the *International Public Management Journal* and the *International Public Management Review* online.

This book grew out of the IPMN workshop on Communicable Crises: Prevention, Management and Resolution in an Era of Globalization, held at the Peter Wall Institute for Advanced Studies, University of British Columbia, Vancouver, Canada, August 15-17, 2005.

The topic of the workshop was inspired by the SARS epidemic, an event that epitomizes the incredible speed and connectivity of our contemporary world. As Teri Jane Bryant, Ilan Vertinsky, and Carolyne Smart explain in their essay in this volume, what began in a remote corner of the Guangdong Province became a health crisis that affected local communities throughout the world in a matter of days. Even in the United States, where we had only a few SARS patients and no deaths, the SARS epidemic made heavy demands on our public health services, especially the Centers for Disease Control and Prevention.

Of course, the SARS epidemic and the response of local, national, and international institutions to it have considerable intrinsic interest. This is especially the case insofar as it tests the claim that we are unprepared to deal with a major epidemic, whether caused by bioterrorism or by new or reemerging diseases that are resistant to antibiotics.

We were attracted to this case primarily by its extrinsic implications. First of all, the speed with which the disease spread and its novelty, together with its potential for harm, made it a classic case of crisis management, calling for extremely rapid and accurate diagnosis of the situation and the improvisation of an appropriate response.

Second, the epidemic quickly crossed national borders. This made it an international crisis. By definition, international crises call for voluntary, collective responses on the part of a self-organizing, nonhierarchical network. Hence, the case tests the degree to which situation diagnosis and the improvisation of solutions can be carried out effectively in the absence of an all-encompassing formal organization.

Third, the SARS crisis was an epidemic, and epidemics can be modeled and understood. Many students of crisis management pessimistically assert that:

> We see frequent evidence of how crises outstrip the coping capacity of national governments. The modern crisis does not recognize or respect national borders; it thrives on fragmentation and variety. Its complexity defies governmental efforts to understand its causes, pathways, and potential remedies. The modern crisis does not confine itself to a particular policy area (say health or energy); it jumps from one field to the other, unearthing issues and recombining them into unforeseen megathreats. (Boin, 2004, p. 167)

In contrast, if crises can be categorized, then we can make sense of their causes, pathways, and potential remedies. The concept of contagion, the transmission of an influence from one individual to another, for example, occupies an important place both in biology—specifically in mathematical epidemiology—and in the social sciences. Here it is applied to a variety of processes including diffusion of innovations, social unrest, and financial panic. If a significant proportion of international crises really are crises of contagion (with its implication of exponential growth) and this is not merely a colorful metaphor, then we ought to be able to assess the susceptibility of populations to large contagion events and also formulate strategies for managing them.

Ultimately, however, only the first two issues are addressed by this volume, although both Todd LaPorte and Herman Leonard and Arnold Howitt in their essays think long and hard about the problem of classifying crises. Indeed, most of the articles in this volume focus on the problem of designing and installing adaptive systems that can improvise satisfactory solutions when a crisis occurs. Chris Ansell and Jane Gingrich discuss the "theoretical implications for governmental and organizational responses to challenging and uncertain problems." Leonard and Howitt conclude that the " 'Incident Management System' provides a generally useful and flexible framework—suitable in a variety of disaster types—for coordinating diverse emergency response organizations and personnel, many of whom may never have interacted before being cast together in an emergency." Richard A. Braunbeck and Michael F. Mastria identify "concepts, technologies, and protocols that can be used to improve crisis operations on a global scale." Bryant, Vertinsky, and Smart stress the need for crisis management teams made up of individuals with diverse expertise and local knowledge, and the need to redesign crisis management teams to handle political issues and value choices more effectively. Louise K. Comfort calls for the creation of nested, but nonhierarchical, information networks in which all the participants communicate richly with everyone else. Deborah Gibbons reports on research that tends to confirm these conclusions, as does Claudia Siefert in a careful analysis of the New Zealand practice.

Returning briefly to communicable crises, it seems that the kind of organizational response called for by large scale, international crises is a mirror image of the process by which the outbreak of a new disease converts itself into a world-wide pandemic. On one hand, the spread of a disease takes place through channels, hubs, and nodes—its spread is halted by isolating hubs, severing channels, and immunizing nodes. A human agency, which needs to respond rapidly and accurately to crises, must connect hubs, open channels, and activate nodes. What Alastair Roberts shows in his essay is that this is not the natural response. Most governments choose to manage information, especially potentially embarrassing information, a point echoed in several of the essays included in this volume.

Finally, Clay Wescott and Roxanne Zolin and Fredric Kropp in their essays show what to do to mitigate the economic consequences of large-scale crises after they have passed.

This volume makes a significant contribution to the crisis management literature. It also adds to our inchoate understanding of network governance: temporary teams and task forces, communities of practice, alliances, and virtual organizations. It hints that the distinction between networks and organizations may be somewhat spurious, a matter of degree rather than kind. Indeed, it seems that this distinction may derive more from mental models in which we consistently reify organizations than anything else. Finally, the volume emphasizes the functional importance of leadership in network governance and puzzles over its provision in the absence of hierarchy. As such, it adds to the contributions made by Marc Granovetter (1973, 1983), John Seeley Brown and Paul Duguid (1991), Bart Nooteboom (2000), Paul J. DiMaggio (2001), John Arquilla and David Ronfeldt (2001), Laurence O'Toole and Ken Meier (2004), and others, as well as Nancy Roberts' seminal work on wicked problems and hastily formed teams. The result is a product the editor and the contributors can be proud of. Overall, it is one that will edify, surprise, and delight its readers.

Fred Thompson
Grace and Elmer Goudy Professor of
Public Management and Policy
Atkinson Graduate School of Management,
Willamette University, Salem OR 97301 USA

REFERENCES

Arquilla, J., & Ronfeldt, D. (2001). *Networks and Netwars*. Santa Monica, CA: RAND.

Boin, A. (2004). Lessons from crisis research. *International Studies Review, 6*, 165-194.

Brown, J S., & Duguid, P. (1991). Organizational learning and communities of practice: Toward a unified view of working, learning, and innovation, *Organization Science, 2*, 40-57.

DiMaggio, P. J. (Ed.). (2001). *The twenty-first-century firm: Changing economic organization in international perspective*. Princeton, NJ: Princeton University Press.

Granovetter, M. (1973). The strength of weak ties. *American Journal of Sociology, 76*(6), 1360-1380.

Granovetter, M. (1983). The strength of weak ties: A network theory revisited. *Sociological Theory, 1*, 201-233.

Nooteboom, B. (2000). Learning by interaction: Absorptive capacity, cognitive distance and governance. *Journal of Management and Governance, 4*, 69-92.

O'Toole, L., & Meier, K. (2004). Public management in intergovernmental networks: Matching structural networks and managerial networking. *Journal of Public Administration Research and Theory, 14*(4), 469-494.

PREFACE

Deborah E. Gibbons

Increases in movement and commerce throughout the world escalate the danger that transmissible local emergencies, such as disease and manmade disasters, will spread globally. Although many institutions maintain emergency plans, even organizations that make it their business to deal with disasters may not be fully prepared for large-scale crises. Bureaucracies are built to streamline known and expected tasks, not to facilitate creative responses to future unknowns. Governments often cater to their elite, the public, or the media, at the expense of present and future functionality. Businesses have stakeholders to please, and local politicians may be more concerned about the potholes that irritate their constituents than about the possibility of life- and property-threatening disasters. Even nonprofit organizations, which specialize in helping people who face personal or community disasters, may not be adequately prepared to coordinate with other types of organizations in large-scale crises. As the arena for management of communicable crises expands around the globe, more attention to preparation, coordinated response, and effective recovery is warranted.

In this book, we bring together the perspectives of several experts on crisis response. Each chapter highlights crucial facets of crisis preparation, response, or both, with a focus on major, unforeseeable disasters that require more than a standard response. We hope that this work contributes to theorizing and practical applications that strengthen our ability to anticipate and resolve such crises.

I would like to thank the contributors to this book for helping all of us become better prepared to handle communicable crises in the future than we have been in the past. Thanks to the various emergency responders who have shared their insights and allowed us to tell their stories. Finally, thanks to Larry Jones for his guidance and encouragement throughout the project.

CHAPTER 1

AGAINST DESPERATE PERIL

High Performance in Emergency Preparation and Response

Herman B. "Dutch" Leonard and Arnold M. Howitt

How do we best prepare and organize ourselves in advance, and respond in the moment, to the significant natural and man-made disasters governments are often called upon to address? Some of these disruptions occur sufficiently frequently to be "routine emergencies," allowing the development of organizations and routines and the provision of people, skills, equipment, and resources that are well-designed to address the resulting challenges. By contrast, other disasters involve significant levels of novelty (different sources [or combinations of sources] of damage, different scale, or other departures from prior experience that invalidate standard approaches and require rapid improvisation of response activities). Still other major disruptions begin as routine situations and "emerge" as novel crisis emergencies. In this chapter, we examine these different types of emergencies and their implications for the types of actions, the forms of organization, the nature of decision making, and the forms of preparation that are most likely to lead to the most successful outcomes possible in these differing circumstances.

Communicable Crises: Prevention, Response, and Recovery in the Global Arena, pp. 1–25

INTRODUCTION

Governments are routinely called upon to assist when their citizens are confronted by any of a wide variety of disasters—from floods to earthquakes, pandemic disease to terrorist attacks, fires to tornadoes. Governments are especially likely to be called to respond to the kinds of communicable disasters that are the subject of this book: situations still evolving, where damage is continuing, where we are still (and may be for an extended period) in the grip of the unfolding disaster itself, where we have not yet entered into the "aftermath." Because governments will inevitably be expected to meet reasonable standards of performance in these assistance efforts, most modern governments (in the developed world, at least) expend considerable resources and effort to prepare for such events, and respond when events do occur. The long history of societies coping with recurrent tragedy—unpredictable in detail, but distressingly predictable in general pattern—has taught them a great deal about how to arrange response capabilities in advance and how to deploy them effectively in a moment of crisis. For this purpose, societies have "evolved" fire departments, emergency medical services, search and rescue organizations, famine and other disaster relief organizations, and a myriad of other organizational structures. Each is specialized and professionalized—staffed by well-trained and experienced people who have relevant equipment and tools. Although some degree of confusion and chaos characterizes all significant emergencies, in locations around the world on a daily basis these organizations do good (and often remarkable) work in high-stress, rapidly evolving situations—at least so long as the situations they are confronting fit reasonably within the scope of what they were designed and resourced to do.

Yet sadly, we have also seen instances of woefully inadequate government response. Perhaps the most vivid in recent history is the multiple failures of effective response to the unfolding catastrophe wrought by Hurricane Katrina on the Gulf Coast of the United States in August and September of 2005. Government response to Hurricane Andrew in Florida in 1992 was also slow and disorganized, compounding unexpectedly devastating naturally inflicted damage. These failures are not limited geographically or by the cause of the disaster. Criticism about the sluggish response by the Soviet government to the Armenian earthquake in December 1988, which took 25,000 lives and left half a million people homeless, eventually resulted in an unprecedented opening of the USSR to outside relief shipments and assistance (British Broadcasting Company (BBC), 1988). In some cases—many areas within the South Asian tsunami impact zone in December 2004, for example—local resources were simply overwhelmed by the extraordinary size of the event. In other cases, incompetence, poor coordination, and sloppy execution yielded disastrously inadequate efforts in jurisdictions that should have been reasonably well prepared.

What accounts for whether governments will be able to provide effective responses to unfolding disaster events? How can they best be organized to respond to significant emergencies? What must they do in advance to create the capacities they will need in the face of disasters? In this chapter, we advance five major arguments about how governments need to structure their disaster response capabilities.

First, there are *three different types of disaster situations*. Each presents a different set of challenges in both execution and planning, and yields to different forms of leadership. Each requires different skills and processes for effective performance, and therefore, requires different forms of organization, resourcing, skill-building, practice, and other preparation in advance.

Second, while *all effective disaster responses require excellence in (a) situational awareness, (b) planning and decision making, and (c) execution,* excellence in these domains requires different responses in different types of disasters.

Third, in any significant emergency, *both (a) technical/operational issues and (b) political issues or value choices* need to be addressed. Common forms of organization for disaster response, however, tend to focus principally on the technical issues; they need to be redesigned to handle the political issues and value choices more effectively.

Fourth, *the "Incident Management System" provides a generally useful and flexible framework*—suitable in a variety of disaster types—for coordinating diverse emergency response organizations and personnel, many of whom may never have interacted before being cast together in an emergency.

Fifth, *government is an important part of disaster response, but by no means its entirety.* This implies that governments need to think through both (a) what responses they can and ought to provide; and (b) what they can do to support, enable, accommodate, and adapt to responses by business firms, nonprofit organizations, and organized and spontaneous communal action.

KEY FEATURES OF EMERGENCY EVENTS

Significant emergency events are characterized by high *stakes*—the likelihood of major losses (to life, limb, property, heritage, or other highly valued social or private assets). They generally also exhibit a high level of *uncertainty* about just what the outcomes will be and a high degree of *contingency* (significant variability in the possible outcomes that may result under different choices of action). Much is at stake, and the results will depend on what we do—but we do not know for certain which course of action will be best. This implies that those working on the emergency will be operating in conditions of high stress.

Many types of emergencies arise regularly and are closely related to others that have come before. House fires occur in urban communities sufficiently frequently to be commonplace. Widespread (but relatively mild) influenza occurs several times per decade. Hurricanes—at least up to Category III—come ashore every year. Earthquakes of magnitude 5 or higher take place every day, and of magnitude 6 or higher every week or so. The planet experienced 12 earthquakes of magnitude 7 or above in 2005. An earthquake of magnitude 8.6 struck near the sites of the devastating earthquake that caused the South Asian tsunami and took about 300,000 lives in December 2004, and the earthquake of magnitude 7.6 that took 85,000 lives in Pakistan in October (United States Geological Survey (USGS), 2006).

"Routine" Versus "Crisis" Emergencies

When a particular type of emergency happens sufficiently frequently in an area where people have (or should have) resources to organize and prepare, it becomes a routine event. This does not make it good, and it may still be quite severe—but it does tend to make it potentially manageable. We refer to such situations as *routine* or *familiar* emergencies to emphasize the opportunity that their regularity creates for organized preparation and practiced response. A house fire in a jurisdiction that has a well-resourced and practiced fire department, a moderate earthquake in an earthquake zone in which people have prepared for such events, a typical hurricane in a region where hurricanes are frequent and hurricane preparation is practiced—these are routine emergencies.

By contrast, some of the emergencies we confront are *not* like those we have previously experienced. By virtue of unusual scale, a previously unknown cause, or an atypical combination of sources, responders face challenges in these *crisis* or *novel* emergencies, the facts and implications of which cannot be completely assimilated in the moment of crisis. These emergencies are thus distinguished from more familiar emergencies by the presence of significantly new circumstances and different kinds of intellectual challenges. The 2004 South Asian tsunami in Banda Aceh far exceeded immediately available capacities for response. Hurricane Katrina, with novel combinations of flooding and infrastructure loss, created unusual needs and simultaneously invalidated standard responses. The 2005 earthquake in Pakistan simultaneously created needs and destroyed available capacity. These are crisis emergencies.

The distinction between routine and crisis emergencies would be useful only for academic interests if these types differ in degree alone—if, for example, the appropriate approach to coping with or preparing for the challenges of one were very much like that which works best for the other. But, as we will see in the next sections, the best approaches to these different circumstances are *not* the same—indeed, they are profoundly different.

ROUTINE EMERGENCIES

A wide range of implications flows immediately from the underlying familiarity of routine emergencies. Imagine a serious highway accident in which three passenger cars collide with a jackknifing tractor-trailer on a freeway, injuring six people—three severely—while disrupting traffic for miles in both directions. Emergency calls go out to state police, the fire department, the ambulance service, a nearby hospital, and the highway department. Each group responds and takes care of different dimensions of the emergency. The police take command of traffic flow, routing lines of vehicles past the accident site, and maintain security around the crash scene. Emergency medical personnel minister to the victims, quickly assessing which ones should receive what kinds of attention in what order of priority. Firefighters douse the flames enveloping an auto. Hospital emergency staff, alerted by the emergency medical technicians, ready teams to treat the specific medical needs of the most severely injured victims. Highway department personnel oversee private wrecking crews that remove damaged vehicles from the site. Within a few hours, the the immediate needs of the injured have been addressed, damaged vehicles have been removed from the accident scene, and traffic is once more flowing.

While each highway accident differs in its details, the fact that similar situations have been faced many times before gave us the opportunity to think about and try many possible approaches, choosing and refining the techniques that work best into a set of routine practices. We have developed rules and lessons, trained professionals to use them, provided practice in their application so that they can be deployed quickly and by ingrained instinct. Thus, by preparation, anticipation, and adaptation, we produce excellence in routine emergency response. The key elements of excellent response are:

> - **High Awareness**: Developing a detailed understanding of the
>   nature of this "kind" of situation and an understanding of its key
>   elements—so that we know what facts and observations are relevant
>   and, therefore, which to collect;

> **Comprehensive Scripts**: Well-engineered general "routines" that provide step by step scripts for dealing with the emergency;

> **Modest Customization**: Well-defined methods for adapting the general routine to the specific instance;

> **Precision Execution**: Implementing well-designed and practiced routines precisely and accurately;

> **Well-Defined, Highly-Developed Skills**: Training in the skills necessary to customize and execute the routines;

> **Leadership**: Leaders who are

  • Trained in the knowledge and methods of the situation and response;

  • Practiced at organizing, deciding, and directing execution in this type of situation;

  • Selected on the basis of their prior training, experience, and performance as better able than others to organize and direct responses of this kind;

> **Command presence**: A leadership approach (generally, an authority-based command and control structure) that performs well in directing the customization and execution of the routines;

> **Recognition-primed decisions**: The ability, through training, practice, and operational experience, to recognize patterns of circumstances and trigger appropriate, nearly autonomic responses; and

> **Hierarchical Structure**: An organizational structure (generally, a hierarchical system) well suited to customizing general routines to specific circumstances and executing them effectively.

In short, organizations that perform well in a routine emergency environment are based in a well-defined, well-developed, and ingrained *expertise* about the nature of emergencies of this type, in the knowledge of how to handle them, and in the skills necessary to deploy that knowledge. This expertise is at once substantive, procedural, and organizational. It involves factual knowledge of how situations of this kind evolve and what the key factors are, an understanding of and ability to deploy the relevant response actions and routines, and an ability to operate effectively in an organizational setting. This ensures the development of sufficient understanding of the situation to make decisions and to issue instructions and commands to direct the response. By virtue of familiarity with the type of emergency, we have the opportunity to understand and prepare. Where things have gone well, moreover, we have equipped people and organizations with expertise that will allow them to perform ably in spite of the danger, stress, and urgency of the situation. The essence of a well-prepared response to a routine emergency is that it is deeply rooted in expertise—an expertise that immediately triggers a practiced and well-targeted series of actions.

CRISIS EMERGENCIES

By contrast, in emergency situations with major novelties—that is, in *crisis* emergencies—such comprehensive expertise is, by definition, not possible. When SARS (Severe Acute Respiratory Syndrome) arrived in Toronto in February 2003 as a result of an infected person flying from Hong Kong to Canada, medical personnel were only dimly aware of a then unnamed, mysterious, virulent pneumonia that had been reported in southern China. Within months, before Toronto public health officials gained control of the outbreak, SARS had infected 375 people and killed 44. Many of these cases were contracted in hospitals, as afflicted people arrived in emergency rooms for treatment and passed the infection to other patients and hospital personnel. Normal ways of preventing the spread of respiratory infections in hospitals, adequate for ordinary pneumonia or influenza, fell far short of stopping transmission of SARS. Severely-ill patients who were transferred from community hospitals to specialized treatment centers spread SARS further. Several Toronto-area hospitals were forced to close their doors during the SARS siege because of contamination. These impacts were not the result of ineffective medical practices or incompetent medical personnel; indeed, Toronto has a world-class medical system whose personnel are highly competent. Nonetheless, they were dealing with a new disease, the characteristics of which were poorly understood. Not until hospitals—after several false starts—adopted much more stringent isolation practices, and public health officials invented extensive contact-tracking policies and required intrusive self-quarantine by people who might have been exposed to contagious SARS victims, did Toronto get traction in fighting the outbreak (Varley, 2005).

In a crisis emergency, the presence of significant novelty implies that understanding of the situation, at least at the outset, will be relatively low, and that there will be no executable script or routine that is known or identifiable and that provides a comprehensive, reliable, and fully adequate response. Existing routines are inadequate or even counterproductive. Dealing with a crisis emergency thus means that the response will necessarily operate beyond the boundary of planned and resourced capabilities. It will necessarily be *un*planned (or, at least, *incompletely* planned), and the resources and capabilities will generally be (or seem) inadequate. We can divide the challenges into three phases: first, the establishment of *awareness*, during an "understanding" phase; second, the development of a *design for action*, during a "design" phase; and third, the *implementation of the chosen actions*, during an "execution" phase characterized by implementation of unpracticed actions that go well beyond our existing plans and resources. This process then continues as observations of the results of the actions build understanding of the new situation as it continues to evolve.

Understanding

In a situation with significant elements that people have not faced before, anticipated, or planned for, responders lack general understanding of the circumstances. More particularly, they lack understanding of the parts of the circumstances that might be most relevant. Faced by this form of uncertainty, no individual or small group is likely to be fully "expert." Different people will observe or discover different bits of relevant information, displayed in different ways as events unfold. In a routine emergency, by contrast, responders would have a well-defined sense of what data they need to achieve good awareness of the situation and an observational system for collecting and analyzing information. In a novel crisis, they would lack both a preexisting list of the "parameters" of the situation and a disciplined system for gathering and assessing data. It seems likely, therefore, that an effective process for developing good understanding would involve eclectic and relatively unstructured observation and analysis. A "flatter" organization would be likely to do a better job of observing and assimilating the relevant features of the situation than a more hierarchical structure.

Design

Since, by definition, the situation that is being addressed contains significant novelty—and, therefore, there is no comprehensive script available to address it—a major challenge of effective action lies in improvising or inventing a new approach. This requires both flexibility and creativity. It is likely to include, but not be limited to, the creative combination, in whole or in part, of existing routines, which may become elements of the newly-minted strategies. It must also be relatively unconstrained by what has been done before. In such a situation, organizational authority needs to be sufficiently hierarchical to assure that the pieces of a new approach fit together coherently and will not work at cross-purposes, but the difficulty of elaborating the details of new design elements requires sufficiently decentralized action to permit timely response.

Execution

Since the approach taken will necessarily contain substantially redesigned or newly improvised processes that have not been previously practiced, execution is likely to expose both imperfections in the new design and errors in implementation. Thus, an organization dealing with the novelty of a crisis situation will have to effectively implement new and imperfect routines, learn quickly to catch errors before they unfold further, operate in spite of difficulties and setbacks, and be tolerant of imperfections. In the "design" and "execution" phases, by contrast with the "understanding" phase, it will probably be more effective if the organization has a more hierarchical structure, with more traditional command-and-control, authority-driven leadership—but with a higher tolerance than such a structure would ordinarily connote for imprecision in execution.

Excellence in coping with crisis emergencies, therefore, means dealing effectively with the specific challenges that novel circumstances generate:

> **Low Awareness**: By definition, the novelty of the situation implies that there is less than complete understanding of the circumstances—or even of which circumstances are relevant. Responders do not necessarily know which facts and observations are relevant and, therefore, which to collect;

> *No* **Comprehensive Scripts**: Scripts developed for routine situations may be applicable, but, by definition, there is no comprehensive "playbook" from which the response can be directed;

> **Major Customization**: The existence of significant novelty implies that significant customization or improvisation is likely to be needed. Existing routines may provide useful elements of the response, but may have to be creatively adapted and melded in unusual and unpracticed combinations;

> **Fault-Tolerant Execution**: Because newly improvised approaches or previously untried combinations of existing routines may be implemented, execution is likely to be much less precise than in routine circumstances, which call for more tolerance of imperfections and errors in execution;

➤ **Incompletely Specified Skills**: Since new actions may be taken, skills will not have been comprehensively developed for either the design or the execution of the required response. While training in the skills necessary to use existing routines as elements of the newly developed response will be useful, the need for the relevant skill base for components of what is being invented and improvised cannot reasonably have been foreseen and will not be available;

➤ **Muted Command Presence**: A leadership approach generally oriented to producing collaboration that works for directing the development of understanding and the design through invention and improvisation of a new approach—followed by a more authority-driven approach during the execution phase;

➤ **Cognitively-Driven Decisions**: Given the uncertainties born of novelty and the corresponding lack of available comprehensive routines, decisions cannot reliably be driven by pattern recognition (because, by definition, the patterns are not available). Decision making must proceed through a standard analytical process: the identification of objectives, the development of alternatives, the prediction of likely results from different approaches, and the choice of a best action;

➤ **"Variably Flattened" Structure**: An organizational structure well suited to collecting a broad range of information (because, at least in the early phases, it will not necessarily be clear what information is relevant) and to absorbing and processing it and developing a range of alternatives. This calls for a "flattened" structure, but the necessary ability to execute the chosen approach reasonably efficiently probably calls for a more hierarchical structure.

The essence of effective response to novel or crisis emergencies thus *also* lies in a form of expertise, but in a very different form than the expertise used in routine emergencies. In the face of novelty, no one is a "substantive" expert—no one knows what to do. When no one knows what to do, response leaders, under stress, have to think their way through—developing an understanding of a situation with potentially great and unknown uncertainties, analyzing possible courses of action, and then executing untried, untested, and unperfected sequences of actions. Leading people and organizations through such an intrinsically chaotic experience requires a form of expertise—expertise in *adaptive leadership*, a very different form of leadership than that used by successful leaders in routine emergencies (Heifetz, 1994).

DECISION MAKING IN ROUTINE AND CRISIS EMERGENCIES

The form of decision making that dominates in routine situations deserves further comment, because it frames a central distinction between routine and novel crisis circumstances. In a series of landmark studies of the decision-making behavior of frontline emergency responders, Gary Klein has provided an intriguing set of insights into how decisions are made in routine emergencies by well-trained, experienced leaders (Klein, 1999). As he describes, he began his work trying to show how operational commanders implicitly used the standard rational action decision-making model (rational action model, or RAM). According to this model, one begins by formulating objectives, then developing and analyzing alternatives, then choosing a best course of action, and then monitoring results (and looping back to the beginning) to refine each step as necessary. What Klein found when he interviewed emergency room doctors, fireground commanders, and other highly trained and experienced people managing urgent, high-stakes, high-consequence, rapidly unfolding events was that, in practice, most used nothing like the rational action model. Instead, they based their actions on rapid recognition of the pattern of which the new situation was a part, and moved quickly to the corresponding routines for action. Klein and his colleagues developed what they term the "recognition-primed decision-making" (RPDM) model as a description of how experienced people actually operate. The key to this form of choice-in-action is that it is driven by fitting the current situation against a series of patterns accumulated through training and experience. Each pattern group is associated with a prescribed (and tested and validated) course of action. The particular collection of actions chosen is customized by adaptation in the small to the individual circumstances of the instant event, but the general approach is selected as the accepted approach to this "type" of incident. The "types" are categorized in pattern groups.

People who are trained, experienced, and selected on the basis of prior performance thus have a set of patterns in their heads. When they see a new situation, they tend, more or less automatically and instantly, to fit it into one of the pattern groups that they recognize. Each pattern group, in turn, is associated with a "recipe" for action—which, while it may involve some customization, provides a general template for action.

By contrast, in a novel (crisis) emergency situation, current events do not fit a preexisting pattern. Because they have no prescribed approach, the responders have no choice other than trying to work methodically through the different possibilities. In some cases, it will make sense to think about mitigating the consequences of a potential emergency; in other cases, it may make more sense to work on prevention of these consequences. There is no template or simplified autonomic response to offer. They have to think in detail through priorities among possible objectives, expand the array of available options, analyze the likely consequences of different actions, and choose the best choice, *ex ante*, that they can identify. In short, in the face of novelty, responders are more or less forced to apply the principles of the rational action decision-making model.

THE ROLE OF STRESS

Rapidly evolving, high-stakes situations are intrinsically stressful. Research on the role that stress plays in activating or blocking decision making casts important light on the challenges of managing routine and novel emergencies. Generally speaking, for trained and experienced experts, stress *activates* the recognition-primed decision making that is the centerpiece of decision making in routine situations—up to a point (Klein, 1996; Rudolph & Repenning, 2002; Useem, 1998, p. 60). At least in the early stages as stress rises, recognitional powers become more acute as the hormonal responses to stress activate and "wake up" the sensory faculties and the response capabilities. (This is not true for inexperienced operational people—their performance is lower, and does not improve with stress.) By contrast, stress tends to block higher-order cognitive responses (Janis & Mann, 1977). Thus, for experienced responders, moderate levels of stress can be an asset in routine emergency situations where recognition-primed decision making is appropriate. In true (novel) crisis situations, however, stress tends generally to be a negative influence because of its effects on capabilities for decisions that require the rational action model.

One potentially important implication is that the more general cognitive tendency to "see" the familiar elements in a situation (and to ignore the "novel" elements) may be exacerbated by the stress levels associated with any emergency situation—thus activating and increasing the inclination toward recognitional responses and reducing the forcefulness of cognitively-based engagement. If this is so, then one significant danger of novel situations is that their novelty may be systematically missed or underplayed—and the natural human responses to stress would seem to accentuate, rather than counterbalance, that inclination.

RECOGNIZING NOVELTY AS
A CENTRAL CHALLENGE OF CRISIS RESPONSE

It follows directly from the nature of the differences between routine and crisis emergencies that in order to deal effectively with true crises, the novelty of the circumstances must first be identified and actively engaged. This is more difficult than it might appear. In emergency situations, we commonly turn to traditional emergency response organizations, and the people in these organizations are generally trained to observe quickly and respond. This means they are likely to observe the familiar, rather than the unfamiliar, aspects of the situation. New York City firefighters, on September 11, 2001, heroically fought the fires in the Twin Towers simply as an enlarged version of a skyscraper fire. They missed the novelty of the structural damage high up that would fairly rapidly lead to the collapse of the buildings—an inevitability quickly spotted by, among others, many of the structural engineers who watched the events unfold on television that morning. The New York City Fire Department (FDNY) approached the situation by marginally customizing its existing routines. Bravely and without hesitation, it moved into execution. FDNY did not, in the main, engage the question: "What, if anything, is materially different and novel about this situation—and what implications might that have?"

Novelties, by their nature, are often difficult to spot, because we do not know to look for them, and we do not know what we are looking for when we do. There tends to be a bias in emergency situations to noticing and addressing the routine elements, and to missing the more subtle, but potentially crucial, novel elements. It is essential, however, to identify what is different and what calls for a different form of response. Thus, developing personal and organizational mechanisms for testing the presumption of familiarity is a crucial element of building an apparatus capable of excellence in both routine *and* crisis emergencies. But the difficulty of spotting novelty is not easily solved. Even deciding when we should systematically look for possible novelty in the situation we are managing calls for judgment about the level of *potential* novelty and its implications, because carrying out an elaborate review in a purely routine situation wastes precious time and resources.

SUMMARY OF ROUTINE AND CRISIS EMERGENCY CHARACTERISTICS

Table 1.1 provides a summary and contrast of the characteristics of familiar (routine) and novel (crisis) emergencies. The differences between crisis and routine emergency situations are substantial and crucial. These differences are operationally significant—they imply important differences in the ways that:

Table 1.1.   Summary of Contrasting Features of Routine and Crisis Emergencies

Attribute	Routine (/Familiar) Emergencies	Crisis (/Novel) Emergencies
Situational Awareness	High; well-defined	Low; many unknowns
Scripts	Comprehensive	Fragmentary
Customization	Limited and modest	Central
Skills	Comprehensive	Partial
Leadership		
Understanding phase	Authority-based	Collaborative
Design phase	Authority-based	Collaborative
Execution phase	Authority-based	Authority-based
Command Presence		
Understanding phase	High	Modest
Design phase	High	Modest
Execution phase	High	High
Decision Making	Recognitional	Cognitive
Organizational Structure		
Understanding phase	Hierarchy	Flattened
Design phase	Hierarchy	Flattened
Execution phase	Hierarchy	Hierarchy
Defining competence	Routine execution of trained and practiced scripts	Recognition of novelty; creative improvisation of response; execution of untested actions

- information should be sought (more broadly in a true crisis, with less attention to normal judgments about what information might be relevant);
- leaders should behave (more collaboratively and less through authority in highly uncertain, true crisis situations);
- organizations should be set up from the outset (in true crisis situations, with greater emphasis on the idea that observers in many different places may hold crucial information, and with recognition of the need for a flatter organization to keep from suppressing what subordinates do know that top management should know).

THE SPECIAL CHALLENGES OF EMERGENT CRISES

Many emergency situations occur suddenly and are unavoidably noticeable. A major earthquake, the landfall of a major hurricane, a bomb blast—there is no doubting that something has happened, or when it happened. There may be more or less warning—an earthquake sequence signaled the recent minor lava eruptions of the Mount Merapi volcano complex in Indonesia—but the associated main event, if it arises, will not be subtle or difficult to notice.

By contrast, some forms of crisis do not arrive suddenly. They fester and grow, arising from a background of more ordinary circumstances that often masks their appearance. When SARS emerged in south China in the winter of 2002–2003, it appeared first as a series of unexplained deaths in a region that has, annually, many unexplained deaths. It was only in looking back, after SARS had clearly emerged as a major, definitively identified phenomenon, that its roots could be traced back and seen at all. At the beginning, it was an invisible part of a confused landscape in which a few deaths from an unusually lethal form of respiratory distress were mixed in with the larger, ordinary flow of deaths from pneumonia. When the 1979 nuclear accident at the Three Mile Island power plant in Pennsylvania began, it started as a simple pump failure—out of which spun an increasingly tangled and escalating series of failures and mistakes until, hours later, it was no longer deniable that a major event was underway.

Crisis emergencies that arise from more normal operating conditions constitute a special—and especially difficult—category of crises, which we term "emergent" crises. In assessing many challenging crisis situations, we find early events that were in fact the genesis of the later disaster, but were intrinsically difficult to spot at the nascent stage of development. There had been previous pump failures at Three Mile Island, and these had always responded to the routine procedures that were applied at the time of the crisis. In fact, the initial moves to address the problem at Three Mile Island appeared to have worked. It was not the original pump failure, but the initially unnoticed failure of the operators' responses that created the conditions that spiraled out of control (Perrow, 1984).

There are at least three reasons why emergent crises are particularly difficult to address. First, by nature they are difficult to recognize. Arising from normally variable operating conditions, emerging problems are intrinsically difficult to spot as a break from the normal operating patterns. But two other challenges also arise. When (and if) the problem is spotted, an individual or group with technical expertise in the issue (as it is currently understood) is generally assigned to address it. Through working on it, the responder(s) are likely to take "ownership" of the problem and its resolution. Generally, this will work: the situation will have been correctly diagnosed, the team chosen because of its capacity to address situations of this type, and the response sized appropriately to address the problem. But what if the diagnosis is not entirely correct, or if the standard approach doesn't work, or if the response is too small or too late? Often, experts (and, perhaps even more so, teams of experts) are not adept at recognizing that their approach is not working. Often, they ignore "disconfirming evidence" (i.e., the flow of data tending to show that what they are doing is not working) and "escalate commitment" to their existing approach (see Bazerman, 1998; and Kahneman, Slovic, & Tversky, 1982, for extended discussion of these and related "cognitive biases"). The person or team working on the situation may not only believe (as a result of cognitive biases) that they are about to succeed (with just a little more effort and time) but also feel pressure not to lose face or be seen publicly as incompetent by peers, subordinates, or superiors if they are unable to handle the assigned situation. (For example, investigations of wildland firefighting deaths from transitional fire "blow-ups" frequently find that teams violated firefighting rules that called for disengagement because they did not want to be seen by other teams as having been unable to handle their assigned fire. See, for example, MacLean, 1999.) Additionally, they may resist seeking help. As the experts (the reason they were dispatched in the first place), they may have difficulty imagining who else might be more expert and, therefore, able to help. Thus, a second major challenge of coping with emerging crisis situations is that the initial responder(s), if not immediately successful, either fail to diagnose their inadequacies or resist calling for additional help.

The third reason that emergent crises are challenging is that they present crisis managers with all of the standard challenges of managing true crises—the difficulty of recognizing novelty, the challenge of creativity and improvisation of new approaches and designs under stress, the painful realities of the errors and rough edges that arise when executing new and untested routines. But these standard challenges now arise in the context of organizations and teams that are already deployed and working on the situation. Operationally and organizationally invested in their original approach, they are likely to be resistant to the idea that they need to switch to a different mode of analysis and response to take account of the emerging scale, scope, and novelty of the circumstances. As specialists or experts, they are likely to feel that they are doing as well as possible under difficult conditions, that their approach is working, that they know better than anyone else, and that what they need is more authorization, and less oversight and "help." In a sudden crisis, obvious to all as a crisis, the response organizations may not be as resistant to engagement with others (senior political officials, for example) because they see immediately that the situation makes extraordinary demands and is not "business as usual." In an emergent crisis, however, the initial responders are less likely to see the novelty and more likely to resent the intrusion of those they may regard as untrained and unneeded.

The communicable crises that are the subject of this book may be particularly likely to arise as emergent crises (rather than sudden onset crises) because they involve ongoing processes and continuing evolution of damage and response. The emergence of new and lethal diseases (or disease vectors) is an obvious example: Ebola repeatedly, SARS in November of 2002, and, perhaps, A(H5N1) today, are archetypal instances. Fires are another common source of emergent crises because they nearly always start out small. Large fires that reach significant emergency proportions and confront responders with novel challenges have almost always emerged after a less than completely successful earlier response. They, therefore, typically involve tired and embarrassed responders who have a high (personal) investment in how the situation is seen and managed. These responders may understandably (and perhaps forgivably) lack perspective on the best way to manage now that the fire is emerging with true crisis characteristics, and they may resist and resent the intrusions of others coming into what they regard as *their* decision-making arena.

POLITICAL AND OPERATIONAL ENGAGEMENT IN CRISES

By their nature—their high stakes, urgency, and associated fear and stress—significant emergency events are necessarily political as well as operational matters. The senior policy officials in any given setting are, in some sense, intrinsically political (they are usually directly elected to represent the interests of their constituents, or appointed by and serving at the pleasure of elected officials), and they are generally uncontested in seniority to the operational commanders involved. In effect, they have a choice about how engaged to be and what role to play in any given crisis situation. In routine situations, political officials may be willing to defer to the expertise of operational commanders and to rely on their assessments, decisions, and command systems. In situations that transcend the routine, by contrast, political officials are likely to feel impelled to be engaged, to be involved in decision making and communication about the situation—and perhaps to be (and be seen as) "in charge."

Political officials, on one side, and operational commanders, on the other, may have very different styles and approaches to managing crisis situations (Leonard & Howitt, 2004). Operational commanders are generally quick to make assessments and inclined to act. Recognition-driven, they are prepared to move quickly; and their experience and instincts tell them that delays are costly. Politicians vary widely in their inclination to move quickly to action; but many prefer to keep their options open, to see how the situation evolves, to avoid committing all of their capacity at the outset. In the Cuban Missile Crisis of October 1962, military leaders (the operational commanders in that event) quickly recommended to President Kennedy that he authorize one of several aggressive military responses. Fortunately—given what we now know of the situation at the time, which included the presence of active nuclear warheads on both sides, and given how events subsequently evolved—Kennedy demurred. Instead of acting immediately, he sought other options, waited until the situation evolved, and eventually chose from a very different decision set. The differing inclinations of politicians and operational officials may be a source of conflict at the heart of crisis decision making, and in any case is an important situational feature to which crisis leaders need to pay attention and manage.

This is rendered more difficult, in the United States at least, and to a lesser extent in many other countries, by the fact that nearly any major emergency will involve both multiple *jurisdictions* and multiple *levels of government*, rendering coordination both necessary and highly complex. In the United States, state and local government officials have no formal hierarchical relationship to federal officials; they may both be acting in the same geographic space at the same time with separate or overlapping authority, and differing ideas about what needs to be done and how to do it. In late 2005, Hurricane Katrina presented the world with myriad examples of the imperfections of such coordination, and the resulting snarls and poor performance. The White House report issued in the aftermath of Katrina proudly pointed out that a joint law enforcement coordination center, with senior federal, state, and local law enforcement officials co-located, was established only on September 6—8 full days after the hurricane came ashore (White House, 2006). Eight days seemed, to many, like a very long time to wait for the creation of an integrated law enforcement response in a situation that had cried out for a better law enforcement presence since at least the day before the hurricane came ashore.

In significant crisis events, both political and operational officials will have important—and different—roles to play. True crisis events—in which, by definition, the responders are operating beyond the bounds of what they have planned, practiced, and are resourced for—will necessarily confront senior decision makers with conflicts of *values*. Values issues are intrinsically political in nature and should involve determinations by people with the political legitimacy to authorize, warrant, and defend the choices made. Thus, political officials should be involved in the most crucial decisions involving conflicting priorities, and in the communication to the public describing and justifying the approaches being taken. Operational officials should help to frame those decisions, and should organize and direct the chosen responses, taking responsibility for the most effective possible execution under the circumstances. While these roles interact, and in some cases may partially overlap, governments need to develop effective processes for parsing the tasks and decisions as effectively as possible between these roles. This calls for the presence—and presence of mind—of both political and operational commanders working in concert in significant emergency events.

ORGANIZATIONAL STRUCTURE AND THE INCIDENT MANAGEMENT SYSTEM

The challenges of appropriate parsing of responsibilities between political and operational officials, and the challenges of coordinating multiple jurisdictions and multiple levels of government in the absence of any hierarchical structure of subordination among the governments involved, have immediate implications for practice. To be ready to address both routine and novel emergency circumstances, we will need an organizational structure that is able to adjust to situations of different sizes, and to incorporate variable numbers of jurisdictions and organizations that may have an important role to play in the circumstances. Given the nature of required responses in the face of novel circumstances, this organizational form needs to have six essential characteristics to be robust against both routine and true crisis situations. It needs to be:

> **Flexible in scale**—so that it can address situations of different sizes and, as events unfold, can adjust by shrinking or growing as conditions dictate;

> **Flexible in scope**—so that it can, usefully and effectively, integrate representatives and decision makers from different agency types or jurisdictions;

> **Capable of distinguishing roles**—so that it can appropriately differentiate *political values* decisions from *technical or operational* decisions;

> **Capable of reestablishing situational awareness in the context of novelty and significant uncertainty**—so that it can organize and effectively direct scanning for information, organizing what is known, defining and seeking information about what appears to be relevant and unknown, and processing and disseminating the resulting "common operating picture" to the relevant response officials and organizations;

> **Capable of improvisational design**—so that it can organize a cre-
  ative process of invention, probably combining existing response
  routine elements and possibly developing new ones; and

> **Capable of fault-tolerant execution**—so that it can effectively
  direct and coordinate actions that are previously untested, and
  which are therefore likely to work imperfectly.

The Incident Management System (IMS), now in wide use by emergency response organizations around the world, is well designed as a
foundation for such a comprehensive disaster response organization.
There are many variations on the specific design of IMS, but most share
key structural characteristics. IMS generally calls for a centralized operational authority (the "incident commander," or IC) to have overall
responsibility for design and coordination of the response to the designated "incident." He or she reports to political officials who provide
authorization for the response and who generally define its goals and
scope. The operational response is organized in units reporting to the IC,
generally including four functional groups, each headed by a "chief": (1)
operations, which directs the current execution of activities; (2) planning,
which organizes plans and orders resources for the next operational cycle
and thereafter; (3) logistics, which provides and manages the flow of
resources and people to and from the zones of activity; and (4) finance,
which tracks expenditures and resource consumption. The central staff
team supporting the IC generally includes a safety officer responsible for
safety procedures throughout the operation and a public information
officer responsible for managing the flow of information to other agencies and to the public.

   IMS was originally developed as an organizational form through which
large numbers of firefighters could be coordinated in fighting large wildland fires. Confronted frequently by the challenge of integrating the work
of agencies and personnel from many different jurisdictions and authority
hierarchies, IMS has evolved a mechanism for coordinating at the command level across agencies. In essence, "unified command" consists of a
voluntary association of the relevant commanders, who agree to coordinate decision making, resource allocation, and strategy. Below this level,
IMS works in similar fashion, whether headed by a single incident commander or a plural, unified command. This system has performed to
good effect in a wide range of severe fires and, more recently, other emergencies. When the Columbia space shuttle disintegrated above Texas in
February 2002, it was the U.S. Forest Service, well-practiced in rapidly
deploying and coordinating incident management teams, that organized

the bulk of the search activities to recover evidence, dangerous materials, and human remains from the wide area over which they were scattered.

While IMS was designed principally to organize operational response to routine emergency situations, it has also proven highly effective in circumstances involving more novel elements. The bombing of the Alfred P. Murrah federal office building in Oklahoma City created unprecedented combinations of challenges involving urban search and rescue, crime scene protection and investigation, and multiple conflicts over who had jurisdiction. IMS proved a useful organizational framework within which these issues could be identified, analyzed, and resolved, and through which the resulting decisions could be implemented (M. P. Rounsaville, personal communication, April 2, 2004).

While the IMS is a good foundation for building *operational* response organizations that are robust against both routine and crisis emergency situations, as currently implemented, it does not produce a fully effective framework within which the political issues raised by severe and novel circumstances can be effectively identified and handled. In the San Diego fire siege in October 2003, there were major confrontations between political officials, who felt that they should have some role in decision making, and operational officials, who felt that the issues were largely technical in nature. The IMS system provided no natural way to integrate political leaders' concerns and participation in the decision-making process, nor a means to distinguish which issues called for engagement of political leaders and which, by contrast, were appropriately in the realm of expert operational/technical officials—to the great frustration of both political and operational officials involved (J. Madaffer, personal communication, October 28, 2004).

COORDINATING PUBLIC, NONGOVERNMENTAL, AND PRIVATE RESPONSES

While the effectiveness of governmental response to any major emergency is a key determinant of how well or poorly public welfare is protected, and how quickly damage ends and recovery begins, government is by no means the sole actor or influence on the quality of society's overall performance. Nongovernmental organizations are often explicitly designed and expected to provide assistance. In the United States, the Red Cross is directly chartered by Congress to do so; many other nonprofit organizations, from inside and outside the community affected, play explicit roles in disaster response planning. Private organizations also can and often do bring substantial additional capacity to bear—and they can frequently contribute in ways that governmental institutions cannot. In the aftermath of Hurricane Katrina, actions by private companies like FedEx, UPS, Wal-Mart, Office Depot, and many others played important roles in minimizing losses. Often operating under the discretion of local store and office managers, private companies reduced the general level of chaos, permitting governmental and other organizations to function more effectively and to recover some of their lost capabilities more quickly. Self-help is also quite obviously a prominent feature of response to many disasters. For example, the great majority of people in New Orleans wisely evacuated before Hurricane Katrina came ashore. They did so under a mandatory order, but in most cases by their own means—and many of those who were rescued in the aftermath of the storm either engaged in self-rescue or were helped by neighbors or others who simply pitched in to help.

Beyond well planned, organized intervention of (mostly nonprofit) organizations, disaster response organizations may not welcome decentralized action or regard it as a good idea. Untrained people who attempt to help others in disaster situations may wind up endangering themselves and the additional rescue workers needed to extract them. Often, disaster response organizations focus on what they and their peer organizations are doing, leaving what others are doing aside (and essentially acting as if it were irrelevant) (Curran & Leonard, 2005). Nonetheless, the inevitability of private action by nonprofit organizations, private companies, and individuals (whether neighbors or, sometimes, strangers) suggests that one of the elements of government planning and response should be to anticipate, facilitate, and where possible, direct, these actions in ways that are most likely to be helpful. Taking explicit account of what others might do—and thinking ahead about how to organize, coordinate, and facilitate those actions that might be most helpful—would be a useful capacity for preparedness organizations. Expanding the concept of unified command to include some capacity for coordinating with nonprofit and private sector organizations—and building the infrastructure of agreements and relationships in advance that would make it easier for organizations to work effectively across sectoral boundaries—might have significant pay-offs in a wide range of possible future circumstances.

IMPROVING PREPARATION FOR, AND PERFORMANCE IN, ROUTINE AND CRISIS EMERGENCY SITUATIONS

Our long history of experience with emergencies, ranging from the small and routine through the large and routine, has led us to build disaster response organizations that provide generally effective performance against routine challenges. These organizations tend to be highly professional, well-trained and practiced, hierarchical, and deeply rooted in substantive expertise and skills for addressing their assigned routine situations.

Episodically, however, we confront situations of significant novelty—by virtue of their scale, unusual sources of damage or a combination of sources, or because they involve eventualities that we have not seen or thought about before (whether or not we should have). The mechanisms that we have constructed for routine situations do not perfectly fit, nor do they constitute full preparation for, such events. These true crisis events—which involve coping with novelty—require systems for rapid information search and analysis, improvisational design, and then "good enough" execution.

IMS, as a general approach for organizing in the face of emergency circumstances, provides a good foundation for building a system that is robust against routine and true crisis situations. IMS was developed for, and generally is well-designed for, routine emergencies. But, just as it can stretch to address larger events, so it can also stretch to take on events of a different kind. Indeed, it probably provides the best organizational structure that we are likely to have available to address such events. But current practice does not always ensure that IMS implementation will be capable of coping with the novelty and improvisational demands of true crises. Among the new capacities that need to be designed and practiced into IMS systems, to make them more fully robust against true crises, are:

> **Further developing the means for parsing political from operational challenges**, and for facilitating effective and useful interactions between political decision makers and operational commanders;

> **Developing better means for recognizing and addressing significant elements of novelty**, and overcoming the bias of trained response organizations to focus on and address only the familiar;

> **Developing means for early identification of emergent crises**, and ensuring that they are not allowed to fester and develop;

> **Strengthening mechanisms for (re)building situational awareness** in circumstances with many unknown elements;

> **Building processes to enhance the capacity to undertake creative improvisation of new actions and responses**, including novel combinations of existing elements;

> **Enhancing the capacity to undertake incompletely designed actions with an appropriate level of tolerance for their consequent rough edges in execution**—and the ability to learn rapidly about how to correct for, and redesign quickly in the face of, inevitable imperfections.

While much has been accomplished, a great deal of work still lies ahead to make governmental organizations as effective as can reasonably be expected in the face of events both routine and novel. We can be grateful for the level of performance achieved by well-resourced and practiced response agencies—and still be concerned that we are not fully prepared or organizationally adapted to the novel circumstances yet to be encountered. Building organizations that can master both routine and novel situations is a profoundly important organizational development challenge, but we believe that great progress can be made toward this goal by beginning with an understanding of how routine and crisis circumstances are similar—and how they are different.

REFERENCES

Bazerman, M. (1998). *Judgment in managerial decision making*. New York: Wiley.

British Broadcasting Company. (1988). *Death toll rises in Armenian earthquake*. Retrieved May 18, 2006, from http://news.bbc.co.uk/onthisday/hi/dates/stories/december/10/newsid_2544000/2544077.stm

Curran, D., & Leonard, H. B. (2005, May). *Recovery in Aceh: Towards a strategy of emergence*. Harvard Business School Working Paper #05-082.

Heifetz, R. A. (1994). *Leadership without easy answers*. Cambridge, MA: Harvard University Press.

Janis, I. L., & Mann, L. (1977). *Decision making: A psychological analysis of conflict, choice, and commitment*. New York: The Free Press.

Klein, G. (1996). The effect of acute stressors in decision-making. In J. E. Driskell & E. Salas (Eds.), *Stress and performance*. Mahwah, NJ: Erlbaum.

Klein, G. (1999). *Sources of power*. Cambridge MA: MIT Press.

MacLean, J. N. (1999). *Fire on the mountain: The true story of the South Canyon Fire*, New York: HarperCollins.

Madaffer, J., personal interview with the authors, October 28, 2004.

Perrow, C. (1984, 1999) *Normal accidents: Living with high risk technologies*. Princeton, NJ: Princeton University Press.

Rudolph, J. W., & Repenning. N. P. (2002). Disaster dynamics: Understanding the role of quantity in organizational collapse. *Administrative Science Quarterly*, *41*(1), 1–30.

Kahneman, D., Slovic, P., & Tversky, A. (Eds.). (1982). *Judgment under uncertainty: Heuristics and biases*. New York: Cambridge University Press.

Leonard, H. B., & Howitt, A. M. (2004). In the heat of the moment. *Compass, 2*(1), 18–23.

Rounsaville, Marc P., personal interview with the authors, April 2, 2004.

United States geological survey. (2006). Retrieved May 18, 2006, from http:// earthquake.usgs.gov/eqcenter/recenteqsww/Quakes/quakes_big.php

Useem, M. (1998) *The leadership moment: Nine true stories of triumph and disaster and their lessons for us all.* New York: Three Rivers Press.

Varley, P. (2005). *Emergency response system under duress: The public health fight to contain SARS in Toronto (A, B, C).* Cambridge, MA: Case Study Program, John F. Kennedy School of Government, Harvard University.

White House. (2006). *The federal response to Hurricane Katrina: Lessons learned.* Washington, DC: U.S. Government Printing Office.

CHAPTER 2

ANTICIPATING RUDE SURPRISES

Reflections on
"Crisis Management" Without End

Todd R. LaPorte

This paper reflects on institutional dynamics of "crisis management" in an age where crises may be prompted by both natural disasters and aggressive social predation. Framed as novel "rude surprises" for decision makers and first and second responders, crises vary widely from emergencies in their initial properties. These variations prompt a wide range of unexpected responses and reveal the limited utility of received organizational and management theories to anticipate institutional dynamics and consequences. A thought experiment is posed to explicate these analytical and research challenges and the paper closes with a discussion of four conceptual themes that could inform subsequent design reflections.

INTRODUCTION[1]

Global economic, political, and technological trends assure the potentials for "institutional crises" of such magnitude that international cooperation

Communicable Crises: Prevention, Response, and Recovery in the Global Arena, pp. 27–46

will be needed to limit their damage and possibly their frequency. The emerging literature on institutional responses to emergencies, disasters, and crises signals both an intensifying expectation that political and economic institutions should be able to limit societal damage and speed recovery, and a sense that such capabilities are far more complex and demanding than formerly recognized (see Tierney, 2006; Tierney, Lindell, & Perry, 2001). Preparing to respond to crises, then, calls for much better understanding of these phenomena as they are experienced by institutions and by their operational leaders. Especially wanting are searching evaluations of recent history with cogent applications to training practitioners and to institutional planning processes[2] (for exceptions see the Transatlantic Crisis Management Project, 2003; and Boin, Hart, Stern, & Sundelius, 2005).

An overview that animated a recent conference on this topic proposed that its sprawling literature could be oriented "around four research traditions in the study of crisis management that (combine) somewhat different analytical emphases: (those that stress) threats originating from 'people and groups,' or those originating from '"macro-structural' characteristics of the institutional/organizational systems involved, as viewed from 'operational/technical perspectives' or 'political/symbolic perspectives.' "

Table 2.1 arrays a preliminary ordering attempt[3] ((Transatlantic Crisis Management, 2003). Its vectors splay out across much of organization and management literature as one moves from the practices of normal operations to emergency response, and then to the extraordinary dynamics of crisis containment and recovery. The range is remarkable, the framing categories providing at least an initial sense of order. But when one

Table 2.1.   On Perspectives of Crisis Management

	Operational-Technical Perspective	Political-Symbolic Perspective
Threats from people and groups	Foci: Command and control Consequence management Strategic interaction High stakes decision making	Foci: Threat politics Problem framing Stakeholders' views Institutional cooperation Nature of communication process
Threats due to structural problems	Foci: Complex accidents and natural disasters Local and regional levels Relieve human suffering Time pressure	Foci: Public policy analysis Agenda setting Performance accountability Public legitimacy Interaction with media

samples aspects of these literatures, one finds little that signals deepening analytical direction.

The reflections in this article were prompted by generous invitations from scholars who have been much more deeply engaged than I in wrestling with the practical and conceptual puzzles of understanding how institutions respond to extreme events. My views are very much those of an outsider, a wide-eyed newcomer who has only a modest sense of the received literature and is more or less innocent of the currents within the communities of those who can make first claims to wisdom in this domain. In accepting the invitations, I found a fascinating, unsettling area that rivets the attention. These reflections, presented with little of the patina warranted from a deeper expert, are filtered through the prisms of studying highly reliable public institutions that operate demanding technologies characterized by high capacity and intrinsic hazards where failures may be very costly, and where social risks could extend widely across space and over numerous management generations (see e.g., LaPorte, 1996; LaPorte & Keller, 1996; Rochlin, 1996). Let us see where it takes us.

For this discussion, I distinguish between considering emergencies and responding to crises—that is, the capacity of organizations/institutions to respond reliably to:

(a) well understood, operational situations that if allowed to evolve could result in serious degradation of capacity and loss of resources and/or life (i.e., emergencies), contrasted with those

(b) unexpected situations that produce demands perceived potentially to overwhelm institutional capacities and possibly to inflict severe, irreversible damage to known and unknown sectors of society (i.e., crises).

This view of "crisis" phenomena is both narrower and less stringent than often orients such discussions: to wit, a crisis is a situation in which decision time is short and error disastrous (cf. Boin, Hart, Stern, & Sundelius, 2005). And recent discussions have expanded the range of what might precipitate a "crisis" to include collective behavior that surprises a society's economic and political elites, for example, regional financial disruption or crashes of economic markets. This could be stretched to include political surprises as well, as in the popular overthrow of an established regime, though these "crises" take on a quite different character compared to the episodes usually assigned to the "crisis" category (see LaPorte, 2005).[4]

When "crisis management" is highlighted, the focus is often tightly on *damage limitation* by attempting to assure the institutional capacities needed to respond to unexpected, potentially overwhelming circumstances that are likely to deliver punishing blows to human life, to political or economic viability, and/or to environmental integrity. These are circumstances we experience as **rude surprises**. But crisis management could (and in my view should) also entail searching out the potentials/precursors for unexpected, overwhelming circumstances, then working to understand them. Effective management would also include developing practices and operational capacities so "crisis potentials" are reduced to less threatening emergency challenges. If this is successful, the range of circumstances that would produce crises narrows, thus reducing potential spikes in public anxiety that come from a sense that social institutions may falter in the face of seriously problematic demands.

The requisites of effective management vary considerably as the operational demands shift from normal, more or less understood, routinized activities to those needed to assure confident responses to understood emergencies. Both normal and emergency activities call for practiced processes founded on an array of recognized skills, coordinating arrangements, accounting techniques, and, in the end, structured organizational patterns that can be learned and transferred from one work generation to the next. And these practices can be interpreted to citizens and to institutional leaders, much as fire prevention and fire-fighting requirements can be described to those who must authorize and pay for them. Effectiveness in realizing these capacities depends centrally on clear understanding of normal working environments and potential threats and the organizational actions needed to reduce and/or limit damage where emergency situations occur (LaPorte, 2005). When these well-ventilated knowledge bases are present, the result is a reasonable degree of certainty about what to do and about the circumstances an organization faces in responding. If well functioning organizational units are able (with skills and resources) reliably to act on this understanding, public confidence is warranted (LaPorte & Metlay, 1996).

The conditions noted so far are generally met in most of what public organizations do—when they engage in normal operations. We expect these functions to characterize administrative systems and bureaucracies we depend upon—even as commentators voice animus about the resulting highly predictable stasis. Indeed, efforts to provide "emergency services" take on many of these predictable qualities—qualities that soothe organizational members and the public as they (and we) seek reassurance in familiarity. Yet one of the lessons learned from reflecting on crisis experiences is that *the more crisis prone the situation, the more deeply surprising and unpredictable it is*—a key condition orienting my comments here (Tierney, Lindell, & Perry, 2001).

CHALLENGES OF "OTHER MANAGEMENTS"

In considering the requirements for emergency and crisis modes of management, I assume two background factors to which I shall return:[5]

- Normal, emergency, and crisis response capabilities (when they exist formally) are likely to be *bundled* together within the same organizations. That is, only a few organizations will see themselves as predominately crisis managers without significant emergency and normal organizational functions as well. Since each of these functions is likely to be associated with different norms and specialized practices, they signal significant imperatives to develop smoothly functioning, "multi-cultural" organizations.

- Emergency and crisis management functions are likely to be seen by most organizational members, and certainly by the public, with a relatively high degree of dread accompanied by serious legislative and public "attention deficit disorder." This has important implications (and dysfunctions) for how public discourse is shaped and evolves.

These background factors of bundled functions and dread color all attempts to join confident, well exercised *emergency management capacities* with the less familiar institutional processes of *"crisis management."* In the first instance, a good deal of emergency management involves working out the processes to identify the onset of recognized operational deviations, nurturing highly reliable organizational responses to them, and establishing damage control capacities to limit organizational liability for unavoidable disruption. Of particular importance here is the tendency for political overseers to press emergency managers to add areas of monitoring and response (often initially prompted by a crisis) where the "loss of control" seems to pose serious risks and damage to agency operations, mission accomplishment, and fitness for the future.

When formal demands grow for responding *effectively to crises*, the conditions of "bundled functions and dread" also affect the dynamics of developing capacities within and between organizations to respond to dangerous, uncertain hazards and, recently, to engage destructive predatory intent. One of the key lessons learned from experiencing crises is that *institutions are confronted with great ambiguity and the "fog of technologies gone opaque."* To remain on the coherent side of chaos requires (a) highly flexible capacity and permission quickly to recombine the organizational capabilities needed to address novel, previously unknowable challenges and, often, (b) seeking out lessons that allow new domains to be included (later) in emergency management processes.[6] Another arresting likelihood is that crises, because they are *novel and surprising experiences for the affected institutions*, are intrinsically difficult for organizational actors to absorb into the context of normal operations or emergency management functions, especially for large, complex (technically oriented) organizations. The implications from an institutional perspective are profound. Organizational learning will be mostly based on *inductive* experiences of failures in past "surprise response reactions," for there will be little credible *deductive* basis to design future oriented, proactive preparation. Furthermore, as noted below, crises vary markedly in their characteristics and, hence, in the variety of institutional capacities needed to respond confidently.

The institutional challenge is remarkable: Success, so to say, rests on understanding *conditions that maintain the institution's capacity to recombine capabilities quickly—with little margins for error—in the face of unpredictable, potentially dire circumstances, that is, rude surprises.*

Clearly, crises come in a variety of types. Their intensities and character of harm vary, as do the qualities of information about institutional capacities related to one crisis or another. Do these variations matter? It is difficult to argue that the conditions needed to maintain the continuities of mature, efficient organizational processes of normal operations, emergency preparedness, *and* crisis response capabilities are independent of variations in the differences between crises. At the same time, there seem to be few attempts to provide a systematic framework for developing institutional capabilities (see for exceptions, Rosenthal, Boin, & Comfort, 2001; Boin, Hart, Stern, & Sndelius, 2005).

Table 2.2 nominates properties of crises that have strong implications for organizational design when political and agency leaders consider enhancing the crisis management capacity of their institutions.[7] Each of these conditions poses rather different organizational puzzles as they vary from one sort of engagement with external pressures or another. One can imagine that as these conditions gather in different combinations, so vary the management challenges that confront the institutions charged with responding to the crises. What follows are reflections on the analytical challenges inherent in deepening our understanding of institutions as they face potential crises.

The two sets of factors are grouped in terms of the expected severity and concentration of the effects of anticipated crises and the quality and accessibility of knowledge needed to understand and then respond to them as they unfold. The more severe the crisis (higher cumulative scores) and the less confidence in and accessibility of information and causal knowledge about the particular crisis (again the higher the score), the more likely institutional disarray and systemic collapse. In general, (a) the more devastating, abruptly delivered, concentrated, and short term the feared effects, and (b) the less confidence in knowledge

Table 2.2.   Properties of Crises: Institutional Design Factors

Factor Varies On a 1-5 Scale	
Public Perception	
a. Consensus on seriousness of the crisis.	From weak, equivocal **to** very strong **
Variations in the Feared Effect	
b. Overall magnitude.	From destructive but not debilitating **to** devastating, potentially irreversible.
c. Speed of crisis unfolding	From evolving over several management generations **to** abrupt and rapid.
d. Propagation of effects	From spreading over unpredictable terrain **to** concentrated.
e. Perceived duration of effects	From many management generations **to** relatively short term.
Information About Causes, Consequences, Responses	
f. Knowledge of causes and consequences.	From available, only needs to be assembled **to** unknowable in the time frame of response.
g. Mix of information for diagnosis, remedy.	From only public information needed **to** information predominantly from secret sources.
h. Consensus on utility/credibility of information.	From strong consensus **to** conflicting, competitive disagreement.

** *Note:*   If consensus is very strong, this trumps everything else as an influence on institutional dynamics.

about causes and consequences, (c) the more secret the information about remedies, and (d) the more disagreement about the credibility of information, the greater the strain, conflict and institutional paralysis and more likely panic behavior of elites. It is unlikely that these factors run together in the directions suggested. Rather, crises are more likely to exhibit different mixes of properties. As these mixes vary, one has a sense that the limits of received conceptual—and practical—wisdom are rather quickly reached.

COMBINATIONS AND ANALYTICAL CONSEQUENCES[8]

Crisis situations present to first responding institutions (a) a wide variety of "crisis properties," and (b) an unusual degree of uncertainty about the specific mix of these conditions. These two characteristics highlight the need for means *to embrace potentially dreadful surprises within an overseeing environment which honors false starts as well as systematic learning*.

To the degree this assertion is defensible, what analytical vectors result? (Set aside, for the moment, the extreme unlikelihood of such organizational norms.)

Let us propose a thought experiment in which some of the eight factors in Table 2.2 are varied along, say, 5-point scales. Then imagine the institutional dynamics (deduced from whatever institutional theories attract you) that might follow if "crisis combination" *a* or *b* or *c* occurred within different "operational and political contexts" (x, y, and z.) Here is a brief illustration (see Table 2.3.) To make this manageable, hold four factors constant (a, d, f, and i).

For each "crisis" assume there is: a moderately strong consensus that it is very serious (factor a/3), with regional effects (d/4); and that knowledge is patchy about its causes and effects (f/3), with information available from credible but competing sources (i/4).

Now posit three cases (A, B, C) varied in terms of the other four (4) factors (see Table 2.3).

Consider the differences in institutional dynamics were the properties of crises to vary as indicated in Table 2.3 (scored on a 5-point scale, 1–5):

Table 2.3.   Factors Parsed—Some Held Constant, Others Varied.*

Factors Held Constant	*Strength (1-5) for Cases A, B, C*		
a. Moderately strong consensus on seriousness of the crisis (3);			
d. Regional propagation of effects (4);			
f. Patchy knowledge of causes and consequences (3);			
h. Competitive sources of useful information (4)			
Case Varied Factors	*A*	*B*	*C*
b. Overall magnitude	devastating (5)	destructive (3) not debilitating	destructive (2) but reversible
c. Speed of crisis unfolding	abrupt, rapid (5)	expected w/in 2 mngt generat.(3)	slowly over 4+ pol generat. (2)
e. Perceived duration of effects	short term (5) 5–10 years	moderate (3) 10–20 years	indeterminate (1) mgt generat.
g. Mix of information for diagnosis, remedy	only public (1) information	equal mix (3) public/classified	mainly (5) classified

Note: * See the appendix for a more formal display of these factors.

The *overall magnitude* for these crises ranges from:

Devastating (5), to Destructive but not debilitating (3), to Reversibly Destructive (2)

The *speed at which they unfolded* ranges from:

Abrupt, rapid onset (5), to one that is expected to become apparent within two management generations (say 14 years) (3), and another not expected for four or more political generations, 24 + years) (2).

The *duration of effects* of these crises is perceived to range from:

Only a short time (5–10 years) (5); to a moderate 10–20 years (3) to stretch indeterminately into the future for many management generations. (1)

The *information needed to respond/recover* ranges from:

Information fully available from public sources (1), sources that are mixed equally from public and classified sources (3), to sources that are mainly from highly classified (5).

Now consider, in your deductive mind's eye, the dynamics that would unfold if a crisis, say, of mix A or B or C, were to be visited upon an administrative and political culture that interests you and you know well.[9] If this administrative setting includes a number of agencies, for example, the combination of air traffic control drawing in the Federal Aviation Administration (FAA), the National Transportation Safety Board (NTSB), and a wide swath of U.S. air carriers, so much the better. Now, add detail to the analysis by making explicit those first responders whose operating responsibilities *cross* jurisdictional and national borders. One could imagine, for example, something of the rude financial surprises that involve a number of institutions and different national environments.

If you have begun imagining several cases—even with these simplified variables from which to deduct institutional, decision maker, and operator responses—you are likely to sense a series of daunting tasks. As you jot down your "seat of the pants" expectations, be sure to include their analytical, conceptual, dare I say theoretical, justifications. How confident are you regarding your predictions? How robust are their conceptual groundings?

Facing emergencies (challenges that had been experienced before) with these varying characteristics would prompt different institutional dynamics, perhaps different emphases of skills, decision processes, and very likely different relations with stakeholding groups. Even if it were limited, prior experience would very likely have resulted in the development of at least some emergency coping response capabilities. This would lead to a sense of anticipation and perhaps even a practiced capacity to deal with the sorts of hazards associated with the feared events.

But crises are, by definition, rude, upsetting surprises, novel circumstances that seem likely to overwhelm existing capacity. They present unexpected challenges about which there cannot be much forward planning because the particulars could not have been predicted. Learning to embrace surprise becomes a useful survival strategy.

ARRESTING PUZZLES

The general characteristics of crises noted above lack adjustment for specific context. Indeed, the tacit frame of reference assumes the presence of a wide range of properties associated with large scale, nationally based institutions rooted in advanced industrial society. Until recently, this may have been justified, I suppose, when examining crises through the period of the Cold War. But, within this decade, a type or class of crisis has emerged that presents particularly puzzling qualities, especially in terms of institutional design. These crises are notable for they involve rude surprises of a particularly troubling nature: the surprises that attend a novel sort of "*fluid terrorism*," especially those associated with suicide terror, or "martyr operations," that have become a means of attack used by some groups oriented toward radical forms of Islam. (We return to this point in Theme Two below.) A mainly post–9/11 phenomenon for U.S. citizens, the crises prompted by these threats combine aspects that confound and amplify the intensity of other qualities.

(a) The U.S. and European institutions face adversaries whose motivations *no longer include a deep attachment to physical survival* as a defining element in their notions of self-interest.

(b) Our adversaries' organizational bases are *not firmly grounded within national systems* of legal and police activities, and national institutions are less effective as means of control.

(c) There are means to *deliver very significant economic and social destruction* more widely than at any time in history. Indeed, in a sense we have gloried in this accomplishment of globalization.

(d) Partly as a consequence, there is the sense of apprehension, *repressed public fear and a kind of free floating dread* that is amplified by "terrorist attacks."

(e) Finally, in response, we see the need to be very broadly prepared, across a much wider range of "first responders" than in the past, at a *much higher level of operating reliability* than has ever been demanded of public institutions or private enterprises.

When challenges *threaten very rude surprises,* characterized by many of the factors noted just above, how do the cases spin out in the settings you know best? From what *theoretical/conceptual bases can confident expectations be derived to anticipate the institutional challenges* associated with them?

Ruminate—deductively—about the dynamics implied. These exercises are likely to show that our insights about managing *to prepare for surprises* are weakly founded. If this is to improve, we need to find ways of framing the matter that provide grounds for research and experiment.

TOWARD DISCUSSION THEMES

This article has taken us unexpectedly at an angle from the vectors of highly reliable organizations, and public trust and confidence, that I had imagined I would follow.[10] The results are more speculative and more worrisome. Below, I nominate several derivative *themes* that raise questions of concept, research, and practice. How could they be expressed in terms of the substantive domains of interest in the social sciences and for purposes of public policy?

Theme One: Managing to be Rudely Surprised (for a Hundred Years?)

In a sense, "crises management" is a contradiction in terms. Rude surprises are not managed; responses to them can be. From an institutional view, the challenges are not only to be prepared, in advance, to do things one knows you will have to do, but to have capacities at-the-ready, so to say, to be combined in unforeseen ways with other capabilities, perhaps from other domains of civil society, as the parameters of the new crisis unfold.

A central question could be: What institutional conditions need to be assured so that rapid recombinations of organizational capacity (and sometime added functions) can be realized? What patterns of incentives would assure self-organized, flexible adaptation to rude surprises for an *unforeseeably long future?* (see LaPorte, 2004; LaPorte & Keller, 1996)[11] Second, to what degree could an *institutional culture of effective emergency response impede the development of a culture embracing uncertainty and surprise?*

The analytical dimensions of addressing these questions are formidable. Novel combinations must usually emerge while normal operations continue. Much of what is nominated as "best practice" for regular public organizational operations leads in the direction of close internal control, limiting slack resources, and transparent, usually punitive external accountability.[12] It is difficult to see how these properties of public institutions result in the capacity quickly to crystallize novel relations between formerly separate functions as the parameters of a rude surprise become evident.

The sustained effectiveness of U.S. institutions to develop emergency response capabilities, perhaps anticipating small surprises and incipient crises, should be reviewed on two counts. How have responding institutions attempted to develop a culture of emergency response (that includes preparation for surprise)? We see attempts to do both in some U.S. state emergency response operations, wildfire-fighting experience, and the U.S. Federal Emergency Management Agency's (FEMA) insistence that nuclear power plant operators conduct bi-annual, full-scale simulations of disaster response decision making. These simulations include ALL of the decision makers likely to be involved, were there to be enough loss of containment of nuclear radiation to warrant the evacuation of adjacent communities. There are similar experiences in the ways the U.S. Centers for Disease Control and Prevention (CDC) assemble the relevant agencies and non-governmental organizations to respond to the discovery of new communicable pathogens (e.g., SARS epidemic). Less admirable experience is found in the United States' tentative initial response to HIV infections.

To what degree can emergency preparedness be accomplished in ways that do not inhibit preparing for rude surprise? This would encourage the potential for ad hoc authority patterns, the availability of resources beyond those needed for everyday activities, and a working environment that minimizes the fear of post hoc criticism and institutional retribution for trial and error learning that necessarily accompanies rude surprises.

Two propositions derive from injunctions in pursuit of normal operations and effective emergency response capabilities with regard to the conditions outlined in the crisis exercise (above). I state these in a bald form.

- The more productively efficient the organization that is called to respond to a crisis, the less capable it will be in dealing with untoward surprise (see Auerswald, Branscomb, LaPorte, & Michel-Kerjan, 2006).
- The higher the consensus about the seriousness of the crisis and the need for rapid response, the more likely serious errors will be made.[13]

Another aspect of "crisis management" also confounds: There is a very low likelihood that any particular network of institutions will actually experience a crisis. When they do, they are likely to incorporate the lessons they learn into their subsequent suite of *emergency* processes. By iinstituting such practices, these institutions are *likely* to *limit* the potential for recombination in the face of unlikely next surprising crises.

It follows that the institutional energy and resources needed for ready responsiveness to untoward surprises will be difficult to assure from one generation to the next. Why, it will be argued, prepare for surprises that are unlikely to confront you? (Another version of "life is short," heed the probable.) This is especially difficult when overseers suspect that surprises are unlikely. Much of what public institutions do is strongly affected by the behavior of political overseers and legislatures. What roles do agency or ministry leaders and legislatures play in assuring the institutional conditions needed continually to respond effectively to serious surprises? We know a good deal about the dynamics of political overseers that work to constrain, sometimes paralyze, agency behavior. These dynamics are precisely the reverse of what would be needed in the face of rude surprise. Considerable work is needed on the potential for overseers' norms that would *increase* the likelihood of institutional flexibility and novel cooperation. Two aspects come to mind, noted here without elaboration.

- Examine the changes in *accounting practices* that would reward, under defined conditions, flexible institutional responses. These would allow for a better understanding of how unauthorized expenses, without formal review, could be incurred rapidly without fear that, in the aftermath of the crisis, those who provided "unauthorized" assistance would discover they could not be reimbursed— essentially being punished post hoc for flexible behavior. To the degree this is expected, and is believed to have occurred, it is the basis for the "bean counting lament," reluctant cooperation, and residual institutional bitterness.

- Understanding the effects of media behavior (themselves performing an overseeing function) on *inhibiting* institutional cooperation, and ad hoc responses to rude surprise.

Theme Two: When the Surprise is Predatory—With a Sacrificial Twist!

In the past, "crisis management" has tacitly assumed that crises would be the result of natural forces and/or unintended human action. Most discussions of these topics include rude surprises that originate from collective behavior of society's economic and political elites, for example, regional financial disruption, crashes of economic markets, and the popular over throw of an established regime. Now as we peer into the future, we must also consider the recent substantial increase in the propensity for humans to prey upon their own kind. Short of organized military action, this predatory activity can wreak sufficiently unexpected destruction to become a new source of crisis. To what degree does social predation add confounding complications when public institutions attempt to prepare gracefully for rude surprises—surprises that now can originate from within their own or other civil societies?

Within the past 5 years, the United States has, for the first time, experienced such a predatory situation, one that interjects security concerns into the mix.[14] The West's confrontation with radical Islam is producing serious and complicating concerns about how public institutions should establish confident emergency responses and, particularly, how they might incorporate processes that prepare the public for predatory crises. Two of the factors in Table 2.2 speak to this situation: the mix of publicly available versus classified information needed to prepare for and/or respond to rude, nasty surprises; and the credibility of the information sources that are available.

Without dwelling here on the importance of these two factors (indeed, readers may wish to add others that stem from predatory sources of crises), it is clear that increasing proportions of classified information needed for understanding and responding to novel threatening surprises set in motion institutional reactions and operating dynamics that are themselves quite difficult to predict. What effects do variations in these factors have on the capacity of institutions to elaborate the norms and develop the facility to recombine resources in the face of novel, nasty surprises? One significant aspect of this is to account for the effects on "crisis management" requirements as a society's technical and institutional infrastructure becomes increasingly interdependent on the province of homeland security and defense agencies. This is particularly interesting as one considers differences among political cultures.

The newly emergent conditions of social predation, which the United States especially seems to confront, represent major hurdles for American institutional preparedness for emergencies and rude surprises. One characteristic is particularly confounding and, when joined by the others, mounts major challenges. Some adversaries' motivations *no longer share with us a deep attachment to physical survival* as a defining element in their notions of self-interest. Nearly all Western concepts of cooperation, deterrence, and social conflict are rooted at least tacitly in this premise. All of our organizational strategies have been based on implicitly accepting the notion of *"physical survival as self-interest."* When we apply them to many of the situations we now confront, errors in predicting adversarial behavior result. Some of these errors produce what amount to tactical crises for those who are the objects of predatorial attack. Providing the institutional capacity to recombine capabilities in the field, when these assumptions are relaxed, becomes a major challenge.

Theme Three: When Rude Surprises are Transborder

The spate of workshops and conferences convened broadly around the crisis/disaster management theme offer an "existence proof" that when the effects of crises spill across national boundaries, analysts and operators have only modest confidence in how to proceed. If confident projections are asserted in public pronouncements, they are almost always rooted in one analytical ideology or another, which, of itself, generates sufficient disagreement to erode general confidence.

Pose this situation in the form of a null hypothesis: Institutional responses to threatening surprises in one nation will be very similar to those in other nations. The only response has to be, *"not likely."* Then the analytical challenge is to identify national conditions that account for differences that we *already* see and should expect to color reactions from the representatives of various national analytical communities.

Another way of putting this is to wonder: In each of the countries affected by a particular crisis, what intranational conditions enable highly discretionary institutional behavior—in service to self-organizing recombination of public capacity as the lineaments of a rude surprise unfold? There is no reason a priori to suppose they will be the same conditions in each country. What national institutional patterns that nurture cooperative behavior *within* the nation also act to inhibit (a) highly discretional behavior *among* national agencies, and (b) *among* agencies of other countries?

In this vein, what conceptual frames would give analysts confident bases for nominating the several most telling national institutional properties from which to predict different patterns of "crisis response" dynamics? Would, for example, these include systematic differences between countries with traditions of common law compared to those following code law? And the list surely would quickly expand to consider the variations in internal incentives, work rules, accounting practices, and so forth; but which aspects of each category? How could the choice be justified conceptually?

All of these can be scrutinized in terms of the inhibiting or enabling effect on self-organized recombination. As far as I know, this way of understanding the effects of consistency and control maintaining processes on institutional responses to surprise (unknowns, sometime unknown unknowns) has not been of interest. When considering "crisis management" in the future, it should be. As national differences become better understood, one suspects that both the opportunities and difficulties of analysis, and then operational adjustment and training, will be much more apparent.

Theme Four: "Crisis Speak" and Design Frames?

In writing this article, the regular language of organizational analysis did not serve me very well either in terms of concepts or in effective means of describing the dynamics one can imagine when managing to embrace rude surprises. There is clearly a need to think carefully about the analytical terms of reference, the views the public, and especially overseers, hold about what is possible and what could be expected in the evolution of "managing in the midst of crisis," as well as a need for a dialect of crisis response evaluation—in parallel to the current language of productive efficiency.

Public management communities now think warmly about increasing productive efficiency and performance management in the public service. This is a domain well known to academics and practitioners of public management. What would become of this discussion if criteria for efficiency also included, say, efficiencies of *crisis response and recovery*, that is, assuring situations that result in intrinsically less damage from crises over many generations of operations? When technical efficiency improvements reduce slack resources, these are no longer available to facilitate taking up new functions, to cover unfamiliar coordination costs, or to invest in distilling lessons learned from the new rude surprise. Could there be a way of framing "crisis preparation/embracing costs" so that they can be included in strategic planning? These are in a sense the costs associated with having uncommitted financial reserves and, as importantly, the costs of not planning *in advance* to encumber 100+ percent of executives' time for each year. In some situations, executives calculate that up to 20% of their annual actual decision time was spent on problems that were novel and unexpected.

A related challenge would be straightforwardly designing technical and operational systems to fail gracefully. In terms of anticipating rude surprises, this would entail designs that facilitated institutions' capacities to reduce maximum damage *if* they confronted a really rude surprise and lost control of their dynamics. This tactic is sometimes featured in military hardware systems and other operations depending on intrinsically hazardous technologies. Fail-safe or safe failing systems intrigue engineers, though this is rarely proposed for the design of large-scale public institutions, or put forward as what should be done for public policies, say in genetically modified food, national pollution control, or ecological protection programs.

When the roots of fearful failure implicate social or political predators, then institutional design for "failing gracefully" takes on an additional objective: thinking through the development of "predator confounding systems." This, of course, is an important element in considering emergency systems—getting ready to do what one must to anticipate damage from known processes. Preparing to embrace unpredictable, predator prompted surprises is likely to be quite different—and difficult to explain to most overseers currently "on watch."

Finally, and most puzzling, are the design implications of preparing confidently to *embrace rude surprises for a number of management and political generations*. Crises that unexpectedly arise from natural and unintentional human sources will occur without end—the institutional demands stretching far into the future. It is possible that their magnitude will grow, and responding to them will be increasingly costly in both economic and social terms. At the same time, it is imaginable that crises of predatory origins will also continue for many political generations and grow in anxiety-arousing potential. From administrative and policy vantages, this means enhancing short-term response effectiveness while reenforcing the development of long-term, highly reliable capacities that exhibit institutional constancy. This involves signaling to the public that the institutions the public depends upon will be able repeatedly to show they can respond to rude surprises, adapt to novel situations, limit damage, and effectively draw lessons from the fearfully unexpected events in ways that improve the emergency response capabilities of each of a number of succeeding generations. This is perhaps the most difficult of the many, nearly insurmountable challenges embedded in the intention to improve "crisis management." It calls persistently to maintain appropriate levels of social watchfulness, and to purposefully engender enough social anxiety to guard continually—generation after generation—against extreme events.[15]

AN AFTERWORD WITH SKEPTICISM

There is a hopeful cast to dialogues of the kind illustrated in this book on crisis management. An obvious need is framed, energized discussions go forward—members of the choir engage each other. This is a good thing; we charge our batteries for the long pull ahead. At the same time, some attention could be fruitfully devoted to a counter view—explicating the present institutional conditions that load the dice against much more than rhetorical gain in deepening our understanding of the institutional elements that facilitate optimal responses of rude surprises even within.

APPENDIX: IMAGINARY MIX OF CRISIS PROPERTIES*

Factor	Strength (1-5) in Case		
	A	B	C
a. Consensus on seriousness of the crisis	strong (4)	strong (4)	strong (4)
b. Overall magnitude	devastating (5)	destructive (3) not debilitating	destructive (2) but reversible
c. Speed of crisis unfolding	abrupt, rapid (5)	expected w/in 2 mngt generat.(3)	slowly over 4 + pol generat. (2)
d. Propagation of effects	regional effects (4)	regional effects (4)	regional effects (4)
e. Perceived duration of effects	short term (5) 5–10 years	moderate (3) 10–20 years	indeterminate(1) mgt generat.
f. Knowledge of causes and consequences	patchy, (3) some available	patchy, (3) some available	patchy, (3) some available
g. Mix of information for diagnosis, remedy	only public (1) information	equal mix (3) public/classified	mainly (5) classified
h. Consensus on utility/credibility	competitive (3) credibility	competitive (3) credibility	competitive (3) credibility

Note: * Variable factors in italics.

NOTES

1. A less developed version of this paper was used for the Conference on Transatlantic Crisis Management, Adirondack Conference Center, Syracuse University, August 6–10, 2003, sponsored by the Center for Crisis Management Research and Training (CRISMART), Swedish National Defense College, the Crisis Research Center, Leiden University, and the Trans-boundary Crisis Management Project, Maxwell School, Syracuse University.

2. Exceptions are the work of Trans-boundary Crisis Management Project, Syracuse University, the Crisis Research Center, Leiden University, and the Center for Crisis Management Research and Training (CRISMART).

3. From the orientation overview for the Conference on Transatlantic Crisis Management.

4. These reflections were initially cobbled together before Hurricane Katrina struck New Orleans and triggered a flood of commentary regarding catastrophe—an event whose intensity goes beyond most of what we usually regard as a crisis. I have not explicitly engaged with the order of institutional surprises associated with this extraordinary event, though much of what I include here pertains to the institutional challenges associated with catastrophe.

5. These are introduced without justification. I invite readers to add others.

6. An example is the realization that a major postemergency responsibility is the provision of mental health services to the affected communities.

7. I invite the reader to nominate additional factors. Notably absent here are conditions that stem from the differences in national institutional patterns and dynamics. These become important when preparing general capacities to respond trans-national crises. For the moment, these sources of variation are bracketed. I return to them below.

8. These reflections now become more cryptic. The analytical vectors proposed here produce an unexpected matrix of puzzles, too many to explore in moderate length. The Themes section extends some of them.

9. For simplicity's sake, I have arranged the factors in these three cases varying mostly from more to less intensity. Of course, reality rarely affords such simplicity. Patterns that scramble the intensity of these factors are more likely, analytically more interesting—and much more demanding.

10. The original draft title was "Reliable Behavior and Institutional Constancy in the Face of Future, (Transnational) Crises: (Requisites of Public Confidence?)."

11. The long-term pressures from environmental changes, along with radical Islam I noted, signal the relevance of our work on institutional constancy.

12. As an aside, framed this way, following the familiar path of seeking "best practices" takes on an odd cast. Best practices usually refer to processes, and so forth, in which there is considerable confidence, for they have been tried out repeatedly in similar situations, then distilled and used again. Rarely, if ever, would this situation characterize crisis learning.

13. In part, this results from the compression of attention and the degradation of analysis due to perceived time constraints.

14. Notably, these complications have been encountered in Europe for decades. Americans have much to learn from this history.

15. Pointed out by Todd M. LaPorte, private communication.

REFERENCES

Auerswald, P., Branscomb, L., LaPorte, T. M., & Michel-Kerjan, E. (Eds.). (2006). *Private efficiency, public vulnerability: Protecting critical infrastructure.* Cambridge, MA: University Press.

Boin, R. A., Hart, P. 't., Stern, E., & Sundelius, B. (2005). *The politics of crisis management: Leadership under pressure.* Cambridge, MA: University Press.

LaPorte, T. R. (1996). High reliability organizations: Unlikely, demanding and at risk. *Journal of Crisis and Contingency Management, 4*(2), 60–71.

LaPorte, T. R. (2004, February). *Elements for long term institutional stewardship in a hazardous age.* Views from a "Stewardee" session on Institutional Challenges for Long-Term Stewardship of Contaminated Sites, Association for the Advancement of Science, Seattle, WA.

LaPorte, T. R. (2004, April). *Considerations of "Suicide Terrorism": Social predation with a sacrificial twist.* Paper presented to the Critical Incident Analysis Group, School of Medicine annual conference on countering suicide terrorism: Risks, responsibilities and realities, University of Virginia.

LaPorte, T. R. (2005, December). *Preparing for untoward surprise: Lessons yet to be learned—Post Katrina and Post 9/11.* National symposium on risk and disasters: Lessons from Hurricane Katrina for American life, rebuilding The Gulf, Washington, DC.

LaPorte, T. R., & Keller A. (1996). Assuring Institutional Constancy: Requisite for Managing Long-Lived Hazard. *Public Administration Review, 56*(6), 535–544.

LaPorte, T. R., & Metlay D. (1996). Facing a deficit of trust: Hazards and institutional trustworthiness. *Public Administration Review, 56*(4), 341–346.

Rosenthal, U., Boin, R. A., & Comfort, L. K. (Eds.). (2001). *Managing crises: Threats, dilemmas, opportunities.* Springfield, IL: Charles C. Thomas.

Trans-boundary Crisis Management Project, Syracuse University, the Crisis Research Center, Leiden University, and the Center for Crisis Management Research and Training (CRISMART). (2003).

Tierney, K. J. (2006, March). *Hurricane Katrina: Catastrophic impact and alarming lessons.* Symposium on real estate, catastrophe, risk and public policy, University of California, Berkeley, CA.

Tierney, K. J., Lindell, M. K., & Perry, R. W. (2001). *Facing the unexpected: Disaster preparedness and response in the United States.* Washington, DC: Joseph Henry Press.

CHAPTER 3

TECHNOLOGICAL TRANSFORMATION OF LOGISTICS IN SUPPORT OF CRISIS MANAGEMENT

Richard A. Braunbeck III and Michael F. Mastria

This chapter identifies and explores logistical frameworks that leverage technology to overcome problems associated with coordinated logistics operations during crisis management. Over the past 10 years, there have been significant advances in Radio Frequency Identification (RFID), satellite, and other related asset visibility technologies. These advances are mature enough to significantly increase the probability of achieving a useful Common Operational Picture during emergency response activities. Recent crisis response operations that would have benefited from improved asset visibility include the Indian Ocean tsunami, the Pakistani earthquake, Hurricane Katrina, and those related to the Global War on Terror. In each of these cases, multiagency involvement, both foreign and domestic, compounded the complexity of asset tracking and communication protocols. The establishment of a logistics-tracking framework that provides adequate asset visibility, while maintaining operational security, will greatly increase the effectiveness of future crisis response operations. The proposed logistics framework serves as a viable solution for common logistical problems encountered by industrialized nations while conducting crisis response

Communicable Crises: Prevention, Response, and Recovery in the Global Arena, pp. 47–82
Copyright © 2007 by Information Age Publishing
All rights of reproduction in any form reserved.

operations. The framework identifies concepts, technologies, and protocols that can be used to improve crisis operations on a global scale.

INTRODUCTION

As evidenced by recent large-scale disasters, significant shortfalls exist in the emergency response capabilities of the United States and the international community. In the United States, the response to Hurricane Katrina uncovered several systemic problems associated with coordinated logistics. These problems hindered the ability of response professionals to create an atmosphere of trust and confidence among those affected. Logistical failure was recognized as a major contributing factor to the overall response breakdown, particularly the absence of reliable, secure, and appropriately transparent asset visibility. By asset visibility, we mean the capability of crisis response personnel to access timely and accurate information regarding the location, status, identity, and requirements associated with available resources (The White House, 2006, p. 44).

Coordinated logistics is a pivotal component in the conduct of effective crisis management. The goal of coordinated logistics should be to maximize efficiency with respect to the allocation of available resources. To achieve this, the right people within each agency or organization need to be communicating and monitoring the same situational picture. Done well, multiagency coordination can provide a tremendous positive impact. Done poorly, it may yield severe negative results. This research identifies and explores relevant technologies and their potential roles within existing and developing frameworks designed to facilitate coordinated response to large-scale crises. In recent years, there have been significant advances in RFID, satellite, and other related asset visibility technologies. Of particular value are technological advances that increase the probability of achieving a useful common operational picture during emergency response activities.

The overall effect of multiagency involvement has served as a primary trigger for our research. The level of simultaneous interaction required from various diverse entities compounds the complexity of asset tracking and related communication protocols. As a mitigating factor, it is imperative to maintain an appropriate focus on the concept of "open architecture" because it encourages and facilitates modularity, economies of scale, and decreased learning curves, all factors that contribute to lower costs. Doing so will have a profound effect on the costs associated with emerging and developing technologies. The establishment of a logistical framework built on the concepts of open architecture, reliable asset visibility, and operational security, will greatly increase the effectiveness of future crisis response operations and provide the assurance that is necessary for the success of any crisis response system.

Given the state of technology in today's world, there is no reason why governments should not be able to provide better crisis response. Wildfires, earthquakes, tornados, hurricanes, tsunamis, and terrorist attacks are all realities throughout the world. Some question the United States' ability to respond effectively. Others believe that America has strong logistical capabilities with respect to crisis management. Despite the shortfalls of the Katrina disaster response, the tools and resources to achieve the desired state of readiness already exist and could be exploited. Whether the right decisions will be made depends on the leadership at the highest and most critical levels. The United States has implemented innovative logistics solutions in the past. The Liberty Ships and the Pacific Campaign of WWII, the Berlin Airlift, and the Desert Storm preinvasion build-up are a few examples. But, as we all have probably experienced, you are only as good as your last failure. It is now time to set forth on the next large-scale, innovative logistical solution. The logistical frameworks and associated technologies that are explored can provide the groundwork and background for crisis response logistical programs in the United States and throughout the world.

LOGISTICS DURING CRISIS MANAGEMENT

Asset Visibility and the Common Operational Picture

Relief efforts in response to recent large-scale disasters such as the Indian Ocean tsunami (December, 2004), Hurricane Katrina (August, 2005), and the Pakistani earthquake (October, 2005) have confirmed the need for more effective logistics operations during crisis response.

A study conducted by the Fritz Institute, a San Francisco-based nonprofit organization that works with humanitarian relief organizations and the private sector to identify solutions to complex operational challenges, concluded that the tsunami relief effort was marred with logistical problems. Some 100 officials in charge of logistics operations were surveyed at 18 of the largest humanitarian organizations that participated in relief operations. Sixteen of these organizations reported that, at the time of the disaster, they suffered from shortages of experienced logisticians within the South Asian region. Only five of the organizations claimed to have access to integrated computer software that allowed for the tracking of resources. Many of the groups did the best they could with what they had, tracking resources manually or through the use of generic spreadsheet programs. The survey also found that, while many of the organizations made an effort to coordinate with local authorities and the military, only about half reported efforts to coordinate with other relief agencies. This lack of coordination is believed to have contributed to many of the logistical bottlenecks that hindered relief operations (Jensen, 2005).

Considerable advances in communication, satellite and RFID technologies offer viable solutions to several traditional logistical problems. Reliable in-transit visibility, coupled with improved interagency communication and coordination, has the potential to provide significant benefits to all stakeholders. The need for these benefits is especially apparent during the critical lifesaving hours following a disaster. The proper application of in-transit visibility can greatly increase the probability that a useful common operational picture will be achieved during crisis response operations. Without it, the chances of providing assurance during chaos will be significantly diminished.

A common operational picture allows identical, relevant information to be shared by more than one command, agency, or authority. It facilitates collaborative planning and coordinated operations by providing all echelons the ability to achieve a high level of situational awareness (Joint Chiefs of Staff, 2005, p. GL6). Relevant information could be as broad as a nation's entire stock of small pox vaccination and as detailed as the last known location of a pallet of Meals-Ready-to-Eat (MREs). While conducting crisis management activities, critical time-sensitive information could be the difference between chaos and order. Within the logistics function of an Incident Command Center, asset visibility is the key component that contributes to a useful common operational picture. Figure 3.1 illustrates how systems and agencies linked by an integrated communications network can use and share information about resources, thereby allowing accurate, real-time asset visibility, a key requirement in the effective flow of material logistics.

Logistics Operations in Support of Hurricane Katrina

To identify the most promising courses of action for the implementation of an integrated crisis response logistics model, we must glean insight from the most advanced existing frameworks. Equally important is recognizing the most recent and comprehensive example of crisis response where these frameworks were fully tested.

Several serious concerns were publicized during the Hurricane Katrina disaster that led to the perception of an ineffective federal response system. The sheer magnitude of the storm was such that certain effects of its power were impossible to effectively mitigate (The White House, 2006,

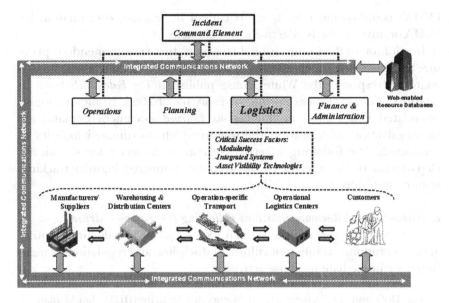

Sources: DSCC, 2005; NIMS 2004; NRP, 2004.

Figure 3.1.   Conceptual integrated framework.

p. 34). However, tools that could have mitigated many negative effects of the storm and its aftermath were not exploited (Newman, 2006). Although there were few deaths from long-term exposure or starvation, and the international response was minimal, Hurricane Katrina is a useful case study. This particular disaster tested and pushed many response functions to and, in many cases, past their breaking points. State-of-the-art response assets and protocols were employed on a large scale, and there were unprecedented levels of media coverage and data to analyze (Reuters, AlertNet, 2005).

Logistical tracking is one of the only major shortcomings that former FEMA director Mike Brown pinpointed during the September 27, 2005, congressional hearings held to "Investigate the Preparation for and Response to Hurricane Katrina" (Library of Congress Congressional Record, 2005). Logistical tracking becomes increasingly important as the size and scope of the subject disaster increases. If a disaster only covers a square mile, most logistics can likely be disbursed from one central and secure location. As the disaster area increases, there is a greater requirement for more complex logistical tracking and planning. Because assistance from FEMA and other federal agencies is more commonly required during large scale emergencies, logistics tracking is a central concern in

FEMA's coordination role. If assets cannot be tracked, coordination by FEMA or anyone else is effectively unattainable.

In addition to the Congressional Hearings, there was tremendous pressure to provide further answers as to why Katrina relief efforts were inadequate. In response, the White House published *The Federal Response to Hurricane Katrina, Lessons Learned* in February of 2006. Numerous logistics-related issues cited in the *Lessons Learned* document demand an increased effort to transform the way in which coordinated logistics is conducted. The following excerpts emphasize the need for significant Department of Defense (DoD) involvement, improved logistics tracking systems and overall asset visibility.

Logistics-Related Recommendations Following Hurricane Katrina

The DoD has the most sustained experience in conducting contingency operations. Its inherent culture of discipline and regulations is well-suited for immediate response activities.

> The DoD and the Department of Homeland Security (DHS) should plan and prepare for a significant DoD supporting role during a catastrophic event. The DoD's joint operational response doctrine is an integral part of the national effort and must be fully integrated into the national response at all levels of government. DoD should have a contingency role and a requirement to assist DHS with expertise in logistics, planning, and total asset visibility. (The White House, 2006, p. 94)

The National Guard has an accepted and tried role in crisis response. They have within their own state and neighboring states that provide them with insights less likely achieved by standard national U.S. military forces. Many capability limitations inherent within the National Guard can be met through the use of designated federal military personnel and resources. To realize these capabilities, a structure must be created to optimize cooperation and coordination.

> DoD should consider fully resourcing the Joint Task Force State Headquarters to address capabilities gaps and to enhance readiness. Enhance National Guard capabilities by resourcing and fully implementing Joint Force Headquarters (JFHQ) State. JFHQ-State transformation is key to rapid deployment of National Guard forces in response to a catastrophe. (The White House, 2006, p. 95)

Asset visibility can be achieved using common standards throughout the integrated supply chain. As part of a useful common operational picture, asset visibility positively contributes to decision-making processes by allowing the most efficient allocation and distribution of life-saving resources.

The Department of Homeland Security, in coordination with State and local governments and the private sector, should develop a modern, flexible and transparent logistics system. (The White House, 2006, p. 98)

Many commercial products were offered to FEMA during the Hurricane Katrina response. The difficulties of entering these items into the federal supply chain left many of them unutilized. Compatible asset visibility systems increase the likelihood that items donated by or purchased from commercial business entities concurrent to the crisis response will be effectively exploited.

DHS should partner with State and local governments, other Federal agencies and the private sector to develop an efficient, transparent and flexible logistics system for the procurement and delivery of goods and services during emergencies. "The new logistics system developed in concert with State and local governments, and the private sector should be transparent to all managers within the system (Federal, State and local governments and the private sector). The system should be comprehensive so that the full range of logistical requirements and the flow of goods and services can be tracked from provider to receiver. (The White House, 2006, p. 98)

In any operation, there is value in clearly defining hierarchical and cooperative relationships among all stakeholders. For crisis response activities, this becomes even more important because time spent deciding who should make decisions is critical time wasted.

DHS should establish a Chief Logistics Officer to oversee all logistics operations across multiple support functions. The Chief Logistics Officer (CLO) would be responsible for developing and maintaining an integrated supply chain management system. This system should be structured in ways that are compatible with the structure of the National Incident Management System. The CLO would be responsible for logistics technology and software solutions that allow emergency managers to have visibility of all assets in the supply chain and to be able to access those supplies. A CLO should also be established in each homeland security regional office. (The White House, 2006, p. 99)

Drawing on the DoD's experience in developing logistics systems for the DHS will reduce friction and miscommunication among all crisis response agencies. Cooperation between the two agencies before a disaster will provide critical benefits toward cooperation during a disaster. Personnel exchange programs are an effective way to achieve this working relationship in a sustaining manner.

> DoD should detail logistics planners to DHS to assist in developing this logistics system. DoD and DHS should review and consider supply chain management best practices in developing the DHS logistics system. DoD should assist DHS in developing its logistics system; train DHS personnel in logistics management; exercise the DHS logistics system; and assist operating DHS' logistics management system until a fully mature capability exists. (The White House, 2006, p. 99)

The sovereignty of state governments in managing crises within their own state is a critical concept in any process transformation that incorporates changes in the federal scope of action or authority. Incentives may be needed to pressure states into accepting and meeting federal requirements.

> DHS should require State and local governments, as a condition for receiving Homeland Security grants, to develop, implement, and exercise emergency evacuation plans and to cooperate fully with all Federal evacuation activities. Consideration should be given to revising the Stafford Act to restrict reimbursement eligibility to only those States that have met basic performance requirements for critical functions such as mass evacuation. (The White House, 2006, p. 100)

The need for DoD integration in hurricane response is not a post-Katrina concept as some of the previous excerpts imply. The need for transformational integration of DoD assets was recognized prior to Katrina. The excerpt below shows the concerted yet underdeveloped attempt to coordinate FEMA and the DoD. Within this limited cooperative framework, the DoD was still able to provide useful asset visibility support to FEMA during the Hurricane Katrina response.

> Well before Hurricane Katrina struck the Gulf Coast, the Department of Defense (DoD) prepared for the 2005 hurricane season. Based on prior assistance for hurricane recovery operations, on August 19th the Secretary of Defense approved a standing order to prepare and organize for severe weather disaster operations. This order expedited the pre-positioning of senior military representatives known as Defense Coordinating Officers, to act as liaisons with other governmental organizations in the projected disaster area prior to an event. The order also authorized the use of DoD installations as logistical staging areas for FEMA. U.S. Northern Command directed a number of emergency deployment readiness exercises prior to FEMA requests, spending training funds to preposition response capability. Once officially activated and deployed, DoD provided logistics support to

FEMA, helping the Agency to track items in motion. (The White House, 2006, p. 130)

The Federal Government has explored, and become more knowledgeable about, existing deficiencies and corresponding solutions. Logistics, command structure, discipline and heavy DoD involvement are major themes of the *Katrina, Lessons Learned* document. While this government document provides a realistic assessment of the situation during the Hurricane Katrina relief effort, other sources are needed to provide a complete picture.

Redundancy and Communications

During an emergency, responders often do not have the luxury of time to recover from a system or device failure. If an asset tracking device or system fails, the emergency situation will likely be over before repairs or remediation can be put into place. Additionally, if time is spent on recovering the tracking system, the lost time may hinder operations to the extent that it would be better to do without the tracking system altogether. When a system fails, it is often better to move forward using any redundant tracking system available, even if it does not provide the accuracy, timeliness or clarity of the primary system (C. Nutting, personal communication, December 7, 2005).

One way to achieve redundancy in asset tracking is through the duplication of functionally identical tracking devices or systems. An example of this would be the placing of four passive RFID tags per pallet of a tracked asset. This arrangement will allow each of the pallets' vertical sides to have a tag, thus affording quicker reading without searching for a tag. This also allows item identification if one or more of the tags is damaged or obscured. Another way that redundancy can be achieved is to utilize distinct and dissimilar tracking devices and systems. For example, the use of passive RFID tags on a pallet could be bolstered by a satellite transponder on the trailer that contains the pallet. Additionally, the truck that is moving the trailer may use CB radio or a cell phone to provide regular location updates. This practice of using redundant means of communication can be very important during various emergencies where communication system failures are common.

During natural disasters, as in traditional military operations, conditions exist that can easily disable required power supplies and communication equipment. If backup systems are concurrently operating or can be quickly brought on line, the mission can continue with limited adverse interruption. One way to minimize the necessity for redundancy is through the strengthening of existing or future logistics tracking systems.

A good example of this is the use of mobile satellite communications, which are less vulnerable to probable threats.

Decision Support Systems

Good decision making requires accurate information processing. Too much disorganized information can create a significant challenge during emergency response efforts because excess information can oversaturate those who are trying to make decisions. Precise and highly pertinent information promotes effective decision making, especially in emergency situations. If decision makers spend too much time evaluating exhaustive amounts of unrefined information, they may have insufficient time to effectively act on that information. The use of Automatic Information Systems can help collect, refine, and present large amounts of raw data that can be transformed into actionable information.

A properly implemented Automatic Information System is essential to achieving an effective common operational picture. An Automatic Information System is composed of system software and hardware that provides for collection, storage, retrieval, processing, and sharing of data and information. If an Automatic Information System is designed and implemented properly, it can support most operational scenarios. If not, it can drain time and effort without the essential pay back. There must be confidence and buy-in by those using the system so they take the time to properly input and use the information. Quality outcomes depend on quality inputs.

Information Security

Hurricane Katrina has made it evident that information held by local officials can be dangerous and hamper relief efforts. During the Hurricane Katrina relief effort, logistical tracking information in the wrong hands could, and sometimes did, have negative affects. A letter by Terry Maddox, the publisher of Slidell Sentry-News, described how "Parish President Davis threatened to take all available parish law enforcement personnel, as well as members of the general public, to go to Baton Rouge to hijack FEMA trailers for our displaced citizens" (Maddox, 2005). This sort of vigilante behavior is very dangerous and appears to have hampered relief efforts (Chenelly, 2005). What might a rogue parish president do if he knew there was a truck containing generators and fuel traveling through his parish on its way to a distant distribution point?

On the other hand, information can instill trust and promote cooperation between victims and the emergency responders. If the public and officials know that supplies are heading into their area, they can respond in numerous constructive ways. Victims can clear and prepare distribution centers. Uninjured citizens can bring injured victims to areas where medical supplies will be arriving. If it is known that required supplies are not going to arrive, the local population or leaders can make decisions to conduct an evacuation or ration existing supplies. If trust is maintained, disaster victims are more likely to employ carts to transport the injured and relief supplies, and they are less likely to use those carts for looting. Any time the victims can be made part of the solution, they are less likely to exacerbate the problem. Therefore, serious attention needs to be given to public distribution of information as well as distribution of information to federal, state, and local agencies. To determine how best to address these concerns, we first consider the logistics functions of current response models.

CURRENT CRISIS RESPONSE LOGISTICS MODELS

The design of effective logistics tracking systems is highly dependent on the hierarchical and communication structures utilized by the relevant crisis response agencies. The United States and United Nations both have significant disaster response entities that require complex levels of logistical protocols. Each has realized the need to restructure their logistics entities to benefit from a more coordinated and functional response. Therefore, it is important to analyze how asset visibility technologies work within organizational structures to achieve the best results. In some aspects, the United States and United Nations have developed and implemented technology to fit their organizational structures. In other aspects, they have changed their organizational structures to better meet available technologies. We will now look at how each is currently organized with respect to logistics operations during crisis response.

U.S. Crisis Response Model

The organizational model for the United States is based on the concept of handling incidents at the lowest possible organizational and jurisdictional level. Depending on the nature of the crisis, that level might be the local police department or it might be the U.S. Coast Guard. For federal emergency management purposes, the United States is broken down into 10 regions (see Figure 3.2).

Within each of these 10 regions are prepositioned federal and state assets. During a large-scale disaster, various agencies compete for many of the same resources. The designated agencies alone provide 15 separate

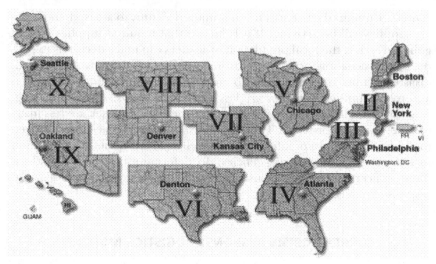

Source: United States Department of Homeland Security, 2006.

Figure 3.2.   Federal emergency management regions.

emergency support functions (ESFs) at various levels of government (see Table 3.1).

When asset visibility is poor, and the perception of scarce resources is high, inefficiency with respect to distribution increases. Support agencies may tend to hoard resources in an attempt to ensure their own sustained operations. Without a common operational picture, response professionals are unable to maximize efficiency when making decisions with respect to resource allocation.

President Bush, in an attempt to strengthen U.S. Homeland Security in February of 2003, issued a presidential directive to the secretary of Homeland Security. Within the order, the secretary was directed to:

(a) Create a comprehensive National Incident Management System (NIMS) to provide a consistent nationwide approach for Federal, State, and local governments to work effectively together to prepare for, respond to, and recover from domestic incidents, regardless of cause, size, or complexity (The White House, 2006, p. 12) and

(b) Develop and administer an integrated National Response Plan (NRP), using the NIMS, to provide the structure and mechanisms for national level policy and operational direction for Federal support to State and local incident managers (The White House, 2006, p. 12).

Table 3.1.   Agencies Competing for Resources

ESF		Primary Department Agency
ESF #1	Transportation	Department of Transportation
ESF #2	Communications	DHS (Information Analysis and Infrastructure Protection/National Communicatiions System)
ESF #3	Public Works and Engineering	DoD (U.S. Army Corps of Enginers) and DHS (Federal Emergency Management Agency)
ESF #4	Firefighting	U.S. Department of Agriculture (Forest Service)
ESF #5	Emergency Management	DHS (Federal Emergency Management Agency)
ESF #6	Mass Care, Housing, and Human Services	DHS (Federal Emergency Management Agency) and the American Red Cross
ESF #7	Resource Support	General Services Administration
ESF #8	Public Health and Medical Services	Department of Health and Human Services
ESF #8	Public Health and Medical Services	Department of Health and Human Services
ESF #9	Urban Search and Rescue	DHS (Federal Emergency Management Agency)
ESF #10	Oil and Hazardous Materials Responce	Environment Protection Agency and DHS (U.S. Coast Guard)
ESF #11	Agriculture and Natural Resources	U.S. Department of Agriculture and the Department of the Interior
ESF #12	Energy	Department of Energy
ESF #13	Public Safety and Security	DHS and the Department of Justice
ESF #14	Long-Term Community Recovery and Mitigation	U.S. Department of Agriculture, Department of Commerce, DHS (Federal Emergency Management Agency), Housing and Urban Development, Treasury, and the Small Business Administration
ESF #15	External Affairs	DHS (Federal Emergency Management Agency)

Source: The White House, 2006, p. 16.

(c)   The presidential order further directed all federal department heads and agencies to adopt and use the NIMS as well as assist the Secretary of Homeland Security in its development and maintenance (NIMS, 2004). Completed in early 2004, the National Incident Management System and the National Response Plan provided a foundation for how the Federal Government would organize itself when called to respond to crises (NIMS, 2004).

An integral and key element of the NIMS is the Incident Command System (ICS). Refined and developed over many years, the concept of the ICS can be attributed to the challenges associated with interagency coordination while fighting wildfires in the western United States. It had been successfully implemented at the federal, state, and local levels for some time prior to being incorporated into the NIMS (2004). The effectiveness of the ICS is a result of its organizational structure that can be customized to manage incidents of varying complexity and size. One main goal of the ICS is to clarify reporting relationships, thus eliminating confusion caused by manifold, and potentially conflicting, information and directions (NIMS, 2004). As shown in Figure 3.4, ICS consists of five major functional areas: Command, Planning, Operations, Logistics, and Finance & Administration (NIMS, 2004).

The NIMS command structure places logistics as one of the core sections within its Incident Command System (ICS). The Logistics Section of

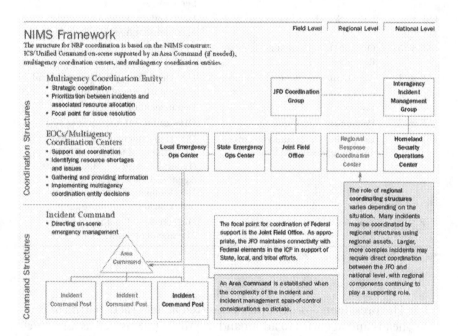

Source: NRP, 2004, p. 19.

Figure 3.3.   National incident management system.

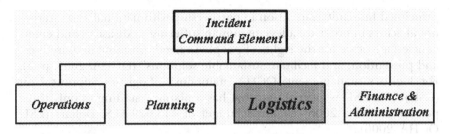

Source: NIMS, 2004, p. 13.

Figure 3.4   Incident command element hierarchy.

the ICS is designed to be flexible in design and function to more effectively and efficiently meet each specific incident's requirements. The ICS command structure calls for an incident command section chief to determine the initial organizational structure of his or her particular section. The organizational structure is then designed to allow transformation to meet the requirements of the particular incident. ICS's organizational structure is modular by nature, allowing for variations in the size, type, complexity, and scope of an incident (NIMS, 2004).

The implementation of modularity within an organizational framework is based on several considerations. First, the form of the organization must be developed to coincide with its function or task. Second, only the functional elements needed to meet the requirements of the specific function should be staffed. Third, span-of-control guidelines must be observed. This requires a high level of organizational and individual discipline and confidence in the plan and those placed in positions of authority. Fourth, functions of any nonactivated organizational element must be performed at the next highest level. And, finally, to keep confusion, redundancy, and wasted effort to a minimum, organizational elements that are no longer required must be deactivated (NIMS, 2004).

Although the overall concepts of the NIMS are reasonable and have been successfully employed in the past, the unpredictable and increasingly complex nature of new situations requires innovative solutions. In addition to the right people, the right training, and the right plan, the right technologies also need to be put into action on a practical level.

United Nations Crisis Response Model

The United Nations' Office for the Coordination of Humanitarian Affairs (OCHA) is responsible to "mobilize and coordinate effective and principled humanitarian action in partnership with national and international actors in order to: alleviate human suffering in disasters and emergencies; advocate for the rights of people in need; promote preparedness and prevention; and facilitate sustainable solutions" (OCHA, 2005, p. 5). For logistics management, OCHA maintains a Logistics Support Unit (LSU). The LSU is a small unit that has a planned staffing of only three personnel and a 2006 requested budget of 443,629 U.S. Dollars (LSU OCHA, 2006).

OCHA's LSU receives primary backing from the United Nations Joint Logistics Center (UNJLC). The UNJLC was formed to provide leadership in assembling and managing humanitarian resources. The UNJLC's formation was motivated by the 1996 crisis in Eastern Zaire where significant problems with resource distribution and cooperation among various agencies became tremendously evident. The UNJLC concept has been effectively used in several United Nations operations including Somalia, Kosovo, East Timor, and Afghanistan. The UNJLC has become more formalized with a permanent standing presence in Rome (UNJLC, 2005).

The UNJLC, initiated in March 2002, supports several UN entities including the United Nations High Commission for Refugees (UNHCR), the United Nations Children's Fund (UNICEF), the World Health Organization (WHO), and the World Food Program (WFP). The WFP acts as the UNJLC's custodian, contributing personnel and assets. The UNJLC's core unit is also housed within the WFP's Operations Department (UNJLC, 2005). The core unit provides the base structure to respond to UNJLC operations. The size of a mobilized UNJLC is kept to a minimum to maintain flexibility. After the decision is made to mobilize the UNJLC, support staff requirements are determined. The staffing requirements are then manned to meet the mission's requirement (UNJLC, 2005).

Because of its joint nature, the UNJLC provides a standardized controlling body for the implementation of technologies across the various UN agencies. The need for a centralized logistics coordination center is a common goal of both the United States and the United Nations crisis response bodies. A primary principle to keep in mind is the common evidence of growing modularity within their structures. Figure 3.5 illustrates the modularity provided by the UNJLC. While these United Nations agencies possess their own in-house logistics section, they can call upon the UNJLC for technical expertise and material support.

Achieving redundancy, modularity, and a common operational picture through asset visibility are the primary motivating factors in the implementation of technology in support of logistical operations during crisis response. Achieving a common vision across various competing and independent agencies is an enormous undertaking. But, powerful tools do exist and even more compelling ones are being developed. So the ques-

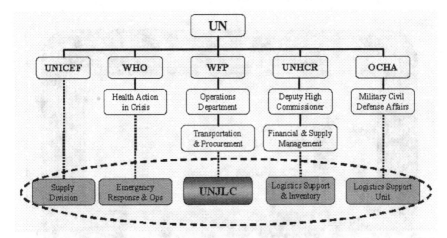

Source: UNHRC, 2004; UNICEF, 2006; UNWFP, 2004: UNWHO, 2006.

Figure 3.5.   Logistical modularity in the United Nations.

tion is not whether we can use these tools, but how to best implement them effectively and efficiently.

OVERVIEW OF RELEVANT TECHNOLOGIES

In this section, we look at relevant technologies that are available and in use by the private sector and various government agencies. In doing so, technologies that directly relate to the enhancement of coordinated logistics operations will be highlighted.

Radio Frequency Identification (RFID)

RFID technology is a means of identifying unique objects through the use of radio frequency transmissions. This rapidly growing and proven technology can support asset visibility during crisis management by allowing data to be captured quickly, efficiently and accurately throughout all stages of the supply chain. Access to reliable information regarding the location, quantity, condition, and description of resources increases the quality of rational decision making at all levels of command. The group of technologies that make up radio frequency identification can be broken down into the three general categories of active, semipassive, and passive RFID. The functional components of an RFID tag consist of a chip,

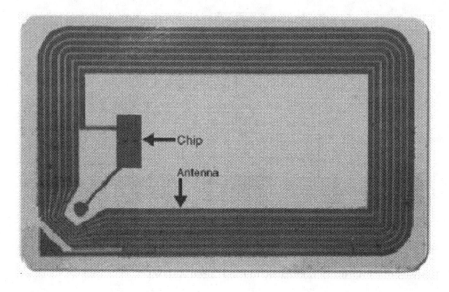

Source: GAO, 2005.

Figure 3.6.   Standard passive RFID tag.

antenna, and in some cases a power supply (see Figure 3.6). The chip holds descriptive information about the item and the antenna is a means of transmitting that information. Table 3.2 provides an overview of the three types of RFID technologies currently in use with common applications and technical specifications (Government Accountability Office (GAO), 2005).

Passive RFID

In many ways, passive RFID is seen as the successor to today's bar code technology. However, passive RFID technology has several advantages over bar code technology. First, passive RFID tags do not require line-of-sight to be read. Also, in many cases, line-of-sight is not required when writing to them. This allows RFID tags to be placed within packaging, thus minimizing the chance of damage or tampering. Second, the read range of most passive RFID tags exceeds that of barcodes. Third, many RFID tags can be read concurrently. For example, a pallet loaded with RFID tagged boxes of blankets, cartons of diapers, and cases of emergency rations can be carried by forklift through an RFID interrogation station and those particular items can be identified and inventoried without any additional operator interaction. Fourth, RFID tags have the potential to store far more data than standard barcodes. Instead of just

Table 3.2.   RFID Tags

ESESF #		
	Active Tag	*Passive Tag*	*Semipassive Tag*
Power source	Battery embedded with tag	Radio waves captured from reader used for both operation communication	Battery embedded in tag for operation and radio waves captured from reader for communication
Tag signal range	Transmits continually or intermittenly with ranges reaching several hundred feet	Only available within range of reader	Only available within range of reader
Signal strength emitted by tag	High	Low	Low
Signal strength required from reader	Low to none	High	Low
Typical applications	Used to track high value items that are being transported over long distance (i.e., rail cars, container ships)	Used for high volume situations where goods pass through a control point (i.e., retail check out counters)	Used to track high value items that are being transported over long distance (i.e., rail cars, container ships)

Source: Meloan, 2005.

identifying a type of product, RFID tags can identify a particular item with its own identification number. With more advanced tags, a particular item's historical data, such as location, temperature, and moisture profile, can be stored and later read (Wilkas, 2004).

There are also challenges associated with passive RFID technology. First, in some ways, the technology is still in the developmental stage. As the technology further develops, there is a great need for common standards. The level of success in developing these common standards will have a tremendous impact on the value of RFID systems today and into the future. The two main dynamic drivers involved in developing standards include the continuous advancements in new RFID technologies and the continuous growth in prospective RFID uses throughout the world's supply chain. The ongoing integration of the global economy makes this standardization even more important (GAO, 2005).

EPCglobal is a leading nonprofit association working to develop effective standards for RFID and other supply chain tracking protocols. EPC has an open membership founded cooperatively between European Article Numbering International (EAN) and the Uniform Code Council (UCC). Its standard model is based on their vision of providing "a simple, compact license plate that uniquely identifies (items, cases, pallets, locations, etc.) in the supply chain" (EPC Global, 2005) which they have trademarked as the Electronic Product Code (EPC). "The EPCglobal Network is a set of technologies that enable immediate, automatic identification and sharing of information on items in the supply chain" (EPCglobal, 2005). The EPC itself comprises sets of numbers, each with a specific purpose (see Figure 3.7).

A second challenge with passive RFID is the initial startup and recurring operational cost. Initial costs include readers (interrogators), writers, network systems, training, and other required material modifications to set up the system. Recurring costs include the cost of the actual tags, equipment upkeep and ongoing training (GAO, 2005).

As the technology has developed, there have been cost reductions due to learning curve and economies of scale. If growth in RFID continues, as many expect, the cost per tag and the associated return on investment will continue to make the implementation of RFID more economically practical (ID Tech Ex, 2005).

More and more companies, including leaders like Wal-Mart, have begun implementing RFID technology into their logistics system (ID Tech Ex, 2005). The next few years will likely determine whether passive RFID will become a widespread industry standard like the Uniform Prod-

---

96 Bit Electronic Product Code

01	0000A87	00015G	000158RHK
Header	EPC Manager	Object Class	Serial Number
8 Bits	28 Bits	24 Bits	36 Bits

Header- identifies the length, type, structure, version and generation of the EPC

EPC Manager- identifies the company or company entity

Object Class- serves the same purpose as a stock keeping unit or SKU

Serial Number- represents the specific instance of the Object Class being tagged

---

Source: Meloan, 2003.

Figure 3.7.   EPC tag.

uct Code (UPC), remain more of a niche technology, or mature in another direction.

Passive RFID Technology Basics

Three primary elements make up passive RFID tags. The chip stores the representative data for the item to which the tag is attached. The antenna receives energy and data signals from an interrogator and can then transmit data from the chip back to the interrogator. The third necessary component of an RFID tag is its packaging. The packaging is used to secure the tag to an item and hold the chip and tag in the proper position (Defense Supply Center Columbus [DSCC], 2005).

A common RFID packaging practice is to attach the chip and antenna on a printable integrated barcode providing backward compatibility (see Figure 3.8). There are also a growing number of dual format reader–interrogators that have the ability to read both RFID and barcode data. This flexibility is vital to many types of operations and can smooth several of the difficulties with any industry in transition from one standard to another. Additionally, the redundancy of dual-technology tags can be of great value. For example, if a tagged label is covered by exterior packaging, the RFID will likely still provide effective identification. If the RFID circuitry is damaged the barcode will most likely still be readable. These types of redundant practices decrease the probability that critical processes will be bypassed if certain aspects of the technology fail (Buy RFID, 2005).

Active RFID

Active RFID encompasses a wide variety of technologies and levels of complexity. Active RFID is generally composed of a battery-energized tag that generates a relatively strong constant or intermittent signal that, in many cases, reaches 300 feet. Some common types of active RFID tags utilize satellite and cellular telephone based transponders. After an active tag generates a signal, then a portable or stationary receiver collects the tag data and can integrate that data into a designated asset tracking and identification system. One of the main limitations of active, as well as semi-passive, RFID tags is their usual dependence on battery power. As battery life and signal handling efficiency have improved, the effective operational life of active tags has similarly increased (GAO, 2005).

Active tags, in one of their simplest forms, provide serial number type data that can be read either while static or in motion. However, active tags can also be integrated with various sensors so they can store and transmit large amounts of descriptive data and conditional parameters such as temperature, moisture content, and impact readings (GAO, 2005).

Active tags are generally more expensive than passive tags, and therefore are more frequently used with high value items or larger amounts of particular items. For example, many rail cars are fitted with active RFID for tracking and inventory purposes. Because of greater costs associated with active tags, they are generally configured to be re-used (GAO, 2005).

Semipassive RFID

Semipassive RFID generally refers to tags that are read by a passive interrogator but also provide additional sensor or specification data. Like active RFID tags, semipassive tags require batteries. Common sensor parameters include temperature, moisture content, and impact readings. Compared with standard passive tags, semipassive tags provide additional benefits at higher costs (Meloan, 2003).

Satellites

As we saw during the aftermath of Hurricane Katrina, existing communications infrastructure is vulnerable to destructive forces. Satellite systems offer redundancy and reliability that can circumvent such problems and therefore deserve serious consideration within logistical frameworks. Several different global positioning and communication satellite systems are currently in use or being implemented. Their far-reaching capabilities transcend existing ground-based communication infrastructure.

When satellites were first developed, they had little impact on the average person. Today, they are instrumental to a wide array of military and private sector operations. In addition to delivering television, telephone and radio signals, satellites are used to map the globe. This capability allows users to precisely pinpoint any particular location on the Earth's surface, an invaluable tool for navigational purposes and asset tracking. With the capability to transfer large amounts of data becoming commonplace, satellites are helping to make the idea of a global connectivity possible. Corporations such as Hughes and Motorola are putting satellite systems into space, which will supply extensive broadband data capabilities. If everything works as predicted, users of satellite broadband will be able to connect to the internet via satellite from anywhere on earth (Whalen, 2006).

The United States' Global Positioning System (GPS) includes 24 NAVSTAR satellites operated by the U.S. Air Force. It is used to track everything from airplanes, vehicles, ships, and personal electronic devices to people and animals. Common applications include: navigation, construction, farming, mining, logistical supply-chain management, package delivery, geological forecasting, emergency services, and biological research (Pellerin, 2006).

GPS tracking can provide real-time asset visibility anywhere with satellite coverage. A GPS-capable device, affixed to a logistical asset, obtains a triangulated fix by comparing distances from various GPS satellites in orbit. After a fix is obtained, a transponder transfers data via communication satellite to a station that can transmit the location information through various communication systems (Land Air Sea, 2005). GPS satellite tracking can provide a secure and reliable tracking system for use in conjunction with logistical planning in areas that have been subject to various forms of devastation (GPS Select, 2005).

Currently, the United States maintains the only truly global, fully operational system. However, the European Union and countries including Russia, Japan, and China are developing their own international satellite navigation systems. International negotiations ranging from financial partnering to interoperability are issues of great interest to all involved (Pellerin, 2006).

Resource Databases/Application Software

Technological advances associated with computer hardware have provided organizations the ability to store massive amounts of information relatively cheaply. However, problems associated with information overload can outweigh the potential benefits of collecting data. Application software provides a means to effectively use large amounts of data. Data mining, querying, and the ability to generate ad hoc reports are some of the tools available to users (GAO, 2005).

Private sector companies like Wal-Mart have demonstrated the feasibility of implementing IT systems that are capable of effectively managing enormous amounts of data. When the cashier scans an item at checkout, the information is stored in a database where it is immediately accessible throughout the supply chain. The information, recorded one time, is then used for restocking, quarterly reports, transportation scheduling, raw material purchases, and so forth (ID Tech Ex, 2005). Giving the appropriate people access to the right information increases

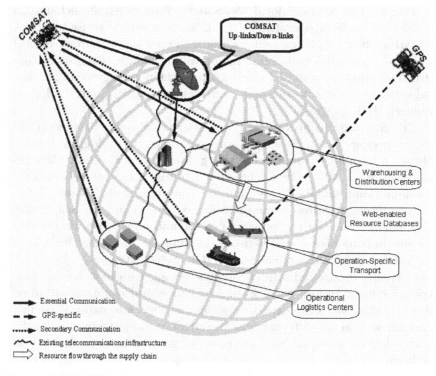

Source: DSCC, 2005.

Figure 3.8.   Communications model.

their ability to make better decisions. It also provides all interested agents the ability to view the same data in real time.

PROPOSED LOGISTICS FRAMEWORK

Integrated Communications Network Model

Recalling the conceptual model presented earlier, Figure 3.9 illustrates how the Logistics Function fits within an overall communications framework.

Perhaps the most essential characteristic of the proposed framework is that of open architectural design. It can operate in conjunction with various existing telecommunications infrastructures or independent of them. By incorporating resource databases and powerful application software, it

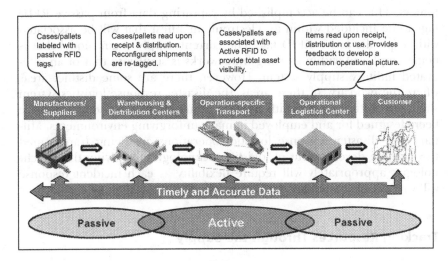

Cases/pallets labeled with passive RFID tags.

Cases/pallets read upon receipt & distribution. Reconfigured shipments are re-tagged.

Cases/pallets are associated with Active RFID to provide total asset visibility.

Items read upon receipt, distribution or use. Provides feedback to develop a common operational picture.

Manufacturers/ Suppliers

Warehousing & Distribution Centers

Operation-specific Transport

Operational Logistics Center

Customer

Timely and Accurate Data

Passive   Active   Passive

Source: DSCC, 2005.

Figure 3.9.   Integrated supply chain.

can easily accept various technologies that adhere to universal standards and specifications. Further, because current satellite systems are capable of operating with various satellite communication devices, several different methods of data transfer can be utilized. This redundant capability affords alternatives that create a seamless logistics process within the overall framework. More importantly, the framework will facilitate the goal of maintaining a common operational picture among all relevant agents and throughout all levels of the supply chain.

Integrated Supply Chain Model

The proposed logistics supply chain can be broken down into five separate stages or components comprising Manufacturers, Distribution Centers, Carriers, Operational Logistics Centers, and the Customer. The following figure shows how both active and passive RFID technology can be integrated throughout the supply chain.

Active RFID technology, including satellite tracking, is generally most effective in maintaining asset visibility between the Distribution Centers and the Operational Logistics Centers. Passive RFID is better suited for tracking assets between the Suppliers and Distribution Centers. It is also better for interactions involving Operational Logistics Centers and Customers. This can be accomplished by capturing data from passive RFID tags to be included within an electronic manifest that will be associated with a specific active RFID tag. The current supply chain model that is being employed within existing frameworks is similar to that of an integrated military supply system. However, there are some distinct areas where the two vary. In these areas, the disaster response logistics system should be better aligned with military protocols as these standards have been designed for and employed in many unforgiving environments. Military and disaster response logistics operations are being transformed through the development of logistics technologies. Applying these technologies appropriately will require flexibility as each incident response will vary according to specific circumstances.

Tracking Resources Through the Supply

Chain Manufacturers/Supplier

The first stage of the integrated supply chain involves the Manufacturers who originally produce and package the required items. These items may or may not be initially or solely produced for crisis response. For example, a plastic tarp manufacturer in Mexico may ship their product to the United States where it could be sold at a Wal-Mart or purchased by the government for integration into an emergency response kit. The tracking process begins with the identification of a requirement and the subsequent creation of a requisition within the Web-enabled database. Ideally, the Manufacturer will be incorporated into the integrated communications network. This will enable asset visibility beginning at the time of initial shipment.

Preferably, the manufacturer will be responsible for tagging the resource with a passive, EPC-compliant RFID tag that may also be encoded with additional value-added data. Examples of additional data might include instructions for use or relevant warnings. Issues of consideration include tag placement and what level of identification is practical (every pallet, every case, or every individual unit). Currently, DoD contracting guidelines require RFID compliance from vendors. Specifically, "the DoD will use and require its suppliers to use EPC Class 0 and Class 1 tags, readers, and complimentary devices" (USD AT&L, 2004, p. 1). Further, "Radio Frequency Identification will be a mandatory DoD requirement on solicitations issued on or after October 1, 2004, for delivery of material on or after January 1, 2005" (USD AT&L, 2004, p. 1).

The process of incorporating tagged items into the crisis response supply chain can be simplified through the utilization of common labeling standards for military, business, and crisis response agencies. Since the

DoD has focused much of its efforts on the adoption of industry best practices and standards, it would be most effective to apply those same standards to the procurement of crisis response resources. Aligning procurement standards with the DoD will facilitate further compliance among vendors, allowing them to label items identically for nearly all government agencies. It will also allow military-specific items to be more easily integrated into any crisis response framework. In addition to facilitating integration, standardization enables flexibility, accuracy, and lower costs (USD AT&L, 2004).

Given that this is the initial stage of the supply chain, decisions and actions made at the manufacturer level can greatly affect the success of the rest of the system. Remedial actions, such as retagging, can and sometimes will need to be performed at subsequent stages. However, these later actions increase the cost and the probability of introduced errors.

Warehousing and Distribution Centers

The second stage of the integrated supply chain involves regional Warehousing and Distribution Centers. This stage covers a wide range of storage and distribution functions and facilities. It includes various commercial distribution centers, long-term emergency supply warehouses, and cross-docking operations. This is the stage where the commercial market most directly interfaces with the crisis response logistical network. RFID technology, utilizing uniform standards, can provide value to crisis response agencies and their suppliers. At these locations, cases, pallets, and containers may be stored, repackaged or reconfigured to meet operational or emergency reserve requirements.

Once a resource arrives at a Warehouse/Distribution Center, it must pass through a RFID interrogator (static or handheld) before it can be included as inventory. Maintaining strict discipline at an entry and exit control point is a key factor in ensuring inventory accuracy. The interrogator records all relevant data and then automatically transfers them to the Web-enabled Resource Database via the existing telecommunications infrastructure or via communication satellites. At this point, the increased inventory level associated with this particular resource is immediately reflected within the database. Anyone with access to the database now has visibility of the resource. When the resource leaves a Warehouse/Distribution Center for transport to an Operational Logistics Center, the resource is read by a RFID interrogator. All relevant information related to the in-transit resource is recorded and immediately uploaded to the Web-enabled Database. The decreased inventory level (as well as the fact that the resource is in-transit) is reflected and could trigger a decision to replenish supplies at a particular location.

Consolidated mission packs are one way to achieve additional efficiency and flexibility. This involves reading in data from multiple items tagged with barcodes, RFID tags, or other labeling, then consolidating those items into one package, case, or pallet, and finally rewriting the consolidated information to a single RFID tag. In most cases this process will be completed in preparation for possible future crisis requirements. However, with the integration of RFID, consolidating crisis-specific mission packs can be conducted much more effectively during the crisis response.

Operation-Specific Transport

The third stage in the integrated supply chain involves Operation-Specific Transport. This component encompasses movement from warehouse and distribution centers to the in-theater depots and operational logistics centers. This transportation piece covers a wide range of possible modes and distances. It could represent multi-modal intercontinental transport utilizing any combination of ship, rail, truck, and air. It could also represent a mule train moving supplies from warehouses located in the cities of Kashmir to Operational Logistics Centers serving earthquake victims in the surrounding mountain regions.

Asset visibility in this stage could be achieved by utilizing stationary readers, active RFID tags, and existing ground-based communications infrastructure. However, in many relevant crisis scenarios, terrestrial data connectivity may be lost. Satellite communication is much less susceptible to destructive forces that are often common to crisis situations. Satellite technology can bypass infrastructure and communicate directly with logistics assets and secure resource database locations. Asset identification and item-specific details can be stored and transmitted from the conveyance or the transport module. The load manifest can be located locally on the conveyance or held remotely at a secure Web-enabled Database site.

While in transit, the satellite transponder—which is attached to a logistics asset, such as a container on a truck, ship, train or plan—periodically receives location data from GPS satellites. It then relays that data to the Web-enabled Database via communication satellites. The resource can be tracked by association with the satellite transponder. If the transponder should fail, the operator of the logistics asset may have the capability of communicating with the command center or directly with the Web-enabled resource database using a satellite-enabled phone or computer.

The U.S. Army has had great success with its Movement Tracking System (MTS) (O'Brien, 2004). The system is being tactically employed in Iraq and Afghanistan. MTS uses GPS and communication satellites to track the location of mobile logistics assets. Comtech Mobile Datacom (the company that developed the system) also incorporated two-way satellite text messaging, a capability useful for rerouting instructions, weather conditions, and other real-time situational data. The requirement for MTS grew out of lessons learned from the first Gulf War, where the U.S. Army experienced insufficient asset visibility with respect to logistics assets and resources (Buxbaum, 2005).

An important evolutionary step for MTS is the military's plan to integrate passive and active RFID technologies into the system. The Department of Defense is in the midst of a massive program to have suppliers place RFID tags on cases and pallets of goods, with the purpose of tracking supplies throughout the supply chain. By incorporating RFID data into MTS, a military logistician will be able to immediately know the location of a vehicle or container as well as its contents. While nearly all of the National Guard's logistics vehicles operating in Iraq are fitted with MTS, relatively few of its U.S.-based vehicles are MTS equipped (Buxbaum, 2005).

Operational Logistics Centers

The fourth stage of the integrated supply chain is comprised of Operational Logistics Centers. While these centers perform many of the same functions as the warehouses and distribution centers of the second stage, they differ in that they are located near or at the disaster site. Here, resources are received from operation-specific carriers and subsequently distributed to customers. The Operational Logistics Centers can vary in size and composition depending on the customer base and the supplies received for distribution. Due to challenges associated with connectivity and power during a crisis, this stage can present great difficulties in implementing RFID tracking. However, it is also where the greatest benefits of achieving asset visibility can be realized.

Upon arrival at the Operational Logistics Center, a resource must be read by a RFID interrogator (static or handheld). All relevant data are then uploaded to, and reflected in, the Web-enabled database via existing terrestrial telecommunications infrastructure or via the communication satellites. Anyone with access to the database has visibility of the resource. Before being distributed to the end user, resources are read into the database where they are reflected as expended items. Figure 3.10 illustrates an Operational Logistics Center layout and one possible RFID interrogation configuration.

Using this configuration, the data associated with incoming and outgoing resources can be captured by various forms of RFID readers to include: vehicle-mounted, forklift-mounted, handheld and static. Maintaining strict control at the RFID read points will ensure the highest level of data integrity, a factor that is essential for useful Automated Information Systems and other Decision Support Systems.

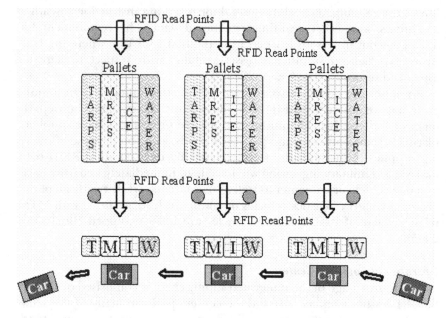

Source: Randon, 2005.

Figure 3.10.   Operational logistics center.

Customers

The customer is the fifth and final stage in the integrated supply chain. Customer is a general term to indicate the point at which the supplies leave the control of the distribution entity. A customer can be a single person in a car, a family on foot, or a church bus obtaining supplies for victims.

The ultimate goal of the supply chain is to provide support to these end users. The ability to tie materials expended to particular end users can provide valuable data to the tracking and distribution system. This data can be used to calculate current or estimate future requirements such as food, transportation, lodging, and medical supplies. However, due to the challenges associated with providing aid to distressed refugees, collecting customer data can be challenging. These challenges could be overcome through the use of personal RFID cards, bracelets, or other wearable devices (Gao, Xiang, Wang, Shen, Huang, & Song, 2004).

Overall, the key to effective utilization of any technology during crisis response is the ability to trace the benefits of the technology directly to the customers. Even if the technology provides reliable total asset visibility throughout the integrated supply chain, if it does not improve the lot of the customer, it is basically unjustifiable. Having access to the information is the easy part. Being able to effectively interpret that information and achieve a useful common operational picture will require skill and training. By maximizing the efficiency with which resources are allocated and distributed, planners and managers can deliver the best possible relief or service to end users.

CONCLUSIONS

Maintaining a state of readiness for unexpected events is a complicated undertaking that requires more than simply publishing a set of policies and procedures. Instead, it will take a sustained, long-term commitment from capable leaders and trained personnel to do what is necessary for the successful implementation of a viable logistics framework. In addition to the three critical success factors introduced in Figure 3.1—modularity, integrated systems, and asset visibility technology—we need specialized training and procurement.

Achieving modularity with respect to structure, resource configuration, and systems will require that the right people be appointed to key positions, people who understand coordinated logistics and the complexities that accompany it. U.S. government officials have acknowledged the need to fully integrate the DoD into the National Response Plan (NRP). They emphasize integration at every level of government (The White House, 2006). This acknowledgement could turn out to be the most critical element toward a successful strategic shift in the way crisis management activities are conducted. Properly incorporated into the NRP, certain U.S. DoD logistics systems and practices would offer numerous benefits (learning curve, turnkey operational abilities, and cost). The salaries of DoD personnel are, in essence, a fixed cost. The missions of existing units can be modified to include crisis response as a core competency. Assigning a primary role to the DoD exploits a highly trained, in-place personnel structure.

The overall manner in which the U.S. military trains and organizes its operations serves as one of the best models for use during crisis management activities. This is mainly due to the culture of discipline that exists within the military and its experience in conducting operations during chaos and war. National Guard and component reserve units are best suited to train for rapid response within each of the Department of Homeland Security's 10 designated crisis response regions. These units can run Operational Logistics Centers, and their military bearing and presence will increase the likelihood of order during a crisis. They possess the necessary discipline, basic skills, esprit de corps, and training opportunities. Any attempt to create this core capability from scratch would face myriad challenges that have already been met by the National Guard.

To implement an effective training program, designated agencies and military units will need to become intimate with logistics procedures and systems. Federal and state governments need to consider long-term budget implications in at least two areas: (1) the procurement of commercial off-the-shelf (COTS) items and (2) the quarterly training of designated national guardsmen, reservists, and emergency operation center (EOC) personnel. Table 3.3 provides some general estimates of critical items and resources, as well as training requirements based on populations within the 10 U.S. Federal Emergency Management Regions. Assumptions used in calculating the estimates follow; population estimates are taken from the U.S. Census Bureau (2005). These ratios of resource requirements to population may serve as benchmarks for designing logistics systems for use by other nations. Adaptations and modifications are likely to be required for use in regions with different levels of existing infrastructure and other resources.

Commercial off-the-shelf products can be utilized to integrate all necessary elements of an effective crisis response logistics system for use by the DoD, DHS, the private sector, and the international community. Military and private sector companies are currently employing effective, comprehensive asset-tracking technologies. As we discussed in the previous section, the U.S. Army has had great success with MTS. Wal-Mart is an industry pioneer and leader in supply chain management. Adopting these and other industry best practices into an integrated, comprehensive, and standardized framework offers proven benefits. In addition to maximizing efficiency in resource allocation and distribution, more information will be available to decision makers. But, unless leaders dedicate adequate attention and effort to sustained training and funding, even the best plan will be impaired.

The next major crisis is coming. It could be a storm, a pandemic, an earthquake, a tsunami, or an attack involving weapons of mass destruction. With any of these real possibilities, a swift and effective logistics response can be greatly enhanced by achieving higher levels of asset visibility. To improve asset visibility and promote a common operational picture, organizational command and control structures and physical resource flows must be tied together through timely and accurate information stored and shared via an integrated communications network. The logistics component of the crisis response framework must be flexible and modular enough to be task-organized to meet the challenges associated with incidents of varying scope and complexity. Several technologies presented here have greatly enhanced the ability to gain a common operational picture. As these technologies mature and new technologies

Table 3.3. Procurement Consideration

DHS Regions	Population per Region	Operational Logistics Centers per Region	Requirement for Satellite Transponders	Requirement for Static RFID Readers	Requirement for Hand-Held RFID Readers	Quarterly Training for EOC Personel
I	20,000,000	100	5,000	400	1,000	2,400
II	29,000,000	145	7,250	580	1,450	3,480
III	30,000,000	150	7,500	600	1,500	3,600
IV	52,000,000	260	13,000	1,040	2,600	6,240
V	51,000,000	255	12,750	1,020	2,550	6,120
VI	35,000,000	175	8,750	700	1,750	4,200
VII	14,000,000	70	3,500	280	700	1,680
VIII	10,000,000	50	2,500	200	500	1,200
IX	45,000,000	225	11,250	900	2,250	5,400
X	6,000,000	30	1,500	120	300	720
Totals	292,000,000	30	1,500	120	300	720

Transponder assumptions for Table 3.3

(1) Estimates are based on the assumption that no more than 25% of a particular Region is affected.

(2) One Module consists of 5 containers loaded with enough life-sustaining resources for 5,000 people per day.

(3) When more than 25% of a particular region is affected, containers will be involved in multiple trips per day to Logistics Operations Centers either within their Region or within neighboring Regions.

RFID reader assumptions for Table 3.3

(1) The above estimates are based on the assumption that no more than 10% of a particular region is affected.

(2) One Logistics Operations Center can service up to 20,000 people/day.

(3) In the case where more than 10% of a particular region is affected, assume that Logistics Operations Center assets will be pulled from neighboring Regions.

(4) Assume 10 hand-held Interrogators per Logistics Operations Center.

(5) Assume 6 Static Interrogators per Logistics Operations Center.

Training assumptions for Table 3.3

(1) Assume 24 National Guardsmen, Reservists, and other State EOC Personnel are needed to operate one Logistics Operations Center.

(2) The above estimates are based on the assumption that no more than 10% of a particular region is affected.

(3) One Logistics Operations Center can service up to 20,000 people/day.

(4) In the case where more than 10% of a particular region is affected, assume that Logistics Operations Center assets, to include personnel, will be pulled from neighboring Regions.

become available, the primary question should always be how it will affect customers. In this case, the customers are the victims whose lives and property will be at stake. Creation of a common operational picture using a modular, flexible, and integrated logistics system can dramatically increase the likelihood of a successful response effort. The time for action is now, before the next major crisis comes upon us.

REFERENCES

Buxbaum, P. A. (2005, February 18). *Tracking logistics transformation: The army's movement tracking system for logistics is also saving lives by identifying the location of friendly forces*. Retrieved March 21, 2006, from http://www.military -information-technology.com/article.cfm?DocID=807

Buy RFID. (2005, October 26). *Symbol 915 MHZ hand-held reader MC9000-G*. Retrieved May 7, 2006, from http://buyrfid.com/catalog/product_info.php/ products_id/181?osCsid=e405b18a6598c29527091cb2518cccef

Chenelly, J. R. (2005, September 02). Troops begin combat operations in New Orleans. *Army Times.com*. Retrieved December 30, 2005, from http:// www.armytimes.com/story.php?f=1-292925-1077495.php

Defense Supply Center Columbus. (2005, April 20). *DoD radio frequency identification policy & implementation strategy presentation*. Retrieved May 7, 2006, from http://www.dscc.dla.mil/downloads/psmc/April05/PSMC_rfid.ppt

EPCglobal. (2005). *Frequently asked questions*. Retrieved May 7, 2006, from http:// www.epcglobalinc.org/about/faqs.html#5

Gao, X., Xiang, Z., Wang, H., Shen, J., Huang, J., Song, S. (2004). *An approach to security and privacy of RFID system for supply chain*. Retrieved May 7, 2006, from http://ieeexplore.ieee.org/iel5/9531 /30211/01388318.pdf?tp=&arnumber=1388318&isnumber=30211

Government Accountability Office. (2005, May). *Information security, radio frequency identification technology in the federal government, 6*. Retrieved May 7, 2006, from http://www.gao.gov/new.items/d05551.pdf

GPS Select. (2005). *The fleet tracking solutions people*. Retrieved December 30, 2005, from http://gps-select.com/index.html

ID Tech Ex. (2005, July 13). Cost reduction in retailing and products using RFID. Retrieved May 7, 2006, from http://www.idtechex.com/products/en/articles/ 00000205.asp

Jensen, B. (2005, June 22). *Logistical problems marred tsunami relief efforts, report finds*. Retrieved May 6, 2006, from http://philanthropy.com/free/update/2005/06/ 2005062202.htm

Joint Chiefs of Staff. (2005, August 22). *Global command and control system common operational picture reporting requirements, GL-6*. Retrieved May 6, 2006, from http://www.dtic.mil/cjcs_directives/cdata/unlimit/3151_01.pdf

Land Air Sea. (2005). *Land Air Sea 7100 real time GPS tracking with nationwide coverage*. Retrieved December 30, 2005, from http://www.landairsea.com/products/ 7100.html

Library of Congress Congressional Record. (2005, September 27). *Select bipartisan committee to investigate the preparation for and response to Hurricane Katrina.* Washington, DC: Government Printing Office.

Logistics Support Unit United Nations Office for the Coordination of Humanitarian Affairs. (2006). *OCHA in 2006, emergency response coordination.* Retrieved March 15, 2006, from http://ochaonline.un.org/ocha2006/chap2_1.htm

Maddox, T. (2005, October 2). *More progress in St. Tammany Parish.* Retrieved December 29, 2005, from http://www.wicknet.com/slidell-covington-update.lasso

Meloan, S. (2003, November 11). *Toward a global internet of things.* Retrieved May 7, 2006, from http://java.sun.com/developer/technicalArticles/Ecommerce/rfid/

National Incident Management System, U.S. Department of Homeland Security. (2004, March 1). *National Incident Management System, 1-28.* Retrieved May 6, 2006, from http://www.dhs.gov/interweb/assetlibrary/NIMS-90-web.pdf

National response plan. (2004, December). Retrieved May 6, 2006, from http://www.dhs.gov/interweb/assetlibrary/NRP_FullText.pdf

Newman, J. (2006, May 3). Report Details Katrina Communications Fiasco. *Los Angeles Times.* Retrieved May 6, 2006, from http://www.latimes.com/news/printedition/asection/la-na-katrina3may03,1,3532430.story?coll=la-news-a_section&ctrack=1&cset=true

O'Brien, K. M. (2004, July). *Estimating the effects of radio frequency identification tagging technologies on the army's war-time logistics network.* Air Force Institute of Technology Thesis, AFIT/MLN/ENS/04-09.

Pellerin, C. (2006, February 3). *United States updates global positioning system technology; New GPS satellite ushers in a range of future improvements.* Retrieved May 7, 2006, from http://www.globalsecurity.org/space/library/news/2006/space-060203-usia01.htm

Randon, F. (2005). *U.S. army corps of engineers, disaster program manager, emergency support function #3, public works and engineering-intergovernmental action plans serving the esf #3 community: Federal to local.* Retrieved May 11, 2006, from http://www.englink.usace.army.mil/igp/doc/briefing/Briefing_ESF3_Intergov_Action_Plans_with_notes_pics_no_BU_30_Jun_05.ppt

Reuters AlertNet. (2005). *International Red Cross deploys more than 80 experts to Hurricane Katrina response.* Retrieved May 17, 2006, from http://www.alertnet.org/thenewsmemphotoalbum/11259222310.htm

UNHCR. (2004, September). *Organigram: Departments/divisions/service at headquarters, 1, 8.* Retrieved May 7, 2006, from http://www.unhcr.org/cgi-bin/texis/vtx/admin/opendoc.pdf?tbl=ADMIN&id=3b91fca74

UNICEF. (2006). *Procuring Supplies for children.* Retrieved, May 7, 2006, from http://www.unicef.org/supply/

United Nations Joint Logistics Center. (2005, October 4). *UNJLC brief light, 1-2.* Retrieved May 7, 2007, from http://www.unjlc.org/9639/index_html/2005-10-04.9166758138/view

United Nations Office for the Coordination of Humanitarian Affairs. (2005). *OCHA in 2005, Activities and extra budgetary funding requirements, 5*. Retrieved May 7, 2006, from http://ochaonline.un.org/DocView.asp?DocID=2230

United Nations Office for the Coordination of Humanitarian Affairs. (2006). *About OCHA, logistics support unit, military, civil defense and logistics section.* Retrieved May 7, 2006, from http://ochaonline.un.org/webpage.asp?Page=663

UNWFP. (2004). *About WFP, internal organisation.* Retrieved May 6, 2006, from http://www.wfp.org/aboutwfp/downloads/organigram_full.pdf

UNWHO. (2006). *Health action in crisis.* Retrieved May 7, 2006, from http://www.who.int/hac/about/HAC_organigram.pdf

U.S. Census Bureau. (2005). *Population by State.* Retrieved May 6, 2006, from http://factfinder.census.gov/servlet/ThematicMapFramesetServlet?_bm=y&-geo_id=01000US&-tm_name=PEP_2005_EST_M00090&-ds_name=PEP_2005_EST&-_MapEvent=displayBy&-_dBy=040&-_lang=en&-_sse=on

USD AT&L. (2004, July 30). *Memorandum, Radio frequency identification policy, 1–23.* Retrieved May 7, 2006, from http://www.acq.osd.mil/log/rfid/Policy/RFID%20Policy%2007-30-2004.pdf

United States Department of Homeland Security. (2006). *Federal emergency management agency, regional contacts.* Retrieved, May 6, 2006, from http://www.fema.gov/about/contact/regions.shtm

Whalen, D. (2006). *Communications satellites: Making the global village possible.* Retrieved May 7, 2006, from http://www.hq.nasa.gov/office/pao/History/sat-comhistory.html

The White House. (2006). *The federal response to Hurricane Katrina: Lessons learned, 16, 34, 44, 94–95, 98–100, 130.* Retrieved January 20, 2006, from http://www.whitehouse.gov/reports/katrina-lessons-learned/

Wilkas, J. (2004). *Evolving from bar code to RFID in the supply chain, 1–7.* Retrieved May 7, 2006, from http://aanza-autoid.com/sitebuildercontent/sitebuilderfiles/Moving5.pdf

CHAPTER 4

IMPROVING DISASTER MANAGEMENT THROUGH STRUCTURED FLEXIBILITY AMONG FRONTLINE RESPONDERS

Claudia Seifert

Recent catastrophes, such as terrorist attacks and Hurricane Katrina, show the importance of continually improving disaster management on a local, state, and federal level. During disaster responses, the actions of individuals are crucial to rescue lives and to avoid further losses. Disaster management planning is often conducted from an abstract, theoretical viewpoint rather than by integrating the experience of first responders. This chapter illustrates basic components of successful disaster management using examples from individual experiences of first responders in New Zealand. Because of their dispersed population and variation in terrain, disaster management in New Zealand requires a decentralized structure, frequent interagency collaboration, and a high degree of community involvement. First responders know how to manage an emergency with or without the presence of government personnel and centralized resources. As a result, the practices that have developed in New Zealand may provide guidance for crisis preparedness and response in many circumstances where disasters preclude routine

Communicable Crises: Prevention, Response, and Recovery in the Global Arena, pp. 83–136
Copyright © 2007 by Information Age Publishing
All rights of reproduction in any form reserved.

reactions. In this chapter, actual experiences are woven with existing theory into a generalizable model that can be applied to disaster management in a variety of situations.

INTRODUCTION

This chapter illustrates significant factors in successful disaster management by integrating theoretical principles with insights and stories from first responders in New Zealand. The country's geographical isolation and sparse population require the application of special advantageous disaster management principles, which are generalizable to a variety of situations. A general model of disaster management organizes the chapter. The model consists of three main parts that connect findings from academic literature with stories from individuals who are involved in disaster management in New Zealand. The stories are taken from in-depth interviews conducted with a senior civil defense member and a trained, voluntary radio communicator in Dunedin, New Zealand.

Some of the insights on disaster management in these stories might seem trivial. However, the importance of individuals to disaster management systems and principles is often underestimated. Postanalysis of disaster management often reveals that individuals make small mistakes in disaster situations that seriously aggravate the problem, and these errors are often easily avoidable. Therefore, it is important to gain an understanding of individual experiences in disasters.

New Zealand, located southeast of Australia in the South Pacific Ocean, is known for its cutting-edge approach to public management. About the size of Colorado and consisting of two islands, New Zealand has a population of roughly 4 million people. Approximately 76% of the population lives on the North Island. The civil defense system discussed here applies to the district of Dunedin, located on the South Island; the main components of this system, however, are shared throughout New Zealand. Sometimes New Zealanders refer to their location as "the periphery of the periphery." Its isolation and sparse population often impact disaster and emergency planning in ways that provide interesting insights for developing crisis management techniques.

Since there has not been a major disaster in New Zealand for more than 25 years, most stories presented here deal with smaller incidents. To extend insights from New Zealand to challenges of major recent disasters, I will reference responses to the September 11th, 2001, terrorist attacks and to Hurricane Katrina, including the flooding that followed, in the Southern United States in 2005.

A GENERAL MODEL OF DISASTER MANAGEMENT

The following model was developed from current literature and interviews with first responders. It begins with organizational structure, coordination, and communication; the second section addresses organizational memory relationships and training; and the third section discusses community involvement and resources in disaster management. All of these components affect individual perceptions of disasters, as well as stress levels in the response situation, which in turn influences the response quality. This model is not exhaustive, but provides a framework from which to study and explore the contributing factors in successful disaster management.

Perception and Stress Levels

All three components of the model influence the perception of the disaster and the stress level, both of which are crucial determinants of how successfully the disaster or emergency is handled. Research shows that the perception of a problem influences the subsequent action to address it (Dutton & Jackson, 1987). When perception of threat decreases, perception of control increases (Dutton & Jackson, 1987; Tjosvold, 1984). Moreover, Weick (1988) asserts that the accuracy of perception influences the variety of solutions applied to a problem. A more effective solution will improve the disaster situation, while an inferior solution might aggravate it. Generally, if responders perceive the disaster as increasingly manageable and controllable, the level of stress will decrease (Weick, 1988). Reduced stress levels, in turn, result in improved decision making (Rudolph & Repenning, 2002; Weick, 1988). Here, it is assumed that stress has a negative impact on decision making and disaster response quality. Research shows that a low or moderate level of stress has initially positive effects on performance, but with rising stress levels, the quality of decision making will begin to deteriorate (Gladstein & Reilly, 1985; Rudolph & Repenning, 2002; Yerkes & Dodson, 1908). Because disasters are exceptionally disturbing events, we may assume that stress levels will be high initially. Perception of increasing control, lower stress levels, and a resulting higher response quality

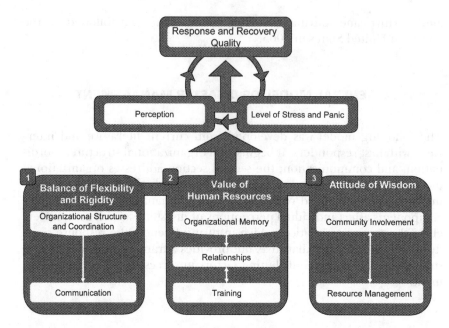

As seen in Figure 4.1, the general model of disaster management consists of three main components (organizational structure, coordination, and communication; organizational memory, relationships, and training; and community involvement and resource management). These three components influence the perception of control and the stress level in a disaster, which in turn help determine the quality of the response.

Figure 4.1.   A general model of disaster management.

reinforce each other (Rudolph & Repenning, 2002; Weick, 1988). For example, response quality increases when the response is timely.

Organizational Structure, Coordination, and Communication

Most disaster management agencies—whether small, volunteer emergency outfits, or governmental institutions—need an organizational structure that allows them to execute and coordinate responses to a wide variety of disasters as effectively and efficiently as possible. Organizational structure and planning are closely linked with the type of communication used in a disaster response. For example, if the structure is centralized and hierarchical, decisions require contacting the central entity, and communication is likely to take the form of command rather than exchange (Comfort, 1990).

Success of an organizational system often hinges on the balance between rigidity and flexibility. Rigid forms of coordination (produced by a centralized organizational structure and communication system) generally allow for a fast response, but they limit creativity. Creativity and improvisation, however, are often necessary in disasters because individuals are confronted with unfamiliar and chaotic situations (Comfort, 1990; Staw, Sandelands, & Dutton, 1981). Flexibility in the system enhances creative problem-solving that can improve performance under uncertainty. Overall, successful coordination helps responders to gain a feeling of increasing control over the situation, and the disaster therefore seems less overwhelming.

Organizational Memory, Relationships, and Training

Rich and vivid organizational memory positively affects the quality of disaster response. Rich memory has the potential to increase the accuracy of perception in disaster situations (Weick, 1988). In turn, if responders understand the unfolding disaster and its consequences, they are likely to find more suitable solutions than they would without the knowledge of past experiences (Weick, 1988).

Rich and vivid organizational memory can be developed only if relationships between members are strong and turnover is low (Anand, Manz, & Glick, 1998; Brandon & Hollingshead, 2004; Weick, 1988). Strong relationships can be pivotal when it comes to decision making in life-threatening situations. As Weick (1993) explains, strong relationships among first responders facilitate decision making under extreme conditions.

One way to strengthen relationships and pass on organizational memory is disaster management training. Training plays a vital role in disaster preparedness (Drabek & Hoetmer, 1991; Paton, 1996). Often the training sessions, whether they are disaster simulations, seminars or informal meetings, not only provide knowledge and skills, but also facilitate and strengthen relationships among responders. In addition, training can increase the perception of control in a disaster situation. As Peterson and Perry (1999) validated in a study on disaster training, successful exercises decrease the perceived danger associated with the task of managing a disaster.

Hence, all three components are intertwined; training and rich organizational memory increase the accuracy of perception in disaster situations. These activities increase the confidence of responders to deal with chaotic and overwhelming situations.

Community Involvement and Resource Management

Interviews with first responders revealed the importance of community involvement and resource management, which link to Weick's (1993) notion of "attitude of wisdom." Community involvement facilitates successful disaster response (Comfort, 1990; Gillespie, 1991; Scanlon, 1991; Uden-Homan Walkner, Huse, Greene, Gentsch, & Atchisonet, 2005). In a disaster situation, passive victims must become active responders in the community. This shift is not only necessary to alleviate damage directly caused by the disaster but also to prevent aggravation through indirect problems in the community such as looting (Comfort, 1990). Past experience with disasters demonstrates that the majority of victims are rescued by friends, neighbors, passersby, etc., because professional emergency response organizations are gravely overburdened (Scanlon, 1991). Like disaster training, community involvement increases the perception of control over a potential disaster and often reduces stress levels because individuals understand roughly how to respond. Simple techniques often make an enormous difference in disaster preparation. In earthquakes, for example, victims often flee without shoes and step on broken glass. Foot injuries are extremely common, and prevent community members from helping in the critical first hours. Therefore, advising the community to keep a torch and a pair of shoes readily available at night can greatly improve the response effort. Through straightforward preparations such as these, individuals provide structure for a chaotic and complex situation. Additionally, simple but helpful tasks can be easily performed even in a stressful situation, while complicated provisions are more difficult under stress (Weick, 1988). When even minimally prepared, communities perceive a disaster as more manageable. This, in turn, reduces stress levels and improves disaster response.

Similarly, an attitude of self-sufficiency towards resource management influences the response quality. Interviews demonstrate that using existing infrastructures creatively often triggers better solutions than an abundance of external resources. The coordination of resources is an enormous task in disaster management and frequently a larger problem than acquiring resources (Comfort, Ko, & Zagorecki, 2004). Weick (1993) showed that creative use of resources is essential to cope successfully in disaster situations. Resource management and community involvement are intertwined; involving the community, using existing infrastructures and materials as resources, and promoting an attitude of self-sufficiency increase the amount of perceived control and reduce stress.

THE BALANCE BETWEEN FLEXIBILITY AND RIGIDITY IN DISASTER MANAGEMENT

Disaster response systems are traditionally characterized by a centralized structure and command relations, and often involve a few expert decision makers rather than the entire community (Comfort, 1990). More recently, however, researchers tend to advocate an approach involving flexibility, improvisation, and decentralization (Comfort, 1990; Mendonca, Beroggi, & Wallace, 2001; Weick, 1993). Both systems have certain advantages and disadvantages, and the optimal balance between rigidity and flexibility of disaster and emergency management structures is widely discussed (e.g., Comfort, 1990; Comfort, Ko et al., 2004; Gladstein & Reilly, 1985; Nunamaker, Weber, & Chen, 1989; Staw et al., 1981; Weick, 1993). The tradeoff between flexibility and rigidity is evident in three important aspects of disaster management: organizational structure, coordination, and communication.

Organizational Structure and Coordination

If unprepared for a threat, individuals, groups, and organizations tend to respond with rigid behavior, which is often maladaptive (Nunamaker et al., 1989; Staw et al., 1981). Rigidity is expressed in two different ways: constriction of control and restriction of information (Staw et al., 1981).

Regarding constriction of control, individuals may opt for well-learned or habituated responses when confronted with threat (Hermann, 1963; Weick, 1988). Moreover, groups and organizations faced with threat tend to increase cohesiveness, leadership support, pressure for uniformity, and higher standardization and formalization (Hermann, 1963; Smart & Vertinsky, 1977; Staw et al., 1981). This shift to a more mechanistic organizational structure is meant to facilitate coordination and centralize decision making. This behavior, however, frequently proves maladaptive in uncertain or complex situations (Argote, 1982; Kiesler & Sproull, 1982; Quarantelli, 1988). Constriction of control prevents the individuals closest to the incident from having the authority to act, even when they are more competent to handle the situation (Perrow, 1984; Weick, 1988). Creative and improvisatory solutions involving a decentralized structure with independent decision makers are often advantageous.

Organizations facing threat often relinquish critical information processing capacity. Disaster research reveals that individuals tend to follow dominant cues in threatening situations and are likely to filter new information in a way that is compatible with the present and dominant perception (Comfort, Dunn, Johnson, Skertich, & Zagorecki, 2004; Dunbar & Goldberg, 1978; Smallman & Weir, 1999; Staw et al., 1981; Tjosvold, 1984; Vaughan, 1990). These responses are predominantly triggered by anxiety and stress (Hermann, 1963; Staw et al., 1981). Under these circumstances, premature consensus can support suboptimal solutions and aggravate the situation.

Given the problems associated with constriction of control and restriction of information, organizations and institutions that deal with disaster and emergency situations on a professional level should have a structure in place that counteracts these maladaptive forms of rigidity (Comfort, Dunn et al., 2004; Gilbert, 2005; Gladstein & Reilly, 1985; Kouzmin & Jarman, 1989; Nunamaker et al., 1989; Perrow, 1984; Smart & Vertinsky, 1977; Weick, 1988).

How do we accomplish this in practice? What are the implications for organizations that deal with crises on a daily basis, such as the ambulance, fire, search and rescue, and civil defense units? How rigidly or flexibly should these organizations be structured? Can these designs be planned beforehand, and how are they applied? We can begin to address these questions by considering some practical examples.

Regarding emergency units, Weick (1993) reports that some organizations, such as the National Park Service firefighters, are extremely flexible, have no formal structure in place, and rely on improvisation. The organizational design of these firefighters is described as a nonstandard "eclectic assembly of compromises" built of discretion and mobility. In contrast to the Forest Service (firefighters) where people do everything by the book, "the Park Service has no books; it puts a premium on the individual. Its collective behavior is tribal, and it protects its permanent ranks" (Weick, 1993, p. 640). Compared to the rigid structure prevalent in traditional firefighting, the Park Service firefighters are more likely to find creative solutions to problems. Additionally, Weick (1993) asserts that these firefighters will respond better to a collapse of their organizational structure during a large-scale disaster because they are accustomed to finding improvised solutions.

While flexible design allows for better handling of unpredictable and chaotic situations, a rigid design produces higher efficiency when the task is structured and familiar. Overall, it is easier to plan a rigid system than one that allows for improvisation and flexibility, and traditionally, response units are rigidly designed. As the Park Service firefighters demonstrate, however, it is essential and feasible to plan for flexibility, improvisation, and creativity when designing an organizational structure for crisis response.

A system that leaves room for frontline personnel to act independently and creatively, while still integrating individual actions into a coherent overall scheme, seems to be most appropriate for coping with disaster situations. In practice, however, such a system is extremely challenging to create.

The Meaning of the "Coordinated Incident Management Systems" (CIMS) for First Responders

In New Zealand, this challenge was addressed explicitly, on a national level, with the introduction of the Coordinated Incident Management Systems (CIMS) in the late 1990s (New Zealand Department of Internal Affairs, 2005). Throughout New Zealand, CIMS is widely accepted, regularly taught, and applied by all relevant organizations. So far, application of CIMS has proven successful and its application has been continuously adapted to make it effective for different organizations (see the report of the New Zealand Police, 2005). New Zealand has not been confronted with a major national disaster since the introduction of CIMS, however, so the system's success has only been tested in smaller incidents.

CIMS is not a New Zealand invention, but based on the Incident Command System (ICS), developed in the United States (California) during the 1970s. At present, the United States uses an expanded and renewed version of the ICS called the "National Incident Management System" (NIMS), developed as a response to the September 11, 2001 terrorist attack (9/11).

The purpose of systems such as CIMS and NIMS is to enable multiple response organizations to work together as a team during an emergency. In New Zealand, CIMS is now used by all emergency services and management organizations throughout the country, including the Ministry of Civil Defence, the New Zealand Police, New Zealand Search and Rescue, fire services, St. John Ambulance, and the Department of Conservation (Ministry of Health, 2004; New Zealand Department of Internal Affairs, 2005; New Zealand Police, 2005). Key elements of CIMS include the use of common terminology, effective and timely crisis communication among organizations, efficient deployment of resources, coordination of skills and knowledge, and modular organizational structure with prescribed functions, scaled according to the size of the incident (Ministry of

Health, 2004; New Zealand Department of Internal Affairs, 2005; New Zealand Police, 2005).

In the United States, NIMS was most recently tested after Hurricane Katrina struck New Orleans in August 2005, but the management of the hurricane was harshly criticized in the media (e.g., Corn, 2005; Lipton, Drew, Shane, Rohde, DeParle, & Pear, 2005; Yourish, Stanton, & Tate, 2005; Zwerdling & Sullivan, 2005). Although Katrina was predicted, and the disaster planning started before New Orleans began to flood, response was not optimal. Some of the plans regarding food, water, and security fell apart before their activation. The National Guard troops waited outside of New Orleans for an official chain of command to be established—while the 100,000 people trapped inside the city urgently needed help. This bureaucratic approach hindered emergency units trying to alleviate the situation. It has been reported that trucks loaded with thousands of water bottles were not allowed to unload because they did not have official authorization. Helpers complained that they were held up with paperwork during the crucial first two or three days (Lipton et al., 2005; Zwerdling & Sullivan, 2005). These problems reflect forms of maladaptive rigidity.

Does this mean that NIMS failed? Was it designed poorly? Would it work in New Zealand in a nationwide disaster? There are many ways to approach these questions, but interviews with civil defense staff and trained volunteers in Dunedin show that individual interpretations of these systems are crucial to their functionality. Systems such as NIMS and CIMS incorporate excellent ideas, but in the Katrina incident, NIMS did not allow for or encourage autonomous decision making. How do first responders in New Zealand interpret CIMS? What does a modular organizational structure mean to a trained volunteer? How, in practice, is responsibility assigned and delegated? How does the rural firefighter understand the term "effective deployment of resources?" Has the radio communicator in a small town even *heard* of CIMS/NIMS or its special terminology?

As the final report of the independent and bipartisan 9/11 commission concludes, "civilians and first responders will again find themselves on the front lines. We must plan for that eventuality. A rededication to preparedness is perhaps the best way to honor the memories of those we lost that day" (National Commission on Terrorist Attacks, 2004, p. 323).

For systems such as CIMS and NIMS to work successfully, first responders must interpret these systems in a way that allows them to work effectively—individually and in teams across organizations. From the postanalysis of Hurricane Katrina's management, it seems that NIMS was interpreted as a rigid and formal bureaucratic structure that is imposed on emergency organizations.

The following quotes reflect the interpretation of CIMS by a senior staff member for (named Paul in the following) New Zealand Civil Defence:

> The Coordinated Incident Management System (CIMS) is really just a philosophy of how you structure your own emergency response so that the terminology and the functions for the structure are common for all emergency organizations. This means that the police, the fire, the ambulance, and a lot of other agencies that respond as part of a civil defense emergency all understand the structure that will be applied. For a larger emergency, a so-called Incident Controller will be determined who coordinates the emergency. In particular, it means that somebody is answering the controller, that you have a planning and intelligence function, and an operations and a logistics function.
>
> The task of civil defense in each city or town is just to populate those functions to a far greater extent than, for example, the emergency services would do in a road accident. All the emergency services in New Zealand use the same structural outline, but they have less people and organizations involved in them than there would be in a large-scale disaster. By the time we get to a major emergency, we have a huge number of people and organizations within each of those functional headings. So the CIMS structure is one that can grow. It is designed that way. It uses common terminology so that everybody understands what the structure is and what their role is within it.
>
> In addition to the common terminology for certain functions and positions within CIMS, there is also an actual color code that everybody is familiar with. This means that the civil defense people who work in the emergency headquarter wear different colored vests with their position on the back. Therefore, if somebody is looking for the manager of communication, they look for a green vest with "Communications" written on the back. And the controller gets to wear pink—very bright day glow pink! Consequently, if you are not the head guy you go looking for the one that is wearing the pink vest. And everyone knows that. The person who is in charge puts the jacket on. There are things like shift change and you have got a different person doing that job, that doesn't matter. You go looking for that vest and that is the person who is in charge.

As these quotes demonstrate, CIMS is a way to organize and coordinate an emergency. In New Zealand, CIMS is not only used in large-scale disasters but also in small incidents, and is therefore regularly practiced by professional emergency organizations. Having practice in responding to less-threatening situations can help to establish a more flexible and knowledge-rich system. Thus, applying CIMS in every emergency and disaster situation regardless of size is advisable.

Implementing a nationwide system is considerably easier in a small country, such as New Zealand, than in the United States Even in the

United States, the goal is to apply a universal system that allows different organizations to work in a coordinated fashion in an emergency. In practice, however, this is not yet the case nationwide. The report of the 9/11 commission and the analysis of Hurricane Katrina's management showed a lack of interagency coordination among local, state, and federal responders. In New Zealand, CIMS has been used since the early 1990s, while, in the United States, NIMS was introduced in 2003 after 9/11 (Homeland Security, 2004). Although NIMS is based on precedent incident and emergency response systems, its nationwide adoption remains in progress. Recently, the department of Homeland Security published two reports that outlined how NIMS can be integrated into local, tribal, and state emergency operation plans and standard procedures (Homeland Security, 2006a, 2006b). Nationwide, multilevel establishment of NIMS will improve overall coordination and structure for responding to future large-scale emergencies.

A large-scale disaster, however, will most likely involve both trained and untrained volunteers. These volunteers are often crucial to help save lives and assist professional emergency workers. It is therefore important to understand what a system such as CIMS means to volunteers and how it is applied to the individual. David, who is a voluntary radio communicator supporting Search And Rescue and Civil Defense, states:

> Regarding CIMS, you have to be careful with three words here: trained, skilled, and familiar. If you put a structure like CIMS in place, people will say, "Everybody is trained in CIMS," and that is true. Yes, I'm trained in CIMS, which means that I've been to two courses ... As a result, it does not worry me if someone is talking about CIMS during the emergency.
>
> In my understanding, CIMS is an evolutionary structure ... it is alive. In my understanding, it is a living being and not a fixed structure. CIMS can be as simple as one man. He is in charge—end of story. However, it could be one man with sub-people doing multiple tasks. Those tasks tend to be divided into specific groups. In order for the system to grow within those groups, tasks will be shed to other people as the structure escalates, so the structure spreads.
>
> Although CIMS has the effect on people that everybody starts using these definite terms about each position, I don't think that this is the core idea behind it. I don't see it as that. I see it as training people to evolve a structure that works.
>
> Now the most crucial situation to use CIMS is when the police, fire, and ambulance all arrive on one site. Who is in command? That is where CIMS comes in—and that is where it is important. All those professional organizations are highly trained with CIMS. The CIMS structure is what police and ambulance and fire can use everyday. So they can become skilled at that, and it works fine with them.

In contrast, trained volunteers, like me, use it so little that I have trouble remembering the details of it. But as long as someone there can remember the structure and say, "He is the such-and-such manager," I will accept all that, because it comes back to me. That is the difference between being trained and skilled and being familiar. Familiar is use, skilled is having used it a lot and trained is just having heard about it.

So, overall it is a sensible system. However, it needs to be melted down at my level with experience, and it needs to be applicable for me in a practical situation. In a large-scale emergency, for example, you will have these different names of all of the different people doing different functions. I cannot remember the names of it. I know there is 'Operations,' 'Logistics,' etc. I think that we, as volunteer radio communicators, are under 'Operations,' but I don't mind. They can fit us anywhere they like. We just have to be prepared to accept the structure.

This statement illustrates that professional organizations can become skilled at adapting the CIMS structure through regular applications, so that they can instruct volunteers. For those who support emergency and disaster operations on a voluntary level, it is necessary to be familiar with the terminology used and the philosophy behind the system. A system such as CIMS can only work if it is regularly applied and integrated with professional and nonprofessional response organizations and agencies on a local, state, and federal level. In the following story, CIMS is applied in a small-scale incident: a rural fire emergency. This example illustrates the basic idea of CIMS:

A small example of using CIMS is a fire emergency that happened a few years ago. In Dunedin, Civil Defense is also the first responder for rural fires, which are the vegetation fires out in the country areas. A few years ago we had a whole series of six disconnected fires going at the same time in a similar area. As first responder, the regular New Zealand Fire Services were dealing with some of them as well as our rural fire crews. The fire occurred in an area that was very bad for radio communication because of the mountainous terrain. In consequence, we did not quite know where all of the regular fire fighters were and whether they were dealing with the same fire as our rural fire fighters. So we had quite a messy situation, ineffective fire fighting, and a potential of people getting hurt because of the lack of communication amongst them, as well as out to us. Next, based on CIMS, we, as Civil Defense, activated part of our operational organizations and said, "This is getting serious. We need to get a coordinated approach to these fires." Then we called in representatives of the ambulance, the regular fire service, the rural fire service and some additional people to the Civil Defense headquarters. These representatives formed a bit of a headquarter team. And it was astonishing to see that within a very short time of putting those people together to manage the incident as one emergency of one organization, we knew exactly where everybody was. Before that, the regular fire services could not communicate with their people because their radio communication did not work, but our radio did. So after we all met in the headquarters here, we talked to our rural fire crews who were able to talk locally to their crews and to the regular fire fighters.

It turned out that we did indeed have some of the fire service crews fighting the same fire as our crews, just in a different part of it, and they did not know that. Then we sorted out the priorities, diverted some of those resources to different places, and the management of the whole incident was much better.

So it is a very small-scale example, but it shows what a difference it makes with organizations working separately compared to when they come together and work in a coordinated fashion. And it was surprising how quickly we began managing well once we brought people in one place.

This regular application allows participants to become familiar and skilled with the system. One could argue that it is easy to use CIMS in a bush fire, but large-scale disasters pose a different challenge. Large-scale disasters, such as 9/11, are so devastating that they are often completely incomprehensible for first responders. They are what Weick (1993) calls a "cosmology episode." A cosmology episode is a disruption that shatters our basic assumption of how the world and the universe work. We mostly assume that events unfold in a rather orderly way. If we would expect a major disaster any minute, we would not be able to lead our lives as we do. In a major incident, such as 9/11, these basic assumptions collapse, as well as our capability to understand or rebuild these assumptions (Weick, 1993). As such, no one had expected—during the incident—that a second plane would hit the World Trade Center, or that the towers would collapse. These events were beyond imagination. In the heat of a cosmology episode, professional response organizations are gravely overburdened and it is extremely difficult to coordinate relief efforts. This makes it even more important to practice systems, such as NIMS or CIMS, regularly in small-scale incidents.

The firefighting story above also highlights another facet of disaster management coordination: horizontal collaboration. As the example shows, a coordinated response across different organizations was more efficient than the uncoordinated scenario.

The need to improve collaboration among the various agencies involved has been clearly identified in the disaster and emergency management literature (e.g., Caro, 1999; Polivka, Dresback, Heimlich, & Elliott, 2001; Thieren, 2005). This is, however, easier said than done. The U.S. Department of Homeland Security states:

NIMS provides a consistent template to enable Federal, State, local, and tribal governments and private-sector and nongovernmental organizations to work together effectively and efficiently to prepare for, prevent, respond to, and recover from domestic incidents.... To provide for interoperability and compatibility among Federal, State, and local capabilities, the NIMS will include a core set of concepts, principles, terminology, and technologies covering the incident command system; multiagency coordination system; unified command; training. (U.S. Department of Homeland Security, 2004).

Practical examples, however, show that the regular application of NIMS in the United States and its integration on a state and local level have not yet been achieved. Investigators and observers acknowledged a lack of horizontal collaboration in both 9/11 and Katrina. Regarding 9/11:

The FDNY (Fire Department of New York) and the New York Police Department (NYPD) each considered itself operationally autonomous. As of September 11, they were not prepared to comprehensively coordinate their efforts in responding to a major incident.... The FDNY, PAPD (Port Authority Police Department), and NYPD did not coordinate their units that were searching the WTC complex for civilians. In many cases, redundant searches of specific floors and areas were conducted....It is clear that the lack of coordination did not affect adversely the evacuation of civilians. It is equally clear, however, that the Incident Command System (predecessor of NIMS) did not function to integrate awareness among agencies or to facilitate interagency response. If New York and other major cities are to be prepared for future terrorist attacks, different first responder agencies within each city must be fully coordinated, just as different branches of the U.S. military are. Coordination entails a unified command that comprehensively deploys all dispatched police, fire, and other first responder resources. (National Commission on Terrorist Attacks, 2004, pp. 285, 321–322)

Regarding Hurricane Katrina:

FEMA officials expected the state and city to direct their own efforts and ask for help as needed. Leaders in Louisiana and New Orleans, though, were so overwhelmed by the scale of the storm that they were not only unable to manage the crisis, but they were not always exactly sure what they needed. While local officials assumed that Washington would provide rapid and considerable aid, federal officials, weighing legalities and logistics, proceeded at a deliberate pace. (Lipton et al., 2005)

These examples underpin the importance of horizontal collaboration. In New Zealand, CIMS determines the lead agency as well as the collaboration of all other parties involved. As Polivka et al. (2001) assert, interagency collaboration is usually more acute in rural areas because fewer professional organizations and resources are available. Horizontal collaboration is, therefore, necessary more often than not. This may be advantageous for New Zealand, because agencies here must collaborate more frequently than in countries where ample amounts of resources are available, and emergencies are usually dealt with by specialized professional organizations. A small example from New Zealand illustrates ideal horizontal collaboration under CIMS.

> The lead agency in a larger emergency is often determined by the statutory authority, but it can also change depending on how large the incident gets. If we have a fire outbreak in a rural area, which is basically the area outside the metropolitan designs, the Rural Fire Service is the local authority to deal with the fire. Thus, Rural Fire Service would be the lead agency. However, if one of our fires is also involving a structure, like a farmhouse, then we bring in the New Zealand Fire Services to deal with the metropolitan area involved. In this case, Rural Fire Service would remain the lead agency. The reverse could happen as well. For example, if there is a fire in a house in the metropolitan area, which also involves vegetation, the New Zealand Fire Service is the lead authority ... and they will call Rural Fire Service, which will then work under their authority. This is a very simple example but it illustrates that the two organizations can swap lead authority. If the scale gets to the point where the Civil Defence Emergency Management act kicks in, or to the stage where there is the need to declare an emergency and the organizations themselves say, "We're having trouble managing this," the civil defense structure will be activated.
>
> The former scenario, a declared emergency, will involve a statutory controller who runs a group of experts to manage the emergency. In the latter scenario, a non-declared emergency, civil defense would still operate under the authority of the senior person from the lead agency. For example, recently we had a fire in a large building in the city center. Here, we actually activated the civil defense structure to support the fire services. Thus, civil defense, the police and the ambulance were acting in support of the fire services as the lead authority. Civil defense was helping with the coordination, but the fire was not big enough to be declared an emergency of the kind that civil defense would swap in as the lead agency. So the fire service remained the lead authority. If that fire had extended to several blocks and we had a really big emergency, then civil defense would have declared a state of emergency and the statutory controller would have led the overall organization, leaving the fire services responsible for fighting the fire. This change in lead authority is intended to take the responsibility of coordinating the emergency away from the fire service so that they are able to focus solely on fighting the fire. As a consequence, it would have been the job of civil defense to organize the evacuations, to take care of people who were evacuated, the road closures and other logistical things.

In New Zealand, CIMS does not only coordinate incidents vertically by determining a hierarchy within the organizations, but also horizontally. As the examples showed, this is very important. The majority of larger incidents involve more than one response organization, which makes it necessary to determine a lead agency and a structure that coordinates all parties involved.

Integrating multiple organizations in a coordinated fashion is not only necessary but also the most efficient way to respond to a disaster. As the interviewee above pointed out, coordinating the fire response solved problems "surprisingly quickly." This corresponds to Comfort, Ko, et al.'s (2004) research findings on disaster response efficiency. In a simulation study, results revealed a positive relation between the amount of jurisdiction involved and the efficiency of disaster response operations. This finding is counterintuitive because of the widespread assumption that it is more time consuming and less efficient to involve more parties in a response (Comfort, Ko et al., 2004).

Thus, a system such as CIMS helps to achieve a coordinated response more efficiently because it determines the lead agency as well as the organizational functions that need to be populated. As the fire emergency example showed, coordination achieved a better distribution of resources; a faster response, as well as avoidance of redundancies. Coordinating response efforts among organizations will lead to a perception of higher control over the situation and to reduced stress levels.

Decentralization as a Necessity

As stated above, emergency and disaster management services should aim for a sufficiently flexible and decentralized design that avoids maladaptive forms of rigidity. In Dunedin, decentralization and flexibility might be more a necessity than in other cities because of its particular geographical setting. In terms of land area, with 3,314.8 km^2, Dunedin is one of the world's largest cities. This special geographical feature poses a challenge to disaster and emergency management planning because many outlying communities that could easily be isolated need to be considered. As such, Dunedin has the following response plan for such a scenario:

> In Dunedin, we aim for a more decentralized system in a larges-cale disaster. Civil defense is able to set up smaller versions of the headquarter facility all around the city. So the civil defense facilities can spread out like a satellite system. In New Zealand many years ago, the government stipulated that every school was a civil defense sector headquarters. So in a civil emergency people would focus on their local school, which is generally [a] very good idea because there are schools everywhere and the size and number matches the community. So, when they started doing civil defense training in New Zealand, they based it around the schools, and schools had these little signs

saying "Sector Headquarters—Sector A," for example. That worked out fine and it is still there. More recently, at least in Dunedin, but probably nationwide as well, civil defense has also installed a little handheld radio into the schools. The radio is engineered into a box that is temperature proof, with a battery and mounted on the walls. All the school people as well as the civil defense people know about them. The school radios link in with the general radio communication of civil defense and they are tested quite often. So the schools became the subcenters from the civil defense headquarters.

For example, in an earthquake where the whole city is affected and communities may be isolated, we need to be able to have people managing that part of the city—locally, rather than centrally—because the headquarters facility would just not have the capacity to do it all from one point. So the various communities have to deal with a lot of issues on their level. They, in turn, have even smaller centers, which they are responsible for. These smaller centers are mostly primary schools which are spread everywhere around the cities. Therefore, civil defense trains people to run those smaller centers. They learn just how to do the usual checks in an emergency and to look out for minor problems at the community level. They would escalate any bigger issues to the next level, the coordination centers of their community. These coordination centers deal with the resources that the Headquarter assigns to them. If they have the need and capacity, the coordination centers may escalate information and requests for more resources in the systems to the civil defense headquarters. So it is a triage type system. The headquarters should only be managing the really big issues, and it is aimed for the coordination centers or the smaller civil defense Post in the community to deal with smaller issues—or with all the issues they have the capacity to deal with.

For example, Middlemarch, which is in Central Otago, has a team that can manage the impacts of a large-scale disaster locally. The same applies to the Peninsula, which could be easily isolated in a disaster such as an earthquake. The Peninsula, which also is part of Dunedin city, has a center down there as well, so that they could manage most of the issues down there. These outlying areas have to have their own capability because they are further away and could possibly be isolated. Comparing the Dunedin setting with Auckland, for example, shows the implication for different management techniques in emergencies. In Auckland you have the whole seven sub-cities closely together. They are all dependent on the same resources. They are all one big physical block. Therefore, they can probably manage things much more easily for a far greater number of people because the city is not so spread out. The population density is much greater, as are the resources. We have a very sparse population with huge distances in between; therefore, we have to manage slightly differently.

On the one hand, Dunedin's rural setting and the large land area poses a challenge to emergency and disaster management. It is more difficult to communicate and coordinate if the disaster affects isolated communities. On the other hand, a rural setting also forces disaster and emergency planners to build a decentralized system and intensify the involvement of communities in the planning scenarios. As Uden-Homan et al. (2005, p. 106) point out, limited public funding historically results in a tradition of higher community involvement or "community-centered volunteerism" in rural settings. As will be shown later in this chapter, this tradition of a higher degree of community involvement, which is born out of necessity in New Zealand, is a highly useful and significant aspect of a successful disaster and emergency response. Lessons learned in disaster planning for widely dispersed populations that depend on community involvement may be fruitfully applied to a variety of circumstances where governmental responses may be limited or delayed.

To summarize, several authors emphasize the need for decentralized decision making in disaster response operations (Hermann, 1963; Quarantelli, 1988; Weick, 1988). Often, the lack of decentralized decision making means that the overall ability to address the problem is reduced (Perrow, 1984; Weick, 1988). Under conditions of high uncertainty and high heterogeneity among training and experience of first responders, a decentralized system is preferable (Comfort, 1990). These conditions are prevalent in most large-scale disasters. The majority of first responders are civilians because professional services are heavily overburdened. Therefore, a decentralized system that allows responders to take action and exchange information quickly should be applied to large-scale disaster situations.

Rigid Thinking as an Obstacle of Disaster Management

As illustrated above, maladaptive forms of rigidity can greatly impair successful disaster and emergency management. The management in Katrina showed signs of maladaptive rigidity, such as bureaucracy and the lack of independent decision making. In New Zealand, interpretation of CIMS seems to be rather flexible and has been cited as an "evolutionary living structure." Moreover, the broad geographical setting of Dunedin encourages decentralization, a higher degree of independent decision making, and community involvement.

The balance between rigidity and flexibility is not necessarily determined by organizational structures or physical settings. Sometimes, forms of maladaptive rigidity result from the way people think. As Weick (1988, p. 306) states, "once a person becomes committed to an action, and then builds an explanation that justifies that action, the explanation tends to persist and becomes transformed into an assumption that is taken for granted." This is what Weick (1988) calls "enacted commitment." Thus, enacted commitment increases rigidity in thinking. On the one hand, this creates more clarity and structure; on the other hand, the strong commitment to an action creates a "blind spot" because this course of action is basically free of doubt (Weick, 1988). The following example of the Abbotsford landslide shows how enacted commitment increases rigid thinking, creates a blind spot, and impairs effective disaster management:

> The Abbotsford Landslide occurred in Dunedin in 1979. Although no lives were lost in the landslide, 17 people had to be rescued from the area, and 69 houses were destroyed or damaged.
>
> Here, early reports existed that the area of Abbotsford proves prone to landslides and, therefore, should be considered unsuitable for residential purposes. The reports of 1940 and 1946 state that "the Abbotsford mudstone is more prone to slide than almost any other formation in the Dunedin district. ... The weathered mudstone is very prone to mass movement. Most of the land surface, even when gently sloping, shows signs of earth flows."
>
> However, in 1948, Town Planning decided that the area was generally suitable for housing purposes. Taking the previous warnings into account, the plan suggested that parts of the area should be planted in trees and residential development should be restricted. Although this plan was made public and officially accepted, it disappeared. It was then replaced with another which ignored the residential restriction. The warning reports were forgotten by all concerned, and it was assumed that Abbotsford is suitable for housing purposes even though smaller landslides had occurred around Abbotsford. When later, in 1968, one Abbotsford house developed rather strange and rapid appearance, then disappearance, of cracks, it was attributed to causes unrelated to mass movement even though there was continuing movement and cracking in the house. After the big landslide occurred in 1979, opinions of witnesses varied on the reasons for the early damage to the house. Some witnesses still believed that the damage should be attributed to causes unrelated to the landslide, such as the nearby debris-carrying stream. Others believed that the early cracks in the house stemmed from mass movement. The Royal Commission of Inquiry into the Abbotsford Landslip Disaster supported the latter interpretation. (Gallen, McCraw, & Roberts, 1980, pp. 9–73)

This disaster illustrates enacted commitment. Following the belief that it was safe to build houses, warning signs such as cracks in the houses and landslips in neighboring areas were attributed to causes other than mass movement. These opinions remained even after the landslide occurred. This rigid thinking prevented early counteraction. If the earlier reports on land instability had not been ignored, the landslip could have been anticipated earlier. Fortunately, nobody died in the landslip, but many lost their houses and belongings. By the same token, a smaller example shows another way in which enacted commitment can undermine systems such as CIMS. David reports:

There was a strong flood in Invercargill. The Dunedin civil defense team contacted the Invercargill team who was managing the flood and said, "We've got all our resources here—jet boats, radios, radio personnel, whatever you want. Just call us!" Invercargill replied, "No, no, no everything is fine here—everything is under control."

At the same time, one of the volunteer radio communicators of Dunedin happened to be on holiday in Hawea and was on his way to Invercargill to visit his son. So he drove down there and thought, "Oh! I'll just pop in to Civil Defense Headquarter and see how things are going." Everyone knew there was a flood. So he went in there, came out, got on the radio to Dunedin and said: "Get 30 radio operators down here straight away! They are deadbeat. They all want to go home to see their families. They are all absolutely stuffed. They have been going 24 hours without a relief." So we shot 30 radio operators down from Dunedin who could go in there. As long as someone fed them, they could keep going because they knew their families were safe in Dunedin. So why didn't they call us for help earlier? The command did not want to ask for help because to him it meant that they were not prepared. You understand? It's a conflict.

I don't know what word you use to describe this behavior, but it is some sort of conflict between asking for help and pride. And the same might apply to Dunedin or other places, too. I am pretty sure that Dunedin would not like to ask for help from outside. But they bloody know they'd have to and they would—I hope they would.

But it would be very easy to politically think, "If I ask for help, the news media will say we were not ready and we did not have enough resources." So that is an enemy—one of the big enemies. Politics and looting would probably be the worst enemies of efficient emergency and disaster management.

It seems that the Invercargill civil defense team excluded the possibility to call for support from outside a priori because they were committed to deal with the emergency themselves. This is just a small example where nobody suffered harm and no further consequences occurred. However, under different circumstances, exhausted personnel or understaffing can add more problems to an already difficult situation (Perrow, 1984; Weick, 1993). Further, factors such as politics or the media can trigger commitment to counterproductive actions that significantly undermine emergency response.

Similarly, forms of rigid thinking can be found in the response to Katrina. Here, New Orleans Mayor Ray Nagin has been widely blamed for delaying a mandatory evacuation which was issued well after the hurricane was predicted to be in category five (the highest category) (e.g., Hsu, 2006; Lipton, 2006; Russell, 2005). Moreover, without consulting emergency and disaster experts first, Nagin urged citizens to come back to the city as soon as possible (Russell, 2005). In hindsight, it proved to be unsafe for citizens to return that early. Both of Nagin's controversial decisions were seemingly motivated by his concerns regarding the economic impact on New Orleans' businesses and tourism (Nolan, 2005).

Whether resulting from the media, politics, or the reliance on basic assumptions, rigid thinking impairs preventive actions and aggravates the disaster. To address rigid thinking, it is necessary to challenge our basic assumptions and the motives upon which we make decisions in a disaster. As Weick (1993) suggests, it is necessary to adopt an attitude of wisdom that allows us to be open and curious enough to deal with changing conditions. This attitude excludes extreme confidence as well as extreme cautiousness because both extremes lead to a closed mind. Attempting to be open-minded during disaster, planning for the worst-case scenario and questioning basic assumptions will avoid forms of rigid thinking. If responders are more open to uncertainty and changing situations, accuracy of perception will increase and allow for a better disaster response.

Traditional disaster response has been prone to rigidity. As such, organizational structures such as NIMS and CIMS have been interpreted as a chain of command rather than an evolutionary structure. In addition, centralization is prevalent although research and experiences show the advantages of a decentralized system. These factors result in forms of rigid thinking, which impair the success of disaster response. In contrast, flexible organizational structure that allows decentralized decision making is more likely to increase the perception of control over the disaster and to reduce stress levels. Moreover, flexible thinking increases the accuracy of perception and allows for finding preventive solutions. Both an increased perception of control and reduced stress levels lead to an improved disaster response.

Leadership

As indicated above, leadership roles in large-scale disasters are often unclear because multiple organizations and agencies are involved. Systems such as CIMS and NIMS attempt to clear doubts about leadership and facilitate cross-agency collaboration. Strong leadership can be crucial in disaster management. In crisis or disaster situations, authority tends to move to higher levels. Consequently, leaders have more influence in crisis situations that in noncrisis situations (Hamblin, 1958), and charismatic leadership is especially likely to occur and influence performance in the onset of crisis situations (House, Spangler, & Woycke, 1991; Pillai & Meindl, 1998). Although systems such as CIMS and NIMS are designed to clarify leadership, the response to Katrina has been criticized for failing to do exactly that (e.g., Lipton et al., 2005).

Even if clear leadership is established, it can be destroyed under the pressure of a disaster situation. For example, in the Mann Gulch Fire disaster, the firefighter lost direction when circumstances required a switch in leadership (Weick, 1993). The role change was clarified with all firefighters, but the newly appointed leader was unfamiliar with this role. Because of role change in leadership in combination with an unexpectedly large fire, the role structure of the firefighter crew collapsed. As Weick (1993) concludes, there are two crucial reasons to prepare everyone for leadership change. First, emergency responders on all levels should be prepared to accept a change in leadership. Second, everyone should be prepared to take on a leadership role. In this "virtual role system,"

> each individual in the crew mentally takes all roles and ... in the manner of a holograph, each person can reconstitute the group and assume whatever role is vacated, pick up the activities, and run a credible version of the role. (Weick, 1993, p. 640)

In general, flexible leadership design is better for emergency response than the more traditional structure in which one person is in charge most of the time (Comfort, 1990; Weick, 1993). CIMS allows and requires changing leadership, as David illustrates:

> There is at least one feature of CIMS that someone unfamiliar with it would find strange: namely that leadership can switch. I have seen it happening in Search and Rescue operations. I have watched it several times. You escalate the incident and a new guy comes in. It means that the person who is currently running the operation will shed a whole section of his duties to this guy as he escalates the functions and gets more people in. For example, we had a search exercise up the coast. When leadership changes, you see the current leader taking the new fellow away and briefing him. Then he says, "Now this is what we've done and this is where we are and this is what you are going to cover. This is your lot. I'm now handing that formally to you and you are now in charge of this whereas I've been doing it up until now." So, yeah, CIMS does work, providing the people are all relatively familiar. All agencies will accept a change of leadership because they all are a part of the planning. They understand very clearly that there will be a change of lead authority in that point and they will be part of the overall management of the civil defense emergency.

Provided that responders on all levels are trained and familiar with CIMS, they are prepared to accept and understand the change of leadership. However, CIMS does not clearly state that every individual or organization needs to be prepared for leadership. Whether CIMS is able to establish a functional "virtual role system" depends again on the individual interpretation of it, the way it is enacted, the way it is taught, and how it is actually applied on a practical level. In New Zealand, this interpretation and practical application seem to be similar to Weick's (1993) suggestions. As David puts it:

> I give you a little story that reflects my understanding of leadership in CIMS. Let's assume I am on holiday at a beach in New Zealand away from my home town. If a civil defense emergency happens in that location, a flood for example, then I would expect that an outcome of CIMS is people who are prepared to say: "Okay, fine, we've got a situation here—I am going to take control." I think that is more important than training people in doing things. That is far more important. It is better to have someone come along and say: "I've got the skills and I will take control." In the first-aid training, they will tell you that this is the first thing. You go into an accident. First thing you say is: "Is first aid here?" And they will say, "No, no, no!" So you will say: "I am here and I will take control." And you've got control. Everybody will give it to you. The same applies in a civil defense emergency. They will respond to a person who takes leadership. Now, once you establish that, you are the leader. You've got all the tasks and you have to shed responsibilities. It is like growing a business, I suppose, you are going to grow so you have to shed responsibilities and build the structure. And that is what CIMS does.

This is exactly what a few people did in the New Orleans Hurricane aftermath. They ignored bureaucracy and official coordination structure in order to fulfill the original goal of NIMS: helping the victims.

> On Aug 31, Sheriff Edmund M. Sexton, Sr., of Tuscaloosa county, Alabama, and president of the National Sheriffs' Association, sent out an alert urging members to pitch in. "Folks were held up two, three days while they were working on the paperwork," he said. Some sheriffs refused to wait. In Wayne County, Mich., which includes Detroit, Sheriff Warren C. Evans got a call from Mr. Sexton on Sept 1. The next day, he led a convoy of six tractor-trailers, three rental trucks, and 33 deputies, despite public pleas from Gov. Jennifer M. Granholm to wait for formal requests. "I could look at CNN and see people dying, and I couldn't, in good conscience, wait for a coordinated response," he said. He dropped off food, water, and medical supplies in Mobile and Gonzales, LA, where a sheriffs' task force directed him to the French Quarter. By Saturday, Sept. 3, the Michigan team was conducting Search and Rescue missions. (Lipton et al., 2005)

As the sheriffs in the U.S. moved to fulfill the intent of the incident management system despite bureaucratic impediments, systems such as CIMS should be interpreted as a structure that allows establishing leadership and acting flexibly. Ideally, the nature and severity of the incident should determine the lead agency. If all agencies and voluntary responders are trained with the system, agencies are prepared to accept the leadership role. Moreover, agencies and individuals need to be prepared to fully accept a change in leadership. For example, if a small emergency escalates into a larger one, the authority switches from the local fire service to the civil defense team. Everyone has to be prepared to accept this new lead agency.

A functional virtual role system allows for a flexible leadership design. If individuals and organizations are prepared for assuming a leadership role as well as for accepting changes in leadership it is less likely that a system of responders disintegrates or, as with Katrina, leadership remains unclear and actions become hesitant. If this virtual role system is working, responders will increasingly perceive more control over the situation and experience reduced stress levels. Both advance the quality of the disaster response.

Communication in Disaster Management

To coordinate a disaster relief operation efficiently, communication is crucial. At the same time, communication is usually severely distorted and impaired, especially in large-scale disasters. The number of communication channels decrease during a crisis, a problem which often accompanies an information overload (Hermann, 1963; Staw et al., 1981). Taking a brief look at the comments regarding communication in Hurricane Katrina, it becomes evident how severely a disaster can affect communication:

Telephone and cell phone service died, and throughout the crisis the state's special emergency communications system was either overloaded or knocked out. (Lipton et al., 2005)

In addition, Comfort (1990) asserts that communication in disaster management requires a balance between exchange and command. Whereas command relationships are faster and more efficient, they usually result in a lack of collaboration among the different agencies involved. Exchange relationships achieve a higher degree of collaboration and are better suited to deal with uncertainty. Maintaining exchange relationships, however, is more time-consuming. Traditional disaster management is prone towards command relationships with a centralized system that involves a few experts rather than the community (Comfort, 1990, p. 93). This approach seems to have been prevalent during the response to Katrina:

Rather than initiate relief efforts—buses, food, troops, diesel fuel, rescue boats—FEMA waited for specific requests from state and local officials.

"When you go to war, you don't have time to ask for each round of ammuni-
tion that you need," complained Colonel Ebbert, the city's emergency operation director. [FEMA] attributed some of the delay to miscommunications
in an overwhelming event. (Lipton et al., 2005)

National Guard troops in other states sat ready, waiting for orders that
never came. Instead, they were told to wait for an official plan and a chain
of command to be established. (Zwerdling & Sullivan, 2005)

A decentralized strategy involving exchange relationships is more
promising, especially when the situation involves high uncertainty, low
training and little experience of responders (Comfort, 1990; Mendonca et
al., 2001). A simple communication exercise that recently took place in
Dunedin demonstrates communication failure in command relationships.
As one of the radio communicators recalls:

Recently, Civil Defense undertook a communication exercise in Dunedin.
The exercise involved the Civil Defense Headquarters as a command center,
all the schools which are Civil Defense Sector Headquarters, as well as the
Emergency Communication Unit (ECU). The ECU is a mobile communication center that has probably 20 radios in it and a lot of aerials, antennas, etc.
    For the purpose of this exercise, we assumed that telephones are all dead,
cell phones are out and we only have radio communications. However, that
means for isolated communities such as Port Chalmers, for example, that
there is only one communication device talking to Dunedin Civil Defense
Headquarters. And Port Chalmers shares the same channel with all the
other outlying communities which also have only one channel for communication. They are all on a party line. This means that the whole city is on the
one channel to get to headquarters. In this centralized system, communication would be, for example, as follows.
    Port Chalmers contacts the Headquarters radio operators and says: "We
have a problem with 16 people trapped there-and-there.... What do you
want to do about it?" Next, this message goes into the command room
because the radio operators are only conveyers and therefore cannot make
decisions. The message therefore goes into a big pool and someone might
find it and say: "We've got that message...." Then they do the thinking
about it in the command room and eventually get back to the radio communicator. In a centralized system the communication does not work the way
such as: "Can I scratch my head?" "Yes, you can". Instead it goes: "Can I
scratch my head?" Then the radio communicator says, "I'll ask Fred."—
"Fred, can he scratch his head?"—"Yes, he can!"—"Yes, you can!"
    Using this centralized system in this exercise became total chaos, and it
was only an exercise! Therefore, it was an excellent exercise because it
showed the problems. However, part of the difficulties was also that a lot of
new people were involved in this exercise. They are trained operators, but

they are not trained per se on civil defense, which is good because that is the way it will be.

So this exercise proved that a centralized system with a very thin communication structure cannot work. If your communication structure gets that thin because there are no landlines and no cell phones, then you cannot have centralized command. Because the communicators can't do it! They just cannot carry the traffic. They proved that that night.

So it did not work. It cannot. The ideal way to communicate under circumstances like that is to say, "Port Chalmers has got a problem with this and that," and one guy will reply: "Okay, go and talk to Port Chalmers on another channel!" Then you allocate them a channel, and they talk to each other. The only safe channel is a quiet channel where there are only quick and fast messages. We recently started to change some of the radio communication technology in a way that allowed more direct communication. Here, the task for a radio communicator is not to be a conveyer, but to provide a radio network for the persons involved in the emergency. We do that mostly for Search and Rescue.

So, in conclusion, as the communications gets thinner, your command must move out, must decentralize. Now what does that mean in an emergency? What it means is that the person, the "Johnny-on-the-spot," is going to make some pretty big decisions. Let's assume you come across a car accident with four injured people involved; then you are going to make some pretty serious decisions. There are four persons injured and you need to decide whom you are going to help. You can only help one; there is only one of you! So you make some pretty serious decision, and someone might die because you chose to go here! And the same applies in a civil emergency. "Johnny-on-the-spot" has got to make some pretty serious decisions. Now, if you train your people to want verification of headquarters before they do anything and there is no or little communication, then the victims certainly die.

This example again illustrates the impact of failing communication in disaster relief operations. As illustrated, a centralized system based on command relations is likely to break down in a large-scale disaster because many communication channels are unavailable and therefore available channels are overloaded. As shown, this implies that those people operating at the frontline need to have the authority to make decisions instead of waiting for "an official chain of command to be established" (Zwerdling & Sullivan, 2005). Thus, communication needs to be more oriented towards exchange relationship and direct communication.

Interim Conclusion

In conclusion, disaster research and practical experiences point towards adapting more flexible structures for organizational structure and

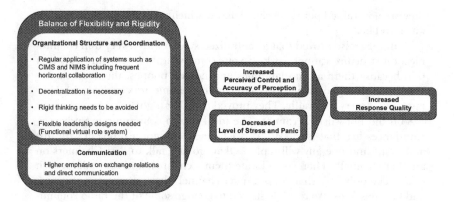

Figure 4.2.   The role of organizational structure, coordination, and communication in disaster management.

communication in disaster management. The following five recommendations are suggested to accomplish this. First, as has been shown above, system such as CIMS or NIMS are able to deliver such a design if they are interpreted accordingly. To make these systems functional, it is important to regularly apply them not only in major disasters, but also in small scale emergencies. This includes frequent horizontal collaboration when more than one agency is involved. Second, decentralization becomes necessary in major disasters. Here, a centralized system that constricts control proved maladaptive. Third, rigid thinking can often delude the finding of better solutions in disaster management and can aggravate the situation. Planning for the worst-case scenario and keeping an open mind by regularly questioning basic assumptions regarding emergencies will help to avoid rigid thinking.

Fourth, leadership designs should adopt a higher flexibility by gravitating towards a functional virtual role system (Weick, 1993). It is vital that response organizations are prepared to adopt a leadership role. However, it is equally important that responders are prepared to accept a change in leadership and support the lead agency. Finally, communication should shift towards exchange relations and direct communication in large-scale disasters.

All these actions contribute to an increased perceived control of the situation. In addition, avoidance of rigid thinking will also increase the accuracy of perception. As outlined in this section, these measures also help to reduced stress levels. Perceived control and declining stress levels both contribute to a better disaster response.

ORGANIZATIONAL MEMORY, RELATIONSHIPS AND TRAINING IN DISASTER MANAGEMENT

As the interviews with emergency management workers showed, organizational memory, interpersonal relationships, and training are strongly linked in practice. For example, the lead organization should possess sufficient organizational memory to distribute responsibilities and consult the various experts for the relief operations. Organizational memory is likely to be higher if the persons involved know each other well and/or for a longer period of time. Here, training not only provides skills for disaster management; it also strengthens relationships among professional and volunteer emergency workers.

Organizational Memory

In the context of emergency and disaster management, two types of organizational memory play a vital role: transactive memory and institutional memory.

The concept of transactive memory comprises the ability of group members to store information about the knowledge, skills, and expertise of other group members, which they then can consult on (Anand et al., 1998; Wegner, Guiliano, & Hertel, 1985). Therefore, in an organization in which people know about each other's expertise, the "cognitive burden on each individual member is reduced, yet a larger pool of information is available to each member than could be managed by any one person alone" (Brandon & Hollingshead, 2004, p. 633). As becomes evident from this definition, transactive memory is intertwined with regularly maintaining relationships among all members of the organization(s) involved in disaster management. The following story depicts this concept in a Search and Rescue context in Dunedin:

> Search and Rescue (SAR) in Dunedin is largely run by trained volunteers. However, Search and Rescue takes place under the authority of the New Zealand Police. Therefore, there is usually one police liaison officer involved. The search operation will be triggered by a command center. The police liaison officer or SAR officer will set up an environment for search. The first person that will be triggered is a search advisor who is also a volunteer. The SAR officer knows who has the expertise that is required for the respective type of incident. If it is a marine incident, he will call a marine advisor. This advisor would be, for example, very well trained in the ways of the sea around Dunedin. If it is an incident in Taieri Mouth, there is another specialist down there. There are a lot of these Advisors around here. At one stage, they paged for a Search Advisor who was away on holi-

day. He rang them back and gave them the advice via phone because he knew the area so well that he could talk them through it by phone. The search advisor actually tells the police the best action to take.

We all know who the experts are because it is a developed structure. The Police and the SAR officer have built up that structure. It is a network now. We know each other. If I meet the SAR officer on the street I say "hello!" to him. As far as I am concerned he is SAR and not a police man. He is just a guy who could turn buttons for us in the police, and he has a lot more experience and more details. He is in the core, whereas I sit just with communication. That is really important—you've got to focus on your own stuff.

A similar example can be provided by the civil defense employees. One of the civil defense core tasks is to maintain a vivid transactive memory:

The full time civil defense staff maintain regular contact with all the organizations that would be involved in a large-scale emergency in the city. We know most of them personally. It is our role to make sure that all those organizations understand what their job is during an emergency. We do that through a series of planning committees that we set up with all the organization that fall into a particular discipline. For example, all the medical people come together, which they normally would not do. So normally the hospital people are a separate entity to the general practitioners and the pharmacies. They all do their own thing. But we bring representatives of all of those organizations together and say, "How are you going to combine your resources and work in a coordinated fashion to deal with all of the injured people that need to be dealt with in a major emergency?"

As a result of that, they develop an emergency plan under our guidance. We also get them to provide us with a list of resources and we maintain databases of the resources that they own and require so that we have everything ready here when the people who will manage the medical aspects of the emergency come in. They and we have all the contacts for all the people who provide medical services, and they have listings for the resources that they might need to access to do that. We do not try to do it for them and so we do not manage the resources per se. All we do is facilitate the planning process and in an emergency make sure that there is a management structure that they operate within. Our task is to know about the experts. We get all these experts in each field to help us manage the overall event.

In a small event you would only have one person with a sufficient scale of expertise to manage the event as an individual. However, when it comes to a citywide emergency you actually need a much broader scope of expertise. So we replaced a single Incident Controller in the CIMS structure with an Incident Controller plus an Advisory Group who bring in more expertise. We know who has which kind of expertise. We have established an activation system where at any time of day or night we can contact those senior people from the various organizations. Initially there are about 25 people. They get contacted first and will report to this emergency operation center within 45 minutes. They act as a team to manage the emergency. We practice that regularly, and for every person we have at least one alternate. Generally, we try to have two alternates, and for some positions we even have three or four back ups to avoid that we do not have somebody from one of those disciplines to act as part of the managing team.

As becomes evident from this little example, civil defense acts as a coordinator and therefore needs to maintain a transactive memory. Under normal circumstances, large-scale disasters are rare events for a town or a region. In that case, the coordinating entity, here the civil defense team, needs to ensure transactive memory is updated regularly. In the example above, this is achieved through regular training that is not only important for learning and practice skills but also for maintaining a transactive memory, or, in other words: to know each other and to know what the others know.

Another form of memory influencing the success in disaster and emergency management is institutional memory (Weick, 1988). Institutional memory can be defined as the stored knowledge within the organization (Moorman & Miner, 1998). If institutional memory is rich, diverse, and present among members of the organization, it positively influences the perception of problems and decision making in a crisis (Weick, 1988). Disasters are chaotic and complex events that vary strongly with individual perception. Establishing institutional memory requires conducting postanalysis of events, storing them in a database, and teaching or narrating them within the organization to pass it on to new members. Thus, institutional memory is easier to establish when turnover is low and the relationships between individuals are strong. In addition, someone has to do the work of documenting past events in a form that is usable for coming generations. This requirement may seem trivial and easily solvable. However, past experience shows us that the practice looks differently. Smith (1984, p. 908) for example, cites one of his interviewees (Beal) who was part of the National Security Council of the White House:

> There is no, I repeat no, institutional memory available at the highest level of government for crisis management. If you were to walk into my office and say, Beal, your job description is crisis management, show us the database on crisis management, the answer, folks, is that there isn't one. This means that in every single instance—I don't care whether it's the Falklands or Lebanon or Poland—every single (team member) begins anew because you can't draw at the highest level on institutional memory. (Smith, 1984)

Thus, institutional memory is not a given in organizations that are concerned with emergency and disaster management. Civil Defense in Dunedin, New Zealand, implements the following activities to establish institutional memory:

Even with the smaller events, we do a debrief to learn what we can. The same applies to the exercises. In addition we try to gain more knowledge from disaster and management workers in other regions. For example, last year, there was a big flood up in the North Island. We brought down some of the senior people that have managed those floods for a seminar here. There was a seminar for all the emergency services as well as a separated and much more concentrated workshop for the Advisory Group. So we built on the experience of people who recently had to manage an event and said: "What have you learned? What have you got to tell us about that?"

To conclude, it is important to build organizational memory. Transactive memory increases the effectiveness of disaster response coordination. Dispatching the right experts to places where they are of most help directly improves the disaster response. In addition, if responders are dispatched wisely, they are more likely to deal with a problem that matches their expertise. This helps to reduce stress levels and increases perceived control over the situation. Institutional memory reduces the likelihood of repeating past mistakes and increases the accuracy of perception by transferring insights from similar incidents of the past to current responders (Weick, 1988). Accuracy of perception increases perceived control, reduces stress levels, and improves ability to address problems.

Relationships

Establishing rich organizational memory depends on the strength of the relationships among people involved in disaster management. In organizations with high turnover, for example, relationships among members decrease and organizational memory is hard to maintain (Smith, 1984). It is not enough just to work together; the quality of the relationship can be pivotal in disaster situations. As Weick (1993) states, it is important that emergency workers build a cohesive group beyond the requirements of the task fulfillment. For example, emergency workers that are able to fight a fire together might not trust each other sufficiently to stick together when the situation escalates beyond expectations. These relationships that make or break with the task fulfillment are also referred to as "non-disclosive intimacy" (Eisenberg, 1990; Weick, 1993). Nondisclosive relationships between emergency workers are related to problem solving and even survival in disaster situations (e.g., Weick, 1993). Regular contact, socializing, and low turnover can increase the quantity and quality of relationships in an organization. Therefore, I was interested to learn about the relationships in Civil Defense and other emergency organizations in Dunedin, New Zealand:

Within in the planning committees that span across emergency services of different fields, some of those people would deal with each other in the day-to-day course of business. Some of them would never have met and talked about managing emergencies together if it wasn't for the structure that we provide. I guess that the city is small enough that it makes it reasonably easy to bring all the senior people from all the organizations together. We do that on a weekly basis. We have about 15 of those planning groups of different disciplines from rescuing, communications, medical, public health, engineering, etc. They all meet within their disciplines. In addition, the respective chairs of each group meet together as the Controller and Advisory Group. The bigger meetings only take place three times a year. We bring them together for planning as well as for an exercise. We do that for more than 20 years already. So we have been doing this for a long time. After the exercises and meeting, we always provide them with some food and drinks so they can socialize. Over time, members of each team change, of course. This is particularly true for emergency services where they often transfer around the country and get new people. But they come into a team that is already functioning pretty well, so it helps a lot. The continuity helps a lot.

Similarly, David states that the Search and Rescue network is not only a group of people that pursue the goal of finding and rescuing someone. He sees it also as a group of friends.

In the setting of emergency services and management, it is important to get a sense of community working within a group. In an emergency team like that, it is camaraderie. Like, when we get a search, I meet a whole group of people that I might not meet otherwise. But they are all friends, they are associates, they are compatriots, we all understand each other. The moment you cease to have that camaraderie, you start to get political intrigue, and it will destroy itself. But once you have a network like that in a community working, it works! It is self-perpetuating until someone gets destructive. And there is no one destructive around here.

As these examples illustrate, strong relationships are important during large-scale disaster responses. Being in a group of friends means another source of feedback, another pair of eyes to judge the situation, and another source of ideas. In a disaster situation, strong relationships help to reduce stress levels by providing a trusted source of feedback or trusted colleagues to help solve problems. Advantages of Dunedin include the small size of the population and regular training that facilitate relationship building. The next section will further illustrate the importance of training and its practical application in New Zealand disaster management.

Training

Training of emergency services workers to increase crisis and disaster preparedness is widely researched in crisis management. Research suggests that problems such as restriction of information, rigidity in responses, and lack of decision readiness can be ameliorated by providing adequate crisis training (Alexander, 2003; Mitroff & Alpaslan, 2003; Mitroff, Shrivastava, & Udwadia, 1987; Nunamaker et al., 1989; Uden-Homan et al., 2005). Training not only improves the skills that are needed in a disaster, but also instills confidence in emergency workers. Increased confidence in escalating, unexpected, and chaotic situations will help to reduce stress levels, which in turn allows the individual or groups to find better and more creative solutions (Paton, 1996; Weick, 1988, 1993). Training through exercises and simulations can increase the familiarity with the potential disaster and provide affirmation because of perceived control. This, in turn, also reduces the level of stress in a disaster situation.

In a corporate context, Barnett and Pratt (2000) assert that dealing with self-induced threats will produce expansion of control instead of constriction and generation of knowledge instead of restriction of information. In short, they say that practice sessions result in a more flexible and organic structure instead of a rigid response. Simulating threatening situations in a safe environment might be a tool that allows for more flexible designs to emerge, including the generation of knowledge and expansion of control. These designs could then be included in a real emergency.

Training is a substantial part of Dunedin's disaster preparedness plan. A small example is the mobile Emergency Communication Unit (ECU). Although there is no special training on it, it is used regularly, which helps to maintain skills and find potential technical problems faster:

> The ECU is available not only for Search and Rescue but also for any event that we (the radio communicators) want it for as long as no one else is using it. So it becomes a multitasked unit. The advantage of that is that it is being used quite frequently. So if there is anything wrong with it, it is usually being picked up reasonably quickly. There are a wide group of people who know all about it. If Dunedin got flattened by an earthquake and CD headquarters was dead. One of us—there are probably five to seven drivers—would go and get it. It is stored out of town. We would take it to the hilltop and set up communications for CD. The same applies to the radios installed in the school. They are also used rather often in order to train people as well as to pick up any technical problems reasonably quickly.

Dunedin is rather rigorous about running exercises and simulations. Usually, professional emergency workers are highly skilled and trained regularly in their domain. However, those who would be part of the Advisory Group in a large-scale emergency represent organizations such as hospitals, pharmacies, building control and so forth, and are, therefore, not professional emergency workers. It is important to provide regular training for them. A senior civil defense staff member illustrates how these training exercises are conducted:

We do several exercises for the Advisory Group. We usually have one long and several short exercises per year. The last long exercise ran for a week. We wanted to know that everybody would be available. We kicked the exercise off at Monday 1:30 to 2 a.m., after the weekend where most of the people involved would be back home in bed. They knew that an exercise was coming, but they did not know when. So we started the process at about 1:30 in the morning and by 2:30 we had the Civil Defense Headquarter fully activated. All of them had to be here within 45 minutes. We gave them a scenario and said: "So this is what is happening."

They had had some lead up information about the developing situation. In this exercise, we practiced a flooding emergency. We would send them envelopes with severe weather warnings, for example, before the exercise was kicked off in the night. Of course, this is not exactly how it would be in a real emergency. One of them joked and said: "Well, it was a bit unreal. I was on the golf course when I had to open one of my envelopes. It was a bright sunny day and the message said: It is pouring with rain now."

By the time they came in here, we had all the information displayed on the status boards and the maps in this facility. Some of them were a bit grumpy about being woken up a bit early in the morning, but they all then worked for about three hours on the scenario. Making decisions, contacting their organizations to check on what resources would be available to respond if this was a real emergency. Eventually we gave them some breakfast and sent them off to work and they did their normal day's work. We had a team during the day that worked on all of their decisions and the changing scenario. The Advisory Group came back at four in the afternoon for another two hours. Here we told them the result of their decisions. We also informed them about increasing rain and said: "So here is the new situation. Make some decisions!" First of all we practiced making decisions as part of that Advisory Group. Then we modeled the results of the decisions and they had to keep managing that. We did that for three days of emergency. Afterwards, we went into a recovery phase for the next two days. Here they had to begin managing the recovery from the event. Throughout this exercise, they got very used to working together as a team in order to manage the event.

We do a mini version of that—a one-day or half-day exercise—every year where we activate them and bring the key team in. We test the activation system at least twice a year, once during working hours and once after hours. The aim is to get 90% of the people within 45 minutes during working hours and within an hour after hours to the Civil Defense Headquarters. This is counted from the time we start contacting the whole list to the time that everybody is here in this facility.

We also have training for the satellite structure, which involves the schools as well. Here we use the councilors and the community board members at their respective levels. We will train them along with their local police and fire. Most of them do not have ambulance, but they have a doctor in the community. And they become the small manager, the equivalent of the Advisory Group. So we train them and we run exercises for them. We also provide training for the people who work at the primary schools. We use the Boards of Trustees there who are elected to run the primary schools. Because it is their facility, they know it well; however, the government owns it and, therefore, we are allowed to use it as an emergency center. The Board of Trustees is responsible for managing the facility; they have got the keys and they know the community. We train the Board of Trustees every three years after elections. In addition to the training, to make it very easy, we have posters of instructions in every school. They get in, unlock the school, and they will find about five or six big instructions to worry about, and they do those things. The poster also shows how they can contact the coordination center, which is the next level up.

We have not had any large events in the last 25 years. So that makes it much more important that we run those simulations. It is important that everybody actually gets some practice, because they are not doing it for real at the moment.

Even if citizen and professional emergency workers cannot be prepared fully for the chaotic, complex, uncertain and extreme conditions they would face in a real disaster, training helps to increase awareness and to reduce the feeling of helplessness. If no training is provided, the disaster or crisis can be aggravated through the actions of individuals. Two small stories illustrate how important it is to provide even the most trivial training and what can happen if this is missed:

Untrained volunteers can become a liability.... Even though it might sound trivial, you need to have a certain expertise on how to use sandbags. We had an example down in Balclutha in a flood about five years ago. Here the local community just placed one sandbag on top of the other down the side of the Clutha River, which is a pretty big river. So they had a wall of sandbags, which was only one sandbag deep. Then the water came up against the sandbags and they were just lucky that the pressure of the river did not tip all the sandbags over and cause an even bigger problem. As a result of this, we started training a group of people in how to sandbag with a proper structure. So that involves sandbagging with more walls than one so it can't fall over. This trained group of people now can go out and supervise those who have to put the sandbags there.

Even though it is a simple task, it was something the community did not have the expertise for. That is another area where we have to provide that expertise, because nobody day-to-day is out there building sandbags walls. So we trained contractors on how to sandbag. Not because they will do it, but because they will supervise it. These contractors are people who work as builders or in roading. We now use concrete mixers to fill sandbags rather than people with shovels. These contractors have also got equipment and the staff that are used to working physically.

Seemingly trivial tasks become essential during a disaster response, so advance training of coordinators can be crucial.

Interim Conclusion

Organizational memory, relationship building, and training are closely intertwined necessities of disaster management. Vivid transactive memory, in which the skills, knowledge, and resources of organizations and experts are updated and known to those who are likely to coordinate the disaster response, can be achieved through regular contact, meetings, and training sessions. In addition, responders need to establish a rich institutional memory in which lessons learned from previous disasters are stored. Because large-scale disasters are rare events, potential responders must learn from the experiences of others.

Furthermore, it is vital to encourage strong relationships between responders. Trust enables better solutions in chaotic and devastating situations. Being among trusted team members also decreases the stress level. A trusted colleague in a disaster means another source of feedback, another source of ideas, and another pair of eyes to judge the situation. Relationships can be strengthened by shared social events, training sessions, or regular meetings.

Finally, training is a vital component of disaster management for experts and for volunteers. Training and simulations allow responders to broaden their skills and knowledge regarding complex as well as simple tasks. In addition, training has important side effects of establishing organizational memory and building relationships.

All three components—memory, relationship, and training—are linked to perception of the disaster situation and stress levels. Vivid transactive memory allows for faster coordination of experts and resources where they are most urgently needed. Matching responders to a familiar task that corresponds to their expertise decreases stress levels, increases perceived control, and improves overall response quality.

A rich institutional memory increases the accuracy of perception and reduces repetition of past mistakes. Responders are more likely to recog-

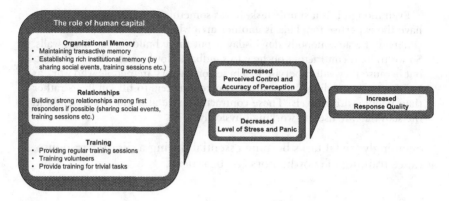

Figure 4.3.   The role of organizational memory, relationships, and training in disaster management.

nize problems or situations that they have heard of previously. They are better able to identify and address the right problems, so they avoid worsening the situation by pursuing salient distractions.

NEW ZEALAND'S CULTURE AND ITS IMPLICATIONS FOR DISASTER MANAGEMENT

In New Zealand, disaster management in general and resource management in particular differ somewhat from continental countries due to the geographical setting. As mentioned before, New Zealand is characterized by its isolated location and the sparse population, which impact disaster and emergency planning. In a major disaster, New Zealand is not easily accessible to bring in resources from outside. In addition, a lot of people live in rural areas isolated from the bigger cities. This applies particularly to the South Island. In Dunedin, for example, this issue has been addressed with the satellite structure.

The geographical setting influences the way of life which, in New Zealand, often includes living remotely. This way of life has an influence on how people perceive the world and on their general attitude towards life and death. This general attitude also plays a role in disaster management (see, for example, "attitude of wisdom" and "cosmology" by Weick, 1993). The following examples will illustrate that further. Living in more isolated settings seems to have a positive influence on self-sufficiency, which is beneficial for disaster responses. It should be noted, however, that these insights are based on interviews and impressions gained from living in New Zealand and not from a statistically valid and reliable study.

Community Involvement as a Necessity

As a result of its isolated geographical setting, New Zealand needs to rely on its communities for disaster and emergency management. With only 4 million people spread around the country, it would be uneconomical to establish large professional organizations for disaster relief. As mentioned above, Dunedin trains representatives of medical organizations for the Advisory Group in a large-scale emergency. Schools are used as command centers, and members of the schools' boards of trustees are trained along with their community doctors. Similarly, civil defense uses the expertise of city council staff instead of relying only on professional emergency workers:

> We have to use the community structures rather than the resources that the government might own. For example, when anybody gets employment with the Dunedin City Council, part of their job description says that they might be required to do civil defense duties. They get trained during work hours, and they also get paid if we use them in an emergency as though it was their normal work. So they are not untrained volunteers. What we use them for, again, is their every day expertise. For example, if they are experts on administration, then we will bring them in for administrative support of the Advisory Group and other operation groups that work from the civil defense headquarters. There are a number of categories of what we train people for. For example, the middle management people are trained to be sort of managers, so that they can actually take responsibilities for an element of the emergency. However, the majority of them are support staff, and they are trained in all of the administrative and clerical processes. They also learn about the Headquarters facility. They know where the stationery is, what forms need to be filled in, and about some of the communication functions that can be used. They also know how to start the generator if the power fails. They know where the portable toilets are if the sewerage is failing. In short, they can do all that sort of routine work that helps this place function to support the experts so that the experts don't have to worry about that.
>
> So, we have the philosophy of using those community groups, like the councilor and community people, in the outlying areas instead of professional resources. Overseas they often would have enough emergency services staff to deal with the emergencies or disasters. But we haven't got the resources and there are not that many police or fire personnel in the city. We also don't have a military base nearby that would be a big source of manpower or equipment. Our army is mainly a territorial force with volunteers.

A lot of them come from vital jobs that need to be done during an emergency. So the military is not an additional resource either.

Even though it might sound like a disadvantage to use the community and its infrastructure instead of professionally trained emergency service staff, it has undeniable advantages. In the following example, Paul illustrates how basic community involvement can make a big difference in responding to disasters:

> In winter of 1980, we had the Taieri floods that lasted eight weeks. The farming community at that time had not developed a stock movement plan for floods, and so the emergency organizations from the city had to come in. They ordered the local farming community to move the stock and cattle away. The situation required a fast decision, and the logical thing to the emergency service staff from the city seemed to be moving everything to the next highest point. This was the flood-free highway. So the farming community together with the emergency workers moved all the stock on the highway.
>
> That meant that there were cows, bulls, and sheep and all sorts of other things on the highway, which closed a vital road link. In addition, there is not much grass to eat on an asphalt highway. So they had to bring in hay and feed the cattle on the highway for a couple of days. At the same time, they tried to fill up stock trucks and move the cattle somewhere else. As a result, the whole incident became one of those big logistics operations that did not need to have happened if the farming community had been involved in the planning. After that incident, the farming community was involved in the planning and developed a stock movement plan. It turned out that the farming community would have found a better solution than the highway. They would have moved the stock west instead of east, on the slopes of the Maungatua Range. This will get the stock out of the flood and there would still be green paddocks. It is again an example that you need to get the right people involved. If you get the local people, they know which area is going to flood first, for example. So they know which stock you have to move away first, etc. Therefore, if you bring in people from outside, they might make mistakes that could have been easily avoided.
>
> I think, if we ever have a widespread emergency, we will have to go to a decentralized management using the communities and the satellite system. But the fact that the emergency manager is their known representative in the community will probably achieve a lot more compliance within the community.

Whereas community involvement is a necessity in New Zealand, the idea of stronger community involvement was established in the United States in 1985 and is now used to varying degrees in different areas. In the United States, so-called "Community Emergency Response Teams" (CERT) are formed to prepare and train the community. The high effectiveness of CERT or other forms of community involvement is illustrated in this simple calculation:

> For example, in a city with 100,000 people, usually only five fire stations and two police stations are staffed, with perhaps forty firefighters, ten fire trucks and thirty police on duty. This is adequate for normal emergencies. In normal rescues, rescuers outnumber victims four to one, and can respond in minutes. A typical rescue is completed in a half hour. In the above community, if a mass emergency traps or injures just two percent of the inhabitants, there are instantly 2,000 victims, many with injuries. The telephones will fail from overload. Roads, bridges, electricity, and other services may fail, hampering emergency services and interfering with fuel and material supplies. If only professionals respond to that mass emergency and there are 2,000 victims, there will be 1,000 hours of rescues, divided by ten trucks, or about 100 hours. As many as three-quarters of the victims could die while waiting for rescue. After an hour and a half, untreated victims of shock would begin to die. After one day, trapped children would begin to die of thirst. After two days, trapped adults and shut-ins would begin to die of thirst. Most of these deaths could be prevented by simple rescue and first-aid procedures. In these environments, CERTs are far more effective than untrained civilians. With less than 40 hours of training, an amateur disaster service worker becomes qualified to perform about 95% of needed emergency services. This means that 95% of the rescues and life-saving triage and first-aid procedures can be completed in the "golden day," the first 24 hours when rescues and first-aid are most likely to succeed. (Wikipedia, last updated 2/11/2005)

The positive effects of community involvement have also been noted in the relief operations of the California earthquake of 1989, as opposed to other earthquakes in which the community was not informed (Comfort, 1990). Similarly, Katrina's disaster management was tremendously supported by many civilians from within and outside of New Orleans. The support of civilians is crucial in disaster situations in which professional emergency organizations are overburdened (Hurricane Katrina Heroes, 2006). Community residents that are hit by a disaster should be converted from passive victims to active participants in the disaster recovery process (Comfort, 1990; Uden-Homan et al., 2005). If residents perceive themselves as passive victims, uncoordinated individual activism can cause even more conflict to the existing crisis (Comfort, 1990). As a result, imposing professional emergency service groups on the local community and controlling rather than involving the local residents can prove destructive.

To conclude, community involvement harnesses the knowledge of those who are closest to the potentially affected geographical setting. A prepared community relieves professional emergency responders by shifting citizens from passive victims to active participants. Community involvement can significantly reduce the losses and damage of a major disaster.

Resource Management With No. 8 Fencing Wire

In a large-scale disaster, New Zealand would have substantially fewer resources than continental countries. This is a disadvantage in some respects; however, it triggers a particular attitude that positively affects disaster and emergency management planning. Paul describes the particular situation of New Zealand:

> I think one thing about our size and our isolation goes in our advantage. Particularly in terms of the size of the city where it is very easy for us to get all the key people from the various organizations and get that management group together. And so that is a manageable thing.
>
> What we lack, I guess, is the ability to bring in a lot of resources whereas in continental situation you've got land-based resources incoming. We are very isolated and we do not have very many resources. I went to Turkey as a part of a team after the 1999 earthquake. We saw more heavy equipment sitting idle around the place, that had been brought in to move the rubble etc., than we could assemble in the whole of NZ. And that was just in one small part of Turkey. It's because they have more resources and can move them very easily. In New Zealand we have to be much cleverer about doing things with what we've got. Like Ernest Rutherford said: "We have no money, therefore we must think."
>
> Therefore, we probably have to rely much more on the planning and the community networks than on having resources. We see that perhaps from the American situation, where the Federal Emergency Management Agency seems to be able to come in with a huge resource to set up a very sophisticated management system for a big emergency. We don't have the equivalent of that in NZ. There are no big resources that can go in to somewhere and take over. So we have to be much more self sufficient that way.

Being forced to think more creatively about the few resources at hand leads to a higher degree of community involvement, as illustrated above. Being able to improvise and find creative solutions in chaotic situations can be very advantageous in a crisis. Weick (1993) refers to this characteristic as "improvisation and bricolage." He asserts that

> reativity is figuring out how to use what you already know in order to go beyond what you currently think.... Thus, when situations unravel ... bricoleurs proceed with whatever materials are at hand. Knowing these materials

intimately, they then are able usually in the company of other similarly skilled people, to form the materials or insights into novel combinations. (pp. 639-640)

This attitude becomes evident in the following quote by David about resource management:

Resources are what you can find. The point is if you allow bureaucracy to dictate to you that you are not allowed to do anything unless you are told, you might as well just tell people to sit at the beach and let the tide run over them. Who is going to do that? I figure it comes back to seeding people in the community to take control. You won't have resources when you are in an emergency. Resources are what is lying around you.

We need to use the resources we have. New Zealanders are renowned for being "Number-8-Fencing-Wire–people."[1] What it means is, in the old days when you drove along in your car and the car broke down, people would be able to fix the car with a piece of a Number 8 fencing wire. They'd go and cut it off the farm's fence. So, New Zealanders and Australians are a bit the same, became sort of known as people where resource is whatever is lying around. Like a farmer's fence or a bit of wire lying around. They use it to fix things. That culture comes from living remotely with nature. Now, that culture lives at the bottom of New Zealand; it doesn't live at the top. If you go to the top of the North Island and someone is sick, they will say, "Oh, the government has got to come and fix me, I'm sick...." That sort of thinking is not good, it is not healthy.

Another thing, it's a bit away from what we are talking about, but it still reflects on emergencies. If you take a child in New Zealand that has lived on a farm, you will find that they have a very balanced view on life. However, if you went to a city center at lunchtime and an old lady drops dead on the footpath and there are school children around, everybody will say: "Take the children away! Take them away! A dead body!" But on a farm the children see dead sheep, see sheep having a lamb, lamb dies … life and death—it's all natural. Inside society we protect people from that. No, you could take Katrina, where some of the people just must have been mind-blown because of the amount of death. Well, I suspect I would be with the *amount* of death. But it must have been doubly bad if you hadn't seen *any* death. So society tends to protect people from things and then blame them if they make the wrong decisions.

Thus, it could be expected that New Zealanders might be more self-sufficient than others when confronted with a disaster because the people are aware that they need to rely on themselves with the resources at hand rather than await an outside rescue. Moreover, those who are not physically impacted might be more self-sufficient in surviving even if essential services are down. This attitude of self-sufficiency is supported by Dunedin civil defense campaigns. Paul states:

> We try very strongly through publicity to get the message across to people that they need to be able to look after themselves and their home without power, without water, without sewage for at least three days. Some Kiwis (as New Zealanders are often referred to) will manage that very well. A lot of people go tramping and camping here for example and they probably have the skills to do that. The same applies to the more outlying farming communities. The fact, that these people are self-sufficient relieves our welfare workers. Often welfare staff has to look after those who lost essential services but are not physically impacted by the emergency.

David shares the same view:

> When you've got a situation, where a person goes to sea in a boat and the boat sinks, I believe that the person must consider his or her life lost. That's the first premise, that the life would be lost. So anybody saved is a real bonus. But nowadays the thinking tends to be that everybody has to be saved, otherwise it's a disaster. This kind of thinking is largely due to the media. It trains people to have the wrong thinking. I'm getting worried about the blame psychology, which is news media driven and liability driven. They want to crucify somebody; there is always somebody who's got to be at fault.
>
> I can give a simple illustration. I talked to an academic once when Dunedin and Queenstown had a lot of snow and he was saying that the police in Queenstown were bad. I asked him why he was thinking that. He replied, "Well, last weekend I went to Queenstown and I got stuck in the snow and the police didn't come to help me out." At that point there was so much snow in Queenstown and Central Otago that the police had been begging people all week not to go to Queenstown. This person had gone in spite of the warning, got stuck, and expected the police to come and get him out. And you know what he said? He said, "I had to rely on a passerby!". Hang on! I would have expected the passerby way ahead of the police. In other words, are we thinking that the police and other emergency organizations are the knight on the white horse all the time for everything? They are not. The knight is really the next friendly person that comes along. The sense of community; using your neighbor and helping each other seems to be going right out the back door. Yet, my philosophy is, I'll spend a day out trying to help somebody who has got lost in the bush. Might be me next time. So people will help people. Police are too busy controlling people to help people in an emergency.
>
> Usually, down here you have a lot of people who are more philosophical, more rural, and more primitive. They are not trying to make a point; they are easy to imply. This is why it works well, for example, to include them into an emergency operation.

Hence, the basic assumption that an official institution is responsible for ensuring personal safety at all times can have strong negative consequences in a disaster or emergency situation. David Corn[2] writes in an article on Hurricane Katrina (2005):

> We are not safe.... It was frighteningly too easy to realize that the authorities—local, state and federal governments—cannot effectively handle any of the nightmare scenarios.... A nuclear detonation? An assault on a chemical weapons plant? Heck, could the government even deal with an outbreak of avian flu among humans?... In an event of a calamity—whether caused by nature or by terrorists—we cannot expect the government to respond competently. It is scary out there.... If we are on our own, it would be better to know that now rather than later.

This just reflects what was referred to above as "the wrong sort of thinking." Of course the United States is not safe; neither is the rest of the world. However, it helps if people are more self-responsible, organized, and informed about potential hazards and coping mechanisms than just to wait and blame the governmental institutions. Even within New Zealand the attitude is slowly changing from self-sufficiency to completely relying on official institutions. As Paul reflects:

> But it is changing and we have got a group of people now coming through who—whilst they live with this nature, etc., they mainly live in the city situation. Look what happened in February this year when some of the storm water couldn't be coped with and we had surface flooding. People were saying, "Why didn't the city stop this?" Well, this was a one in a hundred year event and people weren't prepared to cope with it. So there is less acceptance of natural events that go beyond the point where somebody is looking after them on their behalf and that is a bad thing. That is a very bad thing.

> New Zealanders always prided themselves on being self-sufficient and able to deal with things on their own. However, I think this attitude is changing as we get more urbanized and get more dependent on buying stuff from overseas rather than making it. If something breaks down you are buying some new stuff rather than repairing it, which is what we used to have to do when we were more isolated from the rest of the world. I don't know if we are quite as self-sufficient as we would like to believe. I think the Health and Safety Act is increasingly interpreted by a lot of people: Somebody else is responsible for ensuring my safety wherever I am. So all of these things are going to begin having an impact of how self-sufficient and competent people can be to look after themselves.

Because New Zealand is limited regarding the amount of resources, the people may be creative out of necessity. The community seems to be more self-sufficient in a setting such as New Zealand, thereby relieving the welfare workers and requiring fewer resources. Given that a large-scale emergency is likely to overload government resources in any nation, creative use of existing infrastructures may be crucial for resource management in disaster responses. Another aspect of resources management that is vital to improve response operations is the coordination of resources.

> In addition to that, we have training programs where we bring the politicians in. It is very important to tie them in. They are the interface to the media and therefore they need to be involved in the planning. Often politicians will go out to the media and ask the rest of the country for support. For example, they will ask to donate goods for the affected communities: "Everybody has lost their furniture, their bedding, and clothing, so send us the goods you can spare!" So all of a sudden, container loads of old clothing, old bedding, and all sorts of stuff arrive and it is actually something that only adds to the workload during that time.
>
> When we had a big flood in the Southlands, for example, politicians used the media to ask for help and an Auckland service group sent a container load of fresh food down, including vegetables and fruit. However, at that point in time, the local community could not manage to make the food available for the community. They just did not have the capacity for that. Distributing the goods as well as controlling that it is appropriate became another liability for the community. In addition to that, it kills an already suffering economy. So, instead, it makes more sense to send money so that people go to the local grocer's shops and buy their food. This keeps the businesses viable. They already might have some arrangement to re-supply that shop. So instead of establishing a parallel distribution system it is best to use the normal networks.

Following Hurricane Katrina, simply delivering food and water to those trapped in the city became a major problem of coordination. In a large-scale disaster, resources might be distributed redundantly to some places and not at all to others (Comfort, Ko et al., 2004). Although it seems counterintuitive, donating physical resources, for example, can place a burden on local communities rather than bringing relief. Similarly counterintuitive is the observation that the amount of money raised for disaster relief often exceeds the amount that can effectively be distributed. Even distribution of monetary resources is difficult in large-scale disaster responses (Comfort, Ko et al., 2004). As the response to 9/11 showed, abundant monetary resources were available from around 450 different organizations. However, many victims could not obtain the monetary support they needed (Comfort, 2002). It is important to plan a system that focuses not only on the availability but on the distribution and coordination of resources. This is most important near the beginning of the disaster when demand for resources is highest but availability and distribution of resources is lowest (Comfort, Ko et al., 2004).

Interim Conclusion

There needs to be a stronger emphasis on community involvement and wise use of available resources. Community involvement should aim to transform members of the affected population from passive victims to active participants. The process can begin by assuring that the population achieves a higher degree of self-sufficiency. Involving the community in disaster response can increase the perceived control of the individuals and reduce stress levels. It brings to bear the community's special knowledge of the area in a joint search for solutions. Finally, community-based leadership can facilitate buy-in from local people as they implement recovery efforts.

Resource distribution can pose a greater problem than resource availability, so planners need to focus specifically on ways to coordinate resource distribution. Existing assets and infrastructures should be used more creatively for disaster responses, as illustrated from the Dunedin example. Overall, community involvement and resource management are both linked to a general attitude of wisdom. As David states, sole reliance on the governmental institution promotes high dependence and lowers self-sufficiency. No matter how well a community, a state or a country is prepared, a large-scale disaster can overwhelm response institutions. In that case, no one can be guaranteed safety. If we are aware that we live in a

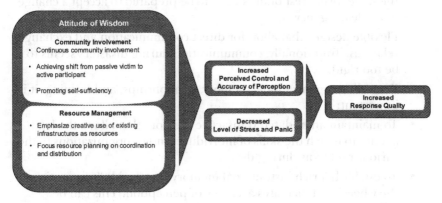

Figure 4.4. The roles of community involvement and resources in disaster management.

constantly changing environment with a certain degree of unpredictability, we might learn to be more self-sufficient and self-responsible.

CONCLUSION

This chapter explored several aspects of successful disaster management by connecting the academic literature with real-life experiences. We may draw several conclusions from this analysis.

Regarding organizational structure, coordination, and communication, the following recommendations are suggested:

- Regular application of systems such as CIMS/NIMS in every emergency, whether on a local, state or federal level.
- More flexible interpretation of systems such as CIMS/NIMS by first responders. Too often, these systems have been interpreted too rigidly and were not understood well by first responders.
- Regular application of CIMS or NIMS that includes horizontal collaboration. It is necessary that different agencies practice to work together even in small-scale incidents.
- Challenging our basic assumptions and planning for the worst-case scenario to address maladaptive forms of rigid thinking. Here, brainstorming sessions or sharing past experiences of "cosmology episodes" might contribute to becoming more flexible.
- Functional, virtual leadership system that prepares responders to share leadership as necessary. Ability to assume leadership is essential in a disaster situation and therefore needs to be encouraged. By the same token, responders need to be prepared to accept a change in the lead agency.
- Flexible designs that allow for direct communication and exchange relations. Traditionally, communication during disasters seems to be too rigid.
- Regarding organizational memory, relationships, and training, it is important:
- To maintain an updated transactive memory that allows the lead agency to match the skills of individuals and/or organizations to the various problems during disasters.
- To establish a rich institutional memory that avoids "reinventing the wheel" and increases accuracy of perception. This can be achieved through social events, training sessions, seminars on past disasters, and databases of accumulated knowledge.

- To strengthen relationships amongst first responders. This might be accomplished alongside development of institutional memory through social events, training sessions, and seminars.
- To provide responders with regular training on disaster management such as exercises or simulations. It is, however, equally important to provide volunteers with training for basic skills and seemingly trivial tasks.

Finally, recommendations for community involvement and resource management include:

- Strong involvement of the community in disaster planning. Whereas community involvement is a necessity in New Zealand, this is not the case for most continental countries. Therefore, it is even more important to rigorously and systematically involve the community in disaster planning. This can be achieved by a number of actions as, for example, outlined by Gillespie (1991) and Scanlon (1991).
- Creative use of existing assets and infrastructures. This includes involving the community and drawing on public facilities, such as schools, for disaster planning.
- Promoting an attitude of self-sufficiency to the community and emphasizing mutual aid among neighborhoods. For example, rather than providing the population with false illusions of safety and promoting reliance on governmental institutions, encourage people to plan for their own well-being in case of an emergency.
- Focus on resource coordination and distribution.

Most of these factors are not new to disaster management. The more it is surprising how little they are applied in reality. In New Zealand, the circumstances reflected in Rutherford's saying, "We have no money, therefore we must think," seem to force disaster management planners to apply some of these insights. In particular, decentralization, community involvement, and training self-sufficiency are strong parts of New Zealand's disaster management. Many of the stories deal with small-scale incidents and seemingly trivial problems, but examples showed that even these small problems can be magnified in large-scale incidents.

This chapter showed that everyone can contribute to improving disaster responses. On a governmental level, systems such as CIMS/NIMS can be designed with an appropriate balance of rigidity and flexibility. They must be rigid enough to integrate responses to large-scale disasters into an overall organizational structure. They must be flexible enough to respond to frontline personnel relatively independently and immediately. On a state or local level, responders should emphasize the integration of their organizations into a higher-level incident management system and encourage a high degree of interagency collaboration. Finally, on an individual level, getting involved in disaster management within the community is a vital but feasible step that greatly improves the likelihood of positive outcomes following a disaster.

ACKNOWLEDGEMENTS

I acknowledge, with thanks, the interviewees in Dunedin for their time and support in conduct of this research. I also thank Deborah Gibbons and Timothy Gibbons for their thoughtful assistance and review of this chapter. Research for this study has been supported with funds from the Department of Management, University of Otago.

NOTES

1. "A rhetoric of frontier inventiveness is imbedded in the New Zealand idea that anything can be fixed with #8 fencing wire. Ernest Rutherford, the nuclear physicist, has become legend as "the story of a Kiwi genius." His favorite aphorism, "We have no money therefore we must think" adorns workspace walls and is ironically invoked" (www2.sjsu.edu/depts/anthropology/svcp/SVCP8wir.html, retrieved December 5, 2006).
2. David Corn, is the Washington editor of *The Nation* and the author of *The Lies of George W. Bush: Mastering the Politics of Deception*.

REFERENCES

Alexander, D. (2003). Towards the development of standards in emergency management training. *Disaster Prevention and Management, 12*(2), 113–123.

Anand, V., Manz, C., & Glick, W. H. (1998). An organizational memory approach to information management. *Academy of Management Review, 23*(4), 796–809.

Argote, L. (1982). Input uncertainty and organizational coordination in hospital emergency units. *Administrative Science Quarterly, 27*, 420–434.

Barnett, C. K., & Pratt, M. G. (2000). From threat-rigidity to flexibility—Toward a learning model of autogenic crisis in organizations. *Journal of Organizational Change Management, 13*(1), 74–88.

Brandon, D. P., & Hollingshead, A. B. (2004). Transactive memory systems in organizations: Matching tasks, expertise, and people. *Organization Science, 15*(6), 633–644.

Caro, D. H. J. (1999). Towards integrated crisis support of regional emergency networks. *Health Care Management Review, 24*(4), 7–19.

Comfort, L. K. (1990). Turning conflict into cooperation: Organizational designs for community response in disasters. *International Journal of Mental Health, 19*(1), 89–108.

Comfort, L. K. (2002). Rethinking security: Organizational fragility in extreme events. *Public Administration Review, 62*, 98–107.

Comfort, L. K., Dunn, M., Johnson, D., Skertich, R., & Zagorecki, A. (2004). Coordination in complex systems: Increasing efficiency in disaster mitigation and response. *International Journal of Emergency Management, 2*(1–2), 62–80.

Comfort, L. K., Ko, K., & Zagorecki, A. (2004). Coordination in rapidly evolving disaster response systems. *American Behavioral Scientist, 48*(3), 295–313.

Corn, D. (2005). *What went wrong.* Retrieved December 15, 2005, from http://tompaine.com/print/what_went_wrong.php

Drabek, T. E., & Hoetmer, G. J. (Eds.). (1991). *Emergency management: Principles and practice for local government.* Washington DC: International City Management Association.

Dunbar, R. L. M., & Goldberg, W. H. (1978). *Crisis development and strategic response in European corporations.* Toronto, Canada: Butterworth.

Dutton, J. E., & Jackson, S. E. (1987). Categorizing strategic issues: Links to organizational action. *Academy of Management Review, 12*(1), 76–90.

Eisenberg, E. M. (1990). Jamming: Transcendence through organizing. *Communication Research, 17*(139–164).

Gallen, R. G., McCraw, J. D., & Roberts, T. A. (1980). *Report of the commission of inquiry into the Abbotsford landslip disaster.* Wellington, New Zealand: P. D. Hasselberg, Government Printer.

Gilbert, C. (2005). Unbundling the structure of inertia: Resource versus routine rigidity. *Academy of Management Journal, 48*(5), 741–763.

Gillespie, D. F. (1991). Coordinating community resources. In T. E. Drabek & G. J. Hoetmer (Eds.), *Emergency management: Principles and practice for local government* (pp. 55–78). Washington DC: International City Management Association.

Gladstein, D. L., & Reilly, N. P. (1985). Group decision making under threat: The Tycoon Game. *Academy of Management Journal, 28*(3), 613–627.

Hamblin, R. L. (1958). Leadership and crises. *Sociometry, 21*, 322–335.

Hermann, C., F. (1963). Some consequences of crisis which limit the viability of organizations. *Administrative Science Quarterly, 16*, 533–547.

Homeland Security. (2004). *National incident management system.* Version of March 1, 2004, http://www.fema.gov/pdf/emergency/nims/nims_doc_full.pdf

Homeland Security. (2006a). Local and tribal NIMS integration: Integrating the National Incident Management System into local and tribal emergency operations plans and standard operating procedures. *Version 1.0*, 1–33.

Homeland Security. (2006b). State NIMS integration: Integrating the National Incident Management System into state emergency operations plans and standard operating procedures. *Version 1.0*, 1–31.

House, R. J., Spangler, W. D., & Woycke, J. (1991). Personality and charisma in the U.S. presidency: A psychological theory of leader effectiveness. *Administrative Science Quarterly, 36,* 364–396.

Hsu, S. S. (2006, February 12). Katrina reports spreads blame. *Washington Post. Hurricane Katrina heroes.* (2006). Retrieved March 22, 2006, from http://www.katrina-hurricane.biz/hurricane-katrina-heroes.htm

Kiesler, S., & Sproull, L. (1982). Managerial response to changing environments: Perspectives on problem sensing from social cognition. *Administrative Science Quarterly, 27,* 548–570.

Kouzmin, A., & Jarman, A. (1989). Crisis decision making: Towards a contingent decision path perspective. In U. Rosenthal, M. T. Charles, & P. t'Hart (Eds.), *Coping with crises—The management of disasters, riots and terrorism* (pp. 397–435). Springfield, IL: Charles C Thomas.

Lipton, E. (2006, February 13). Republicans' report on Katrina assails administration response. *The New York Times,* p. A1

Lipton, E., Drew, C., Shane, S., Rohde, D., DeParle, J., & Pear, R. (2005, September). Breakdowns marked path from hurricane to anarchy. *The New York Times,* Section 1, p. 1.

Mendonca, D., Beroggi, G. E. G., & Wallace, W. A. (2001). Decision support for improvisation during emergency response operations. *International Journal of Emergency Management, 1*(1), 30–38.

Ministry of Health. (2004). *National health emergency plan: Infectious diseases.* Wellington, New Zealand: Ministry of Health.

Mitroff, I. I., & Alpaslan, M. C. (2003). Preparing for evil. *Harvard Business Review, April, 82*(4), 109–115.

Mitroff, I. I., Shrivastava, P., & Udwadia, F. E. (1987). Effective crisis management. *The Academy of Management Executive, 1*(3), 283–292.

Moorman, C., & Miner, A. S. (1998). Organizational improvisation and organizational memory. *Academy of Management Review, 23*(4), 698–723.

National Commission on Terrorist Attacks. (2004). *The 9/11 Commission report: Final report of the National Commission on Terrorist Attacks upon the United States.* New York: W. W. Norton.

New Zealand Department of Internal Affairs. (2005). *National civil defence emergency management plan order.* Wellington, New Zealand: Author.

New Zealand Police. (2005). *Search and rescue incident management guidelines—Functional roles and responsibilities for land search and rescue in New Zealand using the coordinated incident management system.* New Zealand: Author.

Nolan, B. (2005, August 28). Katrina takes aim. *Times-Picayune,* p. 1.

Nunamaker, J. F. J., Weber, E. S., & Chen, M. (1989). Organizational crisis management systems: Planning for intelligent action. *Journal of Management Information Systems, 5*(4), 7–32.

Paton, D. (1996). Training disaster workers: Promoting wellbeing and operational effectiveness. *Disaster Prevention and Management, 5*(5), 10–16.

Perrow, C. (1984). *Normal accidents: Living with high risk technologies.* New York: Basic Books.

Peterson, D. M., & Perry, R. W. (1999). The impacts of disaster exercises on participants. *Disaster Prevention and Management, 8,* 241–254.

Pillai, R., & Meindl, J. R. (1998). Context and charisma: A "meso" level examination of the relationship of organic structure, collectivism, and crisis to charismatic leadership. *Journal of Management, 24*(5), 643–671.

Polivka, B. J., Dresback, S. H., Heimlich, J. E., & Elliott, M. (2001). Interagency relationships among rural early intervention collaboratives. *Public Health Nursing, 18*(5), 340–349.

Quarantelli, E. L. (1988). Disaster crisis management: A summary of research findings. *Journal of Management Studies, 25*(4), 373–385.

Rudolph, J. W., & Repenning, N. P. (2002). Disaster dynamics: Understanding the role of quantity in organizational collapse. *Administrative Science Quarterly, 47*, 1–30.

Russell, G. (2005, 23/10/2005). Nagin gets mixed reviews. *The Times-Picayune.*

Scanlon, T. J. (1991). Reaching out: Getting the community involved in preparedness. In T. E. Drabek & G. J. Hoetmer (Eds.), *Emergency management: Principles and practice for local government.* Washington DC: International City Management Association.

Smallman, C., & Weir, D. (1999). Communication and cultural distortion during crises. *Disaster Prevention and Management, 8*(1), 33–41.

Smart, C., & Vertinsky, I. (1977). Design for crisis decision units. *Administrative Science Quarterly, 22*, 640–657.

Smith, R. J. (1984). Crisis management under strain. *Science, 225*(4665), 907–909.

Staw, B. M., Sandelands, L. E., & Dutton, J. E. (1981). Threat-rigidity effects in organizational behavior: A multilevel analysis. *Administrative Science Quarterly, 26*, 501–524.

Thieren, M. (2005). Health information systems in humanitarian emergencies. *Bulletin of the world Health Organization, 83*, 584–589.

Tjosvold, D. (1984). Effects of crisis orientation on managers' approach to controversy in decision making. *Academy of Management Journal, 27*(1), 130–138.

U.S. Department of Homeland Security. (2004). *National Incident Management System.* Washington DC: Author.

Uden-Homan, T., Walkner, L., Huse, D., Greene, B. R., Gentsch, D., & Atchison, C. G. (2005). Matching documented training needs with practical capacity: Lessons learned from project Public Health Ready. *Journal of Public Health Management Practice, November, 11*(6), 106–112.

Vaughan, D. (1990). Autonomy, interdependence, and social control: NASA and the space shuttle Challenger. *Administrative Science Quarterly, 35*, 225–257.

Wegner, D. M., Guiliano, T., & Hertel, P. (1985). Cognitive interdependence in close relationships. In W. J. Ickes (Ed.), *Compatible and incompatible relationships* (pp. 253–276). New York: Springer-Verlag.

Weick, K. E. (1988). Enacted sensemaking in crisis situations. *Journal of Management Studies, 25*(4), 305–317.

Weick, K. E. (1993). The collapse of sensemaking in organizations: The Mann Gulch disaster. *Administrative Science Quarterly, 38*, 628–652.

Wikipedia. (last updated 2/11/2005). *Community emergency response team.* Retrieved Febraruy 11, 2005, from http://en.wikipedia.org/wiki/Community_emergency_response_team

Yerkes, R. M., & Dodson, J. D. (1908). The relation of strength of stimulus to rapidity of habit formation. *Journal of Comparative Neurology and Psychology, 18*, 459–482.

Yourish, K., Stanton, L., & Tate, J. (2005). Katrina: What went wrong? Preparation and response. *The Washington Post.* Retrieved November 12, 2005, http://www.washingtonpost.com/wp-dyn/content/custom/2005/09/11/CU2005091100067.html

Zwerdling, D., & Sullivan, L. (2005). *Katrina: What went wrong?* Retrieved November 12, 2005, www.npr.org, http://www.npr.org/templates/story/story.php?storyId=4839943

CHAPTER 5

ASYMMETRIC INFORMATION PROCESSES IN EXTREME EVENTS

The December 26, 2004 Sumatran Earthquake and Tsunami

Louise K. Comfort

Decision making under the urgent constraints of disaster is fundamental to effective governance in areas exposed to recurring risk. While after-action reviews held to assess performance following devastating events repeatedly call for stronger coordination among agencies engaged in disaster operations, such coordination cannot occur without an effective process of communication. Communication has both technical and social components, each affecting the other and producing potential failure as well as probable strength. Failure in technical systems of communication almost certainly triggers failure in organizational performance under the rapidly changing conditions of disaster. Such failures lead to asymmetries in access to communication and timely information exchange that are critical to a community's capacity to adapt quickly to serious threat. This analysis examines the networks of interaction among organizations participating in Indonesian

Communicable Crises: Prevention, Response, and Recovery in the Global Arena, pp. 137–168

response operations following the December 26, 2004 Sumatran earthquake and tsunami. It reveals both clusters of communication exchange and gaps among participating organizations at different jurisdictional levels of operation. A bow-tie architecture that incorporates a continuous feedback loop between actors and the changing environment is suggested as a design for timely disaster communication processes that, in turn, provide decision support for effective action.

THE CASCADE OF EVENTS

South Asia, long a region that has received only intermittent attention in world affairs, urgently commanded the attention and empathy of the international community on December 26, 2004. A massive earthquake, measuring 9.3 moment magnitude on the Richter scale of earthquake intensity,[1] occurred at 0758 (local time) on the Sunda Trench, off the western coast of Northern Sumatra, Indonesia (Borrero, 2005). The earthquake, which ruptured the fault line for approximately 1,300 km, caused a massive uplift of the sea floor of approximately 5 m (Pomonis et al., 2005). This sudden alteration of the sea floor generated a powerful tsunami that affected a dozen nations in and around the rim of the Indian Ocean Basin. The effects of the tsunami varied according to the physical formation of the coastlines, with the waves traveling at speeds up to 500 miles per hour and reaching heights that varied from 2.5 to 30 ms (National Aeronautic and Space Administration, 2005) in areas where the physical features of the coastline focused the waves.

The four nations most severely affected—Indonesia, Sri Lanka, India, and Thailand—suffered different degrees of damage and losses in lives and property. Two of these nations, Indonesia and Sri Lanka, torn by long-running civil conflicts in which internal groups have been seeking independence from their respective national governments, confronted serious challenges in mobilizing disaster operations. In both nations, the ongoing civil conflicts have bred distrust between citizens and governments for decades. The demands of maintaining internal security in regions that urgently required disaster assistance complicated the interactions between the disaster-affected citizens and their respective national governments. Only with international assistance could the massive needs of the devastated regions be met, but with international assistance came 24/7 media coverage by international news networks. National governments, with legal responsibilities for protecting lives and property, were closely observed in their operational response to the disaster, and their activities reported in the media of nations whose assistance they sought. This pattern of international reporting of national and local actions created an environment in which all participants were mindful of the potential for major assistance—and possible harm—based on the validity of information relayed to the international community.

The losses in lives and property in the affected nations were staggering. Indonesia reported a loss of over 237,071 people as dead or missing. Sri Lanka, second hardest hit, reported 30,957 fatalities. India reported 10,749 dead and Thailand, 5,393 dead, approximately half of them tourists from Europe visiting the Thai beach resorts over the Christmas holiday.[2]

The suddenness, severity, and scale of this event captured the world's attention for weeks. On a balmy Sunday morning, people in coastal communities across the region were out in their neighborhoods, many on the beaches. They felt the earthquake as a strong, prolonged shaking event, but were relieved when the shaking stopped, thinking the danger had passed. The damage was worst in Indonesia, closest to the epicenter of the earthquake and in the direct path of the tsunami.

Approximately 30 minutes after the earthquake, the first tsunami wave struck Banda Aceh, Indonesia, without warning. A city of 322,000 residents and capital of the province of Aceh, Banda Aceh is located at the northern tip of Sumatra, some 250 km northeast from the epicenter of the earthquake (see Figure 5.1). Although it is a coastal city, Banda Aceh had no recent experience with tsunamis, and its residents were almost wholly unaware of the risk. When the water first receded from the coastline, local residents did not recognize this unusual event as an indicator of a tsunami, but rather walked toward the beach to take a closer look and pick up the fish that were left behind. When the returning wave engulfed the city, residents were caught by surprise and could not escape the incoming rush of water. The destruction was caused in part by the powerful wave, but also by the crushing force of cars, trucks, refrigerators, and other debris that it picked up along the way. People clung for their lives to trees or buildings, but for many it was too late. The tragic aspect of this event was both the lack of local knowledge of tsunami risk for coastal regions and the lack of an information infrastructure to warn the local authorities and residents of this danger.

The tsunami destroyed large sections of Banda Aceh, heavily damaged Meulaboh, a smaller city on the western coast of Aceh, and virtually erased fishing villages from both the western and eastern coasts of Northern Sumatra. The infrastructure that supported transportation, commerce, education, and the daily operations of communities was almost totally gone. When the water receded, the stunned residents who remained confronted the overwhelming tasks of search and rescue, damage assessment, clean-up, reestablishment of some form of local administration, and coordination of disaster assistance to the remaining population. In early March 2005, nearly 2½ months after the tsunami,

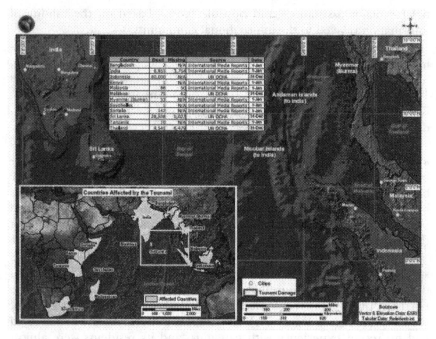

Source: Pacific Disaster Center (2005, http://www.pdc.org).

Figure 5.1   Tsunami damage assessment as of January 2, 2005.

shops had reopened, but there were still massive amounts of debris waiting to be hauled away, and some areas of the city had not yet been cleared of rubble.[3] The local governments were essentially nonfunctional. Many of the local response personnel and public officials were killed or injured in this severe event, and their operations facilities were destroyed. The national government in Jakarta mobilized a national coordinating committee to provide assistance immediately after the tsunami, but emergency assistance had to come from Jakarta, 4 hours away by plane. The scale and scope of the damage in Aceh Province challenged the resources and managerial capabilities of the national government of Indonesia.

Mobilizing disaster operations for the devastated cities, towns, and villages in Aceh was exacerbated by the long-running civil conflict. The people of Aceh have never accepted colonial rule, and the Gerakan Acheh Merdeka (GAM or Free Aceh Movement) has continued to seek independence for the province from the national government of Indonesia. The national government, under a succession of leaders, has sought to suppress the movement with armed force. This conflict, continuing for more than forty years, has engendered a general distrust between the residents of Aceh and the Indonesian Army (TNI). Under national law, the Indonesian government mobilized the TNI to provide emergency search-and-rescue services, disaster relief, and other assistance to the badly damaged regions of Aceh. In conditions where communication was crucial to achieve coordination, effective communication channels had been disrupted, did not exist, or were not trusted.[4]

This urgent, complex environment required a coordinated effort among multiple parties to assist the residents of Aceh and other damaged states across the region. Such an effort could only be established through trusted communication channels that were extremely difficult to maintain under conditions of civil conflict. A similar movement for independence has been operating in Sri Lanka, with the Tamil Eelam (Tamil Tigers) engaged in guerrilla warfare with the national government, also for approximately 40 years. Following the tsunami, both nations confronted severe situations that required a coordinated response from all levels of government. In each nation, initial efforts were made to call a truce in the civil wars in order to focus on the urgent task of aiding the residents of the disaster-affected areas.[5] But initial efforts to resolve the conflicts broke down under the stress of actual disaster operations in both countries. Recent efforts in international negotiation have produced a fragile truce in Indonesia, but the problem of mobilizing an interorganizational strategy of response and reconstruction following the disaster illustrates the cumulative effect of failures in communication, coordination, and capacity for resilience in crisis management.

THE DILEMMA: INTERDEPENDENCE OF COMMUNICATION AND COORDINATION IN EXTREME EVENTS

The interdependence of communication and coordination in rapidly evolving events has been discussed in earlier work (Comfort, 1999; Comfort, Ko, & Zagorecki, 2004). The tsunami events underscore the previous finding that coordination is unlikely to evolve in any reliable pattern without a viable information infrastructure. An information structure that provides sufficient technical support to organizational systems for search, exchange, and cumulative storage of information is essential for real-time problem solving. In crisis conditions, public organizations are confronted with conditions they may never have seen before, yet they have the legal responsibility to protect citizens, provide for urgent needs, maintain order, and return the communities to daily operations as quickly as possible. In large scale catastrophes, such as the earthquake and tsunami disaster of December 26, 2004, the technical infrastructure that supports organizational information processes also provides the means to update operations, correct errors, build relations with participants, and create the essential basis of trust between citizens and government. These processes are critical to creating a "common operating picture" for all participating organizations. Coordination, from previous evidence, occurs most reliably with timely, accurate information search and exchange processes (Comfort, 1999). Without communication, coordination is likely to fail, or worse, slide into coercion, an outcome that defeats the goal of engaging communities in managing their own risks and taking responsible action to solve their own problems.

Designing and implementing communication processes for complex systems is not trivial, especially in situations that include hostile parties. In such situations, more than in ordinary governmental operations, asymmetric information processes hinder coordination and generate further distrust among participating members if they discover that information has not been disseminated in a timely, accurate manner to those who need it and are expected to participate in common action. Designing administrative networks that share information rapidly and quickly becomes a mechanism for building coordination, but runs counter to the purposes of control that most administrative hierarchies seek. The dilemma is whether to support multiway communication with all parties engaged in a common operation in order to foster coordination, or to use one-way communication as a means of control to maintain order in a volatile situation. The former option requires time that is limited in urgent conditions. The latter option leads to asymmetric information processes that hinder coordination among a large group of participating organizations even more. This dilemma is further exacerbated as trust diminishes among participating groups.

Contending Analytical Frameworks for Complex Systems

Coordination in extreme events requires timely, multiway communication processes among the participating organizations. In practice, communication in crisis events tends to be heavily asymmetrical, creating gaps in performance and fragility in the overall system of operations. In large part, this condition is a function of the urgency and severity of the event, but it also indicates a lack of design, failure to acknowledge the vital importance of local knowledge and skills to disaster operations, and lack of investment in a scalable information infrastructure to support system-wide information exchange. Effective communication processes are necessarily sociotechnical; that is, they are supported by technical systems of information transmission and processing designed to facilitate the ready, secure exchange of information within and among multiple organizations to enable coordinated performance of the system.

Persistent inequality of information among participating units and groups in the administrative systems of government has been largely misperceived as a problem of inefficiency or political expediency in governmental performance, ignoring the complexity of the actual problem. Closer examination reveals a much more difficult and complicated set of conditions that impede governmental performance. Summarized briefly, these basic conditions include:

1. Interdependencies among agencies and clientele coping with a specific policy problem

2. Asymmetry of information flow among the agencies responsible for public action

3. Inadequate feedback from heterogeneous clientele to operations agencies

4. Inability of administrative agencies to adjust programs, plans, and resources to changing conditions or to meet urgent demands

5. Unequal participation of agencies and clientele groups in policy processes, leading to increasing inequality in the exercise of power, access to resources, opportunities for redress of errors, and capacity to reframe policy goals and practice

In this profile of governmental operations in disaster environments, the opportunities for self correction are minimized, and the discrepancy between the desired goals and actual performance of administrative agencies grows inevitably over time. Several theorists have addressed the discrepancy between stated goals and actual performance, and have offered different models for analyzing and minimizing it. Interestingly, these models have largely focused on two functions that can be used to improve performance, policy design and information flow, not financial resources or legal authority. The implication, in most cases unstated, is that by changing the patterns of access to information and feedback among participating organizations, one also changes the exercise of authority and consequent flow of resources. Information, considered as a major resource in managing disaster operations, facilitates adaptive change in performance among the units participating in the response system.

The classic concept of design for administrative systems was stated cogently by Herbert Simon (1981) in his book, *The Sciences of the Artificial*. Design is the deliberate construction of an administrative structure that facilitates the achievement of a specific goal in the wider external environment. The newly designed structure consists primarily of a set of procedures and policies that define the exchange of information, marshal the necessary resources, inform the decisions of policymakers, and guide the actions between the policymakers and the environment needed to achieve the desired goal. Although Simon was primarily concerned with designing the internal functions of the organization, in practice this structure became embedded in the wider environment as a vehicle for the achievement of specific policy goals.

Implied, but not fully articulated by Simon, was the assumption that the newly created administrative structure serves the vital function of channeling information both within the constructed organization among personnel engaged in specific tasks and between this organization and its wider environment in pursuit of its stated goal. The new structure thus becomes an agent in the larger network of organizations and groups involved in social action. This adaptive network can be modeled according to Simon's initial conception of administrative organizations as a structured flow of information within a hierarchy of actors that function in an environment of uncertainty and change. While Simon acknowledged the changing environment and informal observation of emerging discrepancies between organizational procedures and requirements for action, he also acknowledged the persistent patterns of human actors, given limited cognitive capacity, to organize information hierarchically as a basis for action. Without design for corrective feedback from the environment into organizational decision making, however, the hierarchical structure of the administrative decision processes tends to exclude information counter to existing procedures and hinder flexible adaptation to changing conditions essential to sustain sound performance.

The hierarchical structure of administrative design advanced by Simon and his colleagues was challenged substantively by a group of theorists who focused on the flow of information that persisted outside of formal administrative structure (Cohen, March, & Olsen, 1972; Feldman & March, 1981; March, 1999; March & Olsen, 1979; Wilensky, 1967). James March and his colleagues, focusing on the practice of administrative organizations, effectively demonstrated the weakness of administrative structures in maintaining control of organizational decision processes, and illustrated vividly how information processes were used to disguise or delay conflicts over competing interests by executives seeking to maintain their control in a dynamic environment. The result, in their sobering analysis, was a pervasive unreliability in administrative performance in dynamic environments.

A third set of theorists addressed the problem of reliability of organizations operating in environments subject to uncertainty and change (LaPorte & Consolini, 1991; Rochlin, 1993; Rochlin, LaPorte, & Roberts, 1987; Weick & Roberts, 1993). The "high reliability" school, initially formed at the University of California, Berkeley, focused on the problem of maintaining highly reliable performance in a single organization under conditions in which failure was not an option. In this conception, the organization itself was a highly structured, carefully designed vehicle for organizing information and action to achieve a very clear goal. The organization itself was a network that often functioned under extreme uncertainty, but managed to maintain its level of performance through the use of clearly defined rules, a shared culture of excellence in performance, timely communication of information, and focused action. This culture was maintained by a program of intensive training, as well as the practice of "heedful interrelating" (Weick & Roberts, 1993) among the participants.

This practice meant watchful scanning of the environment for sudden or unexpected changes that might disrupt performance, and adapting one's actions accordingly. It required that all participants be attuned to the actions of one another and committed to a common goal. Thus, any deviation in expected performance was noticed by multiple actors and met with an immediate response or action taken to offset the change and maintain the expected performance. Heedful interrelating involves primarily a process of self organizing, anticipatory actions on the part of persons who are engaged in the clearly defined, if risky, tasks. When an entire network engages in such activities, it increases the chances for a comprehensive monitoring of critical functions that are central to reliable performance of the system. This network can be modeled as a multiway information flow that maintains reliable action through shared goals and timely communication of critical information. In its current form, this network functions well in highly structured environments, but cannot easily be adapted to wider, heterogeneous social contexts.

A fourth set of theorists focused on the phenomenon of self organized criticality in natural systems (Bak, 1996; Kauffman, 1993; Stauffer & Aharony, 1992). This phenomenon was first observed in physical and biological systems, and describes the process of cumulative introduction of new material into a system until it reaches a threshold point where the entire system transforms itself into a different form or function. The principal distinction between this and other forms of change is that the force initiating change is spontaneous and comes from internal action; it is not imposed by any external force. This type of change can also be modeled as a network, with incoming data (information or material) cumulatively triggering an internal process of reorganization into a design that is more appropriate for the environment. This process can be represented by a lattice in which information is released randomly throughout the network without design, until a sufficient threshold is reached that triggers the reorganization of the components of the system into a new, more appropriate form. This framework mimics the process of change in nature, but it is inefficient in both time and resources and may not produce the desired change.

Carlson and Doyle (1999, 2000, 2002) contrast the theory of self organized criticality with a framework of highly optimized tolerance (HOT). In HOT, design is combined with spontaneous action to achieve system performance that is robust for the purposes for which it is designed, but fragile in unexpected or extreme conditions. This framework reintroduces design as a means of ordering multiscale operations, but retains the flexibility of adaptation that is achieved through real-time communications and continuous learning. This network can be modeled by channeling information through particular nodes for specific purposes to achieve greater efficiency in performance, but it allocates no reserve resources to cover an unexpected failure in the system's operation or the emergence of sudden, urgent demands.

Csete and Doyle (2004) offer a promising theoretical framework that combines feedback processes with simultaneity in transmitting information from heterogeneous sources to facilitate coordinated action in complex environments. Termed "bowtie" architecture, the design identifies key sources of data that "fan in" simultaneously to a central processing unit or "knot" where the data are integrated, analyzed, and interpreted from the performance of the whole system. This new information is then "fanned out" to the relevant actors or operating units that use the information to make adjustments to their specific operation informed by the global perspective. This design is similar to an emergency operations center, where status reports from multiple agencies are transmitted to the service chiefs who review the data from the perspective of the whole community. The set of service chiefs collectively integrate, analyze, and interpret the data from the perspective of the whole community, and then transmit the relevant information to the respective operations personnel, who adjust the performance of their units informed by the operations perspective for the entire system. The process creates a "common operating picture" for the participating agencies.

This theoretical framework acknowledges the importance of both design and self organizing action in guiding coordinated action in a complex, dynamic environment. It can be modeled as a set of networks that facilitate the exchange of incoming and outgoing information through a set of analytical activities that support coordinated decision making. The information flow is multiway, but gains efficiency through integrated analysis and coordinated action toward a clearly articulated goal for the whole system. It operates by identifying the key sources of information, the key processes of analysis and interpretation for the whole system, and the key routes of transmission. It maintains self organizing functions in that personnel, with informed knowledge, adjust their own performance to achieve the best performance for the whole system. Design, self organization, and feedback are central to effective performance of distinct organizational units within the global system.

This theoretical model, using the bowtie architecture, can best be implemented as a sociotechnical system. That is, it would use the facilities of an advanced technical information infrastructure to inform the human decision makers who are responsible for maintaining the daily operations of the community. These facilities include the technical capacity to perform the processes of monitoring, integrating, analyzing, and transmitting information regarding community operations in timely, accurate, and manageable fashion for the human decision makers. The model relies on the human capacity to learn, and uses the design of a technical infrastructure to facilitate the learning process. Communication of information serves as the driving force for the model and transmits a continuous assessment of the status of the system's vital functions in real time. The performance of the system is measured by the shared commitment to informed action among the participants to achieve the stated goal. The elements of the model are illustrated in Figure 5.2.

The question is whether this theoretical model could be fitted to a complex, urgent operations environment, as in the response system to the December 26, 2004 tsunami disaster.

Complexity of Interorganizational Coordination in the Indian Ocean Basin Tsunami Response

The difficulties of establishing functional interorganizational coordination for disaster operations in this event were massive. The international news media publicized the event, with wrenching photos of loss and destruction shown live on nightly television news. Governments, nonprofit organizations, and businesses from around the world offered assistance and pledged donations. Analysts parsed the sequence of events to offer explanations of escalating losses or strategies for assistance. Because complexity increases with the size, scope, and severity of the event, the tsunami disaster was at the extreme end of the complexity continuum. More than a dozen nations were directly affected, each with their own languages, laws, economies, administrative structures, and cultures. Within each nation, multiple governmental and nongovernmental organizations operating across national boundaries rushed to offer assistance and disaster relief. The world community responded to the nations in need with extraordinary generosity and speed.

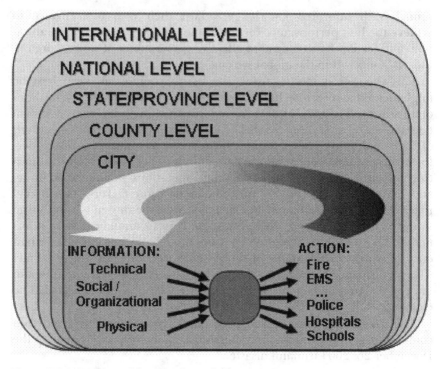

Figure 5.2.   Bowtie architecture for scalable response system.

A content analysis of local newspapers in each of the four major countries documented the size and scope of the task of interorganizational coordination. For the purposes of this chapter, I will report only the disaster response system for Indonesia, based on a content analysis of news articles regarding the disaster reported in the *Jakarta Post*, an English-language newspaper published in Jakarta, Indonesia.[6] From this analysis, 372 organizations from local, provincial, national, and international jurisdictions were identified as participating in response operations, summarized below in Table 5.1.

This set included public, private, and nonprofit organizations, and clustered into nine subgroups across jurisdictional lines: Indonesian governmental agencies, militaries, United Nations programs, national governments; financial institutions, international humanitarian programs, private companies, and other organizations. Of these 372 organizations, 172, or nearly half, were international organizations, seeking to provide support to the 200 Indonesian organizations operating at different levels of responsibility and authority in disaster response operations. Of the total number of organizations, 110 were identified as initiating interac-

Table 5.1.   Frequency Distribution of Organizations Identified in the Sumatran Earthquake and Tsunami Response System, Indonesia, December 26, 2004*

Level of Jurisdiction	Public		Private		Nonprofit		Special-Interest		Totals	
	N	%	N	%	N	%	N	%	N	%
International	104	28.0%	33	8.9%	34	9.1%	1	0.3%	172	46.2%
National	60	16.1%	29	7.8%	26	7.0%	4	1.1%	119	32.0%
Provincial	21	5.6%	3	0.8%	4	1.1%	1	0.3%	29	7.8%
Special region	6	1.6%	0	0.0%	0	0.0%	0	0.0%	6	1.6%
Semiauto region	1	0.3%	0	0.0%	0	0.0%	0	0.0%	41	0.3%
Local	27	7.3%	6	1.6%	12	3.2%	0	0.0%	45	12.1%
Totals	219	58.9%	71	19.1%	76	20.4%	6	1.6%	372	100%

Source of Funding spans the Public, Private, Nonprofit, and Special-Interest columns.

Source: *Jakarta Post,* Jakarta, Indonesia, December 27, 2004 – January 17, 2005.
*Errors in percentage totals due to rounding.

tions with other organizations engaged in disaster operations. These 110 organizations were reported as engaging in 229 interactions, at times with one other organization, most often with several other organizations. This set of interactions is used as the basic dataset for the network analysis.

Interviews with Indonesian officials indicated many more interactions. As well, the Humanitarian Information Center established by the United Nations in Banda Aceh recorded a larger set of humanitarian aid organizations involved in disaster response, and a more detailed list of interactions, especially among the international aid organizations, the United Nations, and the SuperSatkorlak (Provincial Coordinating Committee established for Aceh Province and supported by the Indonesian National Government in Jakarta) and the SuperSatlak (Municipal Coordinating Committee established for the Municipality of Banda Aceh and supported by the Indonesian National Government in Jakarta). This analysis constitutes an initial assessment of the interorganizational response system, based on news reports published in the *Jakarta Post*, the major English language newspaper in Indonesia. While data has limitations, the set offers a daily record of the evolving response system over the first 21 days immediately following the disaster. Figure 5.3 shows the entry of organizations into the response system by date and jurisdiction.

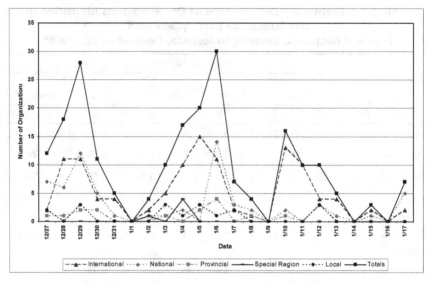

Source: *Jakarta Post*, Jakarta, Indonesia, December 27, 2004–January 17, 2005.

Figure 5.3   Entry of organizations into the full interaction system by date and level of jurisdiction.

International organizations, represented by a dotted line with trian-gles, showed a significant entry into the response system during the first 3 days following the tsunami, dropping on day 4, and increasing steadily again to reach its highest point on January 5, 2005. National organiza-tions, represented by a dotted grey line with diamonds, responded quickly on the first day, dropped slightly on the second day, and reached a point of parity with the international organizations on the third day. Strained by the demands on their resources, the national organizations struggled to organize the response effort in the second week, and invited the interna-tional organizations to participate in assuring the delivery of assistance to the shattered communities of Aceh. This policy decision is reflected in the increase of international organizations (triangles) entering the response system in the second week.

The preliminary evidence from the Indonesian disaster response sys-tem documents the difficulty of communications under the stressful, urgent conditions of these events. Communication was difficult between Banda Aceh and the national organizations in Jakarta even prior to the disaster, given the situation of civil conflict. With almost total disruption of the local communications infrastructure and the influx of hundreds of international and national aid organizations into Aceh Province, communications became critical in efforts to achieve a coordinated response to the disaster. It was difficult to create a common operating picture to inform the multiple actors of a coherent course of action. Rather, multiple operating pictures emerged, as the sectors worked largely independently. Militaries provided logistics, working at the request of the government of Indonesia, but in accordance with United Nations standards for providing humanitarian assistance. International aid organizations were welcomed by the Indonesian government, but also were tasked to follow UN standards for humanitarian assistance in delivering food, shelter, and medical care directly to the disaster-affected communities. International financial institutions interacted with national governments to manage financial contributions, again in accordance with UN guidelines. Following the UN standards meant placing the needs of the disaster-affected people above any single organizational or national goal.

The sheer enormity of the destruction in Aceh Province and the number of organizations involved in offering assistance made it difficult for groups to plan a coherent strategy for coordinated action, let alone implement one. This task was made more difficult by the lack of a common information infrastructure among the participating actors that could transmit urgent information to multiple nations, governments, and groups simultaneously. This vital function meant that organizations and groups often did not know where they could support one another, or where they might provide mutual assistance in reestablishing basic services. Some households and villages were overlooked in the general effort to assist people in need. Small matters that could have been easily solved became larger problems through inattention and delay. The pattern of asymmetry in information processes in this large-scale, multilevel set of disaster operations inhibited the coordination needed to address the urgent problems of the area in a timely way.

This pattern of asymmetry in information processes is shown most clearly in an analysis of the interactions among the international, national, provincial, and local organizations in Indonesia. As Table 5.1 shows, almost half of the organizations participating in the disaster response system, 46.2%, were international and provided welcome funding, expertise, and technical assistance for the badly ravaged communities of Aceh. Yet, the interactions with the disaster-affected communities required knowledge of the local context and language that could most effectively be provided by Indonesian organizations. This situation created mutual dependencies within the evolving response system, where international organizations depended on national organizations for knowledge of the local context and language, and the national organizations depended upon the international organizations for funding, specialized skills, and guidance in meeting international standards for humanitarian assistance. In practice, two networks evolved in disaster operations: (1) an international network that operated under United Nations standards for humanitarian assistance; and (2) a national network that operated under the legal authority of the government of Indonesia. The two networks interacted at critical points in response operations, but in many, if not most operations, acted independently of one another. The inability to coalesce this large set of 372 organizations into a coherent, unified response system reflected the size, complexity, and severity of the event, but also the significant asymmetry in information processes among the jurisdictional levels of authority and action of the networks.

Table 5.2 presents the frequency distribution for the subset of 110 national and international organizations that initiated interactions involving other organizations in response operations during the first 21 days following the disaster.

As is evident from the table, the international organizations initiated more than half of the interactions, with the national organizations initiating more than one-third of the interactions in disaster operations. Painfully evident is the limited role played by the provincial and local organizations that were overwhelmed by the magnitude of the disaster.

To examine the performance of the disaster response system in more detail, I separated the set of interactions into two types, a subset of 100 interactions initiated by international organizations and a subset of 129 interactions initiated by Indonesian organizations, for a total of 229 interactions presented in Table 5.3. Both subsets of initiating organizations

Table 5.2. Frequency Distribution of Organizations Initiating Interactions With Other Organizations in the Sumatran Earthquake and Tsunami Response System, December 26, 2004, Indonesia*

Level of Jurisdiction	Source of Funding									
	Public		Private		Nonprofit		Special-Interest		Totals	
	N	%	N	%	N	%	N	%	N	%
International	41	37.3%	7	6.4%	10	9.1%	1	0.9%	59	53.6%
National	26	23.6%	5	4.5%	7	6.4%	1	0.9%	39	35.5%
Provincial	3	2.7%	1	0.9%	0	0.0%	1	0.9%	5	4.5%
Special Region	2	1.8%	0	0.0%	0	0.0%	0	0.0%	2	1.8%
Local	3	2.7%	1	0.9%	1	0.9%	0	0.0%	5	4.5%
Totals	75	68.2%	14	12.7%	18	16.4%	3	2.7%	110	100%

Source: *Jakarta Post*, Jakarta, Indonesia, December 27, 2004 – January 17, 2005.
*Errors in percentage totals due to rounding.

**Table 5.3. Frequency Distribution of Interactions Initiated by
National and International Organizations Following the
Sumatran Earthquake and Tsunami, Indonesia, December 26, 2004**

System	Public		Private		Nonprofit		Special Interest*		Totals	
	N	%	N	%	N	%	N	%	N	%
International	72	72.0%	10	10.0%	16	16.0%	2	2.0%	100	100%
National	106	82.2%	9	7.0%	12	9.3%	2	1.6%	129	100%
Full	178	77.7%	19	8.3%	28	12.2%	4	1.7%	229	100%

Source: *Jakarta Post*, Jakarta, Indonesia, December 27, 2004 – January 17, 2005.
*Special interest groups include: International: Liberal Democratic Party of Japan;
National: Gerakan Acheh Merdeka (GAM or Free Aceh Movement); Indonesian
Democratic Party of Struggle.

actively engaged other organizations in their disaster response actions. The subset of international organizations included public, private, and nonprofit actors from the world community, and the subset of Indonesian organizations included public, private, and nonprofit actors operating at national, provincial, and local jurisdictional levels.

Figure 5.4 shows a map of international organizations that initiated interactions with other organizations, produced by the UCINET software program (Borgatti, Everett, & Freeman, 2002). The circle nodes indicate international organizations; the square nodes indicate national organizations. The map shows four primary nodes that link with other organizations in the response network: Association of South East Asian Nations (ASEAN); Office of the President of Indonesia; Government of Indonesia; and Military of Indonesia. The United Nations, Indonesian Red Cross, and U.S. Department of State also played key roles in linking other organizations in joint action.

Figure 5.5 presents the map of interacting organizations in the Indonesian national response system. The different jurisdictional levels are represented by different shapes. Circle nodes indicate international organizations; square nodes represent national organizations; up-pointing triangle nodes represent provincial organizations, diamond nodes represent local organizations, and down-pointing triangle nodes represent the national capital district of Jakarta.

The figure shows a sparsely connected network, with four key nodes, president of Indonesia, vice president of Indonesia, Government of Indonesia, and the Indonesian military. Nodes that play linking roles include the Ministry of Health, Indonesian Red Cross, Indonesian National Police, Gadja Mada University, and the Bali Hotel Association, a nonprofit group that coordinated donations from hotels and other

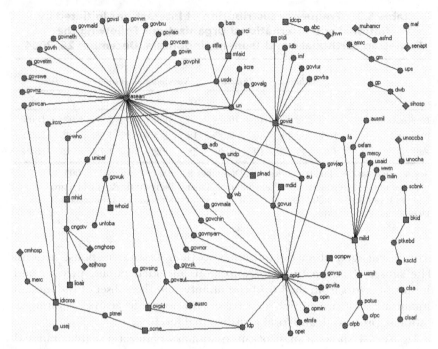

Figure 5.4.   Map of interacting organizations, international response system, Sumatran earthquake and tsunami, December 26, 2004.

businesses located in Bali. Other organizations have only one or two ties to others.

Table 5.4 presents the descriptive statistics for the measure of degree centrality for the national network of interacting response organizations. *Degree centrality* measures the position of each actor in the network in relation to every other actor by the number of ties, or interactions, that actor has with other actors in the network (Hanneman & Riddle, 2005). In this analysis, it means the number of contacts or interactions that a given organization initiated, or accepted, with other organizations. High *degree centralization* means that one actor tends to have more power over other actors in the network, or that the network tends to operate around one or a few main actors. The network centralization for the Indonesian national response network is 17.46%, a relatively low degree of centralization, focusing on the primary actors of the Indonesian government. This finding indicates that many of the actors in the network were operating in subnetworks or independently. The normalized degree statistics show the contrast between this specific network and a hypothetical normal distribution.

Acronym Legend Table for Figure 5.4.

opid	Office of the President of Indonesia	govjap	Government of Japan
govid	Government of Indonesia	govlib	Government of Libya
milid	Military of Indonesia	govmala	Government of Malaysia
idrcros	Indonesian Red Cross	govrus	Government of Russia
idcci	Indonesian Chamber of Commerce and Industry	govsing	Government of Singapore
ovpid	Office of the Vice President of Indonesia	govsk	Government of South Korea
mfaid	Ministry of Foreign Affairs, Id	govsp	Government of Spain
ocmpw	Office of the Coordinating Minister for the People's Welfare, Id	govswe	Government of Sweden
mndpid	Ministry of National Development and Planning, Id	govtai	Government of Taiwan
sgmu	State Gadjah Mada University	govuae	Government of the United Arab Emirates
bha	Bali Hotel Association	govuk	Government of the United Kingdom
adb	Asian Development Bank	govus	Government of the United States
asean	Association of Southeast Asian Nations	hmmal	Home Ministry, Malaysia
ausaid	Ausaid	jbic	Japanese Bank for International Cooperation
ausmd	Australian Ministry of Defense	mfager	Ministry of Foreign Affairs, Germany
ausmil	Australian Military	milmala	Military of Malaysia
cida	Canadian International Development Agency	milsing	Military of Singapore
govchin	Government of China	paris	Club de Paris
govhk	Government of Hong Kong	perum	Perumnas
govin	Government of India	un	United Nations
undfw	United Nation's Development Fund for Women	bbapt	Blang Bintang Airport
undp	United Nations Development Program	cmecp	Cut Mutia Emergency Command Post
unwfp	United Nations World Food Program	muhuni	Muhammadiyah University
usaid	United States Agency for International Development	nadpo	Nanggroe Aceh Darussalam Prosecutor's Office
wb	World Bank	nrpo	Nias Regency Prosecutor's Office

Table continues on next page

Acronym Legend Table for Figure 5.4 Continued

wbcgid	World Bank Consultative Group on Indonesia	sarhosp	Sardjito Hospital
who	World Health Organization	simapt	Sultan Iskandar Muda Airport
aaat	Agency for the Assessment and Application of Technology	tndapt	Tjut Nyak Dhien Airport
bkid	Bank of Indonesia	alc	Alcatel
haai	Home Affairs Administration Institute	appsmg	Asia Pulp and Paper/Sinar Mas Group
hcdfa	House Commission for Defense and Foreign Affairs	bat	British American Tobacco
idhec	Indonesian Humanitarian Emergency Commission	conair	Continental Airlines
idhr	Indonesian House of Representatives	exxon	Exxon Mobile
idnp	Indonesian National Police	ge	General Electric
idoag	Indonesian Office of the Attorney General	motor	Motorola
idsc	Indonesian Supreme Court	pateng	Paiton Energy
mctid	Ministry of Culture and Tourism, Id	seim	Siemens
mdid	Ministry of Defense, Id	sucorp	Sumitomo Corp.
meid	Ministry of Education, Id	unil	Unilever
memrid	Ministry of Energy and Mineral Resources, Id	acs	Aerowisata Catering Services
mfid	Ministry of Finance, Id	astgro	Astra Group
mhid	Ministry of Health, Id	bihs	Binawan Institute of Health Sciences
miid	Ministry of Industry, Id	binsup	Bintang Supermarket
minfm	Ministry of Fisheries and Maritime, Id	gar	Garuda
mjhrid	Ministry of Justice and Human Rights, Id	jatayu	Jatayu
mmtid	Ministry of Manpower and Transmigration, Id	metro	Metro TV
mphid	Ministry of Public Housing, Id	ombak	Ombak Putih
mpwid	Ministry of Public Works, Id	ptper	PT Pertamina
msaid	Ministry of Social Affairs, Id	ptsei	PT Samsung Electronics Indonesia
mssid	Ministry of Social Services, Id	shellid	Shell Indonesia
nccp	National Commission for Child Protection	tepid	Total E&P Indonesia
ndmcb	National Disaster Management Coordination Board	tjc	Toh Jiwa Cargo

nmgaid	National Meteorology and Geophysics Agency of Indonesia	dfs	Dijon Food Specialities
ocme	Office of the Coordinating Minister for the Economy, Id	sb	Sourcing Bali
osmcsme	Office of State Minister of Cooperatives and Small and Medium Enterprises, Id	kbr68	Kantor Berita Radio 68H
osmrt	Office of the State Minister of Research and Technology, Id	lbsb	Lippo Bank Slipi Branch
prescab	Presidential Cabinet	eb	Ecats Bridge
smwe	State Ministry for Women's Empowerment	stc	Save the Children
apo	Aceh Prosecutor's Office	uclg	United Cities of Local Government
app	Aceh Provincial Police	wbf	World Bridge Federation
asndra	Aceh-North Sumatra Natural Disaster Relief Agency	idcba	Indonesian Contract Bridge Association
biag	Bogor Institute of Agriculture	idped	Indonesia Peduli
oga	Office of the Governor of Aceh	idrcres	Indonesian Red Crescent
ogns	Office of the Governor of North Sumatra	muham	Muhammadiyah
praceh	Province of Aceh	wvid	World Vision of Indonesia
sksu	Syiah Kuala State University	sarcr	South Aceh Red Cross Regency
hpapt	Halim Perdanakusuma Airport	cmhosp	Cut Mutia Hospital
jcc	Jakarta Convention Center	muhamcr	Muhammadiyah Community Raido
jpol	Jakarta Police	ldp	Liberal Democratic Party, Japan
ogj	Office of the Governor of Jakarta	golkar	Golkar Party
shapt	Soekarno-Hatta Airport	iddps	Indonesian Democratic Party of Struggle
kuvil	Kuala Village	gam	Free Aceh Movement (GAM)

Source: *Jakarta Post,* Jakarta, Indonesia, December 27, 2004 – January 17, 2005.

Table 5.5 presents the descriptive statistics for betweenness centrality for the network. *Betweenness centrality* is a second way of measuring the relative power of actors in the network. It indicates the number of organizations that need to go through an actor, as an intermediary or gateway to access to information, resources, or authority for action, in order to engage other actors. A high betweenness score means that a

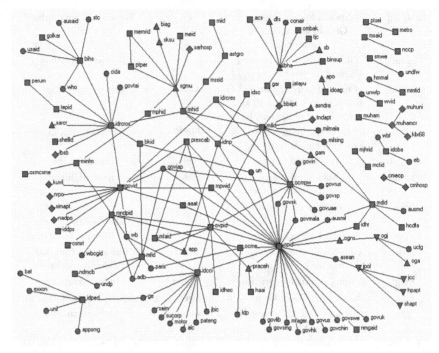

Figure 5.5.   Map of interacting organizations, Indonesian national response system, Sumatran earthquake and tsunami, December 26, 2004.

Table 5.4.   Descriptive Statistics, Degree Centrality, Indonesian National Response Network, Sumatran Earthquake and Tsunami, December 26, 2004

	Degree	NrmDegree
Mean	2.375	1.661
Std Dev	3.193	2.233
Sum	342.000	239.161
Variance	10.193	4.984
Minimum	1.000	0.699
Maximum	27.000	18.881
Network Centralization = 17.46%		

Source: Jakarta Post, Jakarta, Indonesia, December 27, 2004 – January 17, 2005.

single actor may serve as the broker or intermediary for contacts between many other actors. In this analysis, betweenness means the extent to which a given organization stands in a communication path between other organizations, so that it serves as a vehicle—or obstacle—to

Acronym Legend Table for Figure 5.4

opid	Office of the President of Indonesia	govjap	Government of Japan
govid	Government of Indonesia	govlib	Government of Libya
milid	Military of Indonesia	govmala	Government of Malaysia
idrcros	Indonesian Red Cross	govrus	Government of Russia
idcci	Indonesian Chamber of Commerce and Industry	govsing	Government of Singapore
ovpid	Office of the Vice President of Indonesia	govsk	Government of South Korea
mfaid	Ministry of Foreign Affairs, Id	govsp	Government of Spain
ocmpw	Office of the Coordinating Minister for the People's Welfare, Id	govswe	Government of Sweden
mndpid	Ministry of National Development and Planning, Id	govtai	Government of Taiwan
sgmu	State Gadjah Mada University	govuae	Government of the United Arab Emirates
bha	Bali Hotel Association	govuk	Government of the United Kingdom
adb	Asian Development Bank	govus	Government of the United States
asean	Association of Southeast Asian Nations	hmmal	Home Ministry, Malaysia
ausaid	Ausaid	jbic	Japanese Bank for International Cooperation
ausmd	Australian Ministry of Defense	mfager	Ministry of Foreign Affairs, Germany
ausmil	Australian Military	milmala	Military of Malaysia
cida	Canadian International Development Agency	milsing	Military of Singapore
govchin	Government of China	paris	Club de Paris
govhk	Government of Hong Kong	perum	Perumnas
govin	Government of India	un	United Nations
undfw	United Nation's Development Fund for Women	bbapt	Blang Bintang Airport
undp	United Nations Development Program	cmecp	Cut Mutia Emergency Command Post
unwfp	United Nations World Food Program	muhuni	Muhammadiyah University
usaid	United States Agency for International Development	nadpo	Nanggroe Aceh Darussalam Prosecutor's Office
wb	World Bank	nrpo	Nias Regency Prosecutor's Office

Table continues on next page

Acronym Legend Table for Figure 5.5 Continued

wbcgid	World Bank Consultative Group on Indonesia	sarhosp	Sardjito Hospital
who	World Health Organization	simapt	Sultan Iskandar Muda Airport
aaat	Agency for the Assessment and Application of Technology	tndapt	Tjut Nyak Dhien Airport
bkid	Bank of Indonesia	alc	Alcatel
haai	Home Affairs Administration Institute	appsmg	Asia Pulp and Paper/Sinar Mas Group
hcdfa	House Commission for Defense and Foreign Affairs	bat	British American Tobacco
idhec	Indonesian Humanitarian Emergency Commission	conair	Continental Airlines
idhr	Indonesian House of Representatives	exxon	Exxon Mobile
idnp	Indonesian National Police	ge	General Electric
idoag	Indonesian Office of the Attorney General	motor	Motorola
idsc	Indonesian Supreme Court	pateng	Paiton Energy
mctid	Ministry of Culture and Tourism, Id	seim	Siemens
mdid	Ministry of Defense, Id	sucorp	Sumitomo Corp.
meid	Ministry of Education, Id	unil	Unilever
memrid	Ministry of Energy and Mineral Resources, Id	acs	Aerowisata Catering Services
mfid	Ministry of Finance, Id	astgro	Astra Group
mhid	Ministry of Health, Id	bihs	Binawan Institute of Health Sciences
miid	Ministry of Industry, Id	binsup	Bintang Supermarket
minfm	Ministry of Fisheries and Maritime, Id	gar	Garuda
mjhrid	Ministry of Justice and Human Rights, Id	jatayu	Jatayu
mmtid	Ministry of Manpower and Transmigration, Id	metro	Metro TV
mphid	Ministry of Public Housing, Id	ombak	Ombak Putih
mpwid	Ministry of Public Works, Id	ptper	PT Pertamina
msaid	Ministry of Social Affairs, Id	ptsei	PT Samsung Electronics Indonesia
mssid	Ministry of Social Services, Id	shellid	Shell Indonesia
nccp	National Commission for Child Protection	tepid	Total E&P Indonesia
ndmcb	National Disaster Management Coordination Board	tjc	Toh Jiwa Cargo

nmgaid	National Meteorology and Geophysics Agency of Indonesia	dfs	Dijon Food Specialities
ocme	Office of the Coordinating Minister for the Economy, Id	sb	Sourcing Bali
osmcsme	Office of State Minister of Cooperatives and Small and Medium Enterprises, Id	kbr68	Kantor Berita Radio 68H
osmrt	Office of the State Minister of Research and Technology, Id	lbsb	Lippo Bank Slipi Branch
prescab	Presidential Cabinet	eb	Ecats Bridge
smwe	State Ministry for Women's Empowerment	stc	Save the Children
apo	Aceh Prosecutor's Office	uclg	United Cities of Local Government
app	Aceh Provincial Police	wbf	World Bridge Federation
asndra	Aceh-North Sumatra Natural Disaster Relief Agency	idcba	Indonesian Contract Bridge Association
biag	Bogor Institute of Agriculture	idped	Indonesia Peduli
oga	Office of the Governor of Aceh	idrcres	Indonesian Red Crescent
ogns	Office of the Governor of North Sumatra	muham	Muhammadiyah
praceh	Province of Aceh	wvid	World Vision of Indonesia
sksu	Syiah Kuala State University	sarcr	South Aceh Red Cross Regency
hpapt	Halim Perdanakusuma Airport	cmhosp	Cut Mutia Hospital
jcc	Jakarta Convention Center	muhamcr	Muhammadiyah Community Raido
jpol	Jakarta Police	ldp	Liberal Democratic Party, Japan
ogj	Office of the Governor of Jakarta	golkar	Golkar Party
shapt	Soekarno-Hatta Airport	iddps	Indonesian Democratic Party of Struggle
kuvil	Kuala Village	gam	Free Aceh Movement (GAM)

information exchange. The network centralization index is 29.69%, higher than the index for degree centralization of the network at 17.46%. This finding affirms a loosely organized network with many organizations operating in subgroups or independently. A third measure of centrality, closeness, could not be calculated for this network, as it was an unconnected graph. The network statistics confirm observations by experienced disaster managers that the response network for this

Table 5.5.   Descriptive Statistics, Betweenness Centrality, Indonesian National Response Network, Sumatran Earthquake and Tsunami, December 26, 2004

	Betweenness
Mean	166.069
Std Dev	431.057
Sum	23914.000
Variance	185810.250
Minimum	0.000
Maximum	3159.718
Network Centralization Index = 29.69%	

Source: *Jakarta Post*, Jakarta, Indonesia, December 27, 2004 – January 17, 2005.

catastrophic disaster as a national system was very loosely connected. Especially at the local level, response agencies were overwhelmed with the massive task of responding to the needs of the local population.

Analysis of subgroups within the network revealed 16 fully-connected cliques, with significant overlaps among them. The cliques represent subgroups of organizations that engaged in repeated interactions over the course of the 3 weeks immediately following the tsunami disaster. The usual size of the cliques was three organizations or more, although one clique that represented recurring interaction between the Government of South Korea and the Office of the Coordinating Minister for People's Welfare included only two organizations. The set of 16 cliques, with their component organizations, is listed in Table 5.6.

Reviewing this list, as well as the centrality measures, the dominant organizations in this loosely connected network of response organizations are clearly the Office of the President, Office of the Coordinating Minister for People's Welfare; Office of the Vice President, and Military of Indonesia, as each organization participated in five or more of the sixteen cliques. The Ministry of Health and Indonesian National Police each participated in two cliques, and the remaining organizations each participated in one clique. While the data for this analysis were drawn from a content analysis of newspaper articles and do not represent an official record, they indicate the patterns of communication and interaction that likely prevailed in the response system immediately following the December 26, 2004 earthquake and tsunami. In sobering reflection, these patterns reveal an organizational structure for the community exposed to seismic risk with a heavy concentration of authority in national agencies, some interaction with international agencies and national nonprofit organizations, but limited participation from provincial organizations and vir-

Table 5.6.   Cliques Identified in National Network of Interacting Organizations, Indonesian Response System, December 26, 2004 Sumatran Earthquake and Tsunami

1.   Military of Indonesia; Office of Coordinating Minister for Public Welfare; Office of President of Indonesia; Office of Vice President of Indonesia.

2.   Government of Malaysia; Office of Coordinating Minister for Public Welfare; Office of President of Indonesia.

3.   Government of South Korea; Office of Coordinating Minister for People's Welfare.

4.   Government of Japan; Office of Coordinating Minister for People's Welfare; Office of President of Indonesia.

5.   Indonesian National Police; Military of Indonesia; Office of President of Indonesia.

6.   Office of President of Indonesia; Office of Vice President of Indonesia; Province of Aceh.

7.   Office of President of Indonesia; Office of Vice President of Indonesia; Presidential Cabinet.

8.   Office of President; Office of Vice President; Indonesian Chamber of Commerce and Industry.

9   Government of Indonesia; Ministry of National Development and Planning; World Bank.

10.   Ministry of Energy and Mineral Resources; State Gadjah Mada University; PT Pertamina.

11.   Ministry of Foreign Affairs; Office of Vice President, Presidential Cabinet.

12.   Ministry of Finance; National Disaster Management Coordination Board; United Nations Development Programme.

13.   Indonesian National Police; Ministry of Health; Military of Indonesia.

14.   Ministry of Health; Military of Indonesia; Office of Coordinating Minister for People's Welfare.

15.   World Health Organization; Binawan Institute of Health Sciences; Indonesian Red Cross.

16.   Military of Indonesia; Office of Coordinating Minister for People's Welfare; Indonesian Red Crescent

Source: Jakarta Post, Jakarta, Indonesia, December 27, 2004 – January 17, 2005.

tually no representation from the local level. Again, this finding acknowledges the destructive impact of the disaster upon local governments and their inability to function in the period immediately following the tsunami event.

These findings indicate a lack of connectivity among major organizations with responsibility to protect life and property in communities exposed to risk. The findings confirm that a major factor impeding governmental performance in response to this catastrophe was asymmetry in the information flow among agencies responsible for action. In a disaster of this magnitude, no single agency or jurisdiction could mobilize the resources or manage the range and urgency of activities essential for effective response and recovery. Response operations were necessarily interdependent in an event of this scale. Without adequate communication processes in place before the disaster, the capacity for coordination among multiple organizations and jurisdictions declined under the stress and urgency of the event. Without adequate feedback and opportunity for adaptation or revision, the perception, if not the practice, of inequality in access to resources or opportunities for redress of error and the capacity to reframe policy goals and practice likely increased. This case is still unfolding, and further study will bring more detailed analysis.

A STRATEGY FOR CHANGE

Extreme environments require flexible networks of communication that can adapt to change and difficulty. The capacity to adapt depends upon organizational and technical design that enables a shift from asymmetric to symmetrical information processes. This shift requires organizations to acknowledge their limitations in an uncertain environment and encourage the participation of others in their networked search for viable strategies of action. In this approach, communication serves as a means of information exchange, not control. Timely feedback serves to correct error and keeps the evolving response system focused on its primary goal. This interactive process creates a common operating picture for a diverse set of participating organizations. Coordination follows from the common operating picture where all participants can understand the basic goal and adjust their separate performances accordingly.

CONCLUSION

The traumatic events of December 26, 2004 provide an extraordinary context for sociotechnical design and organizational learning. The losses incurred make it a global event, one that no nation can ignore. The suddenness and destruction of this massive disaster demonstrate the fragility of organizational plans in major catastrophes, and the continuing need to review, reflect, and redesign our crisis management plans.

This continuing need to improve the capacity of communities to manage their exposure to risk has generated much discussion regarding changes needed to prevent such an enormous catastrophe from occurring again. The primary strategy proposed has been an early warning system for nations located around the Indian Ocean Basin. The proposed design for this early warning system raises questions of control, access to information, and design for timely feedback to member states. It is critical that the linkage between technical design to facilitate effective communication and organizational processes to support coordination be incorporated into any new strategy for disaster risk reduction. A scalable bowtie architecture designed to support a regional information system among multiple jurisdictions and organizations would enable the member states to manage their shared risk more effectively.

ACKNOWLEDGMENTS

I acknowledge, with thanks and appreciation, several centers at the University of Pittsburgh—Office of the Provost, Graduate School of Public and International Affairs, and the University Center for International Studies—and the Pacific Disaster Center, that provided the financial support for this international, interdisciplinary research study on the December 26, 2004 Sumatran Earthquake and Tsunami. I thank my colleagues at Bandung Institute of Technology, Harkunti Rahayu, and Syahril Kusuma, for joining this research team and facilitating the arrangements for research in Jakarta and Banda Aceh, Indonesia. I also thank my young colleagues, Tavida and Tawit Kamolvej, for facilitating the arrangements for research in Bangkok and Phuket, Thailand. I am grateful to Thomas Haase for his diligent and careful efforts to assist me with the content analysis of the news reports and the preparation of the matrices, tables, and graphs. The findings presented in this paper represent an initial report, and research on this complex set of events is continuing.

An earlier version of this chapter was presented at the International Public Management Network Workshop on Communicable Crises: Prevention, Management and Resolution in an Era of Globalization, Peter Wall Institute for Advanced Studies at the University of British Columbia, Vancouver BC V6T 1Z1, Canada , August 15–18, 2005.

NOTES

1. The scientific community has reported magnitudes ranging from 9.0 to 9.7 on the Richter scale for this earthquake. The magnitude of record is usually determined by compiling the magnitudes recorded at different sites, and then recalculating the magnitude based on the full set of information. This process is still underway. This earthquake was, however, the second largest instrumentally recorded earthquake in geologic history.

2. These figures, cited in various sources by the media and professional reports, are the official statistics of the affected governments. They may still change, as the data are reviewed and checked. These figures were cited by Pomonis et al. (2005).

3. Personal observation, field trip to Banda Aceh, Indonesia, March 10–12, 2005.
4. Interview, Deputy Minister for Research and Technology, Jakarta, Indonesia, March 8, 2005.
5. In Sri Lanka, President Chandrika Bandaranaike Kumaratunga issued a call for unity in the nation in order to provide assistance to the damaged communities as quickly and efficiently as possible (Waldman & Hoge, 2004). In Indonesia, the GAM leaders participated in a conference in Helsinki, Finland, and to find a peaceful resolution of the independence dispute. The Indonesian government agreed to support international covenants on human rights, and the GAM agreed to discontinue its struggle for independence, if the Indonesian government would grant them autonomy protected by law (Mahmood, 2005).
6. This content analysis of newspaper articles in the *Jakarta Post* offers a daily record of events and actions taken in reference to the tsunami disaster. It offers only one of many possible perspectives on the sequence of events, but it does provide a chronological record of daily efforts to manage the disaster. Published in Jakarta, the articles focus heavily on national and international actions. It provides limited coverage of the provincial and local conditions and actions.

REFERENCES

Bak, P. 1996. *How nature works: The science of self-organized criticality*. New York: Copernicus.

Borgatti, S. P., M. Everett, G., & Freeman, L. C. (2002). *Ucinet 6.0 for Windows: Software for social network analysis*. Harvard: Analytic Technologies.

Borrero, J. C. (2005). *Field survey: Northern Sumatra and Banda Aceh, Indonesia and after the earthquake and tsunami of 26 December 2004*. Los Angeles: University of Southern California, Department of Civil Engineering. Retrieved April 6, 2005, from http://www.eeri.org/lfe/clearinghouse/sumatratsunami/observ1.php

Carlson, J. M., & J. Doyle. (1999). Highly optimized tolerance: A mechanism for power laws in designed systems. *Physical Review E., 60*, 1412-1427.

Carlson, J. M., & J. Doyle. (2000). Highly optimized tolerance: Robustness and design in complex systems. *Physical Review Letters, 84*(11), 2529-2532.

Carlson, J. M., & J. Doyle. (2002). Complexity and robustness. *Proceedings, National Academy of Sciences. 99*, 2538-2545.

Cohen, M., J., March G., & Olsen, J. (1972). The garbage can model of organizational choice. *Administrative Science Quarterly, 17*(1), 1-25.

Comfort, L. K. (1999). *Shared risk: Complex systems in seismic response*. Amsterdam: Pergamon Press.

Comfort, L. K., Kilkon K., & Zagorecki, A. (2004). Coordination in rapidly evolving systems: The role of information. *American Behavioral Scientist, 48*(3), 295-313.

Csete, M., & Doyle, J. (2004). *Bowties, metabolism, and disease*. Pasadena: California Institute of Technology.

Feldman, M. S., & March, J. G. (1981). Information in organizations as signal and symbol. *Administrative Science Quarterly, 26,* 171-86.

Hanneman, R. A., & Riddle, M. (2005). *Introduction to social network methods.* Riverside, CA: University of California, Riverside. (published in digital form at http://faculty.ucr.edu/~hanneman/)

Jakarta Post, Jakarta, Indonesia. December 27, 2004 – January 18, 2005.

Kauffman, S. A. 1993. *The origins of order: Self-organization and selection in evolution.* New York: Oxford University Press.

LaPorte, T. R., & Consolini, P. M. (1991). Working in practice but not in theory: Theoretical challenges of "High-Reliability Organizations." *Journal of Public Administration and Theory, 1*(1), 19-48.

March, J. G. (1999). *The pursuit of organizational intelligence.* Malden, MA: Blackwell Business.

March, J. G., & Olsen, J. P. (1979). *Ambiguity and choice in organizations.* Bergen: Universitetsforlaget.

Mahmood, M. (2005, February 22). *Opening speech by PM Malik Mahmood, on behalf of Tengku Hasan di Tiro, to the Helsinki Peace Talks held under the auspices of the Crisis Management Initiative.* Retrieved on December 24, 2006, from Acheh Sumatra National Liberation Front Web site:http://www.asnlf.net/asnlf_my/my/asnlf/swedia/pr_asnlf_ 50223ing.htm

National aeronautic and space administration. (2005). Retrieved September 17, 2006, from http://earthobservatory.nasa.gov/ NaturalHazards

Pomonis, A., Rossetto, T., Wilkinson, S. M., Del Re, D., Peiris, N., Koo, R., Manlapig, R., et al. (2005). *The Indian Ocean Tsunami 26th December 2004.* London, United Kingdom: The Institution of Structural Engineers. Retrieved December 29, 2006, from http://www.istructe.org/eefit/files/Indian_Ocean_Tsunami.pdf

Pacific Disaster Center. (2005). *Tsunami damage assessment as of 02 January 2005.* Retrieved September 18, 2006, from http://www.pdc.org/PDCNewsWebArticles/2004SouthAsiaTsunami/Information Products/USDOS_overview_02jan05.pdf

Rochlin, G. LaPorte, T. R., & Roberts, K. H. (1987). The self designing high reliability organization: Aircraft carrier flight operations at sea." *Naval War College Review, 40*(4), 76-90.

Rochlin, G. I. (1993). Defining high-reliability organizations in practice: A taxonomic prologue. In K. H. Roberts (Ed.), *New challenges to understanding organizations* (pp. 11-32). New York: Macmillan.

Simon, H. A. (1981). *The sciences of the artificial* (2nd ed.) Cambridge, MA: MIT Press.

Stauffer, D., & Aharony, A. (1992). *Introduction to percolation theory* (2nd ed). Washington, DC: Taylor & Francis.

Waldman, A., & Hoge, W. (2004, December 30). World leaders vow aid as toll continues to climb. *New York Times,* p. 1.

Weick, K. E. (1993). The collapse of sensemaking in organizations: The Mann Gulch disaster. *Administrative Science Quarterly, 22*(3), 606-639.

Weick, K. E., & Roberts K. (1993). Collective mind and organizational reliability: The case of flight operations on an aircraft carrier deck. *Administrative Science Quarterly, 38,* 357-381.

Wilensky, H. L. (1967). *Organizational intelligence: Knowledge and policy in government and industry.* New York. Basic Books.

CHAPTER 6

EMERGENT INSTITUTIONALISM

The United Kingdom's Response to the BSE Epidemic

Chris Ansell and Jane Gingrich

The debate over the adequacy of the United Kingdom's response to Bovine Spongiform Encephalopathy (BSE)—popularly known as "mad cow" disease—revolves around the British government's diligence in exploring BSE's public health implications, the appropriateness of its actions to safeguard the human food chain, and their communication of risk to the public. The U.K.'s response to BSE and its implications for similar cases are analyzed through the analytical lens of *emergent institutionalism*. BSE presented the United Kingdom with an *emergent problem*—a situation where the identification and analysis of the problem develops concurrently with the presentation of problem symptoms. A critical aspect of a response to an emergent problem like BSE is how well the problem is met by a problem-specific mobilization of people, knowledge, and resources—*emergent institutions*. The U.K's early response diagnosed BSE problem as "scrapie in cows"—an analogy that led public agencies to focus on animal health concerns and to downplay human health concerns. The institutionalization of this perspec-

Communicable Crises: Prevention, Response, and Recovery in the Global Arena, pp. 169–202
Copyright © 2007 by Information Age Publishing

tive led a series of government advisory committees to react slowly to mounting evidence that eating infected beef could cause Creutzfeldt-Jakob disease in humans. Emergent institutionalism offers an alternative to accounts of decision-making error that stress the political agendas of public officials or the macroinstitutional failures of agencies arising from disputes over "bureaucratic turf " or lapses in "command-and-control."

INTRODUCTION

The British government's response to the epidemic of Bovine Spongiform Encephalopathy (BSE)—mad cow disease—has been described by many names: scandal, crisis, fiasco, disaster, failure, scare. In fact, a minor theme in the scholarly literature on BSE concerns whether these epithets are appropriate under the circumstances (Forbes, 2004). In this paper, our primary purpose is not to find fault or assign blame. In fact, the U.K.'s response to BSE is characterized as much by success as by failure. Our purpose is to draw out some of the theoretical implications for governmental and organizational responses to challenging and uncertain problems.

In late 1986, veterinary scientists in the U.K.'s Ministry of Agriculture, Food, and Fisheries (MAFF) were alerted to a wasting condition in cattle at several farms in southeast England. Epidemiological studies suggested that the disease might be spread through the recycling of animal byproducts in cattle feed and pathological investigations indicated that the condition was similar to scrapie—a common, worldwide disease in sheep. Scrapie itself was part of a family of diseases known as Transmissable Spongiform Encephalopathies (TSEs), which includes Creutzfeldt-Jakob Disease (CJD) in humans. These diseases are deadly in both sheep and humans, but had not been previously seen in cattle. What neither the scientific community nor the British government knew at the time was that BSE in cattle could infect humans, producing a variant of CJD (vCJD). This link was not made public by British authorities until March 1996, nearly 10 years after the first cases of BSE-infected cattle were identified.[1] The debate over the adequacy of the response to BSE revolves around the British government's diligence in exploring BSE's public health implications, the appropriateness of its actions to safeguard the human food chain, and their communication of risk to the public.

We analyze the U.K.'s response to BSE and its implications for similar cases through the analytical lens of *emergent institutionalism*. BSE presented the U.K. with an *emergent problem*—a situation where the identification and analysis of the problem develops concurrently with the presentation of problem symptoms. As detectives and clinicians appreciate, the clues or symptoms of a case or illness often present themselves in partial or idio-syncratic ways. Cause-effect knowledge about emergent problems is often limited and weakly grounded. And, of course, problems do not stand still; they change constantly. Diagnosis of emergent problems is often described as nonroutine, ill-structured, poorly defined, uncertain, com-plex, even "wicked." With the advantage of hindsight, it may be easy to see that institutional responses are often poorly adapted to the actual character of emergent problems. We argue that a critical aspect of a response to an *emergent problem* like BSE is how well the problem is met by a problem-specific mobilization of people, knowledge, and resources—*emergent institutions*.

Much of the current criticism of governmental response to public problems—both academic and political—appears to us to focus on self-serving interests of public officials or on macroinstitutional failures of public agencies. Decision-making errors are seen as arising from the "motivated bias" of public officials who have downplayed or ignored critical information to further a political agenda or they are attributed to macroinstitutional problems like "bureaucratic turf" or "command and control failure."[2] These criticisms often provide compelling narratives and typically suggest a fairly straightforward analysis of what needs to be fixed. Claims of motivated bias, for instance, lead to demands for greater oversight or to the creation of more independent institutions, while macroinstitutional failure requires centralization, the creation of new coordinating bodies, or broad reorganization. Although systematic data on the success of past reforms is quite limited, there is often a sense among both academics and practitioners that these reforms often provide only superficial remedies (Thomas, 1993). We acknowledge that in many cases "capture" or "command and control failure" may provide an entirely appropriate criticism, but we also follow Vaughan (1996) in suggesting that the compelling quality of such narratives may gloss over more nuanced institutional dynamics. Our analysis of how particular institutional configurations "emerge" in response to emergent problems is, in part, an attempt to focus more attention on these dynamics.

In the BSE case, claims of motivated bias and macroinstitutional coor-dination failure are prominent criticisms of the U.K. response. One ver-sion of the motivated bias argument is that the science in the BSE case was manipulated for distinctly political purposes (Bartlett, 1999; Miller, 1999; Millstone & Zwanenberg 2001). Another version invokes wish fulfillment: in the face of uncertainty, decision makers simply drew the conclusions that best fit their own agenda (Beck, Asenova, & Dickson 2005). Ulti-mately, these biases are attributed to MAFF's conflict-of-interest between protecting human health and promoting agricultural interests (Zwanen-berg & Millstone, 2003, p. 28). The failure of MAFF to adequately inform and cooperate with the Department of Health is also attributed to this conflict-of-interest (Gerodimos, 2004).

In this paper, we develop an argument that puts the governmental response in a different light. We certainly do not deny the possibility for either motivated bias or macroinstitutional failure, but our analysis gives priority to the processes by which a mismatch can develop between emergent problems and emergent institutions. Our argument has three components.

i. We focus on *emergent responses* to public problems. The emergence of a new problem requires the mobilization of a particular and possibly unique configuration of people, knowledge and resources. A particular lab—or even a particular person within the lab—might be the only one that can analyze a certain kind of specimen. Certain types of expertise will be invoked as relevant to solving the problem. Some resources will be available or accessible while other resources lie unused. Particular people, knowledge, or resources are mobilized—and hence organization emerges—as needs or opportunities arise. Of course, preexisting organization provides the basic institutional framework and resources upon which this emergent response draws. But the actual response often cuts across preexisting institutional lines and assembles people, knowledge, and resources in fairly unique configurations. The term "emergent" focuses attention on this problem-specific constellation of resources, relationships, authority, and expertise. In stressing problem-specific constellations of actors, knowledge, and resources, our argument builds broadly on network-style arguments that emphasize the differentiated mobilization of social structure (Ansell, 2006). This perspective leads us to ask: who, in particular, gets mobilized to address the problem?

ii. Emergent responses depend on and shape *problem interpretation*. As emerging social configurations try to interpret novel or ill-specified problems, they must engage in what Karl Weick (1995) calls "sense-making." In other words, they must take an incomplete pattern of clues and symptoms and try to create from it an orderly and comprehensive interpretation of the situation. We suggest that sense-making and mobilization are interactive: who gets mobilized depends, in part, upon an interpretation of what the problem is; the interpretation of the problem depends on who interprets it. This perspective leads us to ask: how are problems and their symptoms interpreted, how does this interpretation depend upon who is doing the interpreting, and how does the interpretation lead certain actors to claim jurisdiction over the problem? Clearly, motivated bias might be relevant in this context. But what appears in hindsight as motivated bias may, from the perspective of emergence, actually reflect either the "decision premises" of those who happen to get mobilized to interpret the problem or the decision premises that grow out of the process of ordering information into a comprehensive gestalt.[3]

iii. Emergent responses undergo processes of *institutionalization* that shape subsequent sense-making. Emerging social configurations are likely to be flexible, temporary, and contingent, but they can nevertheless quickly take on many of the attributes that we associate with institutions. There are two ways to think about this process of institutionalization. The first is to think of institutions phenomenologically as patterns of reciprocal expectations (Berger & Luckman, 1966, pp. 53-67). Institutions are therefore conventions or habits or categories that shape social interaction and cognition. Even flexible, temporary, and contingent social constellations may quickly settle into shared understandings about how to define the situation. The second approach, consistent with the first, draws on the work of Philip Selznick to think about institutions as incipient communities that develop their own sense of rules, norms, and purposes, and endow them with value (Selznick, 1957). Emergent social configurations develop community on the fly, but their patched-together quality may disguise just how important this emergent sense of collective purpose is to their subsequent functioning as a group and their distributed intelligence (Weick, 1993). Our argument is compatible with Rothstein's claim that institutional contexts filter risk perception; however, we emphasize the filters that arise from emergent rather than preexisting institutional contexts (Rothstein, 2003).[4]

We also argue that there is a close and reciprocal relationship between institutionalization and sense-making. How an emerging social configuration makes sense of a problem will depend on what kind of understanding it has developed of itself as a group and how it understands its shared purpose. Reciprocally, "sense-making" may enter directly into institutionalization. As groups form, they may begin to attribute value and purpose to a particular interpretation of the situation. Thus, as new information about the problem becomes available, how does institutionalization affect subsequent sense-making? Our perspective expects path-dependent consequences to follow from differential mobilization, sense-making, and institutionalization. As summarized in Figure 6.1, this path-dependence may ultimately lead to a poor fit between emergent problems and emergent institutions.

Readers may wonder how this argument differs from a traditional group think model. Group think has been described as the process whereby groups come to "premature consensus," as a consequence of deference to hierarchical authority, desire to avoid divisive conflict within the group, or peer sanctions to conform to group norms (T'Hart, 1990). In invoking the importance of sense-making and group processes, our concept of emergent institutionalism shares important features with the group think model.[5] However, the groupthink model typically begins by presuming the existence of a group and then reasons from the character of the group to tendencies to premature consensus. Our approach, however, stresses that sense-making also shapes the emerging character of the group. Thus, sense-making can be encoded in the very fabric of the group (institutionalization) and—as in the case of NASA described by Vaughan (1996)—may lead the group to become resistant to anomalous information even when the conditions postulated by group think models are not present. From our perspective, the key to understanding the BSE case is to appreciate that an early interpretation of the problem as an animal health problem shaped subsequent group formation, subtly influencing the decision-making premises later observed. Even this statement makes the process sound more linear that we believe it is: we see emergence, institutionalization, and sense-making as coevolving in mutually interdependent fashion.

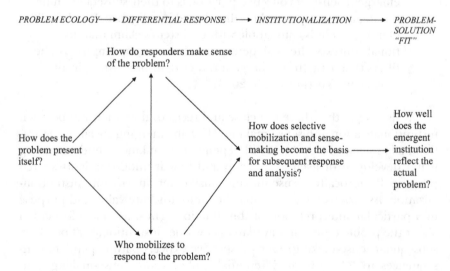

Figure 6.1.   Emergent institutionalism.

EARLY MOBILIZATION AND SENSE-MAKING

In late 1986, two cases of a wasting disease in cattle were referred by the local Veterinary Investigation Centre (VIC) to the Neuropathology Section of MAFF's Central Veterinary Lab (CVL). The CVL diagnosed a "scrapie-like" disease and the Chief of Neuropathology, Dr. Gerald Wells, quickly informed the chief of the CVL's Pathology Section, Dr. Raymond Bradley (S71: 13; PR 3.1.37).[6] As Bradley noted: "The lesions of the brain revealed in both cases were similar to those in sheep suffering from scrapie." We argue that the CVL vets made sense of this unknown disease by drawing an analogy with scrapie—a well-known affliction of sheep. Bradley and Wells were to become the core of an emergent cross-departmental group within the CVL that gradually formed in late 1986 and the first half of 1987 to make initial investigations into the disease (see Figure 6.2). The scrapie interpretation gradually became a basic decision premise for this group, affecting their subsequent information-processing and institutional response.

Scrapie is a common disease of sheep with a long history. It is also one of a class of diseases known to scientists as Transmissable Spongiform Encephalopathies (TSEs), which include Creutzfeldt-Jakob disease in humans (CJD). These diseases attack the brain, producing microscopic holes in brain cells, and ultimately lead to death. Scrapie is familiar to the agricultural community and has important economic consequences, but based on long historical experience it is regarded as non-transmissible between sheep and humans. The possibility that this was a form of "bovine scrapie" was a key point of reference for the veterinary scientists at the CVL. Since scrapie was a well-studied affliction, the use of scrapie as a reference point was quite reasonable. However, in hindsight, it is possible to say that sense-making around scrapie led the emerging BSE community to categorize BSE as primarily an "animal health" risk—thereby underestimating the risks to human health and focusing attention on the implications of a "bovine scrapie" for the export industry.

In drawing the analogy between scrapie and what came to be known as BSE, it is important to understand the reference that these veterinary scientists were making.[7] As one of the CVL pathologists, Dr. Jeffrey, points out in his testimony, vacuolation (holes in tissue) is a symptom of many different kinds of disease, but TSEs present a specific form of vacuolation (S64: 8, Annex I: 5; see also S65: 8). Therefore, to draw attention to the similarity with scrapie is to distinguish this case from a broader class of "spongiform encephalopathies."[8] To categorize it as "scrapie-like" is to send a much stronger signal about what the cases meant—a TSE commonly observed in sheep, but previously unknown in cattle. As Dr. Watson, Director of the CVL, noted at the time, one of the implications of the

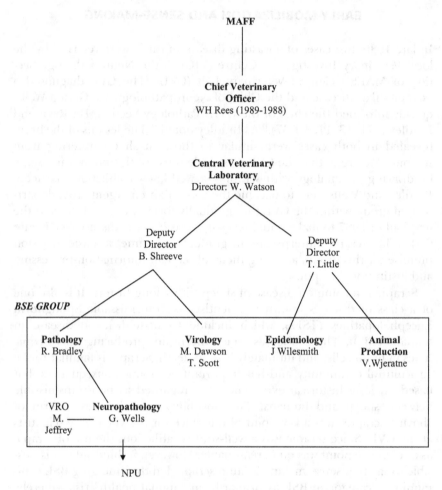

Figure 6.2.   The emergent institutional response to BSE, 1986-1988.

specific type of lesions was that "This condition is immediately associated in people's minds with scrapie in sheep."9

This diagnosis of a scrapie-like disease in cattle fed back into an emerging sense of community among these researchers. The Philip's report quotes a note from Dr. Bradley, who wrote: "At present, BSE is regarded as a major discovery to the cattle industry that will when reported bring deserved prestige to MAFF, ADAS, the CVL and the workers involved" (PR 3.1.39). The Philip's Report notes: "It seems that the scientists at CVL had demonstrated a degree of self-congratulation in having identified the new disease which struck no chord with Mr. Rees [Chief Veterinary

Officer: CVO], who could all too well see its wider implications" (PR 3.1.38).

For both Bradley and Rees, the possible damages to the cattle industry from this "scrapie-like" disease were their primary focus, guiding much of their subsequent behavior. Fearing the negative consequences for export markets, their concern led to sensitivity over characterizing the disease as "scrapie-like."[10] These "wider implications" led to strong controls over information within the CVL. An article reporting on the BSE cases authored by Dr. Wells was not circulated to veterinary investigation officers until June 1987 and it was not until May 1987 that Wells made a presentation to a closed meeting of the Medical and Veterinary Research Clubs (PR 3.2.46).[11] Ministerial level officials were not brought into the fold until June 1987.[12]

The control on information also delayed collaboration with the Neuropathegenesis Unit (NPU), one of the leading centers in the world for the study of TSE in both animals and humans. Dr. Hugh Fraser of the NPU had learned informally in January 1987 that the CVL was beginning to see cases of "scrapie in cattle" (PR 3.2.21).[13] However, Watson, in conjunction with Bradley, had decided not to consult or even talk with the NPU at this early stage (PR 3.2.25; 3.2.49). It was not until Wells' closed-door presentation to the Medical and Veterinary Research Clubs, with NPU's Dr. Kimberlin in attendance, that a discussion about the NPU's future role ensued (PR 3.2.48). Even then, Bradley asked CVL participants not to talk with the NPU (PR 3.2.49).[14] Subsequently, however, informal contacts with the NPU did begin to emerge and they began to play an important role (S65: 29).

Formal and informal contacts—mostly within the CVL—gradually developed and led to a more authoritative analysis of the new disease. Wells sent tissue samples to Mr. Scott and Mr. Dawson in the Virology Department to be analyzed for "scrapie-associated fibrils" (SAFs), tell-tale signs of scrapie (S65: 25), and he discussed the cases with pathologists at the Royal Veterinary College (S65: 26). He also discussed the cases with Mr. Wilesmith, head of the CVL's epidemiology unit, and Dr. Vernon Wijeratne, a veterinary geneticist in the Animal Production Department (S65: 30; S71: 16). He also kept the CVL Director Watson and Deputy Director Shreeve informed of developments. In early June, Watson asked Bradley to be the BSE coordinator and referred to a "BSE group" that included Wells, Dawson, Scott, Wilesmith, and Wijeratue (PR 2.56). In mid-June, a formal and informal relationship was established between NPU and CVL around a new BSE research program. Kimberlin and Wells were the contact points between the NPU and the CVL (PR 3.2.72).

An emerging sense of ownership of this problem can be detected in the guarded nature of the CVL staff. In May 1987, Bradley circulated a memo discussing how information ought to be disseminated (PR 3.2.34).[15] Item five reads:

> When a publication is made it should, apart from giving an authoritative scientific account, give acknowledgement to those contributing to the knowledge in an agreed fashion and indicate to the reader the teamwork necessary to identify, recognize and describe such new conditions ie the importance of surveillance in the SVS which is conducted jointly by the VIS and CVL in the context of the current investigation. (PR 3.2.34)

In Selznick's terms, we can see that the diagnosis of the problem was becoming infused with value.

We can also see an emerging internal regulation of the group. In early July, for instance, a memo from Bradley to the CVL's BSE Group, warned about the control of information:

> It is important however that the Group itself operates responsibly and particularly ensures that information to which it is privy is not communicated directly or indirectly outside the Group and particularly not to non-MAFF personnel. (PR 3.2.82)

The Group had a "duty" to correct false information in order to protect the cattle industry (PR 3.2.94). As communication between Wells (CVL) and Kimberlin and Frasier (NPU) began to confirm similarity to other TSEs, specifically scrapie (PR 3.2.97), controls on information claiming the similarity of the disease to scrapie were relaxed. However, reticence about publicizing this link remained. In October, the head of VIS, Dr. Cawthorne, sent a memo to regional veterinary officers instructing them not to refer to the condition as "bovine scrapie" (PR 3.2.117) and scrapie references were banned even after veterinary officers were allowed to publish notes in local bulletins (PR 3.2.177-88).

A fascinating situation report from Wells to Bradley indicates the way that this group was coming together to take ownership of this issue and insisting on a degree of autonomy and scientific integrity (PR 3.2.61). The report was a response to a decision of the CVO, Rees, to reject part of Wells' report. A key point of contention was the condition that all reference to scrapie be dropped (PR 3.2.61; see also 3.2.63). Although Wells had urged caution in the early stages of diagnosis, the confirmation from the NPU bolstered his belief that the connection was authoritative. The article by Wells finally came out at the end of October and made the issue more widely known (PR 3.2.119-3.2.121).

The CVL had one qualified epidemiologist, John Wilesmith. In May 1987, Watson, Director of CVL, invited Wilesmith to investigate the epidemiology of BSE (PR 3.3.3-5). Soon thereafter, Wilesmith rolled up his sleeves and started to visit farms and producers to carry out an epidemio-logical analysis of known cases. His study searched for "common factors" across the cases as a way of attributing possible causation. By process of elimination, he rejected both genetic and toxic factors. The only common factor, Wilesmith ascertained, was cattle feed and he suspected Meat and Bone Meal (MBM). His analysis was one of the great successes of this period and formed the basis for the introduction of the ruminant feed ban (RFB) later that spring. However, his analysis also contained two key errors: he argued that BSE was likely a form of scrapie that had crossed the species barrier and that this probably resulted from changes in the rendering process in the early 1980s (PR 2.3.32). Neither point has proven to be true, but these arguments formed the basis of a number of later decisions about how to proceed.

Wilesmith also surmised that the geographical incidence of the disease followed a pattern explained by a "common source." The common source theory was built on his view that the source was scrapie diffused through MBM. In hindsight, this turns out to be wrong and it is likely that the ori-gin was a genetic mutation in a single cow (a single source) that was then transmitted through recycling in MBM.[16] The CVO at the time chal-lenged Wilesmith's understanding of the common source theory, though without upsetting its status as the conventional wisdom (PR 2.3.39). The assumption led the CVL to overlook the infectiveness of subclinical ani-mals.

A major implication of the convergence of a relatively closed group of veterinary scientists around the scrapie theory was that they viewed this new disease as an animal health rather than a public health problem (PR 3.5.16; 3.5.29). Watson reported that at the time he considered BSE "the most serious problem in the livestock industry we were likely to encounter since foot and mouth disease in 1967" (PR 3.5.9). In a confidential note to Watson and Shreve in December 1986, Bradley pointed out that:

> If the disease turned out to be bovine scrapie it would have severe repercus-sions to the export trade and possibly also for humans if for example it was discovered that humans with spongiform encephalopathies had close associ-ation with the cattle. (YB 86\12.19\1.1)

Note that while pointing to potential health effects, Bradley does not envision a serious problem of human food safety. Wells reports that no one talked about the risk to human health (PR 3.5.11). The BSE Group "was concerned with the animal health risk posed by BSE and the com-mercial implications that this might have" (PR 3.5.12).[17]

From a public health point-of-view, it was possible to interpret the evi-dence of "bovine scrapie" in a more sinister light. If the origins were sheep scrapie, then the appearance of the disease in cattle represented cross-species transmission—something scrapie was not supposed to do. If scrapie could cross one species-barrier (sheep to cow), then why not another (cow to human)? This logic was apparent to at least Mr. Cruickshank in MAFF's Animal Health Division. But as the Phillips Report observes: "Not all shared Mr. Cruickshank's appreciation that the identification of scrapie as the origin of BSE carried adverse implications for human health. On the contrary, most found the scrapie theory reassuring" (PR 3.5.165).

Although superbly competent on animal health effects, the veterinary group within CVL appeared oblivious to human health implications of the disease. When questioned about links to the Department of Health (DH), Bradley and others pointed to the fact that they had assumed a routine channel to DH through Mr. John Bell, Senior Veterinary Officer at the State Veterinary Service. He was liaison to the Communicable Disease Surveillance Centre (CDSC). But "no one had informed Mr. Bell that BSE had potential implications for human health, so he did not, it seems, think to mention it on one of his routine visits to the CDSC at Colindale" (PR 3.5.139). This failure of routine communications illustrates how emergent institutions do not merely reflect preexisting institutional structure.

As the first sick cows appeared, state veterinary experts diagnosed the disease as bovine scrapie. Was this motivated bias? Early sense-making certainly led to a bias, but was it "motivated" bias? Without a doubt, the BSE group was deeply worried about impacts of a bovine scrapie on British industry, and this concern shaped their view of the importance of the new disease. But were they motivated to draw this conclusion by their solicitude for the British cattle industry? It is plausible that the vets' sense that the scrapie diagnosis could enhance their personal and institutional reputations might have clouded their judgment. Overall, however, a stronger case can be made that the scrapie diagnosis simply made sense of the emerging problem to state veterinarians. Subsequent control of information and failure to appreciate human health implications—rather than being evidence of science manipulated for political purposes—*followed* from this sense-making.

INSTITUTIONAL EMERGENCE, PHASE II:
INDEPENDENT ADVISORY GROUPS

As a consequence of the CVL's animal health focus, the Department of Health (DH) was not informed of the BSE situation until March 1988— nearly fifteen months after the CVL first became aware of the new disease

(PR 3.5.2-5).[18] When MAFF finally wrote to Sir Donald Acheson, the Chief Medical Officer (CMO), it was to request his advice on whether sick animals should be banned from human consumption (PR 3.5.60). Whereas the CVL had responded to BSE in light of their experience with scrapie, Acheson immediately responded in light of his experience with CJD (PR 3.5.63). Fear of media attention and "public concern" led Sir Donald to suggest that an expert committee be set up to provide advice on public health. The resulting advisory committee, the Southwood Working Party (SWP) would become the first of three independent advisory committees created to advise the government on BSE. Following the establishment of the BSE group within the CVL, these independent advisory committees were the most important institutions to emerge as problem-specific responses to BSE. Between 1988 and 1996, the government consulted these three advisory bodies on nearly every major decision regarding BSE.

The use of independent advisory committees to address concerns about human and animal health became a defining feature of the U.K.'s response to the BSE problem. These committees, however, exhibited a number of features that led them to further institutionalize the scrapie analogy and, consequently, to downplay the human health consequences of BSE. Their membership, assigned role, and in some ways basic structure reflected the initial judgment—based on early sense-making—that a scrapie-like disease did not seriously threaten human health. Without questioning the good faith and diligence with which these committees approached their task, their limited investigatory role and subtle dependence on agency resources prevented them from seeing the full picture. At the same time, their eminence and reputed independence reinforced the authoritative nature of their claims.

In response to the inquiry from MAFF, Sir Donald, the Chief Medical Officer, suggested that Sir Richard Southwood, an eminent professor of zoology at Oxford University, chair a joint MAFF-DH advisory committee. Sir Richard, in turn, suggested three other prominent scientists, none of whom were experts in TSEs, to serve on what would become known as the Southwood Working Party (SWP).[19] The secretariat included Mr. Wilesmith and Mr. Lawrence from MAFF and Dr. Hilary Pickles from the Department of Health (see Figure 6.3). The secretariat played a key role in providing information, which meant that much of the knowledge gained during the process of early sense-making was directly transmitted to the committee.

This process was repeated in two additional advisory committees. The Tyrell Committee was founded on the recommendation of the SWP that an expert committee be created to advise on BSE research priorities. After some discussion, MAFF, DH, and Sir Richard agreed to ask

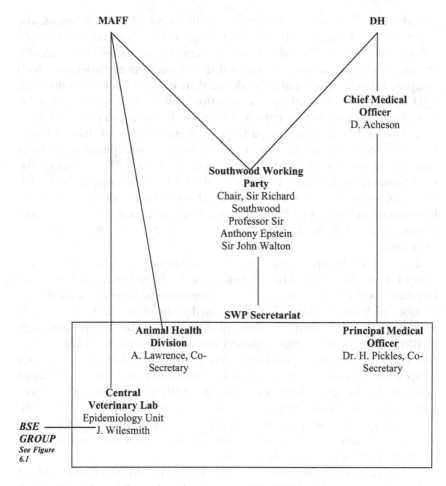

Figure 6.3.   The southwood working party, 1988-1989.

Dr. David Tyrrell, director of the Medical Research Council's (MRC) Common Cold Unit, to serve as the chair of the new committee on research into BSE. The other members of the Tyrrell Committee included Dr. Watson of the CVL, Professor John Bourne, Director of the Institute of Animal Health, Dr. Robert Will, a consultant neurologist from Western General Hospital in Edinburgh, and Dr. Kimberlin of the NPU. Dr. Pickles of DH and Mr. John Maslin from MAFF served on the secretariat.

Following the publication of the Tyrrell committee's interim report, MAFF and DH agreed to establish a standing advisory committee, the Spongiform Encephalopathy Advisory Committee (SEAC). In contrast to the SWP and the Tyrrell Committee, SEAC was not expected to produce regular written reports (although it did produce two), but rather to operate on an ad hoc basis. SEAC was given the wide remit "To advise the Ministry of Agriculture, Fisheries and Food and the Department of Health on matters relating to spongiform encephalopathies" (PR 11.4.11). For administrative simplicity, MAFF suggested reconstituting the Tyrell Committee as a standing body, and Dr. Tyrell was the first chairman of the committee. The members of the committee were largely the same as those on the Tyrrell committee, although the composition shifted over time as the new CMO, Dr. Calman, (who followed Sir Donald in 1991) added new members to further emphasize human health.[20] MAFF and DH were linked to SEAC as both observers and members of the secretariat, which initially included Bradley of the CVL and Pickles of DH with Pickles and Mr. Lowson from MAFF forming the secretariat (See Figure 6.4). Through continuity of personnel, SEAC was built upon the earlier institutional foundations of the CVL group (Watson and Bradley), on the SWP (Pickles), and the Tyrrell Committee.

Since the Tyrell Committee played a less central role and was essentially reconstituted as SEAC, we focus our analysis on the SWP and SEAC in the remainder of this section. In initially establishing the SWP as an expert committee, Sir Donald hoped that having an independent source of advice would support his stance on human health—a logic later followed by the Tyrell committee and SEAC. Sir Richard took his role of creating "independent" scientific advice extremely seriously, describing the group as "fiercely independent" (S 1:2; S 1: 21). Since the problem was still ill-defined, Sir Richard insisted on a broad remit and explicitly sought a committee of generalists (PR 4.1.12; S 1: 3).[21] The institutional qualities of the SWP included its claims of a distinctive character ("independence"), autonomy (a broad "remit"), and a certain kind of competence (eminence in science, generalist perspective). SEAC played a similarly independent role in advising government and it too was constituted by respected and independent scientists.[22]

Yet the institutionalization of both groups was rather narrowly-based. Both the SWP and SEAC involved a group of eminent generalists working on a voluntary basis who were asked to provide input in the form of scientific advice. Therefore, the groups' role was necessarily very circumscribed.[23] While the independence of the SWP and SEAC meant the government was often dependent on them for advice, their limited time and expertise in agricultural and TSE issues and their ad hoc nature meant that both groups were also critically dependent on MAFF and DH for information. Indeed, Sir Richard, head of the SWP, protected a more limited role for the group, rightfully seeing its role as not extending to any kind of administrative follow-up. Thus, the group was not, in

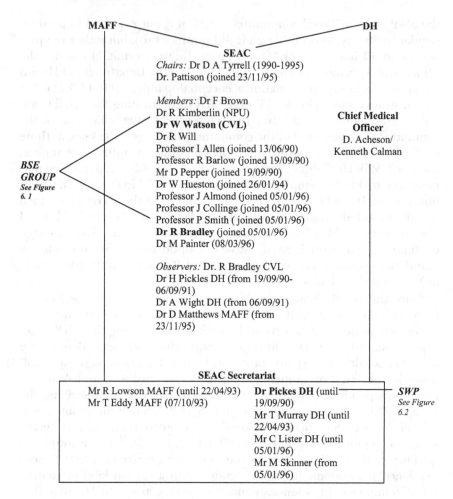

Figure 6.4.   SEAC, 1990-1996.

Selznick's terms, a "going concern." Although SEAC was a standing body, and over time it recognized its role as more directly linked to policy, it too saw itself as limited to evaluating scientific advice – not providing detailed policy evaluations or original research (PR 11.4.89-90).

These groups were also dependent on the secretariat to provide much of the necessary information, particularly on detailed issues such as the implementation of MAFF's control measures. Much of the information provided to the SWP and SEAC and its later utilization was therefore strongly linked to the interpretation of senior officials in MAFF and DH (PR 11.4.45). Both the SWP and SEAC were heavily linked to the early CVL groups through their secretariats (see above). More importantly, the secretariats also helped with the drafting of various group reports, and the minutes of SEAC's meetings were widely circulated to senior officials in MAFF and DH before being finalized. As a result, the role the advisory groups were supposed to play—to independently review the emerging evidence around BSE—was built on dependence on both information and interpretation provided by MAFF, and to a lesser extent DH.

Finally, and more subtly, another form of institutionalization occurred. While the SWP and later SEAC were given a wide remit, MAFF and DH agreed that they should be joint MAFF-DH working groups in order to alleviate fears about human health (PR 4.1.6).[24] This strategy subtly reinforced the limited attention given to human health concerns. As the departmental lead for DH during the SWP and much of the SEAC period, Pickles proved herself an energetic and forceful figure in pursuing the public health implications of BSE. Yet the decision to downplay public health concerns by making the SWP and SEAC joint MAFF-DH committees and external to government essentially institutionalized a very limited public health approach. Consequently, DH made only a limited investment in the project. For 1988-89, for example, only 5% of Pickles's time was projected for attention to BSE (S 115: 12).[25] In addition, although assigned as the departmental lead, Pickles's role was essentially subordinate to the advisory function of the committees. While she pursued information aggressively and kept other DH divisions notified in writing of key issues, there was little "institutional emergence" within DH more broadly. Thus the infrastructure built up around the SWP and SEAC represented *the* core institutional response to BSE as a public health problem.

At first glance, the structure of the advisory groups seems appropriate to address these broader theoretical issues. As groups of eminent scientists operating outside MAFF with a more general set of scientific expertise, the SWP and SEAC appeared well-suited to ask the "big picture" questions about BSE and offer a periodic critical review to the assumptions underpinning MAFF and DH's approach to BSE. In fact, the actual set up of the SWP and SEAC undercut its ability to play this role.

First, MAFF and DH's dependence on the SWP and SEAC to provide ongoing assessment of technical issues and to legitimate government decisions meant both groups were drawn into assessing many detailed issues of which it had little knowledge or expertise. The SWP, and to a much greater extent SEAC, were asked to comment on issues as diverse as the safety of milk, the transmission of BSE to cats, and proper head splitting practices—often receiving decontextualized information about the problem at hand, given little time to reflect, and having no real access to outside experts. As a result, both groups were poorly suited to address the detailed operational questions about the degree of risk BSE posed, but in acting as 'independent' advisory committees their advice carried significant weight and created a degree of complacency in MAFF and DH about the risks posed by BSE.

Second, the SWP and SEAC's dependence on MAFF and DH often undercut their ability to play their intended role of providing an audit of the evidence and thinking through its larger implications for the risks posed by BSE. Both groups, but in particular SEAC, were bombarded by a series of questions regarding operational issues. As a result, news of a growing body of evidence challenging the "scrapie theory" of BSE was received in a piecemeal way alongside more pressing questions on the 'day to day' BSE issues. This limited their ability to critically evaluate emerging evidence. In SEAC's case, its close involvement and dependence on MAFF eventually created a shared sense of purpose and value, and (like the CVL group) it began to identify strongly with the scrapie theory rather than provide a critical evaluative voice.

Third, the SWP and SEAC's very existence gave policymakers in MAFF and DH a false sense of reassurance around the risks of BSE. As an emerging problem, BSE required extreme vigilance to both the operational issues and the broader theoretical risk assessment. The independent advisory role of SWP and SEAC convinced MAFF and DH that their approach to BSE was correct. However, as stated above, both groups were poorly suited to evaluate the day to day issues and as a result did a poor job in examining the "big picture" questions, which meant that MAFF and DH's complacency was built on a weak foundation.

The inability of SWP and SEAC to fully play their intended role, while reinforcing the sense that they were, resulted in two key failures in addressing BSE as an emerging problem. First, SEAC—and MAFF and DH—failed to recognize the implications of a growing body of evidence challenging the scrapie theory of BSE. As a result, the recognition that BSE was not caused by scrapie and did not behave like scrapie—and therefore that BSE might pose a more serious risk to human health—did not come until 1996, despite emerging evidence to the contrary beginning in the early 1990s. Second, the SWP and SEAC's lack of clear understanding of the implementation of control measures often obscured differences in understanding of risk among SEAC, MAFF and DH, and led to a delayed recognition of the problems of implementation. We address each of these two failures in turn.

Evaluating the "Big Picture"—A Growing Resistance to Anomalous Evidence

Both the SWP and SEAC were asked to evaluate the core assumptions regarding BSE. The operation of both groups, however, tended to reinforce, rather than critically reevaluate, early sense-making around BSE.

Although one of the core tasks for the newly formed SWP was to examine the scrapie theory, the framework for the SWP's analysis was in large part set by the earlier process of sense-making. On May 19, 1988, prior to the first meeting of the SWP, Sir Richard, Sir Donald and Dr. Pickles met to devise a list of twenty questions about BSE and a further six questions about BSE and human health. These were then "answered" by MAFF and DH officials and circulated before the first meeting of the working group (PR 4.1.25). While the questions and answers flag uncertainty in the state of knowledge around human health, they also clearly define scrapie as the reference point for BSE and reiterate many of the early conclusions developed in the CVL.[26]

This framing did not mean the SWP was completely in agreement with CVL. In their first meeting, the SWP discussed concerns about the nature of the BSE agent and agreed that they should play it safe and assume BSE was more dangerous than scrapie (PR 4.2.2). This decision led them to make four interim recommendations that were sent to MAFF the following day: to establish a working party into research on BSE (the Tyrell Committee), to conduct experiments with scrapie in meal to test the hypothesis that scrapie was the source of BSE, to conduct epidemiological work on the offspring of BSE cows, and to make BSE a notifiable disease (and therefore subject to compulsory slaughter) (PR 4.2.4).

This early decision making is interesting in that it shows how the scrapie theory was both contested and yet the core of decision making. A statement by Dr. Pickles in a memo to the Health and Safety Executive is instructive in summing up the ethos of the SWP at this early stage: "although I think we all deep down believe there is no human risk, but with the present state of knowledge about these sorts of agents it will take years to prove it. And of course we might be wrong" (PR 4.3.5). The scrapie theory provided reassurance, but not necessarily complacency, and the SWP was willing to consider a range of measures and research programs aimed at ascertaining risk.

While the SWP went much further than the BSE group in the CVL in raising concerns about both the scrapie theory and the implications of BSE for public health, their final report essentially repeats the scrapie analogy and downplays much of the uncertainty around this issue. This occurred despite Sir Richard's recognition that this knowledge was uncertain:

> There was no, or virtually no scientific knowledge concerning BSE available at this time. We worked on the basis that scrapie was the most likely cause of the BSE epidemic; we had to base our advice on the science relating to scrapie at that time. (PR 4.10.27)

Moreover, the report fails to deal with a number of key issues--most importantly, the safety of subclinical animals entering the human food chain and the safety of feeding ruminant protein to non-ruminants (e.g. pig and poultry).

The failure to communicate uncertainty is symptomatic of the way the SWP related to its sponsoring institutions. First, the report reflects the direct influence of MAFF and the CVL. Wilesmith had played a critical role in the early process of sense-making in the CVL, and his analysis as a member of the SWP secretariat formed a large core of the report itself. Indeed, his early epidemiological analysis is essentially repeated in the SWP report. While several members of the SWP expressed concern about components of Wilesmith's analysis, they did not feel in a position to dissent and did not subject the analysis to a full peer review (PR 4.9.8; PR 4.10.98). Here is where the self-limiting role of the Working Party is probably at work: the role of these eminent scientists was to probe the science, but their responsibility did not extend to collecting or reanalyzing basic data. In addition, the CVL kept this information closely guarded. The original sense-making was therefore reproduced under the auspices of an independent review, adding to the authoritative basis of these ideas.

Second, both MAFF and DH were facing multiple problems with respect to animal and public health. Although concerned about the risk of bovine products to human medicines, DH had to balance this with concern about an erosion of public confidence in the safety of medicines. Pickles communicated to Sir Richard that reasonable action would be taken with respect to medicines, and he was convinced to describe this risk as 'remote' in the final report. This codified a risk assessment based in part on assurances of action, but in failing to specify these actions the statement on risk implied that there was very little risk to medicines. MAFF also exerted influence on Sir Richard to ensure that particularly damaging statements were not included. In an initial draft of the report, the SWP raised the question of whether any animal protein should be fed to herbivores, in effect, questioning the practices of the entire rendering industry.[27] While Sir Richard resisted further drafting assistance from MAFF, the statement was not present in the final report.

Millstone and van Zwanenberg (2001) suggest that this influence demonstrates the use of the SWP by MAFF and DH as a 'political resource' or tool. Certainly MAFF and DH used the SWP to legitimate their decisions, but the failure here cannot be narrowly attributed to political manipulation. Both DH and MAFF had reasonable concerns regarding the SWP publication. DH had to balance a theoretical health risk in medicinal products using bovine material with a real risk of a decline of public confidence in medicines. Equally, MAFF had to balance a risk of BSE contaminating pig and poultry feed with the immediate economic and practical consequences of ending the practice of rendering animal protein. These trade-offs were communicated to Sir Richard and the SWP informally, but the logic of this communication was not repeated in the final report. This meant that the formal assurances of the safety of medicines (and the silence on the issue of animal feed) were divorced from the reassurances that sustained them. This failure to fully evaluate MAFF and DH's assumptions and communicate uncertainty around them became more pronounced, and ultimately more damaging, under SEAC. Indeed with SEAC, this process took on a life of its own, as the group looked to protect this early approach rather than evaluate it.

In a press article written only months before the government's announcement of a link between BSE and vCJD, the Chief Medical Officer, Dr. Kenneth Calman, wrote that there was no evidence that beef was unsafe to humans. Sir Kenneth cites the Southwood Working Party report to suggest that beef is safe, given that BSE is similar to scrapie and that the control measures in place have removed any infective parts of the cow (YB 95\12.11\22.1). This action is instructive, as even as those who had worked around the SWP, such as Sir Donald, had by 1995 begun to raise concerns about the validity of these early assumptions, while those in MAFF, DH, and SEAC continued to repeat many of the early CVL and SWP conclusions even as the evidence that supported these came under fire.[28] Table 6.1 demonstrates the tenacity of these assumptions over time, despite the growing uncertainty around them.

Publications between 1989 and 1994 tended to repeat reassurances about the safety of beef and the low risk of BSE to humans based on two factors—that BSE is likely to behave like scrapie and that control measures are effective. While these conclusions were reasonable given what was known about BSE in the early phases, anomalous evidence emerged at quite an early stage. At the first meeting of SEAC, in 1990, the committee discussed evidence that unlike scrapie, BSE appeared to have only a single strain (PR 11.4 Annex). They also discussed experiments conducted by the NPU that demonstrated that the BSE had been transmitted to sheep resistant to scrapie. These experiments showed that so-called "negative-line sheep" had become infected through orally dosed material (PR 6.5.267). Moreover, the evidence began to accumulate in the early 1990s that BSE had a broader host-range than scrapie (i.e., it had spread to more animals), with a number of zoo animals and domestic cats developing clinical symptoms of BSE. This latter development was also dis-

Table 6.1.   Published Conclusions about BSE and its Risks from Expert Advisory Committees[i]

	Southwood Working Party Report (2/1989)	SEAC's letter to Sir Donald Acheson (7/1990)	SEAC's Interim Report on Research (4/ 1992)	SEAC's Second Interim Report on Research (7/95)
Cause of the disease	BSE is likely from a common source (9), increased exposure to scrapie agent due to changes in sheep population and rendering likely caused BSE (11)	Origin "appears to be scrapie affected feedstuffs" (Page 1, 2)	Scrapie "most likely initial source" (3); changes in the rendering process seem to explain the timing of the emergence of BSE	The outbreak probably began because the scrapie agent not well inactivated (35)
Incidence and future course	Disease will continue at the constant rate of 300-400 per month until 1993, assuming no lateral/vertical transmission (15)	Not mentioned	Shows data on the rising number of infections; future course not mentioned (4)	Evidence suggests RFB having an effect; BABs arising from feed in the "pipeline" (40). However important to watch developments to ensure it is not endemic.
Transmission of BSE to cattle	Evidence points to MBM as the 'vehicle of infection' (10)	Not mentioned	MBM likely the cause of the spread (3)	Likely a common source spread through MBM (37)
Similarity of BSE to scrapie	Compared to scrapie—including similarity in pathological changes to the brain (6) and transmission to mice (8)	Appears to be clinically similar to scrapie and likely originated from scrapie (1, 2)	Compared to scrapie; although the report suggests differences[ii]	Extensive discussion of how scrapie operates and the way the PrPs work with scrapie (chapter 1)
Transmission among cows (vertical and lateral)	Uncertain;. studies on maternal transmission are underway; cattle are likely to be dead-end hosts (23)	Not mentioned	Uncertain; no evidence from maternal transmission study that it can occur (12)	Uncertain, may be that cattle are dead-end hosts
Effective Dose for transmission	Not mentioned	Large doses are "undoubtedly" necessarily to transmit to orally[iii]	Not mentioned	Depends on "effective exposure" (infectivity and amount); knowledge on this is emerging (62)

Table continues on next page

Table 6.1.   Published Conclusions about BSE and its Risks from Expert Advisory Committees

	Southwood Working Party Report (2/1989)	SEAC's letter to Sir Donald Acheson (7/1990)	SEAC's Interim Report on Research (4/1992)	SEAC's Second Interim Report on Research (7/95)
Transmission across species	Uncertain; unlikely to spread to non-mammals; unlikely to spread to pets; monitoring is underway (13)	Does not directly mention; does allow for the possibility	Yes; lists range of experiments proving this (9)	Yes; extensive discussion of factors (in donors and recipients) that shape this
Risk to human health	Remote; perinatal transmission is the most effective, and this is unlikely; action to prevent oral transmission should be taken[iv]	Parallel to scrapie suggests oral transmission likely to be unproblematic; control measures further reduce risks (2, 6)	No evidence of an association between animal and human disorders (3)	No evidence of link to humans (74); following SWP they find risk "remote" in part because of the precautionary measures
Safety of Beef	Does not recommend any actions; presumed to be safe	Risk is "minute" (1.2) Will be present in offal, but only in such low levels as to be undetectable in meat	Safe; Committee is satisfied the necessary safeguards are in place to prevent any risk (p.15)	See above; do not recommend any further precautions

i.   The published reports reviewed here are not entirely equivalent statements: the SWP report is focused on evaluating the risks of BSE to human health (PR IBD 1, 2). SEAC letter to Sir Donald Acheson is a statement of SEAC's assessment of the risks relating to beef consumption (it does not constitute a full analysis of risks) but was made public (PR YB 7.24.3.1-3.12). The 1992 SEAC report is focused on highlighting research priorities and evaluating progress since the Tyrrell Committee's first interim report (IBD 2, 13), and finally, the 1995 report constitutes a more comprehensive assessment of the state of knowledge around BSE (PR IBD 2, 21). Despite the differences in intent, length, and audience, we have selected these statements for examination because they are published statements of SWP/SEAC's assessment of risk, and therefore document the understanding of the groups at a given point in time.

ii.   The report suggests that unlike scrapie, there is a single strain of BSE and the incubation period with mice is shorter

iii.   The definition of dose was matter of some misunderstanding; with the Committee reporting to the inquiry they were using a medical understanding of dose that implies the infectivity as well as the amount of the agent (PR 11.4.138).

iv.   The report recommends the destruction of milk from BSE cows; food containing offal is already regulated, thus further action on this is not necessary; they recommend against using SBO in baby food (16).

cussed in MAFF and SEAC. Despite these developments, SEAC's 1992 report makes little mention of the NPU experiments and states "As scrapie is the most common and geographically widespread SE, the scrapie agent is thought to be the most likely initial source of BSE infection" (PR 11.4.708). Table 6.1 demonstrates that scrapie remained the core reference point in 1995 as both *cause* of and *analogy* for BSE.

This resistance to anomalous evidence is explained, in part, by the way early assumptions were institutionalized in the relations between MAFF, DH and SEAC. First, MAFF and DH relied on SEAC as "independent advisors." In February 1992, for instance, the Medical Research Council (MRC) informed MAFF they had experimentally transmitted BSE and scrapie to a marmoset through inoculation (PR 6.5.327). This finding was significant because this was the first instance of transmission to a primate; however, given both scrapie and BSE had been transmitted, it was unclear what the evidence suggested in terms of risk to humans. The dynamic between SEAC, MAFF, and DH is interesting. MAFF did not see the transmission to the marmoset as a matter for concern, but saw independent advice as desirable for purposes of communication to the public and media.[29] SEAC was called in at short notice to discuss the issue, and when they agreed that no further control actions were necessary in light of this issue, the matter was closed.

However, rather than having the chance to review the broader implications of evidence, SEAC was asked to give rapid opinion on a discrete piece of evidence presented in terms shaped by MAFF's own position. As a result, the use of SEAC to solve discrete problems undercut its ability to pursue its role in examining the broader implications of emerging evidence about BSE.[30] Yet SEAC's apparent independence reinforced MAFF and DH's own confidence about the low human health risks of BSE.

Resistance to anomalous evidence also rested on a deeper form of institutionalization, in which SEAC, MAFF and DH increasingly invested their own understanding of BSE with value. The treatment of dissident scientists Professor Lacey and Dr. Dealler is instructive here. Professor Lacey was an outspoken critic of much of the government's policy, who in both public interviews and published material strongly critiqued the government's approach to public health. Both Lacey and Dealler contacted the government at numerous points to raise these concerns. While Professor Lacey's style was often exaggerated, in retrospect he was correct on a number of issues, in particular his critique of the scrapie theory. While MAFF officials did meet with them, MAFF's response demonstrated incredulity bordering on annoyance and focused on rebutting their arguments. This pattern was repeated in SEAC's dealings with Professor Lacey.[31]

While MAFF and SEAC's hostility toward Lacey was fueled in part by his inflammatory style, Lacey was also viewed as a threat in part because he quite publicly disputed the conclusions of the government and SEAC. The way SEAC and MAFF responded similarly to Professor Lacey illustrates a developing relationship between these groups. Behind these statements is a sense of "us against them," with the "us" including both MAFF and SEAC. Thus the independent advisors had become part of a broader institutional structure, which connected SEAC and MAFF not only through information flows but also through a shared sense of ownership of the BSE problem.

The failure of both the SWP and SEAC, to critically reevaluate the early sense-making process and to communicate uncertainty where it emerged, was particularly damaging because the seeming independence of their advice gave further authority to these incorrect assumptions. As MAFF's Minster for Food Safety, David Maclean testified: "I regarded Southwood as our bible ... we had the *Southwood* Report. There was no better or more learned scientific body" (PR 4.11.7). Similar thoughts were expressed about SEAC. Mr. Lowson, the MAFF member of the SEAC secretariat, recalled the Secretary of State, Mr. Gummer, often saying "We ask SEAC what we should do and then we do it" (T 127, 87).

Implementation—Inadequate Knowledge on the Details

While the SWP and SEAC were limited in their ability to critically evaluate the "big picture," they were also limited in their ability to examine more mundane details of implementation and control of BSE on the ground. The SWP failed to approach one of the most critical issues around the spread of BSE—subclinical animals—because of a lack of knowledge about implementation. SEAC did approach issues of implementation but in a partial and often unclear manner.

One of the first things the SWP did was to suggest that animals displaying the clinical symptoms of BSE should not be allowed to enter the human food chain. However, this decision left open the question of what should be done with subclinical animals. The SWP was aware that subclinical animals were entering the food chain and that certain parts of these animals (the spleen, brain, and other lymphoid tissues) were likely to contain some infective material.[32] However, in neither their meetings nor the final report is there a sustained analysis of the safety of meat from subclinical animals.

This stands in contrast to the actions of MAFF. Shortly after the publication of the report, MAFF took the initiative to ban certain offal from human consumption. The specified bovine offal (SBO) ban followed from new information provided to MAFF from the Pedigree pet food company and concerns about how to implement the SWP's recommendation on baby food. Given that the SWP raised questions about subclinical animals, the Phillips Inquiry asks why the SWP did not arrive at this solution themselves. Again, the answer lies in part in the early approaches to the problem. Sir Richard reported that they were uncertain at the time how to deal with the issue of subclinical animals, which potentially included all animals going to slaughter. Sir Richard recalls Sir Anthony saying "What can we do about this? But it is the whole British cattle herd" (PR 4.10.69). In restricting their scope to the scientific aspects of BSE, the SWP had little sense of how the implementation of MAFF policy operated. This division of responsibility exposed subtle differences in understanding risk. The SWP was concerned about subclinical animals but did not pursue it because they saw no practical way to do so, while MAFF (which had knowledge on how to pursue this) did not raise these options because they did not see it as an issue. There is no evidence of MAFF consciously withholding this information; rather, MAFF simply did not think to raise it because it did not (until later) see this as a matter of concern. Behind the reassurances that beef was safe lay different conceptions of what this meant. If Dr. Kimberlin (who was advising the Pedigree company) had not raised this issue, it is likely these differences would have led to a significant delay in halting sick animals from entering the human food chain.

SEAC's evaluation of risk also displayed a diverging understanding of control from MAFF. SEAC's 1995 Report continues to present the regulation on using recycled cow carcasses in cattle feed—the Ruminant Feed Ban (RFB)—as a successful control measure, and plays down concern about the implications of sick cows born after the RFB (BABs). BABs were a concern, because MAFF assumed the RFB would effectively halt the spread of BSE in cattle. Initially, MAFF explained BABs as stemming from a holdover of feed containing ruminant protein produced before the ban, and predicted the number would rapidly fall. Despite growing epidemiological evidence to the contrary and a discussion of BABs at nine of the twenty-eight SEAC meetings between 1990 and 1996, SEAC failed to appreciate the problem of cross-contamination and weak enforcement of the RFB until late 1994 (PR 11.4.354).

Part of the reason that SEAC failed to question much of the evidence around BABs and improper implementation of the RFB was that the common language emphasizing a low risk of BSE to humans and the adequacy of existing controls masked differences in SEAC, DH, and MAFF's understanding of implementation.[33] SEAC's reassurances on the safety of beef were increasingly premised on incorrect views about proper implementation, which MAFF did not correct in part because they saw the risks to meat as minor. Because SEAC was outside of MAFF and did not have the capacity or the will to fully monitor MAFF's implementation, it had no independent means to assess operational issues around implementation. The differences between MAFF and SEAC's views only began to be fully analyzed in mid-1994 when concerns in MAFF began to emerge (PR 1.5. 462).

CONCLUSION

In this paper, we have analyzed the U.K.'s response to the problem of BSE as it emerged between 1986 and 1996. Our theoretical lens has been "emergent institutionalism." We argue that to understand how a government responds to an emerging problem, it is necessary to analyze how incipient institutions crystallize around interpretations of problems. In the BSE case, we describe the development of the BSE group in the CVL, followed by the creation of three advisory committees—the SWP, the Tyrrell Committee, and SEAC. These emergent institutions mobilized a particular configuration of people, knowledge, and resources to respond to BSE, which in turn developed a powerful interpretation of BSE (the scrapie theory); this interpretation then became the basis for subsequent institutional mobilization that eventually reinforced early sense-making.

One of the most important implications of our argument is that problem definition and institutional formation are mutually constitutive. It is natural to think of the relationship between problems and institutions in serial terms, with problems defined by preexisting institutions or, conversely, with institutions created to solve predefined problems. Building on Weick and Selznick, we argue that emerging communities create gestalt-like interpretations of problems—sense-making—that become the basis for a directed sense of institutional purpose. These institutions, in turn, can reinforce this very interpretation of the problem. We have argued that the major problem of the U.K.'s response to the BSE epidemic was an early institutionalization of an interpretation of BSE as primarily an animal health problem. This interpretation was supported by sense-making that emphasized the analogy between BSE and scrapie. The scrapie analogy was first institutionalized in the CVL and inherited by the advisory committees. It encouraged these groups to downplay the human health risks of BSE and proved resistant to revision as anomalous information accumulated.

Ideally, emerging institutions reflect nuanced and flexible responses to the details of emerging problems and mirror the ecology of the problem itself. Yet the emerging institutions may also be inappropriate or incomplete. Strong institutions, in particular, can be both a blessing and a curse. In strong institutions, participants develop a sense of personal and collective responsibility for solving problems as they understand them. Thus, the CVL group aggressively and conscientiously attacked BSE as an animal health problem. But strong institutions can also create what organization theorists call "competency traps." The CVL's response also inadvertently marginalized a more robust response to human health concerns.

Motivated bias and conflict-of-interest may be rife in government, but our concern is that these narratives gloss over the details of success and failure in crisis response. By contrast, emergent institutionalism acknowledges the ambiguous mix of independence and dependence and assertiveness and resistance that characterizes government response to uncertain problems.

ACKNOWLEDGMENTS

We thank participants of UC Berkeley's Organization Behavior Seminar, the International Public Management Network Workshop on Communicable Crises, and the Lucca Institute of Management and Technology for constructive feedback. Special thanks to Arjen Boin, Todd LaPorte, and John Padgett.

NOTES

1. By 2005, 150 U.K. citizens had died from vCJD. See the U.K. Creutzfeldt-Jakob Disease Surveillance Unit, http://www.cjd.ed.ac.uk/
2. Motivated bias is a term used by decision researchers to describe how the motivation to reach a certain conclusion biases decisionmaking judgment (Boiney, Kennedy, & Nye 1997).
3. With respect to BSE, our argument is thus closer to what Seguin (2001) calls a "selective perception" argument.
4. We acknowledge that it may be difficult in practice to distinguish between preexisting versus emergent institutional context. We stress the importance of the emergent institutional context to draw attention to the dynamic relationship between sensemaking, institutionalization, and emergent problems.
5. Rothstein (2003) suggests that "MAFF's adherence to the belief, during the late 1980s and early 1990s, that BSE was not transmissible to humans could be described as a groupthink problem, in so far as officials paid insufficient attention to accumulating contrary evidence that had less palatable implications" (p. 98).
6. We will cite materials from the BSE Inquiry as follows: PR, short for Phillips Report, refers to the 16 volumes of the BSE Inquiry, which is followed by the volume number, chapter number, and the section number within the chapter (this is more precise than page number). S refers to written wit-

ness statements. For example, S65 is the written witness statement of Dr. Wells. Witnesses responded to a specific set of questions from the BSE Inquiry, so the reference also includes an item number that refers to the specific response. T signifies the transcripts of oral hearings. T3, for instance, is the transcript of the oral examination of the members of the Southwood Working Party. It is followed by a page number that refers to a page in the written transcript of the hearings. Finally YB refers to Yearbook, a chronological compilation of relevant documents. All of these materials are available at the website of the BSE Inquiry: http://www .bseinquiry.gov.uk/index.htm

7. Initial steps toward a "scrapie theory of BSE" were the early diagnosis (June 1986), by Dr. Martin Jeffrey, of a form of "bovine scrapie" in a nyala (a cattle-like zoo animal). As Mr. Jeffrey reported in his testimony: "In the nyala brain which I examined, the similarity of the lesions to natural scrapie was striking" (S64: 9). Jeffrey discussed this case with his boss at CVL, Gerald Wells (S64:10) and Dr. Bradley notes that he would have also become routinely aware of the case (S71: 9). In mid-December 1986, Dr. Jeffrey was involved in diagnosing another case of a "scrapie-like spongiform encephalopathy in a cow"—one of the cases reported by Wells to Bradley (Jeffrey S64: 13).

8. Wells, for example, points out that Carol Richardson, another pathologists in the unit, had earlier examined a cow described as having "moderate spongiform encephalopathy." In hindsight, Wells interpreted this as "inconclusive" (Wells S65: 14).

9. June 9, 1987 minute from Mr. Watson titled "Bovine Spongiform Encephalopathy" (YB 87\06.09\1.1-1.3)

10. See PR 3.2.90 and 3.2.91; see also 3.2.40, 3.2.93 and 3.2.95 on export concern. As Dr. Jeffrey reports, his reference to a "scrapie-like" disease in his write up of the nyala case delayed publication until September 1988 (S64: 12). Mr. Rees comments that: "in a broad sense we all had the same attitude to publications at this time i.e. that if the CVL were not happy that there was sufficient information, then premature publication could cause unjustified damage to the industry" (PR 3.2.168).

11. The veterinary investigation officers were important because they were the first line of surveillance in the animal health system. The closed-door presentation to Medical and Veterinary Research Clubs was the first opening to researchers concerned about human, as opposed to animal, health. For example, Dr. Ridley of the Medical Research Council was present (S65: 28).

12. There was also communication between officials in England/Wales and Northern Ireland (PR 3.2.55).

13. The head of the NPU, Dr. Alan Dickinson, also became aware of this news around this time (PR 3.2.23).

14. The Philip's Report criticizes the slowness of CVL to involve the NPU, the U.K.'s leading research center on TSEs (PR 3.2.140). It suggests that CVL either wanted to keep control over the issue for its own prestige or to monopolize referrals of the disease to themselves (PR 3.2.144; 3.2.162). Whether this was because they wanted the glory or wanted to control the spin is not clear, though the Phillips report concludes it is the second (3.2.164-6).

15. Mr. Todd, a veterinarian at the Bristol VIC, wrote to Mr. Bradley about the rejection of a draft article: "Here is a golden opportunity for the Veterinary Investigation Service and CVL to demonstrate to the world that we are performing a function of identifying and investigating new conditions in farm livestock. It would be a great pity if we did not receive the recognition. It would be worse if another groups appeared to be successfully carrying out our functions" (PR 3.2.70).

16. Epidemiological simulation studies now suggest that the disease might have originated as early as 1970. Thus, the cases of the mid-1980's came from a later wave of infection. This is supported by anecdotal evidence from vets who report earlier cases with characteristic symptoms (PR 2.3.46).

17. In discussing risk of cross-contamination in 1988, Mr. Kevin Taylor points out that "the problem was viewed as an animal health problem, not a public health problem" (PR 3.4.141).

18. The Report concludes that: "We believe that Dr Watson, Mr. Rees and Mr. Cruickshank all considered BSE to be MAFF's problem to be resolved by MAFF without the need for outside assistance—or interference—from DH" (PR 3.5.153).

19. These included Professor Epstein (a virologist), Sir John Walton (a neurologist), and Dr. William Martin (a veterinarian).

20. There is one exception—John Bourne (Director of the Animal Health Institute) who was on the Tyrell Committee was not asked to join SEAC.

21. The SWP made a point, in testimony, of saying that they were not "experts" in the sense of specialists in TSE, BSE, or scrapie (T 3: pp.16-20).

22. Between the 5th of January 1990 and the 20th of March 1996, SEAC conducted 28 formal meetings and many informal contacts with MAFF and DH, becoming a central part of the machinery of decision-making around BSE that was respected for its independent role (PR 11.4. Annex).

23. Jasanoff (1997) points out that this reliance on "eminence" to create legitimacy is commonly used in the UK and she provides a broader critique than we do here.

24. "To consider the cause, nature and means of spread of the outbreak of Bovine Spongiform Encephalopathy including its potential implications (if any) for human health and to make recommendations" (YB88/3.23/6.4, cited in PR 4.1.6).

25. Though retrospectively, she reports having used 15% of her time.

26. The first six questions refer to the state of knowledge about scrapie, and the answers to the following 16 questions draw heavily on the scrapie analogy and scrapie theory of origin with over half the questions directly referring to scrapie as a comparative point (PR 4 Annex). Sir Richard also consulted Dr. Hope and Dr. Kimberlin of the NPU, who in large part confirmed the scrapie analogy (PR 4.4.2).

27. Mr. Lawrence apparently "went white" when reading this statement, and MAFF decided to lay out its concerns in a document to the SWP (PR 4.9.24). The practice of rendering animal waste into animal feed provided a major source of waste disposal in the U.K., and the issue of banning animal protein in non-ruminant feed had not been seriously considered

[indeed it was not seriously considered until a pig was experimentally infected with BSE (PR 11.4.310)]. MAFF officials felt that raising questions about this practice would create a major waste disposal problem. In order to communicate this point to Sir Richard, MAFF officials drafted a note estimating the costs and practical difficulties of eliminating this practice (PR 4. 9.25).

28.   In a letter written to Professor Pattison (Chair of SEAC) and copied to Dr. Calman, dated January 22 1996, Sir Donald states:

> "The principal point I want to make is subsequent events have shown that the assumption made in the summary of the South-wood report in 1989 ... that the BSE epidemic is due to the presence of the scrapie agent in meat and bone meal fed to cattle is now less secure than it was then "

thus calling into question reassurances about the safety of beef. (YB 96\01.22\1.1-1.4)

29.   Mr. Lowson in MAFF informed Mr. Gummer that the results were "not particularly surprising and has no implication for human or animal health" but that it was advisable to ask for SEAC advice (PR 6.5.328). The reaction in DH was similar, with more concerns raised about the media/public reaction to the findings than their implications for human health. An informal meeting with SEAC was held on February 27, where Mr. Ridley of the MRC and Mr. Wells described the findings (YB 92\02.27\2.1-2.5). The Committee largely agreed that this did not pose much concern, but raised some issues for future consideration. SEAC's advice was then seen as reassuring that no further action was needed, with Dr. Calman stating :

> We relied very heavily on independent experts' advice to look at the data, give us their views from which we could help Ministers take things forward. They did look at that and concluded that no further action was required at the time (PR 6.5.249).

30.   Given its role in coordinating research and providing scientific advice, much of this work fit within its original remit. However, MAFF and DH also relied on SEAC to a far greater degree than earlier imagined. Members of SEAC reported the task was more time consuming than they originally imagined, with many stating that both the number of meetings and the amount of background reading exceeded their initial expectations (PR 11.4.65-75). Moreover, SEAC was asked to provide advice on areas it was originally not deemed qualified to work on. For instance, in 1990 MAFF began to receive word that Environmental Health Officers (EHOs) were concerned about the practice of head splitting and the removal of the brain from cattle in slaughterhouses. Initially MAFF consulted Mr. Johnston at the Royal College of Veterinary Surgeons to conduct a study because they felt Dr. Tyrrell and SEAC were not qualified to comment on these issues (PR 11.4.248). As concerns continued to be raised though, MAFF turned to SEAC in June of 1990, asking them to advise on slaughterhouse practices. This initiated a pattern where nearly all issues relating

to public health, animal health, research, and increasingly public opinion, were sent through SEAC. SEAC became a hub for not only scientific advice but policy advice, and little action by MAFF or DH was taken without consulting SEAC.

31.   For instance, in an internal memo regarding a new publication by Professor Lacey written in 1993, Mr. Wilesmith stated:

> I feel that we have two basic options for dealing with this tendentious individual who has failed to apply any scientific scholarship to his so-called critique of BSE. The first is to ignore him and hope that he will keep digging his own grave. The second is to launch an all out attack at every opportunity particularly with respect to his published musings. (PR 11.5.72)

Shortly after this, SEAC met with Professor Lacey. The outcome of the meeting was disappointing to both parties, and Dr. Tyrrell reported in a letter to Mr. Bradley:

> On the whole I regard this as an experiment to give an opportunity to a senior academic to return to a normal type of scientific interchange. It has failed, but we did express genuine goodwill and reasonableness and were unambiguously rebuffed. I don't think we should waste any more time or energy on the matter. I certainly don't wish to bother with any more letters. We may well have to expect more substandard behaviour in the future, and I suggest we just ignore it all. (PR 11.5.97).

32.   For instance, there were several discussions during SWP meetings about whether ox-brain should be labeled and repeated discussion of whether the use of offal in baby food should be permitted (PR 4.5.11; 4.7.2). Both the discussion of ox-brain and baby food demonstrate the SWP was aware of food safety issues around subclinical animals and that certain parts of the cow carried more risk that others.

33.   The most glaring of example of this was the miscommunication between MAFF and SEAC on the issue of mechanically recovered meat (MRM). MRM is meat that is recovered through the application of high pressure techniques on the bone, and is used to make burgers and sausages. Part of this meat is recovered from the spinal cord of the cow, an area included in the SBO ban. However, from the beginning of the SBO ban, concerns were raised by EHOs regarding contamination of meat in the process of removing spinal tissue. MAFF sent the question of MRM to SEAC in 1990 with a background document explaining the issue. This document flagged the issue of cross contamination of the spinal cord with the carcass, and raised a series of questions for research; however, it did not clearly spell out the policy options or clearly demonstrate MAFF's knowledge that some cross-contamination was almost inevitable. While considering this paper, SEAC visited two slaughterhouses, where they were shown the successful removal of the spinal cord. SEAC concluded that *if* the rules were followed, there was no need for new regulations on the issue. This advice was sent to

MAFF senior officials and Ministers, in a note by Mr. Lowson, and no action was taken on MRM until 1994. MAFF knew that some of the spinal tissue would be present in MRM, but did not see this as a problem in part because they saw SEAC's reassurances as confirming their own sense that small amounts of cross-contamination were not problematic. By contrast, SEAC was operating under the assumption that no further action was needed because the spinal tissue could be fully removed, thus existing regulation was adequate. SEAC and MAFF were operating on different assumptions about implementation, which was masked in part because of the common language of risk and SEAC's seeming independence on these issues.

REFERENCES

Bartlett, D. (1999). Mad cows and democratic governance: BSE and the construction of a "Free Market" in the UK. *Crime, Law and Social Change, 30*(3), 237-57.

Beck, M., Asenova D.., & Dickson, G. (2005). Public administration, science, and risk assessment: A case study of the U.K. Bovine Spongiform Encephalopathy crisis. *Public Administration Review, 65*(4), 396-408.

Boiney, L, Kennedy, J., & Nye, P. (1997). Instrumental bias in motivated reasoning: More when more is needed. *Organizational Behavior and Human Decision Process, 72*(1), 1-24.

Berger, P. L., & Luckman, T. (1996). *The social construction of reality: A treatise in the sociology of knowledge.* Garden City, NY: Anchor Books.

Christopher, A. (2006). *Network institutionalism.* In S. Binder, R. Rhodes, & B. Rockman (Eds.), *Oxford handbook of political institutions* (pp. 75-89). England. Oxford University Press.

Forbes, I. (2004). Making a crisis out of a drama: The political analysis of BSE policy-making in the UK. *Political Studies, 52*, 342-57.

Gerodimos, R. (2004). The UK BSE crisis as a failure of government. *Public Administration, 82*(4), 911-29.

Jasanoff, S. (1997). Civilization and madness: The great BSE scare of 1996. *Public Understanding of Science, 6*, 221-232.

Miller, D. (1999). Risk, science and policy: Defintional struggles, information management, the media and BSE. *Social Science & Medicine, 49*, 1239-1255.

Millstone, E., & van Zwanenberg, P. (2001). Politics of expert advice: Lessons from the early history of the BSE saga. *Science and Public Policy, 28*(2), 98-112.

Rothstein, Henry F. (2003). Neglected risk regulation: The institutional attentuation phenomenon. *Health, Risk and Society. 5*(1), 85-103.

Seguin, E. (2000). The UK BSE Crisis: Strengths and Weaknesses of Existing Conceptual Approaches. *Science and Public Policy, 27*(4), 293-301.

Selznick, P. (1957). *Leadership in administration.* New York: Harper & Row.

T'Hart, P. 1990. *Groupthink in government: A study of small groups and policy failure.* Baltimore: John Hopkins University Press.

Thomas, C. (1993). Reorganizing public organizations: Alternatives, objectives, and evidence. *Journal of Public Administration Research and Theory, 3*(4), 457-486.

Vaughan, D. (1996). *The Challenger launch decision: Risky technology, culture, and deviance at NASA.* Chicago: University of Chicago Press.

Weick, K. (1993). The collapse of sensemaking in organizations: The Mann Gulch disaster. *Administrative Science Quarterly, 38*(4), 628-652.

Weick, K. (1995). *Sensemaking in organizations.* Thousand Oaks, CA: Sage.

Winter, M. (1996). Intersecting departmental responsibilities, Administrative con

Van Zwanenberg, P., & Millstone, E. (2003). BSE: A paradigm of policy failure. *Political Quarterly, 74*(1), 27-37.

CHAPTER 7

MAXIMIZING THE IMPACT OF DISASTER RESPONSE BY NONPROFIT ORGANIZATIONS AND VOLUNTEERS

Deborah E. Gibbons

Nonprofit organizations provide stable assistance during crises by supporting disaster preparation, coordinating on-site response, and remaining until recovery is complete. Interventions from nonprofit organizations may be particularly crucial when government agencies cannot respond to individual needs, during periods of confusion or intermittent formal support, and through the ongoing recovery period following emergency interventions. Throughout the process, nonprofit organizations and volunteers play key roles in mitigating effects of the initial disaster and preventing subsequent crises. How can government planners, community leaders, and nonprofit organizations best organize to support the activities of unpaid volunteers and voluntary organizations? Although the optimal form of a response network depends on the circumstances, we can identify attributes of disaster response systems that are likely to increase effectiveness. This chapter uses interviews with coordinators, responders and people affected by disasters to explore roles of system design, leadership, and planning as they influence effective and efficient interventions by nonprofit organizations in large-scale disasters.

Communicable Crises: Prevention, Response, and Recovery in the Global Arena, pp. 203–240
Copyright © 2007 by Information Age Publishing
All rights of reproduction in any form reserved.

INTRODUCTION

Operating on the belief that organizational issues can be as important as technical preparedness, we will consider aspects of networks, planning, and teamwork that relate to management of communicable crises and their effects. A communicable crisis is defined here as an unstable or emergency situation that has potential to trigger ongoing disaster. The most likely scenario for a communicable crisis is one in which an incident—such as a natural disaster, outbreak of disease, or terrorist strike—increases the probability of subsequent negative outcomes. For example, an outbreak of severe influenza can cripple businesses, overload health care facilities, and inhibit the flow of resources precisely when those resources are most needed. As more people become ill, fewer responders are available to handle ongoing emergencies, and normal law enforcement and social services become unavailable. Shortages of trained personnel may lead to the collapse of preexisting systems that are necessary to maintain safety and continuity in the community. When normal procedures become untenable and existing systems become overloaded by a disaster, the social capital and resources of nonprofit organizations frequently enable them to provide needed services. Further, nonprofit organizations that are embedded or tied to local communities can serve as gatekeepers of long-term support for recovery. Proactive networking, strategizing, and training before a disaster happens may greatly enhance the likelihood of a successful response. By integrating design principles for success under dynamic uncertainty with lessons learned from practical experience, we may obtain guidelines for crisis management systems.

In this chapter, I will talk about interorganizational networks and their roles in crisis prevention, disaster response, and long-term recovery. Particular attention will be given to attributes of nonprofit organizations that enable them to provide response and recovery aid that cannot be done solely by government interventions. I will emphasize the importance of networks, both planned and emergent, that enhance emergency response efforts. Throughout our explorations, we will hear stories from experienced volunteers, organizers, and experts who coordinate nonprofit organizations working in disaster response and recovery. Some of these people worked in the aftermath of the Hurricane Katrina disaster in the Southern United States in the fall of 2005. Others have long-term experience in disaster management. Their stories will assist us in understanding the roles of interorganizational networks for crisis management and recovery.

HOW DO NONPROFIT ORGANIZATIONS AND VOLUNTEERS FIT INTO DISASTER MANAGEMENT SYSTEMS?

Nonprofit organizations and volunteers provide the bulk of hands-on disaster relief and recovery work. Large nonprofit organizations have expertise in field work, which enables them to implement standardized procedures quickly and route volunteers and resources effectively. In contrast, community-based organizations possess social capital and expert knowledge of the region, which can open doors, attract volunteers, and provide problem solving that would not occur under the direct leadership of an external agency. Alongside the nonprofit organizations, businesses and government organizations bring unique and valuable resources and capabilities. Ideally, responses to large-scale crises should involve a network of complementary organizations working cooperatively toward shared goals.

Nonprofit organizations can be distinguished from business and government organizations by their voluntary nature and legal commitment to return no profits to stakeholders. Nonprofit and volunteer groups that are not associated with governments are termed "non-governmental organizations" by the United Nations and, hence, by many stakeholders and critics. Also called "private voluntary organizations" (PVOs), nongovernmental organizations (NGOs) include all nonprofit organizations that are independent from the government (Shreve & Galli, 2006) along with associations of citizens that share a common interest (Hofstetter, 2006). NGOs tend to be founded on shared values, depend on charitable donations, and espouse principles of altruism and voluntarism, even though some of the more visible organizations have become increasingly professional in recent years (Shreve & Galli, 2006). Although they are sometimes categorized separately, faith-based and secular organizations, advocacy and operational organizations, and relief and development organizations are all included in our working definition of NGOs, nonprofit organizations, and volunteer organizations. These terms are equivalent, and I will use the term "nonprofit organizations" to refer to them hereafter.

Linkages Between State Government and Nonprofit Organizations

Businesses and branches of government can play crucial roles in supporting nonprofit organizations' efforts toward emergency response and disaster recovery at national, state, and local levels. Their interactions with nonprofit organizations influence the quality of response and the likelihood that initial crises will become ongoing disasters. In the United States, federal disaster interventions reflect the long-standing principle that response efforts should first be handled at the state and local level (Federal Emergency Management Agency (FEMA), 2000). This policy of supplementing state and local agencies reflects the federalist roots of U.S. government (The White House, 2006), which places state and local governments firmly in charge of disaster-related decision making. To assist our understanding of state–nonprofit linkages, I consulted Eileen Cackowski, Executive Director of the Kentucky Commission on Community Volunteerism and Service. Years of experience have given her an excellent grasp of principles that facilitate collaborative disaster responses. Interestingly, she defines a disaster response network very broadly, including

> VOAD (Voluntary Organizations Active in Disasters)... faith based organizations, American Red Cross, Salvation Army, fire departments, police departments, emergency services providers, contractors, heavy equipment businesses, owners of four-wheel drive vehicles (used during severe snow storms), fast food establishments (coffee and food for an extended disaster), grocery stores, schools (for shelter and also for kitchen facilities), utilities companies, landscape businesses (extra chainsaws), bus companies, taxies, Amtrak.

We will incorporate several of Cackowski's insights for planning and coordination into our model for successful crisis management.

Local Nonprofit Organizations

Nonprofit organizations range in size from small groups that work in their own neighborhoods to large humanitarian, religious, or educational organizations that operate internationally. Local churches, synagogues, and community organizations frequently maintain interpersonal assistance programs as part of their normal activities. Although most of these organizations don't specialize in crisis management, most of them do have contacts, resources, and a network of volunteers that can respond quickly. Many local churches promote emergency response training among their members, and participate in disaster relief or recovery on a regular basis. To better understand church roles in disaster response, I visited Tuscaloosa, Alabama, where many evacuees from Hurricane Katrina found shelter, food, and support for recovery. In Tuscaloosa, I talked with Timothy Plant, who coordinated response activities of members of Calvary Baptist Church, situated about a mile from a large emergency shelter that operated in the recreation center at the University of Alabama. I also talked with Gary Bonner, who coordinates joint emergency responses by Southern Baptist churches from Tuscaloosa County. In cooperation with FEMA, the Red Cross, and people from many other denominations, members of the Southern Baptist Association of Tuscaloosa County helped evacuees with food, clothing, health care, medical supplies, transportation, child care, furniture, kitchen supplies, relocation, and a variety of idiosyncratic needs. They regularly send trained chainsaw and cleanup teams (to clear storm damage) and feeding units to devastated areas as part of their ongoing disaster response program. Conversations with Plant and Bonner provided many insights into the proactive planning and the ongoing potential of local nonprofit organizations for responding quickly and effectively to future disasters. They also revealed areas where better system design could multiply the benefits derived from such organizations.

Large Nonprofit Organizations

Large relief and development organizations often channel funding from national governments to specific human needs. For example, 532 U.S. and 59 non-American organizations are currently registered as private voluntary organizations (PVOs) with USAID (United States Agency International Development) (USAID, 2006). They obtain grants from the United States government to support humanitarian aid throughout the world. Despite the governmental ties of large development organizations, however, most nonprofits that contribute to disaster relief or recovery do so without direct government support. Some engage in a variety of disaster services, while others tend to specialize.

Advocacy groups lobby for governmental support, and they direct clients to sources of funding or other aid. Operational organizations design and implement relief and recovery activities on the ground. Some organizations, such as Church World Service (CWS), do both. Representing 35 denominations that contribute to disaster response, Church World Service provides immediate and long-term help for victims of disasters in the United States and throughout the world. To better understand the roles and needs of large, multifaceted nonprofit organizations in crisis management, I talked with Lesli Remaly-Netter, who is one of Church World Service's six disaster response and recovery liaisons. She identified a broad variety of strategies that they have developed to maximize efficiency and quality of service to people affected by disasters.

Ad Hoc Volunteer Teams

Alongside existing nonprofit organizations, ad hoc volunteer groups respond to specific emergencies. Volunteer teams often specialize in an area such as medicine, construction, or communication. Following Hurricane Katrina, many such teams traveled to Louisiana or Mississippi to help survivors who remained on site. Many nonprofit organizations that do not generally work in disaster relief also mustered volunteer teams to aid individuals in recovery. To gain better understanding of the roles, experiences, and potential pitfalls experienced by ad hoc teams, I talked with Captain Cesar Nader of the U.S. Marine Corps. Nader went to Waveland, Mississippi, as part of a voluntary military team that erected a wireless communication system in an area where the local infrastructure had been destroyed. Unlike Tuscaloosa, Waveland had few resources and little formal organization for emergency response. Having prior experience setting up large, self-contained facilities in desolate areas, Nader provides several insights into principles that facilitate ad hoc organization with minimal external assistance. As a logistician, he adds some helpful pointers on managing large influxes of goods in a short amount of time.

Hurricane Evacuees' Perspectives on Nongovernmental Response

Throughout the management of a communicable crisis, the primary goal is to assist victims and stop the spread of disaster. This assistance begins with proactive planning, continues through immediate relief, and reaches completion following long-term recovery. To keep perspective on the benefits of various approaches, I talked with three Hurricane Katrina evacuees who traveled from Louisiana to emergency facilities in Alabama. One young man, Joe Kimbrough II, had been a college student in New Orleans before the area flooded. Through an outstanding program offered by the University of Alabama, he relocated to Tuscaloosa and transferred smoothly into courses that were already in progress. Two more evacuees, Kay McGrath and Mac McGrath, left their home in Violet, Louisiana, with a few clothes and personal items. The hurricane and flooding destroyed their house, two cars, and both of their workplaces, such that they found themselves in Tuscaloosa needing long-term assistance. The experiences of these three people serve as references for considering the array of tasks involved in helping someone recover from a disaster.

Kimbrough volunteered in Tuscaloosa for several days and then returned to help in New Orleans for 2 days before applying to the University of Alabama's evacuee program. Asked about sanitation, equipment, and coordination in New Orleans, Kimbrough replied,

> We were using apartments that were still there. We used people's apartments, dorm rooms, and campus buildings.... We were all down there, and it was just kind of like, OK, we are reasonably okay; we have neighbors who aren't. It's our job to do something.... There was no application process to get help.

About the contrast between working in New Orleans and volunteering for the Red Cross in Tuscaloosa, he said,

> The Red Cross knew where they were going with water, knew how to put the beds up, knew how to cram as many people as humanly possible into a very small space. They had plans for gathering clothes, they had plans for getting houses, they had plans for getting work. We on the local level didn't have any of that. It was like neighbors getting together and just helping one another out.

Finally, asked about his own experiences as an evacuee,

> I applied to the University [of Alabama]. The University, getting me in the school, was very, very helpful. I went through a 3-day orientation process in about two hours, and went to class that afternoon. I had a dorm room and an e-mail address and five classes, and I was in class within 3 hours.... They suspended a lot of their bureaucracy.

Kay McGrath has diabetes, and Mac McGrath had a heart attack during the evacuation, so they arrived at the University of Alabama shelter with serious health problems. They encountered welcoming volunteers, volumes of confusing paperwork, and charities willing to provide medicines and health care. The couple received about $4,100 in monetary assistance from FEMA, the State of Louisiana, and Red Cross. Health care, advocacy, diabetic foods, medications, pet boarding, laundry services, extended housing, furniture and household goods, and personal necessities came through a variety of churches and volunteers. "If it hadn't been for the churches, I don't know what we would have done. Some church that didn't even know us came and gave us money so that we could get into an apartment" (Kay McGrath, 2006). Kay and Mac both reported frustration with the paperwork required to apply for government help, but they expressed deep appreciation for a variety of individuals and organizations:

> Kay: We were amazed. People brought us things: toothpaste, blankets, dental floss. They got us clothes and my special

foods because of diabetes. We didn't have anything, and the people from the church came and got me everything I needed.

Mac: Some people were complaining, but I said, "what are you complaining about?" We had Outback and other restaurants, First Baptist Church tried to do red beans and rice like New Orleans, various restaurants came, nearly every restaurant in Tuscaloosa.

Kay: People would come from churches with personal items like shoes. They would ask what we need. They would do our clothes.

The McGraths went on to praise the Salvation Army and Catholic Charities for funding prescription medications, the Good Samaritan Clinic, along with the VA Center and health professionals from Calvary Baptist Church who provided free health care, the Southern Baptist Convention for help provided in Louisiana, the University of Alabama football team, and a variety of unnamed individuals and churches for a variety of good deeds. Kay concluded, "We needed shelter, food, medications, and that came through the community. The government didn't do anything for a long time." Clearly, a complex network arose to meet people's needs during this series of crises.

Coordination of Nonprofit Organizations' Relief and Response Efforts

For a wide variety of organizations, disaster response is one component of a broader mission, and their efforts are mobilized as needed. When a disaster strikes, many seek coordinating instructions from state representatives or federal agencies such as FEMA (G. Bonner, personal communication, March 2006). Others plan their own disaster response and recovery efforts, operating independently until they find partners among their existing contacts or at a disaster site. Some organizations proactively coordinate disaster preparations through groups such as the Voluntary Organizations Active in Disasters (VOAD) or Church World Service (CWS). Others work primarily through denominational hubs such as the Southern Baptist Convention or Catholic Charities. Large nonprofit organizations, such as the Salvation Army, coordinate myriad volunteers and resource deliveries in disparate locations as needed. Yet, even large organizations must adjust their actions to fit the circumstances, and they need assistance with coordination issues that exceed their internal logistics or communication capacity. To be efficient, they must be informed about needs, resources, surpluses, and other responders in the areas where they are working. At the same time, the overall system needs information gained on the ground, which enables oversight, resource routing, and coordination of entire regions.

Required cooperation falls into three general categories. First, there is the actual coordination of services, managing who will be where doing what to mitigate the crisis. Second, there is the distribution of resources, assuring that necessary medications, supplies, and equipment reach the correct destinations without excess. Finally, there may be a need to orchestrate control, including possible quarantines, evacuations, or movement of population subgroups. All of these areas of cooperation depend on timely, accurate information. Transfer of information between people and organizations that lack day-to-day partnerships becomes particularly important when large numbers of volunteers or donations are involved. Blending the skills, resources, and labor of hundreds or thousands of participants into an effective collaboration requires good organization, clear leadership, and sensible preparation.

SYSTEM DESIGN, LEADERSHIP, AND PLANNING FOR CRISIS MANAGEMENT

Organization theorists have identified specific aspects of structure, leadership, and process that contribute to success in rapidly changing, unpredictable environments. Most of this research pertains to individual organizations, but many of the principles can be applied to systems of organizations. Networks research has developed further insights into the pros and cons of various network structures among disparate entities in a complex system. Finally, practical experience of people who coordinate disaster responses has helped them discover approaches that increase success in a variety of situations. By integrating these ideas, we may assemble some useful guidelines for keeping performance high under unpredictable circumstances.

The design of an organization should follow from its mission, resources, competencies, task requirements, and external environment. By analyzing these aspects of the organization, one gains necessary information for planning appropriate structures, communication channels, and task flows. An organization's mission statement outlines its broad goals, and compatible operational goals must be developed at the level of each operating unit. Similarly, the mission of a system (e.g., to reduce likelihood, impact, and recovery time related to a crisis) must be translated into operational goals for components of the system. This is more complicated at the system level than within a single organization because

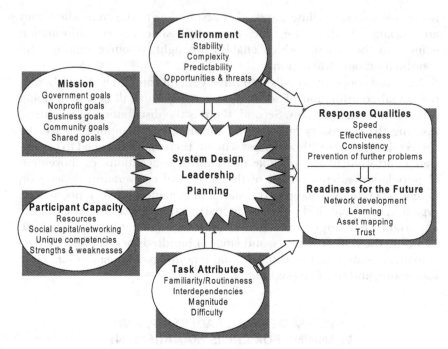

Figure 7.1   Factors related to system design, leadership approach, and planning.

the system's mission must be compatible with many stakeholders' goals. Each component needs to develop strategies, structures, and processes that facilitate its performance within the anticipated operating environment(s). These components must then be coordinated to ensure that each contributes and receives adequate support from the greater system. All of these factors influence optimal choices for system design, leadership, and advance planning (see Figure 7.1).

COMMUNICATION AND CONTROL STRUCTURES: DESIGNING THE SYSTEM

Component integration can be accomplished by centralized control, as is often the case in bureaucratic organizations, including branches of governments. Centralized coordination networks form a hierarchical communication and command system that routes information and decisions through a few tiered hubs. In Figure 7.2a, each field-based cluster represents the multitude of organizations that might work side-by-side

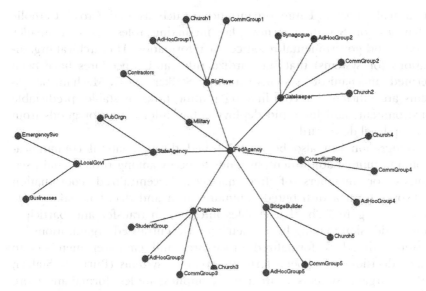

Figure 7.2a.   Hierarchical coordination. Federal Agency coordinates with big players that manage smaller groups. Structure provides rapid top-down communication, standardization, centralized control; limits lateral communication, collaborative problem solving, and adaptation.

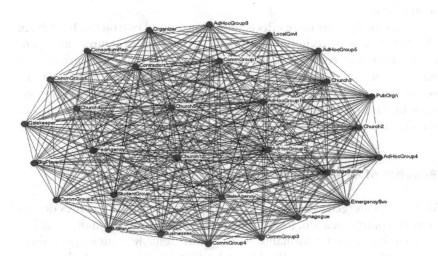

Figure 7.2a.   Decentralized coordnation. All participants in the relief effort are able to coordinate directly with all others. Structure provides ongoing access to information from all sources, facilitates collaborative problem solving, resource sharing, innovation, and adaptation; increases communication costs, may inhibit global strategizing.

in a real disaster. Large organizations, such as Red Cross, Catholic Charities, or Salvation Army, play mediating roles between smaller groups and governmental resources or information. Hierarchical organizations (or systems) that standardize rules and procedures have been termed "mechanistic" systems (Burns & Stalker, 1961). Mechanistic systems are efficient for coordinating routine tasks in stable, predictable environments and for rapid deployment of information or goods from the top level downward.

Integration can also be accomplished through lateral communication and mutual adjustment, as tends to occur among professionals, scientists, or members of free markets. Decentralized coordination networks form a distributed communication and decision-making system (see Figure 7.2b) that enables information transfer and participation in decision making by all members. Decentralized organizations (or systems) that lack formalized procedures and empower members to make decisions have been termed "organic" systems (Burns & Stalker, 1961). Organic systems, as their name implies, are less formal and more adaptable than mechanistic systems. They are particularly appropriate when procedures must be customized, when the environment is uncertain or changing rapidly, and for self-coordination of information or resources among members. Given large amounts of information to filter and analyze, however, the decentralized system will be less efficient than a hierarchy.

System design has huge effects on processes and outcomes. To operate effectively, system components require strategies, structures, and processes that are compatible with their resources, competencies, task requirements, and environmental conditions. These contingencies must be accommodated for each component, possibly using different communication and coordination structures, without reducing the coherence of the overall system.

Benefits of Organic Systems

Within an emergency response team, organic design that includes decentralized communication, joint problem solving, and autonomous decision making increases performance. To operate reliably under uncertainty, organizations need to be flexible and adaptable. To succeed, they must rely on self organization by informed participants who initiate action but adjust their action to that of others operating toward the same goal to achieve a timely, efficient response (Rochlin, LaPorte, & Roberts, 1987). The greater the uncertainty, the more important it is to let competent teams and team members make decisions and forge solutions together as they encounter new circumstances.

Lateral communications help local organizations know which actions to take and how they can accomplish the most in a particular situation. Plant (T. M. Plant, personal communication, March, 2006) addressed this in talking about his church's assistance programs.

> Sometimes people will ask, "why didn't you send a bus down there to pick somebody up, or carry a fishing boat down there [to New Orleans]?" Well, you couldn't even get in there, so that would not be good stewardship of the resources that we had. We sent our financial resources to people that are established and have teams ready to go for this. We sent our human resources in conjunction with the organizations that were already working here.

This is Plant's general approach to relief:

> We have a list of all the social services here, and I've been here for 7 years now, so I know these people. We work in conjunction. Most of them, we support. We do blood drives here. We send money to the Community Services, and we send money to the Salvation Army. We send money to various and sundry social agencies here. That's the same principle. Community Services and the Christian Ministry Center provide food and clothing for people in need. Rather than us having a clothing closet or a food pantry here, which is difficult to administer well, we send money to those people. It's easier for us to send them money and manpower. It is manned by volunteers and we send them down there.... We have a Good Samaritan clinic here that gives free medical care. There are probably 25 or 30 M.D.s within our congregation, and then dentists and optometrists, so we are fortunate we can staff them with medical people.

Plant went on to identify a variety of other partners in ongoing relief activities, where his church sends money to support the most capable organizations for each task. They coordinate nearly all of their volunteer services with others. This integration within decentralized networks enables Plant and other leaders of networked organizations to maximize the results of their members' investments to help others. In contrast, if many organizations remain isolated from the network, the system as a whole suffers.

Beyond routing of volunteers or resources, lateral communications are crucial for people or organizations doing interdependent tasks because the participants need to be able to coordinate in real time. Lateral ties build mutual understanding of the environment, ongoing activities, and opportunities for improvement. Nader describes problems that arise when neighboring organizations lack communication:

They can't see beyond their network, beyond their node. [In Waveland], they didn't know that if they'd just drive 20 minutes there is a facility that can give you ice. You don't have to turn people away, saying, 'we're out of ice, and we don't know where we'll get any more.' Ignorance was another issue that was really catching people—rational ignorance, the inability to know what's beyond you. You didn't have enough communications to be able to know what's beyond you ... that situational awareness, who's on my right and who's on my left. That's one of the things that we work on in the military a lot ... before you move anything, you want to know who's on your left, who's on your right, so you can either reach left or right or back if you need support, or you can join forces to move around a mountain. In this case, you've got to know, and you're stationary.

Without ongoing communication, opportunities for collaboration are lost. Creative solutions to dynamic problems depend on this timely understanding of the situation and the resources available to address it. Implementation of creative solutions then requires freedom for people on the ground to take action.

A mechanistic structure that restricts emergency responders' actions because of prior experiences, rigid rules, or status differences retards their ability to react quickly and effectively to developing situations. Rules meant to facilitate operations during normal times or to standardize response procedures can often destroy the special functions of rescue teams. For example, Comfort (1996) explains how Japanese laws interfered with rescue operations following the 1995 earthquake in Kobe: "existing law kept the dogs from the French Search and Rescue team in quarantine, not allowing them to enter response operations until the fourth day after the earthquake when they extricated dead bodies, instead of living people." In contrast to Kobe's destructive adherence to inappropriate rules, the University of Alabama recognized the value of flexibility for handling Katrina evacuees, as attested by Kimbrough's registration, housing assignment, course placement, and enrollment in classes in less than three hours. Sensible flexibility works; rigid control impedes responsible action at the point of service.

Designing for Creativity, Coordination, and Control

The answer to the control issue, without destroying necessary flexibility, lies in the establishment of guidelines for oversight at the broad level that allows exceptions as needed in practice. Every volunteer group or organization needs coordinating information, and every operation needs leadership that can allocate tasks and access to appropriate groups. Pre-planned community networks can establish good procedures for each group to obtain information and to coordinate roles. Remaly-Netter (L Remaly-Netter, personal communication, 2006, May 2006) emphasizes the importance of community participation in planning and network building:

> Now volunteer recovery organizations are actually helping to educate and train and provide preparation and mitigation venues for non-disaster times. It's morphed into a more comprehensive long-term recovery organization that becomes a more sustainable community organization for disasters. The most important thing, in my mind, is to bring together as quickly as possible community leaders that have their finger on the pulse of what the needs are within their community.

System design also involves establishing procedures that ensure adequate training for volunteers so they will be able to handle whatever they find in the field. The goal is to prepare potential responders so that each person contributes and nobody becomes a liability in a crisis. Cackowski (E. Cackowski, personal communications, May, 2006) comments that

> individuals like to learn and are very willing and ready to learn how to respond in time of a future disaster. The problem is that after 6 months or a year, the training gets dim and the energy level plummets. There should be some sort of information flow and additional training every 60 to 90 days to keep skills sharp.

Along with sharpening skills, training updates keep people engaged with the network. Together, training and proactive self-organization are better than mechanistic control because they enhance the respondents' capacities for creative problem solving and self-management when it becomes necessary. Good leadership before and during the crisis then enables optimal use of the capacities that are present. We will discuss leadership and planning shortly.

While each team needs the freedom to adapt to changing circumstances, the overall system must be monitored for excesses, overlaps, and unaddressed problems. Situational awareness—understanding the details of the environment in which you're operating—is crucial for coordinating large interventions. Following Hurricane Katrina, breakdown of communications infrastructure reduced situational awareness to the detriment of the response efforts (The White House, 2006). Overarching communication channels, often managed by government agencies, must be in place to distribute relevant information to participating organizations, provide asset tracking, and support lateral communications. Hierarchy in this function is helpful so that all information about positions, resource demands, and environmental circumstances can be routed through a central processing station. From there, data can be analyzed, and results can be distributed to the entire system. A risk in routing critical information through a central source is that communication lines may be disrupted, as occurred following Hurricane Katrina. To prevent interruptions in data transfer and processing, redundancy in all key aspects of the system is absolutely crucial. Key aspects include communication technology (radio, telephones, cell phones, internet, messenger systems) and interpersonal relationships (preplanned contact lists, ad hoc partnerships, local grape-vines). Alongside hierarchical communication lines, decentralized com-munication capabilities should be maintained within and among groups in the field (see "Communications" discussion below).

Mechanistic organizing may be necessary when managing untrained or unpredictable volunteers. Workers who lack training and experience require careful supervision and specific instructions. Cackowski recom-mends using a volunteer center or United Way Clearing House to route unaffiliated volunteers to appropriate tasks. She further suggests keeping "Volunteer" notebooks of questions and answers, participants' contact information and expertise, and instructions. Finally, she adds, "We also love computers but, without emergency generator back up, the rule may be a notebook and a flashlight."

In summary, government agencies or large nonprofits are often needed to coordinate resources and information that support the point-of-contact efforts by smaller organizations and volunteers. These func-tions can be facilitated by centralized data analysis and control structures that use standard operating procedures and integrated technology. Com-fort (in this volume) and Braunbeck and Mastria (in the volume) outline specific data management and asset tracking approaches that rely on hierarchical data control systems. In the field, however, decisions should be made by people who are involved with the specific situation. Lateral communication and decentralized control among competent responders enable rapid, effective action. A wise blend of mechanistic and organic structures maximizes the response system's performance.

Figure 7.3 illustrates a response system that balances hierarchical over-sight, information processing, and resource tracking with decentralized communication, collaboration, and decision making in the field. Keeping the hierarchical structure (heavy ties, from Figure 7.1) for information processing and asset tracking, collaborative (light weight) ties have been added to connect organizations working in the same area. These ties sup-port ongoing collaboration, resource sharing, and immediate updates on occurrences of mutual concern. Boundary spanning (medium weight) ties have been added to connect large nonprofit organizations with each other, and to connect military and state agencies with public, private, and nonprofit organizations. Boundary spanning ties enable coordination

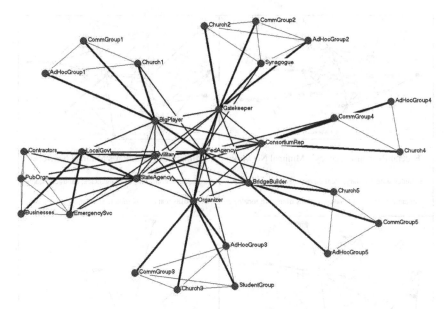

Figure 7.3.   Balancing hierarchy with decentralization in a crisis management system.

across adjoining areas or related tasks, thus avoiding duplication of some services and neglect of others. Finally, redundancy ties have been added between a representative organization from each component of the system and federal (or state) emergency management agencies. These redundant ties support independent communication routes between government coordinators and clusters of local organizations.

To make the structures around representative organizations more apparent, Figure 7.4 displays the ties immediately surrounding the federal government agency, the state government agency, the military organization, and a representative local organization. In all cases, the small number of local organizations represents dozens or hundreds of participants, each of which should maintain a network similar in construction but more complete than the examples depicted here.

LEADERSHIP: STEERING THE SYSTEM

Good leadership in crisis requires unconventional thinking, critical analysis, and recognition of valuable information from a systemic viewpoint

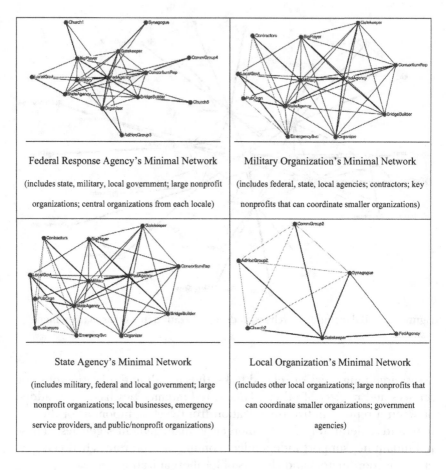

Federal Response Agency's Minimal Network	Military Organization's Minimal Network
(includes state, military, local government; large nonprofit organizations; central organizations from each locale)	(includes federal, state, local agencies; contractors; key nonprofits that can coordinate smaller organizations)
State Agency's Minimal Network	Local Organization's Minimal Network
(includes military, federal and local government; large nonprofit organizations; local businesses, emergency service providers, and public/nonprofit organizations)	(includes other local organizations; large nonprofits that can coordinate smaller organizations; government agencies)

Figure 7.4.   Network structure surrounding representative organization types.

(Mitroff, 2004). In field operations, good leadership requires orchestration of many players and diverse resources, strong information processing capacity, adequate authority to act, and ability to preplan for a variety of possible surprises.

Gathering and Analyzing Data

Organization theorists have long emphasized that rapidly changing environments demand intense fact finding by leaders before they make decisions (Eisenhardt, 1989). An organic structure facilitates broad solution searches by including many people in the process. Hierarchical data collection with centralized analysis can also facilitate broad solution searches by systematically aggregating vast amounts of information into understandable results. Using the recommended combination of hierarchical macrocommunications with lateral ties for specific communications and cooperation, a leader has access to both sorts of information. The extent to which leaders attune to incoming data and relate them to ongoing concerns influences the organization's likelihood of success. This applies at the level of an operational team, a regional coordinator, or a board making decisions about large interventions. Siggelkow and Rivkin (2005) tested effects of leadership teams' "coordinative processing power" under various organizational structures using computational models. They found a consistent positive effect on organizations' speed of improvement and average organizational performance. This effect occurred under various types of structures, with the greatest effects on performance in turbulent (rapidly changing) environments. Good problem-solving behaviors, including broad information searches and continuous updating, are fundamental to successful leadership.

Developing Appropriate Tactics

A good leader must translate strategy into tactical success through appropriately scaled responses. Nader (C. E. Nader, personal communication, March, 2005) explains:

> You have the strategic operation and the tactical, tactical being the smallest level. If you have tactical support, you may serve a smaller number of people, but you are more effective. In this case, when you have a crisis, you have pockets of support requirements. Everybody needs the same stuff, but you can't be in Biloxi, an hour away, to try to give support to Waveland. You have to be where the people are, and for that you would have to be a little more flexible.... The things that I saw that worked in the immediate aftermath were local groups, so trying to massively overwhelm the crisis area with your helos and trucks and boats that may not even get there just shuts down the whole system.... In a crisis, if too many people at the same time are trying to do the same thing, it's like a funnel, and at one point, that funnel gets stuck, and nothing goes through.

A good leader assesses the likely demands and allocates enough, but not too much, personnel and equipment to meet expected needs.

Institutionalizing New Procedures

When unexpected events destroy standard facilities or preclude normal procedures, leaders must develop alternatives. Within a changing mass of people, supplies, and events, some order must be achieved. From organizational theories, we can draw guidelines for implementing improvements in a system. (1) If you can build the necessary procedure into the floor plan or fixed structures, do that. (2) Otherwise, (a) develop procedures, forms, checklists, and norms to support correct implementation of the procedure and (b) institute a monitoring system with incentives to increase the likelihood that people will comply. It is much easier to manage a complex process when the only possible option is the correct one. Failing that, clear explanations and easily accessed instructions are necessary, but not always sufficient to guarantee smooth operations. Nader makes the point that people fall quickly into patterns, so it is crucial when constructing a disaster response to establish logical, thoughtful patterns from the beginning. He gives an example of managing new volunteers in the field:

> It's like walking into a new country, and you have to give them the law of the land. I did this three times in Korea, so I became proficient at avoiding people putting their bags down at the first bunk they found. To create trust, you not only meet their expectations, you surpass them. They don't know what they're doing ... people come and say, 'I'm here to help, what can I do?' If you say, "I don't know," that's it—you've lost the opportunity to gain a helper or a resource, whatever he brought. If they say, "I brought stuff, where shall I put it?" and you say, "ok, drop it there," because you don't know where to put it, you create problems for those of us who are staying because now we have to sort it. Instead say, "You want to drop stuff off? Listen, do me a favor. Drive all the way down; I have a station there. Let me see what you have; do you have a list?" Or, "Why don't you stay here a day? We're going to unload your vehicle ... then we're going to reload your vehicle for you to take it down there." You don't ask them, you tell them.... You give them the orders because in crisis people are willing to take orders, but you have to be quick to pick up the baton. You have to create the law right away and make people believe this is the way it's always been done.... It's one of the things that helped me when I went to check out systems (for the wireless network).... It's all a matter of starting small and trying to meet the needs of the people, hopefully getting the resources you need, and knowing what to do with them. So, you should deploy a small contingency of people originally, as quickly as you can after the crisis, and based on what those soldiers on the ground tell you, those guys who have boots on the ground, then bring in reinforcements in stages.... How do you keep people from going to help their neighbors? You don't. What you do want to do is coordinate them in a way that is more effective.

We gain three guidelines from Nader's experience. First, scope out the terrain and develop a logical plan to set up facilities. Second, as reinforcements and supplies arrive, route them directly into the operations plan. Third, establish consistent norms, be directive, and give clear instructions that channel people into useful behaviors.

MAINTAINING REPORTING STRUCTURES
UNDER CHANGING LEADERSHIP

At the field level, reporting structures and task assignments should be clear to all. Cackowski recommends using colored name tags.

> Color denotes responsibility. I may wear a red, top dog name tag for one event and a yellow "worker" tag for another…. When I check in, I am given the color to represent where I can go and where I should not be!

Other approaches for marking the on-site leader include brightly colored vests, jackets, or hats. Asked what is most likely to get in the way of response efforts, Cackowski replied that egos must be left outside the disaster area. Nader gave similar responses when addressing necessary leadership qualities. He said that leaders should (a) "wear the uniform" that identifies their organization and their role, (b) travel as needed to gain better understanding of the situation, and (c), "augment the people who are already there instead of hoarding the fame."

The Katrina investigation (The White House, 2006, p. 43) found that military capabilities combined with excellent leadership yielded outstanding performance under extreme conditions: "LTG Honoré's leadership, combined with the Department of Defense's resources, manpower, and advanced planning, contributed to the military's success in the Federal response, especially in areas such as search and rescue, security, and logistical support." Even excellent resources must be coupled with good leadership to achieve strong results.

PREPARATION: PLANNING AROUND STRENGTHS,
WEAKNESSES, OPPORTUNITIES AND THREATS

Recent disasters have demonstrated the good will of multitudes toward disaster victims. With plentiful donations and volunteers, coordination and integration become crucial for shaping outcomes. Objective assessments and planning before a disaster strikes can help with this. Cackowski believes that preplanning is the key to successful collaboration under stress. Because every responder should be prepared to lead, she recommends rotating leadership during planning. She also suggests that a notebook containing frequent questions and answers should be provided for the group's emergency communications office. Church World Service places heavy emphasis on disaster planning, and they frequently provide guidance for communities. Remaly-Netter begins with joint goal setting and self-assessment. "What makes long-term recovery organizing different from everything else that happens in your community? This is a new focus, a disaster driven focus. We ask organizations and local leaders to develop a mission statement." She described efforts by Florida communities to organize a sustainable disaster response infrastructure following the hurricanes in 2004. This included establishment of nonprofit organizations that could accept donations, hire staff, and prepare for future disasters. Preexisting organizations were ready to respond rapidly during the 2005 hurricane season because they had prepared in advance.

Following Hurricane Katrina devastation in Mississippi, county-level organizations from Florida sent self-contained relief teams that Nader described as "impressive."

> They had modified trucks to be the communications vehicle, so this thing deploys in a seven-piece module of three vehicles and four trailers. It had a floodlight set, over 100 radios, its own generator, its own computers.... This was the support of the police and the fire department that came with them. They brought their own self-support system. It was impressive. These guys didn't have one bad day out there because they knew what they were in for, they knew what they had to do.

In other words, they were extremely well prepared.

According to Remaly-Netter, many denominations are developing disaster ministries,

> sending teams that will go outside of their own local community. Mission teams are certainly a focus of building that prethought, planning for the future and developing the capacity to respond to disasters outside their community. There's also the need for the long-term recovery organizing, and the VOAD (voluntary organizations active in disasters) at the county level or at the state level, to be sure that they are in the LEPC plans (local emergency planning committees).

Participants in community disaster planning should include people from all stakeholder groups, including public and private organizations, nonprofit organizations, government agents, community groups, and coalitions such as VOAD. Their founding task should be careful self-assessment. What are we good at doing? Where are our weaknesses? What kinds of disasters might we anticipate? How can we as a community design a comprehensive crisis management system?

Objective Assessment

It is important to understand the strengths and weaknesses of participants and of the system at large. It is also important to understand potential threats that may arise during a crisis. Careful assessment of an organization, a community, or a response system and the range of situations they could face is a necessary first step in planning. Contingency plans follow, preferably working on a "worst case scenario" basis to identify adequacy of existing resources and expertise. When the general scenarios have been mapped, delegation of roles and responsibilities brings individuals and organizations into the system.

It is very important to clarify roles that each group or organization is able and willing to fulfill in case of crisis. Their skills and competencies can then be integrated. New participants can be recruited to fill gaps, and coordination mechanisms can be developed to match participants that fill complementary roles. Proactive identification of skills, resources, and capacities speeds coordination of individual volunteers and organizations. Timeliness, in turn, can be crucial for the survival and safety of victims. For example, following the Kobe earthquake of 1995, the survival rate for those being rescued from collapsed buildings dropped from 80.5% on the first day to 21.8% by the third day (Comfort, 1996). Knowing the capabilities of potential responders before the crisis saves time. Likewise, inclusion of local volunteers whose skills have already been developed supports positive outcomes.

Remaly-Netter outlines some goals for community leaders in the planning phase:

> We want leaders thinking, "what would we do if a tornado or flood hit tomorrow? Could we work together to talk about planning or recovery?" The recovery community, at large, is not necessarily advocating for the government to step in and do recovery. They provide assistance through the federal programs and through the state programs for getting dollars. When donated dollars come through the VOAD and through the denominations, we're suggesting that the government agencies be liaisons to the local community leaders. Let the local leaders, the community leaders, become the decision-makers for how they are going to help individuals.

Only through extensive self-analysis and cooperative problem solving will community leaders develop the understanding and the consensus required to handle that level of decision making.

VOLUNTEER PREPARATION

Pretraining of volunteers for skill-based interventions builds an immediately available worker pool. According to Cackowski,

> In any area, non profit human resource organizations, faith based, governmental and private organizations will find it helpful to come together to talk about who the first responder to a disaster really is. Have several scenarios in order to bring ALL of the appropriate people on board. If there is a house fire, the first responder may be the mailman or the neighbor. There should be some sort of training open to John Q Citizen to take care of themselves.

Remaly-Netter advances a similar notion:

> How about a course for high schoolers and utilizing the service hours for preparedness? Colleges and universities, in all disciplines, whether it be health-care or social services, construction, or any of those—the disciplines could all be incorporating all-hazards education as a part of their normal response.

Cackowski emphasizes the point that every volunteer should be part of a response organization: "There is nothing more wonderful than volunteers coming together to help, and there is nothing more frightening than unaffiliated volunteers jumping into the fray." She tells a story about the importance of training people before sending them:

> Here in Frankfort, Kentucky, many offered to be deployed to flooded areas in Louisiana and Mississippi, not having had training of any kind. Prior to being deployed, they were given a multi-hour orientation in what to expect, what clothing and essentials they would need to bring with them, how to complete paperwork for reimbursement, track expenses, etc. The county health department had nurses providing tetanus shots at no charge at the chapter house. In the after-deployment briefing that they all received, they were proud to have been told that they were the only out-of-state volunteers who were prepared, knew what to expect and were not (too) shocked by what they saw or experienced.

Many nonprofit organizations build training into their regular routines. For example, Bonner described training and certification programs offered by the Tuscaloosa Baptist Association for volunteers on their chain saw teams, child care teams, and feeding teams. He mentioned the necessity for emergency response team leaders to receive NIMS "first line single resource field supervisor training." Finally, he described a current program coordinated with another church:

The reason we're doing it there is because they reach a lot of university students. These university students who go to that church want to be trained in disaster relief so they can respond.... Then, when the students graduate from college, even though they are probably only going to be here four or five years, they've been trained. They can go back to their local church, and they might be the ones to initiate this training in their church and get their church actively involved.

By planning ahead, fully training volunteers, and structuring communication and authority patterns appropriately, we can maximize opportunities for success and minimize the likelihood of devastating system failures. Further, by including teenagers and young adults now, we increase the future disaster readiness in their communities.

ADVANTAGES OF NONPROFIT ORGANIZATION INVOLVEMENT IN DISASTER RESPONSE AND RECOVERY

The Duke University Non-Governmental Organization Research Guide (Shreve & Galli, 2006) identifies several strengths of nongovernmental organizations. These include strong grassroots links, expertise in field-based development, innovation and adaptability, participatory methodologies and tools, long-term commitment with emphasis on sustainability, and cost-effectiveness. All of these strengths complement attributes of government and business interventions to bolster crisis response and recovery. We will address them in four general categories: community involvement; flexibility and adaptability; commitment, follow-through and sustainability; and cost-effectiveness.

Community Involvement

Interorganizational Collaboration

Trust among faith-based organizations enables resource sharing and rapid responses that would not otherwise be feasible. For example, the Southern Baptists often leave a food trailer in a disaster area for other groups to use, then retrieve it after the last user calls to say that they have finished. Occasionally, they do not retrieve their equipment. Bonner recalls,

We have responded to disasters locally as well as internationally. Alabama Baptist flew the airlift kitchen to Iran, what was it, three years ago, when they had their earthquake. We actually set up the airlift kitchen to feed Iranians, but after about two weeks there, they decided they didn't want the

Baptists there. So we left the airlift kitchen, and Christians, Iranian Christians, were feeding people there. That feeding unit is located now in Iran, permanently. And we have a new airlift kitchen now in the state.

On the topic of interorganizational collaboration, Bonner continues,

> The state offers some ministries that we can't offer locally. There is a state feeding unit that is an 18-wheeler... We've had good cooperation with FEMA, or EMA here... We are working with Salvation Army; we are working with Compassion Coalition; we are working with—I think there are 29 different organizations.

The ability to partner with other nonprofits, government agencies, and local workers in disaster areas enables nonprofit organizations to adjust their capacity and contribution to suit each new circumstance quickly and effectively.

As nonprofit organizations or volunteers step forward to respond to an emergency, their developing credibility increases their impact. Nader explained the importance of credibility in the formation of an ad hoc response center:

> One case was a local gymnasium where a lady who had lost everything, her house and everything, took over this gym at a local school and began to collect the donations from all these little groups who were coming. She stored them, segregated them, lined them up so people in that neighborhood could come every day and get stuff. Then another group of a doctor, his wife, and a couple of nurses came and asked where they could help. "Oh, go to the gym where this lady, say Susan, she's taking care of the whole neighborhood." So the word spread that this lady was the person to go to. She had credibility. When you have credibility, people say, "that's a more efficient place to go; forget FEMA. I'm going over there." You saw these guys—Scientologists—they decided, "let's go help these people here because we can have a more meaningful effect," and they became worker bees. You'd see them in their yellow shirts, 'Scientology,' and they were just working, working, working. That's an example of how something started out of nothing—just a lady, the community work, and a couple of helpers—and became one of the most important logistical points to the extent that we... set them up with a network so they could communicate. We set up phones so people could call now to their families, say "I'm ok." So, slowly that became a place where people were relying on them for services.... She was probably being the most effective, as far as I could tell. Now, being a logistics guy, I'm thinking, 'why is it that FEMA wasn't as effective?' And again, it goes back to credibility; they were too big, and there was no real plan for the particular needs of that area.

Social and Community Ties

Links between volunteer groups or nonprofit organizations and local people frequently enable use of resources that the government could not obtain. When Kimbrough returned to New Orleans as a volunteer, his group used local apartments, dorm rooms, and campus buildings. They obtained drinking water, disinfectant, and gloves from a local religious group. In short, they relied on personal networks within the community.

Remaly-Netter emphasizes the importance of building links with community members and maintaining those links throughout a disaster response effort.

> The disaster happens locally, and it heals locally. In my mind the most important aspect to our work is to bring together the local grassroots organizations that have money, materials, or human power, to effectively meet the needs of those who have no other resources to recover from the disaster.

When local organizations become involved, myriad resources become available. Crucial among these is social capital. To investigate this on a local scale, I asked Tim Plant what his church is prepared to do in case of a pandemic that overloads the health system. At first, he said that they hadn't thought about this and don't have any plans. But then he started talking about the social structure within their organization.

> As far as a support group, we call it Sunday School. Sunday School is designed for small group Bible study and also for ministry within that small group. We have seven ministers on the staff here. There are 2,300 members. As a Baptist church, we can't staff enough of us to take care of all those people. We have to depend on that small group, as an organization, to take care of the ministry means. For the most part, they do an excellent job of that ... as time goes on, you have to give support with deaths in the family, older parents, all this type of stuff. Most of the support for that goes through that organization. It's designed to deal with a lot.... The maximum [in a group] would probably be 45 or 50 people. We have a deacon that is responsible for every Sunday School class, and I am responsible for the entire organization. I meet with the department directors on a regular basis for communication. We don't have a committee that is the hospitality committee or the grievance committee; that is all handled through the Sunday School organization... The senior adults, anybody over about 60: you can walk into the class, and if there are 15 ladies enrolled in that class and 10 of them are there, they know where the other five are. They know what's going on in their lives, and they respond to those problems.

The church's day-to-day ministry plan, designed with hierarchical macrocommunications among decentralized membership groups, has the capacity to assist every member as soon as a problem arises. Local systems like this, operating in concert, have great potential for rebuilding a community in case of disaster. They may also provide foundations for coordinating good-neighbor responses to disasters that affect adjoining communities.

Volunteer Resources

Community-based networks may include a lot of people, many of whom are willing to help in an emergency. To rally the volunteers, Cackowski recommends having a phone tree "with no more than five numbers for any one person to call." At the city level, existing infrastructure may be expanded to notify residents if needed.

> Our City Emergency Management office now has a reverse 9-1-1 system. Everyone in the city (population approximately 27,000), may now be notified in the event of any need. These needs could include a lost child, severe weather, flooding, or literally any situation that may arise where many members of the community must be notified. Within a matter of minutes, an emergency message may be written, and as fast as you hit "send," all 27,000 residents, businesses, schools will receive a telephone message.

For areas that lack mass-information capabilities, Cackowski recommends asking two or three homebound volunteers to take charge of the phone-tree calls.

Flexibility and Adaptability

Unlike government agencies that embed staff members in rigid and costly bureaucracies, nonprofit organizations have the freedom to structure their operations to fit the circumstances. People-to-people approaches in many nonprofit organizations enable them to identify idiosyncratic needs and customize their services to meet those needs. Fluid partnerships with others allow them to adapt rapidly and effectively. For example, Kay and Mac McGrath mentioned receiving support from a variety of large and small nonprofit organizations, along with businesses, individual volunteers, FEMA, and University of Alabama students. Although their specific needs changed over time, people from the local churches and Good Samaritan Clinic continued to meet the needs as they arose for several months following the hurricane. Ad hoc teams are particularly useful in this regard. A team can be composed for a particular situation, equipped for that task, and deployed without the delays inherent in creating a new task force within a typical government bureaucracy.

Another example of nonprofit flexibility occurred recently when Operation Blessing organized teams of volunteers to deliver mosquito-eating fish to abandoned swimming pools in the South where mosquito larvae were growing (Operation Blessing, 2006b). This simple, organic solution to a potential health hazard depended on cooperation among people from many different organizations, including the local health agency. By destroying the mosquito larvae, this joint effort reduced the likelihood that malaria and other diseases would follow the existing devastation.

Commitment, Follow-Through, and Sustainable Solutions

Many nonprofit organizations exhibit greater concern about the mission than about ownership or recognition. For example, local churches frequently feed thousands of people under the banner of the Red Cross (G. Bonner, personal communication, March 2006). When Operation Blessing conducts relief efforts, they coordinate volunteers from many other organizations, none of which appear to be interested in accolades or media attention.

Organizations such as Church World Service look beyond the immediate need to help communities plan for the future. Very often, nonprofit support continues for several years following a major disaster. For example,

> they were still doing rebuilds eight years after Floyd. Any of those organizations donated human hours for years and years and years after the storm. And this is true all across the country. It's still going on after the California wildfires. It's true in Kentucky and East Kentucky; they are still rebuilding homes from the storms and the flooding back in 2003.
>
> United Methodist Committee on Relief provides a good deal of case management training across the country. They are the premier case management training arm of long-term recovery. They will pull in after a long-term recovery group has been organized and provide training for that local group for case management. Then rebuild teams, such as Mennonite Disaster Services, Presbyterians, and Lutherans, and CRWRC (Christian Reformed World Relief Committee) and Church of the Brethren, and many others, will provide volunteer labor for the casework that has been done. (L. Remaly, personal communication, May 2006)

Cost-Effectiveness

Less bureaucracy means less administrative expense, so more of the donated resources can reach the desired destination. In nonprofit organizations where everyone on a disaster team is a volunteer, administrative costs can be negligible. For example, when the Tuscaloosa Southern Baptist Convention fields a team of volunteers to clear away fallen trees and mud, the effort is coordinated by a voluntary team leader and completed by people who generate no paperwork beyond the initial application and training that were completed before the disaster happened. The local churches, which support disaster relief as one of their ministries, provide training and safety equipment, then cover the costs of the operation. This enables volunteers to apply their skills to the problem without worrying about anything else (G. Bonner, personal communication, March 2006). At Calvary Baptist Church in Tuscaloosa, every dollar collected from members to help Katrina evacuees went directly to aid, usually accompanied by volunteer time from people associated with the church (T. M. Plant, personal communication, March 2006). As this scenario repeats across a region or a nation, relief teams that operate under the sponsorship of larger charitable and religious organizations provide enormous benefits to local communities at no cost to the community or to the government.

A second approach to efficiency arises when large nonprofit organizations use their assets to leverage the time, talent, and resources provided by others. For example, Operation Blessing International Relief and Development Corporation (OBI), which consistently spends over 99% of its money on humanitarian programs (Barrett, 2005; Operation Blessing, 2006a), forms collaborative networks with others:

> We are the intermediary between our donors and the people they seek to help. With that understanding in mind, OBI maximizes the efficacy of every dollar of funding through leveraging. We encourage matching contributions from churches, ministries and other benevolent organizations that are part of our assistance network. (Operation Blessing, 2006c)

OBI also mediates between government agencies and smaller nonprofit organizations and volunteers. From the warehouse where they stored relief supplies for Katrina recovery, OBI was able to "process hundreds of daily work orders; strategize recovery efforts with local government officials, FEMA and partnering agencies; and provide full accommodations to house and feed the hundreds of volunteers arriving weekly." To facilitate volunteer efforts, OBI informs people, via the internet, of needs. They screen applicants who would like to help, and then provide all necessities to accomplish their tasks. Volunteer accommodations include all meals, sleeping quarters in a secure, heated facility, and hot showers (Operation Blessing, 2006a). By interfacing between governmental agencies and willing helpers, this organization maximizes the gain from each volunteer while minimizing wasted donations.

In the area of cost-effectiveness, some organizations seem to perform better than others. The American National Red Cross, the Salvation

Army, and Catholic Charities are three of the largest charitable organizations. The Red Cross, a nonprofit organization chartered by the U.S. Congress to respond to disasters, is known for managing emergency shelters, coordinating the efforts of volunteers, and distributing resources that have been provided by donations during emergencies. Of the nearly $3 billion received in donations for the hurricanes in the Southern United States in 2005, the Red Cross received about $2 billion. Despite their high profile, however, their efficiency and reliability have been questioned following the September 11, 2001 terrorist strikes and the Southern U.S. hurricanes in 2005 (Williams, 2005). For example, in 3 years the Red Cross spent over $500,000 on consultants to polish their image (Salmon & Gaul, 2006). They have had five leaders in 7 years, paying about $2.8 million in severance, plus another $780,000 to the most recently resigned leader (Salmon, 2006). According to Forbes.com's annual report on charities (Barrett, 2005), the FY 2004 salary paid to Red Cross's leader was well over twice that paid to the leader of Salvation Army, and three times the pay of Catholic Charities' leader. Given that disaster needs generally exceed available resources, it is important that we identify to responsible organizations that truly ascribe to the ideals of voluntarism and altruism, with good organizational practices to back them up.

NEEDS OF NONPROFIT ORGANIZATIONS AND VOLUNTEERS INVOLVED IN DISASTER RESPONSE AND RECOVERY

Despite their intrinsic strengths, nonprofit organizations and volunteers that respond to disasters can accomplish more if they have support from government, from the community, and from other helping organizations. This is particularly true with regard to the weaker features of nonprofit organizations, which may include limited institutional capacity and interorganizational coordination, small scale of interventions, or difficulty understanding the broad context (Shreve & Galli, 2006). There are also specialized needs when working in areas that may be devoid of normal sanitation, communication infrastructure, and transportation. Because all of these concerns grow larger given smaller organizational size and/or isolation, we may reasonably assume that they are at least as relevant for ad hoc teams and individual volunteers as for formal organizations. Many of these issues can be addressed through good interorganizational system design, leadership, and planning, as previously discussed. Others require special attention to communication and coordination networks that will remain effective during an ongoing crisis. A few require access to resources that should be shared within a network or provided by government agencies because individuals and organizations cannot effectively maintain them.

Communication Infrastructure

Proactive network building, strategic planning, and volunteer training can establish foundations for cooperation under crisis conditions. Even strong networks and excellent training cannot fully compensate for failures of infrastructure or technology that cut off communications. Communication structures that distribute timely updates to on-site volunteers, donors, victims, and potential helpers are crucial for smooth implementation of relief and recovery activities. A network that supports rapid information transfer without overloading individuals with unnecessary information is ideal. To accomplish this, we need stable infrastructure or alternative media such as dedicated cell phones or radio frequencies. This may be accomplished through preplanning that puts communication technologies in the hands of trained volunteers in each region. When that system is lacking, information transfer may be accomplished through hastily formed communication networks provided by military or other governmental emergency teams.

For example, during the Katrina response, the "Hastily Formed Networks" wireless communication system set up in Waveland, Mississippi, by the Naval Postgraduate School Detachment allowed relief workers to obtain information about rescue operations and supply flows (C. E. Nader, personal communication, March 2006). Teams from Florida also arrived with complete, self-contained communications equipment that supported their activities. This level of equipment may exceed the capacity of community-based organizations, but there are some options suitable for local organizations.

Taking a proactive approach, the Southern Baptist Association in Tuscaloosa, Alabama, is developing its own ham radio network as a backup for communication systems provided by the government. As Gary Bonner explained,

> My understanding is that EMA is going to provide radios to all of us who have teams… but let's say you have thunderstorms and five tornadoes come through from the North end to the South and the communication network is completely disrupted. There's going to have to be some type of radio communication. Even with that, you don't know, because you still have to have towers. Cell phones are useless when you have tornadoes. You start knocking out towers, and cell phones stay tied up. I have a young man who works with the Tuscaloosa County Board of Education, with the computers, who wants to start a ham radio group here…. That's still one of the best ways

to communicate during disasters. You can have small towers at your house, and it would take more than a series of tornadoes coming through to knock them all out. Communication is an area that is going to need more work, right now, than anything else.

Cackowski offered similar advice:

Keep in mind that communications may fail and that you should have amateur (ham) radio operators. There may be organizations of citizens band (CB) operators. We learned during an exercise in Kentucky that the ham operators were the only communications folks that could get through.

Resources that Cannot or Should Not be Maintained by Each Organization or Volunteer Group

These resources include sanitation facilities, communication systems, logistics, and large-scale interventions that require special equipment or yield economies of scale. In some cases, large nonprofit organizations provide the infrastructure for smaller groups or organizations to volunteer effectively, as we saw in the example of Operation Blessing. In other instances, groups of organizations work together to make equipment available to whichever members need it. For large-scale logistics or interoperability issues, military and security forces are particularly well suited because of their ongoing expertise and existing portable equipment.

Security and Other Public Goods

When asked what nonprofit organizations need from government, Bonner replied,

I think anytime you end up with a situation, as you ended up in New Orleans with the looting, that the local law enforcement will have to have help from the state level.... In the case of a disaster where you have hurricanes hitting the Gulf Coast like they hit, you have to have the input from the national government. You have to have FEMA to come in, but I still believe the first response has to be from the local people. If the local people are on top of things, then they can say, "this is what we need. Get us this help, and get it here." Then, at that point in time, the federal government ought to be ready to respond.

Sanitation

The Alabama Southern Baptist Convention provides portable showers and water purification equipment for use as needed in the Southern United States Bonner explained,

[The Alabama Southern Baptist Disaster Relief coordinator] sent a letter saying "we want to give your feeding unit a water purification unit if you will send me two people to be trained on it...." I think there are about 10 different feeding units in this state that will be provided water purification units.... There are some shower units, and generally they are shower units that can be taken different places.... But you don't have enough if you talk about going to many, many different locations. It would be good if each unit could have their own trailer as far as the shower unit and things like that, but then again you'd have to have so many vehicles to pull it. We don't need them all the time. In fact, they would probably be used one time out of every 20 occurrences, so that would be a lot of money to put into that type of situation.

The portable showers and water purification units are stored in different regions of the state to be accessible wherever they might be needed. This approach conserves resources while allowing reasonable preparation on a regional basis.

Although many national and international nonprofits coordinate with local organizations that have water and sanitation facilities available, there are times when local resources fail. In the backwoods of Mississippi after Hurricane Katrina, Nader observed

people that were coming with resources, individual guys who got donations from a church and just set up out there. That did two things. It created more work for FEMA because then you have people coming to help, but they need food, they need bathroom facilities and sanitation. You clog the system even though you have goodies to bring, but if you didn't think, 'How am I going to support myself?' you need water and food. You can only bring so much food on your own even if you come in a big RV. The level of support you brought, and the level of soft support you brought, determines how much of a burden you're going to be in the process.

Sanitation and water, needed to maintain volunteers while they are on-site, are crucial, and often overlooked. Portable sanitation facilities, incorporated into self-contained disaster units or maintained at regional levels, are one solution that has been adopted by many nonprofit organizations. Another answer is to reduce the number of extraneous volunteers at a disaster site. To accomplish this, we need better communications and logistics at the system level.

Resource Management and Tracking

Remaly-Netter emphasized the importance of advance planning among nonprofit organizations, unaffiliated volunteers, and state agencies so that volunteers do not "inundate and make a second disaster happen." Cackowski explained how goods and volunteer services were

handled in Kentucky to minimize the level of effort required at the destination farther south:

> After Katrina the VOAD in Kentucky, for example, was put in charge of
> all donations. Everything. In a very short time they opened empty ware-
> houses, accepted and catalogued goods, prepared pallets that they then
> shrink-wrapped with a contents list for each pallet. The pallets could then
> be loaded on trucks and, at the receiving end, there was no need to go
> through the pallet to see what was there. Appropriate goods went to the
> appropriate place in a very fast, efficient manner. Did that take time? Yes.
> Did that SAVE time? YES! The time saved was more important in the
> Gulf States when the goods were received. One did not have to plow
> through used clothing and magazines to find cleaning supplies. There
> were warehouses around the Commonwealth where goods were either
> brought by individuals or by organizations who collected in another part
> of the region to be palletized.

Sometimes logistics present challenges that exceed the capacity of
large nonprofit organizations or coalitions. Despite excellent efforts to
coordinate with each other, nonprofits need more systematic logistics support. The Fritz Institute, following the 2004 tsunami in Southeast Asia,
surveyed members of 18 of the largest international nonprofit organizations that were active in disaster relief there. They found that the majority
of these very large organizations lacked adequate software for tracking
resources, and that "Competing supply chains for procurement and transportation caused congestion at local airports and roads, taxing already
limited capacity." (Fritz Institute, 2005, p. 4). Their report recommended
development of flexible technology solutions and training of logistics professionals at the national and international level who could be dispatched
to disaster sites as needed. In the case of logistics, the best solution
requires standardized tracking methods administered at the system level
(for more information on development of an appropriate logistics system,
see Braunbeck & Mastria, 2007). The U.S. committee reviewing the
response to Hurricane Katrina concluded that

> The Department of Homeland Security, in coordination with State and local
> governments and the private sector, should develop a modern, flexible, and
> transparent logistics system. This system should be based on established
> contracts for stockpiling commodities at the local level for emergencies and
> the provision of goods and services during emergencies. The Federal gov-
> ernment must develop the capacity to conduct large-scale logistical opera-
> tions that supplement and, if necessary, replace State and local logistical
> systems by leveraging resources within both the public sector and the pri-
> vate sector. (The White House, 2006, p. 56)

Standardized, Interoperable Technology

Along with logistics, technological compatibility must be overseen at the systemic level. Although federal governments and military organizations have the ability to do this, various departments, even within one nation, may adopt incompatible technologies that impede joint action. *The Katrina Lessons Learned Report* (The White House, 2006, p. 43) highlighted this problem.

> The separate commands divided the area of operations geographically and supported response efforts separately, with the exception of the evacuations of the Superdome and the Convention Center in New Orleans. Equipment interoperability problems further hindered an integrated response. Similar issues of bifurcated operations and interoperability challenges were also present between the military and civilian leadership. (p. 43.)

Clearly, we need to develop equipment standards to facilitate joint responses by organizations engaged in crisis management.

CONCLUSIONS

Considerable research effort has been invested to understand organizational designs that facilitate success in unpredictable environments. Years of experience by local, national, and global disaster response organizations have developed processes that parallel the theoretical principles in many respects. By combining theory with practical knowledge, we have identified several guidelines for enhancing performance in crisis response systems that include nonprofit organizations, unaffiliated volunteers, and governmental agencies. Streamlined information processing and data analysis are crucial for success. At the system level, this should follow hierarchical communication channels, but lateral ties remain crucial for coordinating interdependent tasks and sharing information that is specific to a region or activity. Redundancy in all critical functions should be built into the system. At the local level, all participants in crisis management should be included in decentralized collaborative networks. Standardization of communication and tracking technology, identification of assets, and tentative allocation of roles before a crisis can increase the likelihood that disaster will be averted or mitigated.

To achieve an optimal system, proactive planning and training are required. At the community level, these include strategizing, network building, and asset mapping. Among nonprofit organizations, increased communication and coordination of resources could go far to increase the overall impact of their efforts. For ongoing collaboration during crises, backup communication systems need to be in place before a disaster strikes. Ideally, these systems should be arranged to speed top-down information distribution, accommodate lateral communications, and enable bottom-up information flows. The system must include enough redundancy to remain functional if a few nodes become unavailable or overloaded with information.

Mechanistic and organic structures each have a place in large-scale crisis management. A hierarchical structure can provide streamlined information flows from central or lead sources, such as FEMA, DoD, or state EMAs, to appointed gatekeepers in the community. Standardized technology, language, and procedures can be important in the coordination of system components. At the point of service, however, organic structures are crucial to accommodate rapid changes. People on the ground during an event must be able to contact and collaborate with each other without going through a hierarchy. When this capability is lacking, resources are wasted, efforts are constrained, and outcomes are limited.

It is important for nonprofit organizations and volunteers to have the freedom to use nonstandard approaches to solve nonstandard problems, and to organize themselves with regard to space, time, and task as the needs arise. At the same time, they need government or private infrastructure to facilitate information transfer, coordination, and communications. By identifying each organization's response potential and integrating related functions through proactive network building, our response to the next disaster could run much more smoothly than any we have experienced thus far.

REFERENCES

Barrett, W. P. (2005). *Special Report: The 200 Largest U.S. Charities, 11.23.05, 3:00 PM ET.* Retrieved February 7, 2007, from http://www.forbes.com/2005/11/18/largest-charities-ratings_05charities_land.html

Braunbeck, R. A., & Mastria, M. F. (2007). Technological transformation of logistics in support of crisis management. In D. E. Gibbons (Ed.), *Communicable crises: Prevention, Response and Recovery in the Global Arena* (pp. 40-80). Charlotte, NC. Information Age Publishing.

Burns, T. & Stalker, G. M. (1961). *The management of innovation.* London: Tavistock.

Cackowski, E. (2006). Kentucky Commission on Community Volunteerism and Service Director, E-mail correspondence, May 2006.

Comfort, L. K. (1996). Self Organization in Disaster Response: The Great Hanshin, Japan, Earthquake of January 17, 1995. Quick Response Report #78. Submitted to the Natural Hazards Center, University of Colorado at Boulder in partial fulfillment of the requirements for a Quick Response Grant, December 7, 1995. Revised: May 16, 1996.

Comfort, L. K. (2007). Asymmetric information processes in extreme events: The 26 December 2004 Sumatran earthquake and tsunami. In D. E. Gibbons (Ed.), *Communicable Crises: Prevention, Response and Recovery in the Global Arena*.

Eisenhardt, K. M. (1989). Making fast strategic decisions in high-velocity environments. *Academy of Management Journal, 32*, 543–576.

Fritz Institute. (2005). *Logistics and the effective delivery of humanitarian relief.* Retrieved May 29, 2006, from http://www.fritzinstitute.org/PDFs/Programs/ TsunamiLogistics0605.pdf.

Hofstetter, M. (2006). *NGOs and disaster response—Who are these guys and what do they want anyway?* Retrieved May 21, 2006, from http://cdmha.org/ Presentations.htm.

Mitroff, I. I. (2004). *Crisis leadership: Planning for the unthinkable*. Hoboken, N.J.: Wiley.

Operation Blessing. (2006a). *Hurricane relief: Volunteer with Operation Blessing*. Retrieved May 11, 2006, from http://www.ob.org/projects/hurricane_relief/volunteer.asp.

Operation Blessing. (2006b). *Gambusia fish bite back*. Retrieved from http:// www.ob.org/programs/disaster_relief/news/2006/ dr_2006_0420_bugbusters.asp?NP_ID=1772, May 11, 2006.

Operation Blessing. (2006c). *About us*. Retrieved May 11, 2006, from http:// www.ob.org/about/index.asp.

Remaly-Netter, L. (2006). Church World Service Emergency Response Program, Disaster Response and Recovery Liaison. Personal interview, May 2006.

Rochlin, G. I., LaPorte, T. R., & Roberts, K. H. (1987, Autumn). The self-designing highreliability organization, Aircraft carrier flight operations at sea. *Naval War College Review, 40*(4), 76–90.

Salmon, J. L. (2006, March 4). Red Cross gave ousted executive $780,000 deal. *Washington Post*, p. A09.

Salmon, J. L., & Gaul, G. (2006, February 27). Red Cross spent $500,000 in 3 years to boost its profile. *Washington Post*, p. A08.

Shreve, C., & Galli, C. (2006). *Categorizing NGOs. Non-governmental organizations research guide*. Duke University online publication. Retrieved May 22, 2006, from http://docs.lib.duke.edu/igo/guides/ngo/index.htm

Siggelkow, N., & Rivkin, J. W. (2005). Speed and search: Designing organizations for turbulence and complexity. *Organization Science, 16*(2), 101–122.

United States Agency International Development. (2006). *Private Voluntary Organizations Registry*. Retrieved May 21, 2006, from http://www.pvo.net/usaid/ index.html

The White House. (2006). *The federal response to Hurricane Katrina: Lessons learned*, chapter 2. Retrieved May 25, 2006, from http://www.whitehouse.gov/reports/ katrina-lessons-learned

CHAPTER 8

HOW GOVERNMENTS CAN HELP BUSINESSES WEATHER A CATACLYSMIC DISASTER

Roxanne Zolin and Fredric Kropp

Natural disasters, terrorism, or other nonfinancial sources of crisis may lead to economic difficulties that delay the recovery process. Disasters take an enormous toll on businesses, ranging from short periods where no income will be generated, to permanent closure. When businesses fail, the economic repercussions add more negative consequences to a community already struck by disaster. One of the first needs in disaster recovery is distribution of goods and services. One of the first goals in reconstruction is re-growth of the economy. Both of these needs are served by business activity in the community. It is important, therefore, that government bodies assist and interact with affected businesses to increase their chances of survival. What helps or hinders business survival of a cataclysmic disaster? In this chapter, we explore characteristics of government response that can help more businesses survive and prosper in the midst of a communicable crisis.

INTRODUCTION

Large-scale flooding, tornados, hurricanes, earthquakes, terrorism, military actions, and other major disasters—if severe enough—can have cata-

Communicable Crises: Prevention, Response, and Recovery in the Global Arena, pp. 241–264

clysmic effects on communities. They can create enormous damage to people, possessions, homes, infrastructure, and the natural environment. Disasters also take an enormous toll on organizations and businesses, ranging from short periods, where no income will be generated, to permanent closure. Some business owners may decide to rebuild elsewhere, producing additional negative consequences to a community struck by disaster.

A thriving economy has a fluctuating population of new and existing businesses. Businesses are created, grow, change focus, or die, on a regular basis. This is a natural part of the business life cycle. However, the normal stresses of economic cycles, competition, cultural and technological change, and other external threats to business survival can be trivial compared to the sudden losses created by a natural or man-made disaster.

Recent disasters, in the United States and around the world, have brought attention to the importance of quick and effective disaster response. Proper response can save lives, reduce human injury and suffering, protect possessions, preserve buildings and infrastructure, and protect the natural environment from further damage. Quick and effective response is also necessary to the survival of businesses impacted by the disaster. One of the first needs in disaster recovery is distribution of goods and services. One of the first goals in reconstruction is re-growth of the economy. Both of these needs are served by business activity in the community. Therefore, it is important to assist the survival of businesses in disaster areas.

Many, if not most, businesses do not have plans to cope with a major disaster. Even if they do, their plans may be flawed or poorly suited to the actual disaster that occurs. Although the business disaster plans may address a wide range of disasters, particular challenges are faced during cataclysmic disasters, when the whole region's infrastructure may be destroyed. In addition, because official first responders focus on assisting human survival and reducing suffering, businesses often are left to fend for themselves.

Government's first and primary responsibility is to individual life and limb. Nonetheless, it is important to facilitate business recovery, which can provide goods and services, jobs and income for the community during reconstruction. What helps or hinders business survival of a cataclysmic disaster? In this chapter, we will explore characteristics of government response that can help more businesses survive.

Although a wide variety of organizations can be threatened by a natural disaster, the focus of this chapter is on businesses. Our conceptual definition of a business is any commercial, professional, industrial, or service organization that conducts activities designed to satisfy the needs or wants of its customers. Businesses can be publicly or privately owned or controlled. Though we recognize the importance of governmental and nongovernmental organizations (NGOs) whose role is to assist disaster victims, they are beyond the scope of this chapter. For this work, we studied the business response to a natural disaster, but many of the remedies described in this paper could also be applied to man-made disasters.

We first report on interviews with businesses who survived Hurricane Katrina, describing the stages of business response during and after the disaster. Then we show how the business environment created by disasters requires businesses to revisit activities typically associated with the start-up phase of the business life cycle. Based upon this observation, we present a conceptual framework of entrepreneurial orientation and business survival in the context of a cataclysmic disaster. Finally, we propose guidelines for federal, state, and local government to assist postdisaster business survival, and we make recommendations for future research.

Business Disaster Survival

We define business disaster survival as maintaining or resuming business operations during or after a major disaster, such as a hurricane, terrorist attack, or military action. At the time of Hurricane Katrina, there were over 22,000 business establishments in areas of Louisiana and Mississippi that FEMA later designated as flooded or damaged areas. The flooded areas of Louisiana contained 18,078 establishments employing over 300,000 people who earned almost $3 billion per quarter. Many local businesses could be lost forever when their assets are destroyed, employees are dispersed, and markets are disrupted, even if the business has a disaster plan and insurance.

Firms surviving earthquakes are affected by factors relating to the firm, the earthquake, and the postdisaster aid (Dahlhamer & Tierney, 1997). Firm factors include the size of the firm and their financial condition before the earthquake. Earthquake factors include the shaking intensity and disruption of business operations. In terms of postdisaster aid, research indicates a gap in the perceptions of small business owners and government officials about the availability, usability, and effectiveness of public support and assistance following an earthquake (Furlong & Scheberle, 1998).

Disaster preparedness programs typically include evacuation plans, emergency operation centers, and computing disaster plans, but they do not address the issue of business survival (Castillo, 2004). This new area of "Business Continuity is the ability to retain a revenue stream through a crisis" (Castillo, p. 18).

In this chapter, we attempt to answer two questions: What helps a business survive a cataclysmic natural disaster? What can governments do to contribute to business survival?

We interviewed a number of organizations about their experience surviving the Hurricane Katrina disaster. The organizations included large and small, public and private organizations. We will focus on three exemplary organizations[1]:

- Engineering Software: A small engineering software development partnership with about 80 personnel at one location in the disaster zone
- City University: A large educational institution with over 1,200 faculty and 17,000 students at one location in the disaster zone, with the parent organization in Baton Rouge, Louisiana
- Department of Information Processing (DIP): A large public information technology (IT) service provider with approximately 1,500 employees located in the disaster zone, but with counterparts in other locations.

STAGES OF BUSINESS RESPONSE TO CATACLYSMIC DISASTER

When considering survival through a major disaster, it is useful to start by recognizing that the focus of business survivors changes quickly and businesses "shift gears" as time progresses. Following a cataclysmic disaster, there appear to be distinct time frames in which the focus of attention and activity shift. These stages can be described as:

First Hours: Personal Situation Awareness

Businesses gather information in order to develop a better picture of the conditions they face. The situational awareness starts with an assessment of the physical well-being of individuals, expanding to a wider circle of personal relevance. Immediately following a disaster, business owners or managers reported responding like others in the disaster area by first determining that they and their loved ones are alive and unhurt. The business owner or manager might ask first, "Am I alive and unhurt?" Followed by, "Is my family unhurt? Are my friends and extended family unhurt?" Followed by, "Are my business colleagues and employees unhurt?" This investigation of personal situational awareness may stall or stop to respond to the situation if one or more loved ones are injured.

Similarly, the business owner or manager might conduct an expanding circle of questions to establish situational awareness of physical property. In this case, they might ask first, "Is my home undamaged?" This leads to questions like, "Is my car undamaged?" and moves very quickly to questions like, "Is my business undamaged?" One of our respondents assumed that his home and business were destroyed in the flood, when, in fact, they were simply inaccessible. It might take days or months to answer these questions, but we found that business people move quickly from personal to business situational awareness.

First Day: Business Situational Awareness

In this stage, we began to notice the difference between firms with effective disaster plans and those with little planning or ineffective plans.

Department of Information Processing (DIP) reported having an effective plan that was practiced regularly. In this case, the management team evacuated to nearby cities and maintained close contact as they constructed their assessment of the situation.

City University reported having a disaster response plan, but said that they did not know what it contained and it did not address the situation that developed. The plan assumed that the buildings would be damaged, but it did not anticipate that the buildings might be undamaged, but inaccessible. In this situation, a small team formed of people that, by coincidence, worked in the offices of the parent organization and banded together to save the business. This group contained some top management, but also other individuals who volunteered, mainly because they arrived while the team was forming and had useful skills, like Web building and network management.

Engineering Software did not have a formal disaster plan. They reported that, due to the lack of communication between the partners of the firm, both partners operated independently, falling back on their typical roles in the partnership. One partner focused on maintaining client contacts and the other on reestablishing the infrastructure. Thus, Engineering Software, which typically operated in a decentralized manner, reported that their decentralization gave them the ability to make decisions independently, and that was their "saving grace."

Maintaining the organization's identity was an initial focus mentioned by two respondents. Engineering Software did this by making sure the Web site was operational. City University went to their parent organization and asked for resources to assist in survival. Both focused efforts on getting their Web sites up and running to achieve the goal of the next stage: finding people.

DIP employees had practiced their disaster plan. They reported that they had no disruption to their Web site or to their client service.

First Week: Finding People

When they learned that Hurricane Katrina would hit New Orleans, many local residents evacuated to nearby cities such as Houston, Texas, or Jacksonville, Florida. This created the need for the businesses without effective disaster plans to locate top management, key personnel, and employees. Supply chains were broken because key suppliers, with personnel missing, were not able to deliver their inputs. In addition, many retailers closed due to inadequate human resources.

After the hurricane hit and the levies broke, cell phone reception was completely unavailable for some time. As the Engineering Software partner reported, "Anyone with a 504 area code cell phone could not be contacted, and if anyone got a new phone number, no one knew what their phone number was." This firm instituted an 800 conference call number and published a notice to employees on their Web site for an 8:30 a.m. dial-in conference call to locate their evacuated personnel. Within one day, they had located all but 2 or 3 of their 80 employees.

Even at DIP, with effective disaster plans, no one anticipated the complete devastation of the communications infrastructure. They have subsequently modified their plans to have cell phones based outside their local area. They also did not anticipate the situation in which their workforce would be homeless. One of their major challenges was balancing personal needs of employees with business requirements.

First 2 Weeks: Reconstructing Management

City University shifted authority after the first week from the ad hoc business survival team to the reconstructed top management team. DIP established its management team in surrounding cities and began planning for the future. They used the opportunity created by the disaster to implement changes in the system that they had long wanted to make.

For Engineering Software, the challenge was to get back to work. They reported getting a helicopter to bring ice to the police—in exchange for being allowed to go into their building and remove their computers. They then shipped the computers to their people, who were dispersed around the country.

First Month: Reconstructing Strategy

After reconstructing the management team, the next challenge was to develop a new business strategy for the new business environment. The new strategies addressed replacement of destroyed or inaccessible premises, but also identified new business opportunities.

The business survivors could not return to their premises, so they had to identify temporary workspace for their returning employees. Engineering Software rented five workstations in an office that specializing in providing temporary office space and business services. This proved to be an extremely useful strategy because most of the other workstations were rented by the local newspaper. As a result, the company obtained firsthand information from the reporters sharing the serviced office. After the first few weeks, the firm rented temporary office space and tried to secure office equipment from their existing offices, but they had difficulty getting authority to enter the flooded area. Gaining access to quarantined areas was a major problem for these surviving businesses.

City University, whose faculty and students were dispersed throughout the country, could not access their buildings for 2 months. Instead of encouraging faculty and students to return, they asked their faculty to set up online courses. Prior to Katrina, the school had only about 60 online classes, and the administrators hoped that they could provide 1 or 2 hundred classes online. They were surprised to be able to offer 1,200 classes online. As the respondent said, "Maybe the faculty had nothing else to do while they were away from home." The stated goal of the organization was to "keep everybody getting paid" so they could make the case that people were actually working and increase the chances of organizational survival.

With their effective disaster plan, DIP relocated their entire operation to Philadelphia within six weeks. From their Philadelphia data center, they continued to provide services without any interruption.

Some surviving organizations wasted no time in identifying opportunities created by the disaster. Engineering Software started building Web sites for other business survivors, documenting the status of structures, developing graphs of the depth of the flood in different areas, and assessing the percentage of structures impacted by the storm. Thus, the disaster opened the door on many new product opportunities for the firm.

First Quarter: Back to (the new) Business

By this stage, most of the businesses had resumed operations, but their new structures and processes reflected the changed environment. Engi-

neering Software had new business opportunities, DIP relocated to Philadelphia, and City University had developed a new distanced learning
capability.

Based on these observations, we propose that there are a number of
distinct stages of disaster survival leading to reconstruction. At each stage,
the business's focus of attention and its goals change. The time frames
may vary on an individual basis, and these stages may overlap or merge in
some cases. By thinking about these stages, we may be better able to
assess how a business has progressed following a disaster, and where its
attention will turn next.

LEARNING FROM BUSINESS SUCCESS

As these businesses responded to the disaster, their experiences were similar to those of new businesses. The disaster changed the business's
resources and created new opportunities and challenges, plunging each
business into strategy development similar to that required of new enterprises. These surviving businesses had the added advantage of established
relationships, but each made a major change to its business strategy and/
or operations. Rather than focusing on causes of business failure following a cataclysmic disaster, we focus on identifying reasons for successful
survival.

The Small Business Administration (SBA) reports that approximately
600,000 businesses have started every year for the last decade (Timmons
& Spinelli, 2004). These entrepreneurial business ventures (EBV) or
small-to-medium sized enterprises (SME) are important parts of the local
economy, providing jobs and fueling economic growth. Though rates vary
according to industry, more than half of these EBV start-ups fail within
the first 5 years. Business failure is a fact of life.

Experts cite many reasons for the high failure rate. Some of the reasons are internal to the business: lack of management competence, inex-
perience, a lack of strategic focus, poor cash flow management,
uncontrolled growth, and inadequate knowledge of marketing basics. In
contrast, EBVs or SMEs that have an entrepreneurial orientation perform
better than those businesses that do not (Kropp, Lindsay, & Shoham,
2006). Entrepreneurial Orientation (EO) refers to the organizational processes, methods, styles, practices, and decision-making activities
employed by entrepreneurs that lead to new entry (Lumpkin & Dess,
1996; Lumpkin & Dess, 2001; Stevenson & Jarillo, 1990). Entrepreneurial orientation can be characterized by proactiveness, willingness to take
reasonable risks in return for gain, creativity and innovation, a sense of
autonomy, and competitive aggressiveness in running a business (Lump-

kin & Dess, 1996). It interacts with environmental and organizational factors to influence organizational performance (Lumpkin & Dess, 2006).

Entrepreneurial orientation is distinguished from entrepreneurship and it has been shown to be an essential feature of high performing firms (Lumpkin & Dess, 1996). Entrepreneurial orientation includes the process, methods, or style of what the firm does. Entrepreneurship refers to the content of entrepreneurial decisions and addresses *what is undertaken*. Entrepreneurial orientation is particularly important because it is a way of being. For example, firms that are innovative and proactive possess a greater ability to respond quickly to challenges. As we found in this disaster, firms with the ability to respond to change have a greater capability to take advantage of new opportunities.

Although a disaster can suspend business income, it will not suspend the payments a business is required to make. As a result, more money is going out than coming in, potentially creating an immediate and severe cash flow problem. Disruption of electronic transactions, such as credit card and electronic fund transfers, can also make it difficult for most businesses to conduct financial transactions. Lack of cash flow can be overcome if creditors are confident that the business will obtain funds and pay its debts. The focus on survival and maintaining an adequate cash flow is analogous to the experience of SMEs in the early stages of business operations. It requires proactiveness, risk-taking, and innovation—all aspects of entrepreneurial orientation.

Other organizational factors also affect firm performance. The internal organizational factors include the size of the firm, structure, strategy and strategy-making processes, firm resources, culture and top management team characteristics (see Table 8.1). Each of these may affect survival or recovery. One of the most common reasons that small businesses fail is inadequate cash flow. Most SMEs operate on small profit margins and finely timed cash flows of incomes and expenses, making smaller firms more likely to close. Smaller firms could also have a large proportion of their resources within the disaster zone, thus reducing their chance of survival, compared to large multi-national firms for example, whose survival is unlikely to be threatened by a localized disaster.

Table 8.1.   Influence on Business Survival of Specificity of Destroyed Business Assets and Business Size

Specificity of Assets Destroyed	Small to Medium Business	Large Business
Low	Low survival	Medium survival
High	Medium survival	High survival

In addition to entrepreneurial orientation and other internal factors, forces that are external to the firm can contribute to its success or failure. Examples of these environmental forces include competition, the munificence of the environment in which the firms operate, economic conditions, and technology. In addition, sudden shocks to the business environment, such as natural or man-made disasters, can profoundly affect a business's chance of success. As exhibited in recent natural disasters like hurricanes, tsunamis, or major earthquakes, businesses can be forced to close as a result of external shocks. These business failures after a cataclysmic disaster differ from business failures during normal conditions. Business closures due to new competitors entering the market, unfavorable downturns in the economy, or inability to keep up with technological innovation may be much less concentrated than those experienced after a disaster. Disasters that cause the destruction of critical resources, loss of key personnel, or relocation of the market could result in immediate cessation of operations for many potentially interdependent organizations. The loss of business activities then impedes recovery in the community.

SURVIVAL AS A MEASURE OF ORGANIZATIONAL PERFORMANCE

Under normal situations, businesses evaluate their performance by examining metrics such as sales growth, market share, increase in customer base, profitability, return on investment, return on equity, and stakeholder satisfaction. Traditional measures of success—for example, return on investment, return on equity, and market share—are not as relevant to a business after a disaster. Performance goals for businesses after a disaster involve survival and rebuilding. The key question for stakeholders will be whether they want to invest the resources to stay in business and fight for survival.

> *Proposition 1:*   Immediately following a disaster, short-term survival is likely to become the business's major goal.

In the normal course of business, stakeholder satisfaction is measured in terms of return on investment or qualitative measures of personal satisfaction with the business. Following a disaster, stakeholders have to consciously decide whether to keep the business operating or close it. Cressey (2006) proposes that new business fails when the firm's value falls below the opportunity cost of staying in business. If the business's assets are too badly damaged, if it does not seem possible to resurrect the business, or for a myriad of other personal reasons, financial stakeholders may close the business. Therefore, business survival will be dependent on the major stakeholders' perception of the situation.

Proposition 2:   Following a disaster, the personal goals and perceptions of major stakeholders are likely to have a large influence on survival.

If the decision is made to fight for survival, many factors are likely to converge to influence the likelihood of success. Some of these parallel normal operating issues, but others are unique to the postdisaster situation. To understand the interactions among various organizational and leadership attributes as they influence business recovery, we must consider entrepreneurial orientation, environmental factors, and organizational factors.

ENTREPRENEURIAL ORIENTATION

Entrepreneurial orientation includes the "strategy-making processes that firms engage in [to support] entrepreneurial activities" (Lumpkin & Dess, 2001, p. 429). As indicated earlier, Lumpkin and Dess (1996) identify five components to an entrepreneurial orientation: autonomy, innovativeness, risk-taking, proactiveness, and competitive aggressiveness (see Figure 8.1). We discuss each of the components and conceptual relationships between each component and business survival following a major disaster.

SMEs have a higher failure rate in early stages of formation and growth than when they become better established. New enterprise development can be riskier due to entering new markets or introducing new products (Best, 2004). Each of these strategies entails risk in addition to the risks associated with ongoing market fluctuations. Survival is a critical goal of these early-stage SMEs. Previous studies show that firms that have an entrepreneurial orientation outperform other firms and have higher survival rates (Kropp, Lindsay, & Shoham, 2006). Following a disaster, most markets in the disaster area are likely to experience huge fluctuations caused by loss of customers and changing buying habits. Businesses will not be able to carry on "business as usual," with the same products or markets—they will need to change their strategies. Like a new business entering the market, postdisaster businesses must identify new opportunities and create new strategies. Consequently, we propose that SMEs with an entrepreneurial orientation may have a better chance of surviving a disaster.

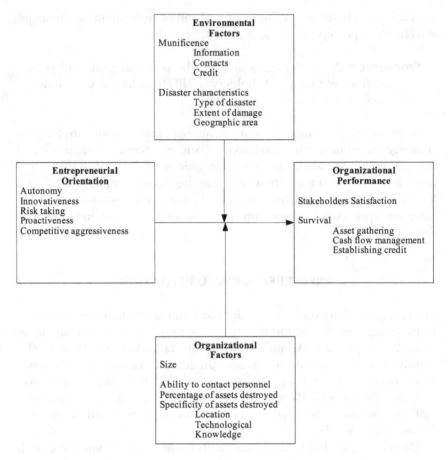

Figure 8.1.   Model of entrepreneurial orientation and business survival following a cataclysmic disaster.

Proposition 3: Businesses with a higher entrepreneurial orientation will be more likely to survive a cataclysmic disaster.

Autonomy

Autonomy is defined as "independent action by an individual or team aimed at bringing forth a business concept or vision and carrying it through to completion" (Lumpkin & Dess, 2001, p. 431). On an individual level, autonomy represents freedom of action. On the firm level, autonomy implies the ability to act with relative freedom from organizational constraints. There are numerous decisions that must be made quickly after a natural disaster. At the same time, by their very nature, natural disasters are disruptive to organizational efficiency. Following a disaster, the ability to act decisively could make the difference between life and death of the business as well as the individual. Time perceptions could be expanded, making quick, right action critical to survival. Therefore, individual members' freedom to act on behalf of the organization, along with organizational autonomy, are likely to impact early recovery efforts.

Proposition 4: Businesses that possess greater organizational autonomy and promote higher levels of member autonomy will have a greater ability to survive a major disaster.

Innovativeness

Innovation and creativity are closely related. Creativity implies doing things in new and novel ways. Innovativeness includes fostering a spirit of creativity, experimentation, developing new processes, introducing new products/services, technological leadership, and implementing new management techniques (Lumpkin & Dess, 2001; Lumpkin, 2002; Kropp & Zolin, 2005). In the business context, innovation also implies doing things in new and novel ways.

By their nature, disasters create unusual, possibly overwhelming situations. Innovation, creativity, and improvisation are necessary to solve problems that may occur. Existing customers may have evacuated, but new opportunities arise to assist the recovery effort. Engineering Software's trade of ice for the ability to access valuable computers and records from their offices serves as a good example of innovation that contributes to survival.

Proposition 5: Businesses that possess greater organizational innovativeness and promote higher levels of member innovation will have a greater ability to survive a major disaster.

Proactiveness

Proactiveness is a forward-looking, opportunity-seeking perspective that involves introducing new products or services and acting in anticipation of future demand. Through discontinuities, disasters create new opportunities. Firms need to be proactive in order to avoid possible threats and to exploit opportunities. This involves a wide variety of activities that include identifying opportunities and market trends, assessing the strengths and weaknesses of opportunities, and forming teams capable of exploiting them (Kropp, Lindsay, & Shoham, 2006). Although entrepreneurs are predisposed to the formation of business ventures to pursue specific objectives (Kouriloff, 2000), they still need to be proactive in seeking out an attractive niche and creating the necessary resources to facilitate new entry (Lumpkin & Dess, 2001). Entrepreneurs need to develop a vision and determine ways to combine previously unidentified components to capitalize on the perceived business opportunity (Bird, 1989; Schumpeter, 1954).

Because proactive firms are forward-looking, they will be more likely to prepare for a disaster. They may be more likely to network, to engage in information gathering, and to react with forethought. Consequently, they may be more likely to survive.

While most people do not anticipate a disaster, more and more businesses do prepare for disaster to reduce the chance that it could destroy valuable resources or the organization itself. Proactive organizations will, in the normal course of business, investigate and develop Disaster Preparedness Programs (DPP) and Business Continuity Plans (BCP) (Castillo, 2004) that include preparations such as:

- Disaster insurance for business income, extra expenses, contingent business interruption, and civil authority denial of access to a business's property
- Information technology protection strategies
- Backup of computer databases
- Duplication of critical assets

Consequently, when disaster strikes, proactive businesses will be better prepared and have a higher chance of survival.

Proposition 6: Businesses that are proactive will be more likely to prepare for a disaster, thereby increasing their ability to survive.

Risk-Taking

There are numerous concepts of risk. Entrepreneurs perceive risk as the uncertainty surrounding potential losses or gains (Forlani & Mullins, 2000). Specific aspects of strategic risk may include venturing into new and unknown territory, committing a relatively large share of assets and significant borrowing (Baird & Thomas, 1985). Entrepreneurs generally accept that entrepreneurship involves risk-taking and are willing to take risks in return for potential rewards. Arguably, when possible, entrepreneurs would prefer to lower the risk aspect of the risk-return equation. Although entrepreneurs are willing to take reasonable risks, they do not like to take extreme or unreasonable risks. Quick reaction to a disaster requires reasonable risk-taking. Therefore,

Proposition 7: Businesses that exhibit moderate risk-taking behavior will have a greater ability to survive a major disaster.

Competitive Aggressiveness

Competitive aggressiveness relates to a firm's willingness to challenge its market rivals to gain market share (Lumpkin & Dess, 1996). Lumpkin and Dess (2001) describe competitive aggressiveness as a response to threats. Competitive aggressiveness implies a willingness to take quick, decisive action. For example, Google has aggressively attacked Yahoo in an attempt to capture market share. Although competitive aggressiveness is more associated with responses to mature markets, competitive aggressiveness against anything blocking the survival goal could be invaluable in disaster response. City University officials felt that initial organizational support would be withdrawn quickly if they did not remain operational. They aggressively focused on finding their faculty and developing Web-based courses. The swift response of their faculty allowed them to continue teaching and to graduate hundreds of students that quarter, despite the hurricane. Thus, competitive aggressiveness in disaster response is more likely to lead to business survival.

Proposition 8: Businesses that are competitively aggressive will have a greater ability to survive a major disaster.

Although entrepreneurial orientation is a valuable business skill in both good times and bad times, it is not the only approach that can assist business survival. While those with entrepreneurial orientation are informed risk takers, risk aversion can be useful if it triggers planning and preparations prior to a disaster.

In the next section, we discuss environmental factors that are particularly likely to affect businesses' disaster survival.

THE EFFECT OF ENVIRONMENTAL FACTORS ON SURVIVAL

Business environments have been compared to battlefields (Peter & Donnelly, 2003). However, there is a big difference between a hostile business environment under normal conditions and in the aftermath of a natural or man-made disaster. The degree of competition in normal conditions can range from cooperation in building a market to friendly competition to extreme, perhaps even hostile, competition. The level of competition can be a function of the stage of market development, resources available, and the competitors themselves. In the extreme, metaphorically speaking, businesses may be at each other's throats.

Following a disaster, the business environment is characterized by drastic changes in demand as consumers congregate at aid stations or evacuate the area. Needs change to products or services needed to survive, e.g., basics such as food, water, medical assistance and transportation. Changes in demand can be accompanied by changes in the ability of most consumers to pay as inflation escalates, cash runs out and employment is interrupted. As seen with Hurricane Katrina, the government may step in to buy goods and services on behalf of the population. Alternately, the government may supply those affected by the disaster with funds, as was done with the government-issued credit cards. In addition to disrupting demand, the ability of most firms to supply goods and services may be radically limited. Thus, following a disaster, the business environment may be characterized by large, rapid change in effective demand accompanied by inability to supply.

ORGANIZATIONAL ECOLOGY AND THE BUSINESS ENVIRONMENT

Theories of organizational ecology seek to explain the number and diversity of organizations in an industry based upon social, economic, and political conditions (Baum, 1996; Hannan & Freeman, 1989). This perspective acknowledges that, due to structural inertia, businesses often do not have time to adapt to changes in the business environment, and that major innovations occur early in the life cycle of organizations and business populations. Thus, like biological organisms, many variations of business are created, some better than others. The successful variations are selected by customers, managers, investors, and government, allowing competitive variations to be retained. Thus, features of the business environment can determine the success and survival of a business.

Lumpkin and Dess (1996) propose that munificence, dynamism, complexity, and other industry characteristics will moderate business performance.

MUNIFICENCE

The scarcity or abundance of critical resources, especially after a natural disaster, can potentially affect the success or failure of a firm. When the environment is not munificent, there is a scarcity of critical resources, which can cause organizational stress and threaten survival (Wiersema & Bantel, 1993). When an environment is munificent, the critical resources are abundant.

A business facing disaster needs more resources than would typically be required during normal business operations. These additional resources include access to broader information, new contacts, and additional credit. The need for information increases because substantial uncertainties have been introduced into the business environment. The need for new contacts increases because the business has to revise its business strategy, often investigating new opportunities. The need for credit increases because old revenue sources are likely interrupted, disaster insurance is unlikely to cover all expenses, and new investment may be needed to address new opportunities. To the extent that the business can find or generate these resources during the crisis and throughout the rebuilding phases, the business has an increased chance of survival. Businesses with better access to relevant information about the situation may be able to recognize and capitalize on new opportunities. This can enhance the probability of success and survival.

In summary, business that can make new contacts who have access to valuable resources will be better able to gather information, learn about opportunities, get help, or form strategic alliances. Businesses that have quicker and easier access to credit will be more likely to survive the cash-flow shortages that are likely to accompany disruptions to markets and operations previously described. Therefore,

Proposition 9: The more munificent the environment in terms of information, contacts, and credit following a major disaster, the greater the chance of business survival.

Dynamism and Complexity

Dynamism refers to the rate or the unpredictability of environmental change surrounding a firm (Duncan, 1972; Miller & Friesen, 1983). A major disaster appears to be the ultimate in dynamism. In the twinkling of an eye, everything can be lost: valuable personnel, facilities, and customers. Environmental complexity relates to the range, variety, and heterogeneity of environmental factors involved in strategic decision making

(Aldrich, 1979; Child, 1972; Palmer & Wiseman, 1999; Wiersema & Bantel, 1993). In essence, it involves the complex knowledge and understanding required to succeed in business. The conditions following a disaster can increase the complexity of everyday decisions by a magnitude. Nothing is normal. There are no routine decisions, conditions are uncertain, everyday tasks are problematic or impossible to complete.

Disasters create sudden shocks that can affect the dynamism and complexity of the business environment. Though these impacts may be extreme in the short term, they may have varying effects in the longer term. Nevertheless, the short-term increases in dynamism and complexity are aberrations to the normal, steady state characteristics of the environment; extreme dynamism, coupled with complexity, could cause stakeholders to cut their losses and withdraw from the market following a disaster. Therefore,

Proposition 10: The greater the dynamism of the business environment, in terms of disruptions to markets and supply of resources, the lower the chances of business survival following a major disaster.

Proposition 11: The greater the complexity of changes to the environment, the lower the chances of business survival following a major disaster.

Industry Characteristics

Industry characteristics include many possible aspects of the industry including type, location, structure, and the competitive nature of the industry. It is possible that some industries have greater survival capacity than others. For example, small local retail businesses could have less chance of survival because their customers have evacuated and may not return. The type of business activity— for example, retail, wholesale, manufacturing, or service—will determine, to some extent, the criticality of lost or damaged assets. For example, one major resource of a retail shop, the loyalty of its local clientele, could be dispersed in a disaster like Hurricane Katrina. Likewise, the major resource of a service business could be its specialized personnel, who may leave the area. Manufacturing and wholesale businesses typically have large investments in plant and equipment that are expensive and can't be replaced quickly, even if the funds are available. Businesses that provide services needed during recovery may benefit from a disaster. These idiosyncratic contingencies between industry and type of disaster are certain to interact with other factors to shape business success and direction during and after a crisis.

ORGANIZATIONAL FACTORS

Organizational factors include size and structure of the organization, its strategies and strategy-making processes, firm resources, and organizational culture. In-depth analysis of organizational factors exceeds the scope of this chapter. Instead, we will focus on factors that are particularly likely to influence business survival. These include the size of the business and the percentage and specificity of lost assets.

Size of the Business

A cataclysmic disaster has a different impact on a large national company or an international corporation compared to a small regional business. A small company that resides wholly within the disaster area may lose all of its assets. A large, distributed company could lose as many people and buildings, but because of their other resources, the loss may not threaten the business's survival.

Proposition 12: Other factors being equal, a large enterprise is more likely to survive a disaster than a small- or medium-size enterprise.

Percentage and Specificity of Lost Business Assets

The type of disaster determines which business assets are damaged over what geographic area. For example, the September 11 attack on the World Trade Center had a very concentrated effect on a very limited geographic area, although the people affected came from all over the world. In contrast, an avian flu pandemic could have a relatively lower physically-damaging effect on a much broader geographic area. A distinguishing feature of Hurricane Katrina was the extremely large geographic area that was almost destroyed. The higher the proportion of critical resources that are destroyed, the more difficult it is to maintain or resume business operations.

The type of resources destroyed is also critical to business survival. All things being equal, a business that sustains damage to noncritical resources is more likely to survive than a business sustaining damage to critical, hard-to-replace assets such as head office and central computer operations and key personnel. The types of assets we posit as most critical are those that have asset specificity to the organization. These assets, such as employees with customized skills, have special characteristics of value to the company, although they may not provide extra value to other firms.

Forms of asset specificity include location specificity, technological specificity, and knowledge specificity (Teece, 1982). Location specificity refers to the investment in local assets, such as facilities or market relationships, and these are the most threatened by disaster. Technological specificity refers to the uniqueness of technology developed by a firm. Assets with technological specificity could be destroyed if they are concentrated in the disaster area. For example, City University held computer backups in downtown New Orleans at the time of Hurricane Katrina. Luckily, the computer backups were not destroyed, but the firm had to get the National Guard to retrieve them one month after the hurricane. Knowledge specificity refers to the unique knowledge held by members of the firm, such as the firm history and culture and ways of doing their work. Assets with knowledge specificity could reside in people, particularly if the knowledge is tacit rather than explicit. Disasters with large human losses could destroy a company's knowledge assets.

Assets with special characteristics cannot be replaced in a short period of time, even if unlimited funds are available. Information systems are a critical asset for all types of businesses. Loss of computer systems is such a threat to businesses that developing disaster plans and business continuity plans are often considered to be part of the function of the Information Technology group in most organizations. Head office is another critical resource for many companies, particularly small businesses and highly centralized companies. Most businesses would be more critically injured by an attack on their head office than on a remote facility or branch. There are a number of reasons for this. Head offices often contains the top management decision-making functions, which are unique, while remote or branch sites are often replicas and might contain less asset specificity.

Proposition 13: All things being equal, the lower the specificity of business assets destroyed, the more likely the firm will survive.

The size of the business could also interact with the specificity of destroyed assets. Table 8.1 shows how the size of the business and specificity of destroyed assets are likely to jointly affect business survival rates. A small business is more likely than a large business to lose a high proportion of firm-specific assets in a disaster. For example, tacit knowledge in the head office of a firm is a highly specific asset. Many small businesses are geographically specialized, with local head offices. When such a business is hit in a disaster, its chances of survival are lower.

IMPLICATIONS FOR GOVERNMENT AND OFFICIAL FIRST RESPONDERS

Surviving businesses can contribute quite early to disaster recovery if officials understand their needs. The stakeholders' decision to continue the business is likely to be influenced by the munificence of the environment in terms of information, contacts, and new business opportunities. By helping businesses to access these resources, government and other responders may increase the likelihood that they will survive and succeed. Some businesses become relatively entrepreneurial during the disaster response, and better information could help them find new opportunities. By enabling local businesses to continue, intervening agencies may hasten economic redevelopment.

In the early stages of disaster response, business needs are similar to individual needs: Find and communicate with family members and employees. After re-forming the management team, the business must build a strategy to recover assets, create temporary premises, and address new business opportunities that arise during reconstruction.

To facilitate this process, government agencies can:

- Create a "one stop" business survival Web site for each major disaster containing:
- A "people finder clearing house" that aggregates the information on the location of survivors from the many aid and recovery organizations
- FAQ and information to assist business to deal with people-finding, communication, and strategy revision
- Information on the location and extent of damage to help businesses create their Business Situational Analysis
- A register of disaster recovery calls for proposals that businesses can apply to work in the recovery effort, with preference given to local businesses in the disaster recovery area
- Create official roles that give business representatives some standing and position in the minds of First Responders. Typical roles might include "Business Principal" to designate a business owner/operator, and "Business Representative" to designate someone acting on behalf of a business during the recovery phase. These roles could have associated responsibilities. For example, there might be

only one Business Representative of each firm, whose responsibility is to liaison with the local police.

- Train government officials and first responders to understand the official business roles and legitimate needs of surviving businesses
- Enable businesses to more easily pass security check points to gain access their physical locations to recover key records and equipment
- Make information about business recovery loans available as early as two weeks following the disaster to allow stakeholders to assess their businesses' potential to survive
- Implement a system that will provide credit to struggling businesses in a timely manner
- Include entrepreneurial disaster response in small business education courses
- Encourage SMEs to develop business disaster response plans and continuity plans
- Publish information on the wide range of disaster events and what can be done to prepare for them

CONCLUSION

In this chapter, our goal was to illustrate how surviving businesses respond during and after a major disaster and to propose steps to increase business survival. Businesses are major assets to local communities because they provide goods, services, employment, and revenues, but they are often overlooked in disaster response. Entrepreneurial businesses can move quickly—from needing help to assisting responders—if they have adequate information and opportunities. By understanding how disasters impact businesses, governments can assist the businesses that can support long-term recovery for the region.

NOTE

1. In all three cases, a fictitious name has been chosen for the organization to protect the confidentiality of the organization and the respondents.

REFERENCES

Aldrich, Howard. (1979). *Organizations and environments*. Englewood Cliffs, NJ: Prentice Hall.

Baird, I. S., & Thomas, H. (1985). Toward a contingency model of strategic risk taking. *Academy of Management Review, 10*, 230–243.

Bird, B. J. (1989). *Entrepreneurial behavior.* London: Scott, Foresman.

Best, R. J. (2004). *Market-based management* (4th ed.). Englewood Cliffs, NJ: Prentice Hall.

Baum, J. A. C. (1996). Organizational ecology. In S. R. Clegg, C. Hardy, & W. R. Nord (Eds.), *Handbook of organization studies* (pp. 78–114). London: Sage.

Castillo, C. (2004). Disaster preparedness and business continuity planning at Boeing: An integrated model. *Journal of Facilities Management, 3*(1), 8–26.

Child, J. (1972). Organizational structure, environment, and performance: The role of strategic choice. *Sociology, 1*(6), 1–22.

Dahlhamer, J. M., & Tierney, K., J. (1997, August). *Winners and losers: Predicting business disaster recovery outcomes following the Northridge earthquake.* Annual meeting of the Toronto, Ontario, Canada American Sociologist Association.

Duncan, R. B. (1972). Characteristics of organizational environments and perceived environmental uncertainty. *Administrative Sciences Quarterly, 17,* 313–327.

Forlani, D., & Mullins, J. W. (2000). Perceived risks and choices in entrepreneurs' new venture decisions. *Journal of Business Venturing, 15,* 305-322.

Furlong, S. R., & Scheberle, D. (1998). Earthquake recovery. Gaps between norms of disaster agencies and expectations of small businesses. *American Review of Public Administration, 28*(4), 367–389.

Hannan, M. T., & Freeman, J. (1989). *Organizational ecology.* Cambridge, MA: Harvard University Press.

Kouriloff, M. (2000). Exploring perceptions of a priori barriers to entrepreneurship: A multidisciplinary approach. *Entrepreneurship Theory and Practice, 25*(2), 59–67.

Kropp, F., Lindsay, N. J. L., & Shoham, A. (2006). Entrepreneurial, market, and learning orientations and international entrepreneurial business venture performance. *International Marketing Review, 23*(5), 504-523.

Kropp, F., & Zolin, R. (2005). Technological entrepreneurship and small business innovation research programs. *Academy of Marketing Sciences Review.* Retrieved December 12, 2006, from http://www.amsreview.org/articles/kropp07-2005.pdf

Lumpkin, G. T., & Dess, G. G. (1996). Clarifying the entrepreneurial orientation construct and linking it to performance. *Academy of Management Review, 21,* 135–172.

Lumpkin, G. T., & Dess, G. G. (2001). Linking two dimensions of entrepreneurial orientation to firm performance: The moderating role of environment and industry life cycle. *Journal of Business Venturing, 16,* 429–451.

Miller, D., & Friesen, P. H. (1983). Strategy making and environment: The third link. *Strategic Management Journal, 4,* 221–235.

Palmer, T. B., & Wiseman, R. M. (1999). Decoupling risk taking from income stream uncertainty: A holistic model of risk. *Strategic Management Journal, 20,* 1037–1062.

Peter, J. P. Jr., Donnelly, J. H., Donnellyr, J. (2003). *Marketing management: Knowledge and skills* (7th ed.). Boston: McGraw-Hill/Irwin.

Schumpeter, J. A. (1954). *History of economic analysis*. New York: Oxford University Press.

Stevenson, H. H. & Jarillo, J. C. (1990). A paradigm of entrepreneurship: Entrepreneurial management. *Strategic Management Journal, 11*, 17–27.

Teece, D. J. (1982). *Some efficiency properties of the modern corporation: Theory and evidence*. Unpublished manuscript, Stanford University.

Timmons, J., & Spinelli, S. (2004). *New Venture creation: Entrepreneurship for the 21st century* Boston: Irwin McGraw-Hill.

U.S. Department of Labor, Bureau of Statistics. (2006). Retrieved March 4, 2006, from http://www.bls.giv/katrina/data/data.htm#3

Wiersema, M. F., & Bantel, K. A. (1993). Top management team turnover as an adaptation mechanism: The role of the environment. *Strategic Management Journal, 14*(7), 485–504.

CHAPTER 9

GLOBALIZATION AND INTERNATIONAL COMMUNICABLE CRISES

A Case Study of SARS

Teri Jane Bryant, Ilan Vertinsky, and Carolyne Smart

Globalization has dramatically changed both how international communicable crises are transmitted and how communication occurs during them. This chapter uses the 2003 SARS crisis to examine how the impacts of individuals' actions are to be managed; how diverse nation-states can best coordinate their crisis responses; and how supranational institutions can improve their effectiveness. The case study focuses on the WHO and three nations that were severely affected by SARS, China, Singapore. While knowledge, communication, authority, and resources are necessary elements of successful crisis management strategies everywhere, cultural, economic, and political differences dictate cross-national differences in strategy implementation. Prior agreements for information and power-sharing are often necessary at both the national and international levels to ensure timely responses to crises. In the case of infrequent but potentially catastrophic crises, complacency is a risk that must be fought continuously.

Communicable Crises: Prevention, Response, and Recovery in the Global Arena, pp. 265–299

INTRODUCTION

An international communicable crisis may originate anywhere, geographically, and then spread across borders, either because of the tight coupling and interdependence of different national systems or through contagion effects such as panic. Examples include the international spread of severe acute respiratory syndrome (SARS) and the Asian financial crisis. Multifaceted globalization has dramatically affected the mechanisms by which transmission of such crises takes place, as well as the processes of communication during such crises. Globalization has shaped the roles of individuals, nation-states, and supranational actors in the emergence and management of crises. These effects, in turn, raise important questions about how the impacts of individuals' actions are to be managed; how culturally, economically, and politically diverse nation-states can best coordinate their crisis responses; and how supranational institutions can improve their effectiveness.

The SARS crisis of 2003 provides a useful setting for examining these questions. SARS and news about it spread rapidly around the world. There was a need to contain the disease's spread in all countries simultaneously since international travel was a potential vehicle for renewed contagion. News spread quickly and largely outside the control of national governments, creating both positive and negative effects within and across nations. Individual actions brought unforeseen and sometimes tragic consequences, highlighting the message that no man is an island in today's tightly interlinked world. The involvement of multiple national governments complicated coordination of responses since each operated in a unique cultural, economic, and political environment, and therefore constructed and managed the crisis differently.

In this chapter, we examine the emergence and management of SARS in three countries that differ significantly in their politico-economic institutions, physical infrastructures, and national cultures. China, Canada, and Singapore each interacted differently with the World Health Organization (WHO) in identifying and managing the crisis. Careful analysis of response patterns allows us to identify the elements that crisis response plans must share across nations and where they must be allowed to diverge to adapt to local circumstances. The WHO was a key supranational player, providing official recognition of events as constituting an international crisis—where international resources are mobilized to contain and mitigate the consequences of the crisis. The WHO's responses were criticized on a number of fronts. We therefore consider how to improve international coordination of communicable crises such as SARS. We also examine the theoretical implications of the case study in understanding more generally the management of crises in a globalized world.

SARS AS AN INTERNATIONAL COMMUNICABLE CRISIS

SARS and the management systems that emerged in response to it possessed all the commonly recognized characteristics of a crisis: a high degree of uncertainty, time pressure, and high stakes (Herman, 1963; Quarantelli, 1988; Smart & Vertinsky, 1977). Moreover, since SARS affected some 28 countries within the space of just a few months, it also had a clear international dimension. The pathogen was transmissible by infected travelers, while fear and, in some cases, panic regarding its possible effects were spread through cross-border communication about its progress.

When SARS appeared, little was known about it. Its epidemiology and pathogenesis were poorly understood. It appeared highly threatening, as its case fatality was 14-15% (it exceeded 50% in those over 65; diabetics were also particularly vulnerable). The possibility that its appearance could usher in the onset of a new worldwide pandemic could not be discounted. Developing an effective diagnostic test and, potentially, a vaccine would take time. While a pandemic is an inevitable recurring event, it is a low probability event in any given year. However, once there is an outbreak, it can sweep through populations with ferocity and speed, and overwhelm the system's ability to contain it. The appearance of a new disease (SARS) to which the population's immunity levels are likely to be low, requires rapid response under conditions of great uncertainty.

The perceived threat to a core goal of most societies—preserving the safety of their population—was high. At first, there was fear of a pandemic, and then when infection rates proved to be lower, there was the recognition of the dire consequences to those infected and those who cared for them as well as the impact of SARS on the economy. Time pressure to decide and respond was felt throughout health care systems around the globe. The health systems in affected areas were strained and, in some jurisdictions, overwhelmed. Organizational routines were overridden, authority structures changed, and harsh measures—at times suppressing civil rights—were legitimized.

SARS: ORIGINS OF A CRISIS

SARS came to the world's attention in February 2003 when the WHO received reports—first unofficially by e-mail and then officially from the

Chinese Ministry of Health—about an outbreak of a severe respiratory illness that had stricken hundreds and killed five in Guangdong province. Lab tests failed to identify known influenza viruses, and the illness was first referred to as "atypical pneumonia."[1]

The disease spread quickly from this base in Guangdong. On February 21, a doctor from the province, who had treated patients with atypical pneumonia, went to Hong Kong for a wedding and checked into the Metropole Hotel. The doctor was hospitalized the next day for respiratory failure, and died on March 4. Several family members and a nurse were infected.

Although he was there for only 1 day, the doctor's brief hotel stay had world-wide ramifications. Over a dozen guests were infected, some of whom subsequently carried the disease with them to Vietnam, Canada, and Singapore, initiating a string of secondary and tertiary infections. This early, pivotal incident demonstrated the importance of the impact of sociocultural pressures on individual behavior. One individual's actions spread the disease from China to the regions where most of the rest of the subsequent cases occurred (including Hong Kong, Vietnam, Canada, and Singapore). He had decided to travel to fulfill a perceived family obligation, even when he knew he had been exposed to a severe and unknown illness, and had begun to show early symptoms (though these seemed to have lessened when he decided to go). There were many similar later cases in other places where individuals, perhaps out of ignorance, placed their perceived social, religious, or professional obligations above their responsibility to safeguard the health of the general public. This case points to the need for public education tailored to the pressures or vulnerabilities likely to induce behavior that is suboptimal from a broad social perspective. These pressures may be social, legal, religious, or monetary (such as fear of loss of income or employment).

Medical staff and family members of the stricken quickly swelled the numbers of infected individuals. Meanwhile, additional infections were occurring in China and among travelers who visited infected regions there; without proper precautions, many then became vectors of transmission in their home regions. By March 22, there were 386 reported cases, in 13 countries on 3 continents, and 11 deaths. Within a few days, this number swelled to over 1,300 cases and 49 deaths as China reviewed and restated its statistics.

On March 12, 2003, the WHO issued a global alert about respiratory illness among health care workers. This was followed the next day by an emergency alert through its Global Outbreak Alert and Response Network (GOARN). On March 14, a GOARN team began arriving in Hanoi to assist in fighting the outbreak there (WHO teams were also later sent to

China and Singapore.) The next day, the WHO issued a travel advisory about the potential for spread through air travel, issued case definitions, and coined the term "severe acute respiratory syndrome," or SARS. Two days later, it set up a nine country network to identify the cause and develop a diagnostic test, as well as networks on practical case management and epidemiology. On April 2, the WHO issued its toughest-ever travel advisory, recommending that travelers to Hong Kong and Guangdong "consider postponing all but emergency travel." Three weeks later, the same warning was extended to Beijing, Shanxi Province of China, and Toronto. Travel advisories were later issued for Tianjin, Hebei Province, Inner Mongolia, and Taipei (eventually all of Taiwan).

The SARS crisis stimulated responses at the local, national, and international levels. Hospitals were closed to new patients and visitors; medical staff undertook extraordinary infection control measures while providing care; those who had been exposed were quarantined, travel was discouraged, and an international collaborative effort was undertaken to identify the causative agent. Private citizens also took their own precautions in affected areas, avoiding crowds and public places, with severe repercussions on the travel, hospitality, entertainment, and restaurant industries. By April 16, the causative agent had been identified by the WHO research network as a previously unknown corona virus. Later research determined it had most likely been spread to humans by civet cats held for sale for human consumption in wild animal markets in southern China; the disease's ultimate point of origin is now believed to have been in bats. By late May, the worldwide total of cases exceeded 8,000, but new cases were dwindling as a result of the aggressive implementation of the measures cited above. All travel advisories were lifted by June 24 and by July 5 the WHO was able to declare that the SARS outbreak was under control.

CROSS-NATIONAL DIFFERENCES IN CRISIS MANAGEMENT

Well-developed literature on crisis management is available in a variety of contexts (for useful surveys, see Bryant, Smart, & Vertinsky, in press; Pearson & Clair, 1998; Quarantelli, 1988; Rosenthal, Boin, & Comfort, 2001). From this literature, one can distill four key elements to successful crisis management:

1. Knowledge or understanding of the nature of the crisis and how to deal with it;

2. Effective communication amongst the actors involved in dealing with the crisis and between them and the public (for useful summaries of best practices in this area, see WHO, 2005a, 2005b);

3. Sufficient authority in the hands of those tasked with taking action; and

4. Human, financial, and material resources that are adequate in amount and available in a timely manner where needed.

While these broad prescriptions seem to travel well, they often have different implications in diverse national contexts. For example, the identities of the actors responsible for dealing with a crisis, the way they communicate, and their expectations of what constitutes good communication may all differ across nations. Thus, although there were definite commonalities across nations—particularly at the micro level, where the demands of medical practice become paramount—differences in culture, political institutions, and socioeconomic conditions also led to telling differences in the way this crisis was handled around the world. Three of the most severely affected locations, China, Canada, and Singapore, illustrate these differences and provide insights into the factors that can influence crisis management.

SARS: THE CHINESE EXPERIENCE

China represents perhaps the weakest node in the international network of contacts through which epidemics spread. Due to its dense human and domestic animal populations living in close proximity to each other, Southern China is a source of many epidemics. Early detection and effective measures to control their spread at the source may reduce the chance of their international spread. However, China's lack of detection capacity and, more importantly, economic and social incentives to suppress communications about suspected illnesses once they occur, increase the probability of the spread of the disease domestically and internationally. The ability of the international community through the WHO to monitor and help control the potential onset of epidemics in China, however, is limited by complex political issues and institutional and cultural differences. The ability of China itself to respond to early warning signals is limited by internal differences in priorities between central and provincial governments, as well as rigidities introduced by multiple overlapping bureaucratic systems dealing with the issue.

The details of the early development of the SARS epidemic in China became known only well after the fact, and some aspects are still not clearly understood. However, enough is now known to reconstruct a rough outline of the sequence of events, with increasing certainty and detail in the later phases of the story.[2]

The first case of what is now believed to have been SARS was recorded in a businessman in Foshan city, a suburb of Guangzhou, in November 2002. As early as November 20, a WHO flu specialist in Beijing heard about a cluster of respiratory cases in health care workers in Guangzhou. He asked for and received tissue samples, but nothing unusual was found since the samples were analyzed for variations on known illnesses. Several more cases of the mysterious respiratory disease appeared in the region throughout December, with an unusually high proportion of the early cases occurring among those involved in the sale and preparation of wild animal meat for human consumption. Each of those cases then spread the disease to several hospital staff. This unusual clustering of cases of an uni-dentified illness was reported by the health departments of Shunde, Heyuan, and Zhongshan to the Guangdong provincial health authorities in early January. However, it is not clear whether these reports were ever forwarded to the national Ministry of Health in Beijing. While no overall alert was issued, the news gradually spread informally amongst medical practitioners. Some hospitals, aware of the rumors, began isolating patients suspected of having the disease early on while others, unaware of the rumors, did not take precautionary measures until much later. Thus, in early February a sick man from Zhongshan sought treatment in several hospital emergency rooms in Guangzhou before he was finally admitted. Unfortunately, he turned out to be a "superspreader"[3] who left a trail of infections at the many institutions he had visited.

Although the disease was spreading rapidly, there was still no official alert. However, the general population seemed to have heard rumors of some kind of outbreak, and there were runs on herbal medicines and vin-egar—the latter incorrectly believed to prevent the illness when boiled to vapor. On February 10, the WHO's Beijing office heard rumors of a strange new illness, and requested details from the Chinese Ministry of Health. A day later, the Ministry reported an outbreak of a respiratory dis-ease to the WHO, but gave few details. The first report from Guangdong authorities on February 11 cited 305 cases and five deaths, but claimed that the situation was under control. That same day, WHO flu specialists from Hong Kong secretly made their way into Guangzhou and obtained tissue samples, but since they were looking for bird flu, they failed to find anything unusual. On February 14, Li Liming, director of the Chinese Center for Disease Control, declared that there had been no new cases since February 10 and that the situation was "under control and not as serious as the rumors say" (McNeil & Altman, 2003). Five days later, his center announced that the outbreak had been caused by chlamydia—a claim that was rejected out of hand by U.S. and WHO experts since chlamydia responds to common antibiotics. Understanding of the evolv-ing situation was further complicated when a family who had traveled to

Fujian province fell ill in Hong Kong on February 19. Their illness was unambiguously identified as avian influenza, which temporarily misled investigators into believing this was the cause of the main outbreak. In addition to the delays in reporting information, the early spread of the virus was permitted by several near misses as investigators failed to identify the illness because it was not of the type they expected to find.

Seriously concerned about the discrepancies between the unofficial news emerging from China and the official accounts, the WHO and the U.S. Center for Disease Control and Prevention sent a joint team to Beijing. It arrived February 23 but was stonewalled for 2 weeks, and left in frustration in early March. Because the WHO is a voluntary organization, it has no power to investigate disease outbreaks without the permission of local authorities, who may not be forthcoming for any one of a variety of reasons that have little to do with health. It was on February 21, while the members were sitting in their Beijing hotel rooms awaiting permission to investigate, that the aforementioned doctor from Zhongshan spread the disease to Hong Kong (and indirectly to several other countries) during his stay at the Metropole Hotel. Here we see how delays in a single jurisdiction can stymie international efforts to stem a threat to the world's health due to jurisdictional confusion and conflicting priorities. While the specifics and intensity of the problem may vary across nations or regions, a clear understanding of the need for prompt reporting, particularly of early cases, and strong incentives to encourage such early reporting must be key elements of any pandemic management plan.

With the mystery illness now reaching several countries on three continents, the WHO issued a first global health alert on March 12, followed by a more emphatic one on March 15. This was a risky action since little was known at that time and a false alarm could seriously damage the WHO's credibility. In retrospect, however, it proved extremely beneficial as the high profile of an alert from the world's premier health organization put the situation front and center on the world stage and moved doctors around the world to begin to take preventive measures, such as isolation of suspected cases, thereby short-circuiting cases of secondary and tertiary transmission.

Meanwhile, in China itself the disease was spreading to other provinces. With Chinese authorities claiming the situation was under control, the lunar New Year travel surge provided additional opportunities for the virus to make its way into the hinterland. With the health care systems in these areas lagging far behind the facilities available in major centers, the disease then spread easily. In some places, hospital staff members, fearing the unknown, refused to work. On March 27, the number of Guangdong province cases reported to the WHO (as of the end of February) was revised upwards to 792.

Despite the rise in cases and the broadening geographical spread of the disease, hospital leaders in Beijing were called into the Ministry of Health and forbidden to publicize the arrival of SARS, so as not to affect "social stability" during the National People's Congress sessions that confirmed Hu Jintao as President and Wen Jiabao as Prime Minister (Rosenthal, 2003a). During this time, the disease spread into the hinterland where health infrastructure is underdeveloped. Beijing city officials finally acknowledged the presence of SARS on March 26, stating that there were nine cases including three deaths; just a week earlier they had vehemently denied SARS had reached the capital (Rosenthal & Altman, 2003). As late as April 3, the health minister announced there had been only 12 cases and three deaths there (Rosenthal, 2003a). On April 10, He Xiong, deputy director of the Beijing Center for Disease Control, reinforced this calming tone, stating that there were only 27 SARS cases in Beijing and that people should not worry (Rosenthal, 2003b). Short-term political expediency was allowed to supersede the importance of the health of the nation and indeed the world as a whole.

Then, however, a whistleblower emerged: A retired military physician, Dr. Jiang Yanyong, released a statement to the media, claiming that there were many more cases at military hospitals in Beijing, some of which also accept civilian patients. WHO officials then met with Vice Premier Wu Yi, receiving a commitment to investigate possible underreporting in Beijing. Suddenly, SARS was a priority. On the weekend of April 12–13, Prime Minister Wen Jiabao evaluated the threat from SARS as "grave" (Eckholm, 2003a). In addition to the threat to the health of the people, the country's international prestige and influence were at stake. The press in Hong Kong criticized China's reporting delays that had resulted in a severe epidemic in the Special Administrative Region. Taiwan, claiming it needed prompt access to WHO services, insisted on receiving observer status in the WHO. This action had been blocked by China for over 30 years, ever since China replaced Taiwan at the United Nations. Furthermore, the prestige associated with China having been awarded the 2008 Olympics was tarnished. The WHO's attention caused the crisis to become costly in the currency which China's leaders have held most dear since the humiliations forced on it by the major powers in the nineteenth century: prestige or, in more culturally-specific terms, face.

The consequences of China's dithering in responding to the crisis were not confined to the international sphere. They included the threat of social fragmentation as individuals, believing something was wrong but not receiving solid information as to what it was or how they should respond, acted in narrow self-interest. The vast population of migrant workers in the major cities, alarmed by rumors, had begun vacating the major cities, risking the further spread of the disease into areas with poor health care. Those who could not flee rushed the stores to stock up on disinfectants, basic foodstuffs, and supposed home remedies. Public places such as restaurants and shopping centers sat empty, and public transit users donned protective masks. Control over domestic events and confidence in the regime seemed to be slipping away. The old system of tight direct social controls from the center had atrophied before a sense of responsibility to one's community had developed to take its place. In a hierarchical, top-down society, there is little sense of personal responsibility to do anything one is not specifically told (or even compelled) to do. Thus, in the absence of reliable information about what was happening, people feared the worst and felt no reason to restrain themselves from whatever behavior they believed was in their own self-interest.

Once it came, the change in policy emphasis was sudden and dramatic. The People's Daily of April 19 carried huge headlines announcing a meeting of the Standing Committee of the Politburo and warning against covering up the SARS situation. President Hu Jintao ran the meeting, highlighting his personal commitment. The Mayor of Beijing, Deputy Party Secretary Meng Xuenong, and Health Minister Zhang Wenkang were promptly dismissed. This move also served to consolidate President Hu's power base, since they were both protégés of his predecessor, Jiang Zemin, who was still a rival. Wu Yi, a deputy prime minister dubbed the "Iron Lady" due to her formidable reputation as a trade negotiator, was appointed to head the anti-SARS effort and was later formally appointed Health Minister, in addition to her existing duties. Deputy Health Minister Gao Qiang assumed de facto leadership of the Health Ministry in the immediate aftermath of his superior's dismissal, and quickly disclosed that there had been more than 200 hidden cases of SARS in Beijing military hospitals; the city's total was revised dramatically upwards to 339 confirmed cases and 402 suspected cases. He also announced the shortening of the traditional May Day holiday to reduce travel and the associated risk of spreading the epidemic. Gao Qiang put Beijing municipal health officials in charge of the anti-SARS effort at all hospitals in the capital, including those normally controlled by the military, and declared, "We will spend as much as it takes to contain this disease." At the same time, he portrayed the problems as the result of administrative errors at the Ministry of Health and jurisdictional conflicts in the capital, where municipal, national, military, and other powers overlap, rather than as resulting from systemic flaws within the one-party state (Eckholm, 2003b). Chinese authorities were able to do what was believed necessary with little attention to the procedural or legal niceties that often hamstring rapid responses in jurisdictions with a more highly developed sense of the rule of law.

Practical measures rapidly followed these organizational changes: Workplaces, hospitals, schools and areas where SARS had struck were quarantined to prevent further exposures, and long-dormant "neighborhood committees" swung back into action to reinforce government strictures on isolation and hygiene issues such as public spitting. Primary and secondary schools were closed, affecting over a million students. By the end of April, some 9,000 Beijing residents were quarantined (Eckholm, 2003c). The new mayor of Beijing, Wang Qishan, was faced with more cases than could be handled at the 17 hospitals designated to deal only with SARS patients. He mobilized 4,000 construction workers from the capital's biggest firms to build a 1,000-bed hospital in 8 days to accommodate the excess (National Adisory Committee on SARS and Public Health, 2003, p. 34). Employers of migrant workers were ordered to hold meetings to encourage them to stay put so they would not spread the disease to their home provinces. Mayor Wang also appeared in a live TV news conference, urging village heads in the large rural zones of greater Beijing to monitor local residents' temperatures, and he requested the postponement of weddings, funerals, and other large gatherings. Internet bars, cinemas, dance halls, and other forms of public entertainment were ordered closed. To head off Taiwan's push for status at the WHO, special permission for a WHO team to visit the island was rushed through within 24 hours "on humanitarian grounds," and on condition that the mission speak only to front-line doctors, not officials or politicians (McNeil, 2003).

New regulations were introduced on reporting and managing public health crises ("Speedy and Consequential," 2003) and many low-level officials around the country were fired or disciplined for concealing information or failing to devote adequate attention to the SARS outbreak. Hundreds of millions of dollars were allocated to pay for the urgent improvement of medical facilities in poorer rural areas and the provision of free treatment to SARS-afflicted farmers and migrant workers. An existing law on infectious diseases was re-interpreted to provide for punishments of 10 years in prison to death for anyone caught deliberately spreading the disease. On April 30, 2003, orders were issued to prevent hospitals from delaying treatment of SARS-afflicted patients pending payment of fees, and the arrest of rumor-mongers was given prominent coverage in the *People's Daily* ("Central Government," 2003, pp. 57-62, 89-91). When faced with a crisis that could no longer be ignored, the Chinese leadership relied on its standard operating procedures for a centrally planned economy and society: propaganda campaigns in state-controlled media, full mobilization of the Party apparatus, and forced diversion of whatever resources were deemed necessary.

This flurry of activity, however, did not meet with immediate and consistent success. In the short run, social fragmentation even accelerated. Panic buying of supplies increased, while migrant workers and students thronged railway stations, seeking to flee the capital. Riots broke out in protest against efforts to build or convert centers for the treatment or isolation of SARS patients in outlying communities without consulting local residents. Local villagers took to erecting barricades to keep out strangers, and insisted on spraying the tires of residents returning home by car. By the end of April, the number of cases had reached 1,550 in Beijing, with 82 deaths, and exceeded 3,600 nationwide (Eckholm, 2003d). The illness even touched the elite itself, with both senior politicians and state-owned enterprise executives and their families among the stricken.

The potential economic toll also looked alarming. The clothing and electronics industries were shaken by the inability of buyers to visit China to inspect samples and shipments when many Western firms banned employee travel to China. May figures for retail sales were down 43% from year-earlier figures (Chen, 2003), hotel business was down two-thirds, and leisure and entertainment by half (Buckley, 2003). J. P. Morgan Chase predicted GDP growth would drop from a 9.9% per annum rate in the first quarter to an annualized 2% in the second (Bradsher, 2003a).

The broad use of quarantines soon had an effect, however, and the number of new cases began to decline. Between May 3 and 5, the daily number of new cases in Beijing dropped from 114 to 69 (Bradsher, 2003b). By May 23, this was down to 15 new cases, with only 11 others elsewhere in the country (Kahn, 2003b). By the final third of May, new cases nationwide averaged only 14 per day (Eckholm, 2003e). Whatever other inadequacies the Chinese response may have suffered from, clearly they were eventually outweighed by the ability to impose and enforce quarantines broadly and strictly, and to divert all necessary resources.

In the end, the economic cost was smaller than predicted. Service businesses were indeed hard hit. However, the service sector is a much smaller share of China's economy than it is in more advanced economies, which limited the overall damage. In June 2003, exports were up 32.6% over May, and industrial output was up 16.9%, as the manufacturing and tradable goods sectors, which make up much more of the economy, promptly shrugged off the effects of the outbreak (Buckley, 2003). Even tourism bounced back quickly. China Eastern Airlines, for example, reported a 162% rise in traffic between June and July, 2003 (Chen, 2003).

The notion that the tide had turned in the battle against SARS became the new theme in press coverage as the regime sought to reassure the population and rebuild its credibility. The *People's Daily* reported that "the people have become more trusting and supportive of the party and government" (Eckholm, 2003d). While this may have been an optimistic interpretation, anecdotal interview evidence suggested that the forceful (if belated) government response did reassure many. News of the riots against SARS facilities was suppressed. Heroes and villains were created. The *People's Daily* vilified a physician who returned from Beijing to his home town in Inner Mongolia, bringing with him the SARS virus that eventually took the lives of his father, mother, and wife, as well as other members of his community (Kahn, 2003a). In contrast, three doctors and a nurse were posthumously awarded the title of "National Outstanding Communist Party Member" after losing their lives in the fight against SARS ("Central Government," 2003, pp. 92–94). Dr. Jiang Yanyong, the man whose courageous disclosure of the hidden cases in Beijing military hospitals had shattered the complacency that allowed SARS to take hold, was conspicuous by his absence from the ranks of official heroes. By June 25, Deputy Minister Gao was claiming credit for the victory over SARS in the name of President Hu Jintao and Prime Minister Wen Jiabao.

Unfortunately, this declaration proved premature. Under pressure from the $100-million-a-year wild animal meat industry, in August 2003, the State Forestry Administration issued a directive that allowed the sale of farm-raised civet cats and 53 other species for several purposes, including human consumption, while retaining a ban on sales of animals caught in the wild ("China Allows Sale," 2003).

In December 2003 through January 2004, a fresh outbreak of SARS occurred. It was much smaller in scale, affecting only four people, and milder in its effects, apparently due to a fortunate mutation in the virus. Nonetheless, the outbreak was a wake-up call that caused the public health machine to swing back into action. One of the cases was a waitress in a wild meat restaurant, and the civet cat cages there were almost all found to have an identical form of the virus ("Fresh SARS Cases," 2004). Links to civets could not be established in all cases, but the authorities in Guangdong were taking no chances this time: the immediate killing of all civets in captivity was ordered (Bradsher & Altman, 2004). Temperature screening of travellers was instituted, and WHO assistance promptly called in from Australia. The spread of the disease was nipped in the bud. With SARS now high on the priority list of the senior leadership, no one was going to risk the consequences of failure due to half-measures.

Yet, China had one more round to fight. A third outbreak arose after two medical students were infected in lab accidents at the Institute of Virology at China's Center for Disease Control. The first student was not, at first, tested for SARS, and spread the disease to her home province of Anhui, where it killed her mother. Since the affected students were not even involved in work requiring direct handling of the SARS virus, suspicion was cast on procedures at the severely outdated lab that was scheduled for replacement (Yardley, 2004). Here again we see the tendency for a high power-distance society's members to fail to take action due to the belief that if it were important to do so, someone "up there" would have said so. This suggests that information programs in such societies must be careful to spell out the exact actions expected of citizens, with the communication coming through channels considered authoritative and credible in the matter concerned. However, once again, prompt action to contain the outbreak salvaged the situation and the WHO declared the outbreak over on May 18, 2004.

China's experience led to two sets of postcrisis changes. Liang and Yue (2004) outline the development of a Public Health Emergency Response Information System (PHERIS) "to facilitate disease surveillance, detection, reporting, and response" (p. 675) as a direct result of the measures enacted to deal with SARS. Lan (undated) emphasizes broader, systemic changes including greater information openness and transparency, and improved cooperation with foreign partners resulting from the deficiencies that the crisis brought to light. A "right to know" has now been acknowledged in municipal legislation in some of the more progressive jurisdictions (Ling, n.d). However, while there are some hopeful signs in this direction, there also has been a strong tendency to revert to the patterns of the past: The newspaper that broke the story of the second SARS epidemic was shut down along with a sister publication that had questioned the handling of the SARS crisis (Kahn, 2004).

China's response to the SARS crisis had strong elements of commonality with efforts elsewhere at the microlevel, but also several elements that reflected its unique cultural and political history. Both Chinese and WHO officials initially had difficulty diagnosing the new disease since they were so focused on finding what they expected (bird flu, pneumonia, or chlamydia) that they were unable to escape the influence of their existing knowledge base and thus overlooked anomalies that would have pointed in other directions. However, while this tendency toward professional conservatism (compounded in China's case by a cultural reluctance to question authority) may have delayed the initial diagnostic phase, it did end up serving a purpose: more than one observer has noted the irony in the fact that in the absence of a medical breakthrough the first major new disease of the twenty-first century was defeated using medical technology from the nineteenth century (quarantine and thermometers).

At a more managerial level, however, China's approach reflected the idiosyncrasies of its history and culture. The initial Chinese response to the outbreak of SARS was hampered by serious shortcomings in the flow of information to responsible authorities both within China and abroad.

In part this was due to the difficulty and ambiguity inherent in diagnosing a previously unknown disease, and in part due to inadequate technological systems for ensuring timely reporting (Liang & Xue, 2004). However, the legacy of China's past also weighed heavily. In Imperial times, civilian and military officials who reported failure often literally paid with their heads. As a result, the information reaching the central government was often falsified for the purposes of self-preservation (Paine, 2003). During the planned economy period, officials further refined their skills at falsifying reports in order to appear to meet or exceed centrally-established economic and social targets, and thereby advance their careers. With the advent of economic liberalization, these tendencies have been exacerbated by the profit motive and corruption that has created a vested interest on the part of local officials in ensuring that local industries such as tourism are not disrupted. A long history of xenophobia also created a habit of secrecy (Ling, n.d.) in which the release of any negative information to foreigners was considered tantamount to espionage. Indeed, the *China Economic Times* referred to the errors made by the authorities, including "delaying, hiding and preventing exposure in the press" as "habitual behavior under this system" (Kahn, 2003b). A WHO report commented that "failure to disclose this information is widely regarded as one of the most striking examples of the grave health, social, and economic consequences, for multiple countries, of late reporting of an outbreak. It is also a striking example of how mismanagement of outbreak communication can damage a nation's political image at the highest level" (WHO 2005b, p. 32).

In a high power-distance society such as China, subordinates, instead of exercising their own initiative in dealing with problems, expect orders to come from above. This cultural trait creates a society that is highly receptive to the type of top-down leadership that was exercised by the Communist Party in China, with directives from Beijing being carried out down to the grass-roots level by the Party apparatus. The eventual success of the system in bringing SARS under control—whatever its contribution to the creation of the problem in the first place—reinforced the legitimacy of this approach both in the leadership and the population at large. However, while some official media, such as the *China Youth Daily*, portrayed the handling of the crisis as a "classroom in which we have felt and forged a national spirit," more critical voices such as historian Xu Jilin suggested that a society which "can only passively depend on government control ... in itself represents a latent crisis" (Kahn, 2003b, p. A8). The argument, echoed by liberal media such as *The 21st Century Economic Herald* (later closed down by the authorities), is that a society that depends only on the head is fragile: it can only develop true resilience when society has the ability to come together at a time of crisis and deal with it autonomously, relying on the rule of law and a sense of community and individual responsibility. Chinese society, which splintered into the pursuit of individual self-interest when under threat, lacks such resilience in this view (Kahn, 2003).

China's reliance on punishments for officials who allowed the disease to spread reflected a long tradition of using the stick rather than the carrot to enforce compliance with central government priorities. Some analysts have suggested that this approach may discourage accurate reporting in the same way STD reporting was discouraged by the public humiliation of sufferers. However, it is consistent with the regime's overall response pattern: Faced with a crisis, to the greatest extent possible, it followed previously successful strategies dating back to the 1950s rather than risk experimentation when its reputation and possibly its fate were put in jeopardy.

SARS: THE CANADIAN EXPERIENCE

Canada's position in the international health arena reflects both the strengths and weaknesses of a midpower, technologically advanced, decentralized democracy. Canada played a significant role in alerting the international community to the early warning signals of the onset of SARS, and helped identify the virus, thus facilitating the potential development of a vaccine. Domestically, however, Canada showed weakness in not responding to the crisis aggressively due to difficulties in mobilizing and coordinating the use of resources to combat the disease. Its response revealed a lack of institutional capacity to deal with crises. Furthermore, its weak position as a midpower country—and lack of attention to and skill in effective and timely communication—resulted in a lack of consultation by the WHO before the imposition of a travel ban that significantly affected the regional economy, despite the presence of many Canadians in the organization. The conflict that resulted between Canada and the WHO reflected significant differences in priorities: The WHO, a health organization, defined the crisis uni-dimensionally while in Canada, socioeconomic (and hence political) consequences assumed a high priority. The differences may also stem from the parochial outlook of a member state compared to the overall systemic view taken by an international organization.

On November 27, 2002, a Canadian Internet scanning system, the Global Public Health Intelligence Network (GPHIN), provided the WHO with one of the earliest warnings of what later became recognized as the SARS outbreak. Between February 19 and 21, Health Canada also began to spread influenza alerts through the Pandemic Influenza Committee, the Council of the Chief Medical Officers of Health, the Canadian Public Health Laboratory Network, and the FluWatch Network. Nevertheless, the nation was ill-prepared when the outbreak spread to its shores just a few days later. The crisis revealed both the strengths and the weaknesses of Canada's public health and health care systems.[4]

The first known Canadian case was an elderly tourist who had stayed at the Metropole Hotel in Hong Kong on the same floor as the doctor from Guangdong. On February 25, 2 days after returning home, she fell ill. She consulted her family physician 3 days later, and died at home on March 5. Her illness was identified as SARS only retrospectively. On March 7, 2 days after she died, her son went to the emergency department of Scarborough Hospital, Grace Division, where he spent more than 18 hours in an open ward awaiting admission, a typical experience in the Canadian system, where overloaded emergency departments are often the first place patients turn to for care. During this time, he exposed several other patients and staff to the disease. Two of these patients subsequently became ill, leading to separate clusters of new cases; soon other patients, health care workers, and visitors were falling ill as well. Family members of the original Scarborough patient were sent to various hospitals in Toronto and generated new clusters at those institutions. Several members of an extended family were exposed while at the Grace Division; a month later it was realized that they had spread the disease to a new cluster in their religious group.[5]

On March 14, the Ontario Ministry of Health and Long-Term Care (OMHLTC) held a press conference to discuss the atypical pneumonia cases, and media coverage began in earnest. Health Canada convened the first information-sharing teleconference of federal, provincial, and territorial public health experts on March 13. These were soon held daily. On March 14, Health Canada sent six experts to assist with the SARS crisis and another eight on April 1. However, due to a lack of interjurisdictional agreements on how these experts could be used, they tended to be underutilized and limited to tasks such as liaison with other provinces and countries. They were withdrawn on April 30. That same day, the federal government opened a 2-day "SARS Summit" in Toronto. While the summit was helpful in promoting a sense of common direction, the government was also criticized for failing to invite many front line individuals who were most involved and knowledgeable.

Affected hospitals began to recognize that they were acting as hot spots for the transmission of the disease; if it was to be prevented from reaching the community at large, aggressive isolation measures would be necessary. Grace Division of Scarborough Hospital closed its emergency and intensive care services on March 25, began refusing new patients, closed outpatient clinics, and banned employees from working elsewhere. Recent visitors to the hospital were also asked to quarantine themselves at home for 10 days. Stringent infection control measures targeted at contact and droplet transmission were also implemented. Before long, quarantines were also imposed on numerous other groups where exposure was feared.

As the crisis peaked, the Ontario government invoked the Health Protection and Promotion Act on March 25, designating SARS as a reportable, communicable, and virulent disease, thereby allowing the authorities the power to track those infected, and order them not to engage in activities that risked spreading the disease. The next day, the premier declared a provincial emergency under the Emergency Measures Act and the Provincial Operations Centre for emergency response was activated. However, a system of joint leadership by two provincial officials with conflicting perspectives and management styles impeded the center's effectiveness. The OMHLTC ordered all hospitals in the Greater Toronto Area (GTA) and in Simcoe County (just north of Toronto) to implement their "Code Orange" emergency plans. This meant suspending non-essential services, limiting visitors, creating isolation units for SARS patients, and requiring the use of protective clothing for health care personnel. Within 4 days, all Ontario hospitals were ordered to implement access restrictions.

Canada's health care system had been under severe financial stress for some time, and public health expenditure had been a low priority. The surge in demand caused by SARS cast an awkward spotlight on the short-comings of the under-funded system. Negative pressure rooms were among the control measures deemed necessary. However, the very limited supply of these was quickly exhausted by March 26, and other rooms had to be converted on a makeshift basis. Shortages of N95 masks and other material also developed, and systems to distribute them were inadequate. Health Canada did eventually procure and supply a large number of N95 masks, but even health care workers who had them were often unable to use them properly. For example, the N95 masks require fitting, but the support necessary to carry this out was not available. Local physicians were often at a loss as to where to obtain the necessary supplies. Eventually the provincial vaccine distribution system was pressed into service to provide them with the equipment required—almost a month after the emergency was declared.

Laboratory capacity also became a sticking point. Toronto's Central Provincial Public Health Laboratory was quickly overwhelmed, and testing was often referred either to local hospitals with strong lab testing capabilities or to the National Microbiology Lab in Winnipeg. While the latter had considerable surge capacity, it was often troubled by inadequate or inaccurate labeling of specimens sent for analysis. In short, ad hoc arrangements had to be made to accommodate the surge in tests required by mobilizing pockets of slack wherever they existed in the system.

The health crisis led to a second, economic crisis as travel to Toronto plunged and hotels sat three-quarters empty. Paul Clifford, the President of the Hotel Employees and Restaurant Employees International Union Local 75, declared that "The SARS outbreak is no longer just a public health crisis, it is a jobs crisis in Toronto ("Toronto's Economy," 2003).

On April 1, a University of Toronto epidemiologist was seconded to the OMHLTC to set up a system to monitor SARS cases. However, he quickly discovered that the software platform available was so antiquated as to be unusable, while staffing was also inadequate. A patchwork of overlapping and incompatible local systems evolved, with many details held in widely dispersed paper files. Data sharing was further impeded by concerns about patient confidentiality and conflicts over jurisdiction. Meanwhile, an Ontario SARS Scientific Advisory Committee (OSSAC) of volunteer doctors and other officials was established to develop guidelines for quarantine and hospital procedures. However, these directives were routed through the hospitals branch of the OMHLTC for translation into official memoranda, and in the process their intent was often distorted, obscured, or lost altogether. To compound the confusion, the public service union also issued its own warnings and directions. It was not until April 3 that family doctors throughout the province received instructions on how they should approach SARS cases: Amazingly, there was no single, unified system for communicating with all the province's doctors. In the end, guidelines were distributed through the Ontario Medical Association's network. They recommended methods for keeping SARS cases away from physicians' offices, where they could infect other patients and staff, and for dealing safely with any patients that showed up anyway.

By late April, these measures appeared to be bringing the situation under control. Canadian officials were therefore stunned when the WHO announced a travel advisory for Toronto on April 23. There had been no prior consultation on this matter, so the decision came as a shock. Dr. Colin D'Cunha, Ontario's Commissioner of Public Health, denounced the decision, claiming, "We are not some rinky-dink Third World country," and Prime Minister Jean Chretien telephoned WHO Director-General Harlem Brundtland to protest (Heinzl, 2003, p. A8). Although initially the WHO stated its travel advisory would be in place for 3 weeks (Heinzl & Chipello, 2003), the WHO, after intense lobbying by Canadian officials from both the political and public health establishments, withdrew it on April 29, and on May 17, the provincial state of emergency and Code Orange status were withdrawn. A $128 million marketing campaign to bring back tourists was launched. While enhanced infection control measures continued, hospitals relaxed some of the most onerous measures. Unfortunately, however, the optimism of the day soon proved ill-founded.

Although it is still not clear how, the illness spread from several geriatric patients in the orthopedic ward of North York General Hospital to other patients, staff, and visitors. Patient transfers then spread the problem to five other hospitals. By May 23, it was clear that a second wave of SARS cases, subsequently referred to as "SARS II," had arisen. Recent visitors to affected hospitals were ordered into quarantine, strict infection-control procedures were re-introduced, the OSSAC came together again, and a SARS operations center was established in the OMHLTC offices. This time, only four hospitals were designated as SARS treatment centers. The tourism marketing campaign was suspended. By the end of May, careful tracking had identified 48 probable and 25 suspected cases of SARS. However, with the understanding gained in the first wave, the second was brought under control more quickly. Despite a few relapses that necessitated quarantines, by midsummer, the outbreak was contained.

Although the WHO was vital in the overall coordination of the international effort to bring SARS under control, its role in the Canadian SARS crisis was much-criticized. The surprise inclusion in the travel advisory of Toronto, where new cases had tapered off, stirred up a storm of controversy, given its severe impact on the travel and tourism industries. The decision was denounced by Canadian politicians, and a team was dispatched to Geneva to argue for the withdrawal of the advisory. The Canadian protests worked, and the travel advisory on Toronto was lifted on April 29—just as the second wave of SARS infections was about to break out. While the initial decision to impose the advisory was criticized by Canadians as "political," with the suggestion that it was included for face-saving political reasons so that China would not feel singled out, the use of political pressure to have it removed—in hindsight perhaps prematurely—seems at least as vulnerable to criticism.[6] Concern for narrow local interests seems to have outweighed broader considerations of the potential impact.

Canada's response to the SARS crisis was handicapped by its governance structure, which has multiple levels of government with no clear hierarchy and an ambiguous division of powers. Even the lowest level was not directly involved on the "front lines," since hospitals are largely self-governing under broad regional supervision. Health care workers were frequently presented with similar requests for information from multiple data gathering agencies, at a time when they could ill afford to be distracted. Even more importantly, by the time information filtered upward through various levels to the federal government and was communicated to the WHO, it was often contradicted by more current information available in the much more rapidly-responding media; as a result, the credibility of official Canadian communications suffered. While Canadians have historically been creative in inventing pragmatic compromises to deal with the awkward jurisdictional aspects of their federation, these solutions have often taken decades to evolve. In a crisis where time is measured in hours or days rather than years, such compromises must already be in place, for there is no time to work them out in the midst of an overwhelming problem; even if a temporary solution is found, it is unlikely to be optimal. Likewise, accommodations must also be reached ahead of time with interest groups such as organized labor to provide seamless delivery of the necessary responses. Canada was fortunate that the crisis did not spread further: Some problems (e.g., lack of lab test capacity) were dealt with by mobilizing slack in other jurisdictions. Had these been under the same pressure, the relief they offered might not have been forthcoming. In comparing the Canadian response to that of, say, Singapore, it is noteworthy that the affected areas in the two countries were effectively very similar (one major metropolitan area and its hinterland with populations of the same order of magnitude), yet the complications of multiple jurisdictions in Canada were nevertheless plainly evident.

Compliance with quarantine orders could not be taken for granted in the Canadian socioeconomic context. A lower level of respect for authority and the financial consequences of lost work led some of those quarantined to go to work or attend social or religious functions anyway, resulting in hundreds of additional exposures which then had to be traced and quarantined. After it became clear that pure voluntarism would be inadequate, health care workers began to call those quarantined at home twice a day and speak to them personally to verify compliance. To deal with extreme cases several "Section 22" orders compelling compliance with quarantine had to be issued, and one man was confined to a hospital room with a security guard to make certain he did not leave (Heinzl & Cherney, 2003). Covering workers' lost wages became a priority to remove incentives for evasion of quarantine orders, and the usual 10-day waiting period for Employment Insurance benefits was waived. Although the problem of inappropriate individual responses due to lack of public information and understanding was not as acute as in China, cases of ostracism of Chinese-Canadians and the children of health care workers were reported.

In the aftermath of the outbreak, Canada undertook several new initiatives to prepare for future public health crises. Hospitals tightened exposure control procedures; new guidelines were circulated to hospitals for implementation in the event of an outbreak; a new federal superministry of Public Safety and Emergency Preparedness under Deputy Prime Minister Anne McLellan was established to manage crises of all kinds, from epidemics to terrorism; and a panel report was published recommending the use of a "values-based decision-making tool" to include consideration of ethical issues when decisions are made on matters such as the imposition of quarantines and the responsibilities of health care workers in epidemics. The establishment of a center for disease control was also recommended.

SARS: THE SINGAPOREAN EXPERIENCE

Given its role as a regional transportation and trade hub, Singapore's vulnerability to the spread of epidemics originating in Southeast Asia is high. To combat this threat, it has been highly responsive to alerts from the WHO, keeping open the channels of communications. A crisis-ready, authoritarian government, compliant citizenry, and a compact city permitted timely mobilization of resources and effective control of the disease.

Singapore was one of the first countries to which SARS spread. Three female tourists, who had been infected by the Chinese doctor at the Metropole Hotel in Hong Kong, were the first source of transmission; one turned out to be a superspreader. They were admitted to hospitals between March 1 and 3, suffering from what was soon recognized to be atypical pneumonia. On March 6, the Ministry of Health (MOH) received word from the WHO that health care workers in Hanoi had fallen ill after treating their case of atypical pneumonia.[7] It immediately passed on the word to hospitals that they should isolate patients and implement stringent infection countermeasures. A press release was also issued. After more cases were found, the MOH formed a SARS task force 2 days later. This was followed by a Ministerial Committee on SARS on April 7.

On March 22, the MOH designated Tan Tock Seng Hospital as the sole institution for the care and treatment of SARS. The Infectious Disease Act was invoked on March 24, authorizing compulsory home quarantine for those exposed. Cameras were installed in the homes of those quarantined to enforce compliance, with severe penalties for evasion. On March 26, all schools were closed; they were gradually reopened between April 9 and April 16, with those for the youngest and most vulnerable being the last to reopen. Visitation of hospital patients was banned. At points of entry and departure, a variety of measures were used to check both the inbound and outbound spread of the disease, including health declarations and thermal scanners. On April 20, a new cluster of infections was found to include a vegetable hawker in a wholesale market; the whole market was closed and the health of 700 people checked, including all stall holders, their employees, and customers who had visited within the previous 2 weeks (Devadoss & Pan, 2004).

At first, hospital staff tracked contacts. When this proved too onerous, given their primary responsibilities for patient care, the MOH established an operations center where National Environmental Agency (NEA) staff used spreadsheets to track contacts. Soon the growing crisis overwhelmed even this arrangement. On April 24, the Defense Science and Technology Agency (DSTA) was called in to staff an expanded operations center with 120 stations at first, and then 250 stations. The makeshift, spreadsheet-based information system for tracking the disease was quickly found to be inadequate. Within 11 days, a team of experts from the DSTA had developed an entirely new system and populated it with data. It was run in parallel with the older system until confidence in it developed. The new system was used to identify contacts the same day they occurred so that quarantine orders could be issued before midnight to prevent exposed persons from going to work the next day. The quarantines were firmly enforced: a 50-year-old man had criminal charges laid against him for leaving his home against orders (Bradsher, 2003b). This system soon proved its worth: When a new case of SARS appeared on September 9, 2003, due to a lab accident, 60 of the patient's contacts were traced within eight hours, and quarantine orders were issued where necessary (Devadoss & Pan, 2004). Throughout the crisis, a single MOH spokesperson spoke to the media—in contrast to Canada, where many senior health care professionals were drawn away from their duties on a daily basis to satisfy the media's curiosity. This may have reflected differences in the level of trust in different professions in the two countries: While Singaporeans may be prepared to have confidence in a government spokesperson, doctors in Canada are much more respected than politicians or bureaucrats, and their participation may have been a prerequisite for credible communication.

Singapore also had several geographical and sociopolitical advantages that positioned it well to respond quickly and decisively to the SARS crisis. As a compact, unitary city-state, communications were simplified due to short distances and the lack of multiple levels of government involvement. Inbound and outbound travel is highly concentrated in one major airport and two causeways, facilitating control of the movement of travelers. Political control has long been vested in a single party, one which has accumulated considerable experience and permeates the entire governmental system to a degree unparalleled in other developed democracies. Whether by preference or resignation to the inevitable, Singaporeans have also developed a culture in which considerably greater intrusion into citizens' personal lives is tolerated: It is hard to imagine North Americans allowing the installation of monitoring cameras in their homes. As a consequence of this high degree of social cohesion, centralization of decision making, and ease of communication, Singapore was able to rapidly and effectively coordinate a powerful response to the SARS crisis. Indeed, where necessary, they could and did literally call in the army. The efficiency of the Singaporean response motivated a WHO spokesman, Dr. Ali Shan Khan, to state, "I can't think of anything that Singapore can do better. Based on the knowledge that they had at any given time, they made the right set of decisions" (Khalik, 2003, as cited in Lim, 2005, p. 2)

GLOBALIZATION AND THE NATURE OF INTERNATIONAL COMMUNICABLE CRISES

Communicable crises, medical, financial or otherwise, have long spread internationally. Where globalization has made a difference is by creating mechanisms that have increased the likelihood of more rapid and extensive transmission: the Internet, mass travel, media with world-wide reach, such as satellite television, 24-hour financial markets, and so forth. This intensification of interdependencies may both put constraints on the domestic management of crises and provide for international synergies (e.g., exchange of information, early warnings, and resource pooling). However, the mechanisms for containment are not automatic and their creation has often lagged behind the growth in means of transmission. Effective containment, now more than ever, requires conscious efforts to establish an infrastructure for domestic and international information exchange and decision making, ahead of the emergence of a crisis.

Globalization has created new channels of communication that have improved the scanning abilities of those who are in charge of preventing the onset of an epidemic from becoming a crisis. The international spread of Internet communications has empowered individuals and NGOs to scan the environment and disseminate their reports globally, thus eliminating institutional "blind spots" induced by rigid professional interpretations, economic interests, and economic or social incentives. These new media mean that information about crises spreads outside official channels, reducing nation-states' control over information. In combination with commercial media, such as satellite television, they have also broadened the geographical attention span of the public: The domestic political environment in a country is now affected by the way the media, NGOs, and the public interpret information about events in distant locations and their domestic relevance.

Clearly, every international communicable crisis involves a sequence of interdependent national crises to which the extant framework of crisis management theories and findings apply. However, a new layer of governance institutions (the international organization or organizations involved) is added. These institutions that traditionally dealt solely with national governments now have increasingly direct access through the Internet and media to publics and information sources in different countries. Information can flow rapidly and uncontrollably across borders, creating pressures on domestic governments to act in response to real or constructed threats. Interactions between states are impeded by differences in institutions and cultures, adding complexity to internal conflicts between agencies that are involved.

IMPLEMENTING BEST PRACTICES IN THE DOMESTIC MANAGEMENT OF COMMUNICABLE CRISES

The ease and rapidity with which crises can move across borders makes a coordinated international response critical to the effective management of a crisis, and this raises the question of how best to achieve the necessary coordination, given the variety of different national approaches and priorities dictated by political, cultural, and economic differences.

Our case studies reveal that some of the individual-level decision-making "pathologies" characteristic to crises were present in various jurisdictions infected by SARS. Selective information processing delayed initial aggressive control measures. Initial responses tended to echo past experiences and actions. As the stress levels and urgency of control increased, decision makers consulted fewer sources of information. Generally, attention focused on salient issues and stakeholders. Thus, for example, in the effort to contain SARS, actions were taken in Toronto that put at risk non-SARS patients who were denied treatment. The WHO has also observed that "some countries battling SARS missed cases of other epidemic-prone diseases, including dengue and Japanese encephalitis" (WHO, 2005b, p. 31).

The experience with SARS highlights the role of the Internet in forcing transparency and providing information. It also highlights, more generally, the importance of transparent communications to educate and encourage the compliance of the population and to reduce the spread of rumors. During the early spread of SARS, numerous individuals who had been exposed to the disease made decisions that had serious, often fatal consequences, both for themselves and others. Had they been better informed, it is likely fewer such tragic actions would have been taken. At the same time, compliance with central authority is largely dependent on acceptance of authority and hierarchy, which were greater in the high power-distance cultures of China and Singapore (Hofstede, 1991). Different communications approaches may be necessary to achieve the level of credibility necessary, as was evidenced by the willingness of Singaporean and Chinese audiences to take direction from government officials, while the more skeptical Canadian audience required information direct from medical professionals.

Open communication channels during a crisis may also serve to reduce psychological trauma and help restore confidence in the system in case of failure. Post-crisis learning can be enhanced by the open provision of all available information and the encouragement of public debates about causes and solutions. Distributional and ethical questions involved in the management of a crisis such as SARS must also be debated, for example, determining the trade-offs allowed between individual rights and collective safety during the crisis, and the issue of postcrisis compensation.

The impact of political differences could be seen in the degree of freedom of action enjoyed by different crisis management teams. While authorities everywhere relied heavily on quarantines, the breadth and rigor of application of this tool varied considerably. Singapore and China both had the advantage of political systems where one central power could, and did, exert its influence effectively to override any jurisdictional conflicts, and marshal whatever resources were thought necessary. Beijing quarantined 10 times as many people per capita as Toronto, while Singapore used electronic surveillance to enforce its isolation orders. (China, lacking such sophisticated technology, relied on human monitoring by the infamous "neighbourhood committees.") Singapore, with a tight, hierarchical bureaucracy, centralized both policy and operational decisions in an efficient and effective manner. China forced compliance at all levels by mobilizing the Party network that parallels, and has the power to supersede, formal governmental structures. This network was able to take action from the top of society (dismissing the Health Minister and the Mayor of Beijing) to its lowest levels, where neighborhood committees could enforce minute compliance with government directives; it could also mobilize the media to manage public perceptions. Canada, on the other hand, lacks such a dominant presence. Even when emergency powers are declared, formally constructing a crisis, the level at which decision-making power is nominally centralized often lacks the means to effectively enforce its will in the short term. This situation highlights the need for interjurisdictional agreements to be in place before a crisis strikes in order to provide a timely and coordinated response.

Differences such as these suggest that while the essential elements of a crisis management plan (knowledge, communication, authority, and resources) may be universal, the details of implementation must be allowed to vary. In one environment, government spokesmen may be credible, while in others, medical professionals may need to weigh in.

One jurisdiction may have a center of authority that can intervene at will, while another may require prearranged contingency plans to be in place for any deviations from normal distributions of powers. Rational development of priorities at the local and national levels may also be made more difficult by externalities created by international contagion, international political relations, the presence of international nongovernmental agents (e.g., multinational corporations or NGOs), the standard operating procedures of domestic bureaucracies, or the media's ability to draw public attention to a particular issue with a high "dread factor," any of which can generate political pressure to devote resources to the prevention of crises with lower probabilities or impacts, or the adoption of suboptimal crisis management responses.

Analysis of our case studies leads to the following observations regarding the four key elements of crisis management identified at the beginning of this paper and how they can best be disseminated in a domestic context.

To provide those dealing with a crisis with adequate knowledge and understanding, they need to have prior training to familiarize them with the existing state of knowledge about both crisis management in general and the types of crises they are likely to face. In addition, since crises are often of a novel or ambiguous nature that requires the development of new knowledge or the making of informed assumptions, they need access to multidisciplinary units that can assist in interpreting the often conflicting data that emerge as the crisis evolves. In this way, the construction of the crisis incorporates all available information, not just that which fits into the conceptual framework of the first professional grouping that encounters the crisis. The Ontario SARS Scientific Advisory Committee was a good example of how such a team can provide a broad cross-section of scientific advice to policymakers.

Effective communication requires a coordinated infrastructure, but this need not be overly formal. Indeed, formal structures, and the physical and human assets that support them, may be among the first casualties of a crisis. Damage to physical infrastructure, or the loss, unavailability, or inaccessibility of key personnel, can disable the most sophisticated arrangements. Thus, it is important to establish broad and deep networks of personal relationships among key players at more than one authority level, and to create proper incentives for the sharing of information.

Empowering those faced with a crisis with the authority to do what is necessary involves several careful trade-offs. There must be a balance between the need for central control and oversight, and the need for units in the field to respond quickly to emerging local situations. This may require the prior development of legal and institutional mechanisms to provide special authority at various levels, and allow for alternative lines of authority and role definitions that are not dependent on a few key individuals in order to give the system the necessary resiliency.

Resource issues include not only having sufficient slack and prepositioned pools of supplies, but systems of incentives and accountability that allow for pooling and diversion of supplies to where they are most needed. For example, it may make much more sense for units to send their limited supplies of vaccine to one location, to help nip an outbreak in the bud, rather than hoard them locally. If they allow the outbreak to spread until it reaches them on their home turf, it may, by then, have acquired dimensions that overwhelm their abilities to respond with these limited local supplies.

A recurring theme in several of these areas is the need for strategic partnerships involving both different levels of government and NGOs. Providing a framework to facilitate such interactions can greatly assist in getting a crisis response off to a running start at a time when every hour may count.

IMPLEMENTING BEST PRACTICES IN THE INTERNATIONAL MANAGEMENT OF COMMUNICABLE CRISES

As with any situation involving externalities, there is a tendency to underinvest in disease prevention. Geographical, institutional, and cultural differences make bilateral and multilateral coordination among nations difficult. Differences in interests make it difficult to coordinate investment and pool resources when there is no imminent threat, especially when domestic health agendas are dominated by high costs and rising demand for immediately visible care, rather than largely invisible prevention. The existing mechanisms for coordination, the WHO and national health care systems, are geared to the onset of highly predictable influenzas, for which immunity levels in the population exist, creating a false sense of security. While public health authorities are concerned about the certain onset of a pandemic sometime in the future, the uncertainty involved in dealing with novel situations requiring novel strategies makes their case less attractive to politicians. Concern for efficient use of scarce health care funds domestically, and suspicion of "free riders" internationally, make investment in both international and domestic capacity less attractive.

Three characteristics of the WHO tended to influence its approach to the crisis: its bureaucratic nature, its identity as an organization dominated by a single profession (medicine), and its political nature as an organization controlled by and responsible to its membership. As a bureaucracy, it has its own agenda and standard operating procedures, which may influence its approach to a problem, regardless of their utility in a specific case. In a grouping of professionals with a deep belief and investment in the tools of their trade, unlearning may be difficult—and vulnerability to the competency trap high—particularly where its beliefs have led to escalating commitment to a particular course of action. Since China was viewed as a constant source of new varieties of avian flu, diagnostic testing at first focused on this disease, perhaps delaying the discovery that the problem was actually of a different nature. On the other hand, it was a standard operating procedure in the medical profession (isolation via quarantine) that eventually defeated the disease when no medical breakthrough was forthcoming. Professional organizations also tend to define problems uni-dimensionally, sometimes thereby precipitating new crises as side-effects of their actions. In the case of SARS, the use of travel advisories was a logical response when the crisis was viewed from a strictly medical viewpoint, but also precipitated economic crises, particularly where the travel and service sector played a large role in the economy. Indeed, some observers felt it went too far in dealing with the SARS crisis. Terence Corcoran, the editor of the (Canadian) *Financial Post* and a widely-cited conservative columnist, argued that "the scale of the measures, including the WHO's travel warnings and other directives, far exceeded the benefits ... the WHO's extravagant impositions and style on more than one occasion appeared calculatingly arrogant ... somebody needs to look at the cost of stopping everything in its tracks using the WHO's methods" (Corcoran, 2003, p. FP 15).

As an international group dependent on its members for direction and resources, it will also tend to reflect the interests of members whose influence is great either by virtue of their power to dominate the agenda through broad influence over shifting groups of members, or through access to superior resources and expertise. Thus, during the SARS crisis, there was extensive collaboration with the U.S. Center for Disease Control and Prevention, despite the very slight direct impact SARS had on the USA. It must also be sensitive to issues that are salient to its members to maintain their continued support. This requirement may have made it more receptive to Canadian lobbying for the withdrawal of the travel advisory. The dominance of Western countries reduces the social capital the institution possesses with respect to its transactions with developing countries.

During the crisis, the major constraint on international collaboration was the strong local incentives to conceal information on the spread of the disease to reduce economic and political impacts. The WHO, with no ability to enforce its decisions, had only a constrained access to information in China, causing significant delays. The power of "naming and shaming" can be used only cautiously by an institution that relies on voluntary compliance by its members. This power is based on the ability to legitimize or de-legitimize the health-related activities of national governments, and to impose economic costs on them. Declaring travel advisories can essentially end tourist and business travel overnight, while "naming and shaming" governments can scare off the multinational corporations (MNCs) that could otherwise bring much-needed foreign direct investment (FDI). Such power is contingent, of course, on there being public interest in the issue at hand, and some degree of sensitivity to economic losses and losses of reputational capital (or face) on the part of the target government. The WHO has also recognized that too extensive use of tools such as travel advisories could create disincentives to report outbreaks. On the other hand, it defends them by observing that "advice on which areas were experiencing local transmission segmented international travel, allowing travel to continue to large parts of Asia. Moreover, when WHO declared an area free of the illness, confidence in this decision brought rapid economic recovery" (WHO, 2005b, p. 36).

As noted above, the WHO's power is contingent on the issue rising to international prominence. Here the Internet and other forms of global communication have given individuals, such as whistle-blower Dr. Jiang Yanyong, unprecedented power to bring an issue to the top of the world's agenda by releasing sensitive information that increases the "dread factor" associated with a given problem, thereby raising its salience among decision makers. This creates a kind of symbiotic power relationship between the WHO and those who have knowledge of information that could prove embarrassing if widely disseminated. The WHO's power is also contingent on some degree of sensitivity to world opinion and economic consequences. Where a xenophobic or irrationally despotic regime exists, such power is likely to be extremely limited. Recognizing its source of influence, the WHO has been quick to offer praise where compliance was forthcoming, thereby rewarding regimes with the legitimization whose pursuit motivated their compliance. It held up Singapore as a model, and lauded China's efforts once it began to take serious action to contain the threat of SARS.

To be better crisis-prepared, the WHO must consider the establishment of independent multinational interdisciplinary crisis management units. These units should focus on the development of crisis management capabilities and infrastructure, both at the national and international levels. As part of this infrastructure, independent monitoring systems in susceptible regions should be established, as well as stockpiles of antiviral drugs. Recent studies suggest that, under certain conditions, the tactical deployment of antiviral drugs might contain, or even eliminate, an outbreak of human influenza ("Catching the Flu," 2005). Stockpiles of antiviral drugs deployed quickly may thus reduce significantly the chance of an onset of a flu pandemic if the infrastructure to administer them properly exists in the region where the outbreak occurs. To respond swiftly, prior bilateral and multilateral agreements, and a comprehensive plan of crisis prevention and management must be in place. In addition, training programs (for example simulations) for their activation must be implemented. The international crisis management units may have parallel national units with responsibilities for developing national response plans coordinated within the international plan. In addition, an international advisory task force—removed from the actual management centers of the crisis—should be formed, with the task of analyzing potential deviations from predicted forms of flu epidemics and developing novel response alternatives. Such interdisciplinary advisory committees will provide direct channels to those in the crisis management/decision centers and to front line units, as well as key stakeholders. This may allow broadening the information flows to the decision makers managing the crisis, without overloading them unnecessarily.

International structures require trust. Trust can only be built if a trustworthy, equitable governance system is in place. The development of a transparent organization open to the scrutiny of NGOs and individual citizens, with processes and procedures developed on a scientific basis after wide consultation with stakeholders, is necessary. The funding of such an organization should be stable and independent of national pressures. The creation of an endowment to which all nations contribute, rather than annual national assessments, might be the most promising funding arrangement.

FINAL NOTE

SARS was not a surprising or a novel type of crisis. Indeed, the traditional means of responding to epidemics served well in controlling and resolving the crisis. Yet many of the pathologies predicted by the framework of crisis management were manifested and the prescriptions for eliminating them applicable. In the case study, we have highlighted the blind spots that resulted from selective information processing (avoiding bad news and its messengers). We have observed the tendency for centralization once a "crisis situation" is constructed and the locus of decision making shifts upwards. This phenomenon, under the circumstances surrounding the SARS epidemics, while narrowing the information base and cognitive processes of key decision makers and isolating them from front line units and stakeholders, helped bring about more coordination. However, the case also shows that rigid bureaucratic structures and territoriality do not evaporate during a crisis and continue to impede an efficient response.

Leadership appears to be critical in helping mobilize resources, breaking constraining routines, reassuring the population, and achieving compliance.

In the postcrisis period, a number of new institutions were established to deal with crises in general, and the possibility of a pandemic in particular. However, the public agenda in most countries quickly moved on to other burning issues of the day, prompting *The Economist* to observe, "given how much money rich countries have spent preparing for bio-terror attacks, it is surprising how little attention they have paid to the possibility of a flu pandemic, which may be likelier and which, if it happens, would probably kill more people" ("Catching the Flu," 2005). Since that time, intense, often daily media attention to the spread of the H5N1 strain of avian influenza around the world has led to renewed attention to the threat of a pandemic and to increases in resource allocations. The challenge will be to maintain this level of vigilance if, as is quite possible, the next pandemic is some years off. The dilemma for crisis managers is that lack of preparedness leads to disaster, but success in averting disaster tends to lead, over time, to complacency that increases the risk and potential severity of future crises.

ACKNOWLEDGMENTS

The authors gratefully acknowledge the research support of the Atkinson Graduate School of Management, Willamette University, as well as helpful comments on earlier drafts of this paper from Denise Werker and Fred Thompson. All conclusions and interpretations are those of the authors, who retain responsibility for any errors or omissions.

NOTES

1. The chronology presented here is based on WHO (2006), cross-checked with media reports and National Advisory Committee on SARS (2003).

2. The chronology in the Chinese case study is based on cross-referencing media reports with WHO (2006), plus the additional sources cited.

3. For reasons that are not yet well-understood, but that may relate to viral load, a small minority of SARS cases seem to account for a disproportionate number of secondary infections, in some cases as many as 100. Such individuals are referred to as "superspreaders," although the WHO prefers the terminology "superspreading events."

4. Except where otherwise specified, the following account is based on chapter 2 of the National Advisory Committee on SARS and Public Health's

October 2003 report, *Learning from SARS: Renewal of Public Health in Canada*, cross-referenced with WHO (2006) and media reports.

5. The experience in British Columbia was markedly different, despite similar origins of transmission. On March 13, another man who had stayed at the Metropole Hotel in Hong Kong was admitted to Vancouver General Hospital. Although doctors there were as yet unaware of the Toronto outbreak, the man was masked and isolated, and therefore generated no secondary cases. Two more cases appeared among travelers from infected regions, but only one case of secondary transmission to a health care worker was recorded. This account focuses on the experience in the Greater Toronto area since this was the focal point of the Canadian outbreak.

6. It should be noted, however, that the criteria for the issuance of travel criteria were themselves open to criticism since they seemed to lack a close relationship to characteristics of the local situation that would create an actual danger to travelers.

7. This section draws heavily on Lim (2005), cross-referenced with WHO (2006) and media reports.

REFERENCES

Bradsher, K. (2003a, April 28). Outbreak of disease brings big drop-off in China's economy. *New York Times*, p. A1.

Bradsher, K. (2003b, May 5). Cases thought to be relapses now seen as other conditions. *New York Times*, p. A8.

Bradsher, K., & Altman, L. (2004, January 5). China to kill 10,000 civets in effort to eradicate SARS. *New York Times*, p. A4.

Bryant, T. J., Smart, C., & Vertinsky, I (in press). The fit between crisis types and management attributes as a determinant of crisis consequences. In J. Starbuck (Ed.), *Handbook of organizational decision-making*. New York: Oxford University Press.

Buckley, C. (2003, July 11). SARS does little to slow China's growth. *New York Times*, p. W1.

Catching the flu. (2005, August 6). *The Economist*, p. 10.

Central government regulations, directives and documents. (2003). *Chinese Law and Government, 36*(6), 30-94.

Chen, D. (2003, August 21). SARS keeps foreign students home, hurting Chinese businesses. *New York Times*, p. A7.

China allows sale of animal tied to SARS. (2003, August 14). *New York Times*, p. A8.

Corcoran, T. (2003, June 19). Look WHO's killing jobs and growth in Canada. *National Post*, p. FP15.

Devadoss, P. R., & Pan, S. L. (2004, August). *Managing knowledge integration in a healthcare crisis: Lessons from combating SARS in Singapore*. Paper presented at the Academy of Management Meeting, New Orleans, LA.

Eckholm, E. (2003a, April 15). Cases of lethal new illness rise sharply in interior region. *New York Times*, p. A6.

Eckholm, E. (2003b, April 21). China admits underreporting its SARS cases. *New York Times*, p. A1.

Eckholm, E. (2003c, May 1). As cases mount, Chinese officials try to calm a panicky public. *New York Times*, p. A10.

Eckholm, E. (2003d, May 2). Illness brings subdued May Day in Beijing. *New York Times*, p. A15.

Eckholm, E. (2003d, May 16). China suspends adoptions and sets edict to fight virus. *New York Times*, p. A12.

Eckholm, E. (2003e, May 31). China says SARS in retreat: Canada has another death. *New York Times*, p. A8.

Fresh SARS cases in China called milder. (2004, January 16). *New York Times*, p. A5.

Heinzl, M. (2003, April 28). The SARS outbreak: WHO will review Toronto advisory. *Wall Street Journal*, p. A8.

Heinzl, M., & Cherney, E. (2003, April 22). In Toronto, containing SARS is gumshoe work. *Wall Street Journal*, p. D3.

Heinzl, M., & Chipello, C. (2003, April 24). Toronto is put on travel watch, angering officials. *Wall Street Journal*, p. D5.

Herman, C. F. (1963). Some consequences of crisis which limit the viability of organizations. *Administrative Science Quarterly, 8*, 61-82.

Hofstede, G. (1991). *Cultures and organizations: Software of the mind*. Berkshire, England: McGraw-Hill.

Kahn, J. (2003a, May 15). Man's virus infects town, killing his family. *New York Times*, p. A1.

Kahn, J. (2003b, May 23). Some Chinese say government's response to epidemic has been too heavy-handed. *New York Times*, p. A8.

Kahn, J. (2004, January 8). Police raid Chinese newspaper that reported new SARS case. *New York Times*, p. A7.

Khalik, S. (2003, May 6). Singapore made "right decisions." *Straits Times*.

Liang, H., & Xue, Y. (2004). Investigating Public Health Emergency Response Information System Initiatives in China. *International Journal of Medical Informatics, 73*, 675–685.

Lim, V. K. G. (2005). *Crisis management and SARS: Lessons from Singapore and Toronto*. Unpublished manuscript.

Ling, L. (n.d). *Open government and transparent policy: China's experiences*. Tianjin University of Finance and Economics Working Paper.

McNeil, D. (2003, May 19). SARS furor heightens Taiwan-China rift. *New York Times*, p. A8.

McNeil, D., & Altman, L. (2003, May 4). As SARS outbreak took shape, health agency took fast action. *New York Times*, p. 1.1.

National advisory committee on SARS and public health. (2003). *Learning from SARS: Renewal of public health in Canada* [Publication Number 1210]. Ottawa: Health Canada.

Paine, S. C. M. (2003). *The Sino-Japanese War of 1894–1895: Perceptions, Power and Primacy*. New York: Cambridge University Press.

Pearson, C. M., & Clair, J. (1998). Reframing crisis management. *Academy of Management Review, 23*(1), 59–76.

Quarantelli, E. L. (1988) Disaster crisis management: A summary of research findings. *Journal of Management Studies, 25,* 373–385.

Rosenthal, E. (2003a, April 10). A Beijing doctor questions data on illness. *New York Times,* p. A8.

Rosenthal, E. (2003b, April 27). From China's provinces, a crafty germ breaks out. *New York Times,* p. 1.1.

Rosenthal, E., & Altman, L. (2003, March 27). China raises tally of cases and deaths in mysterious illness. *New York Times,* p. A12.

Rosenthal, U., Boin, R. A., & Comfort, L. K. (2001). *Managing crises: Threats, dilemmas, opportunities.* Springfield, IL: Charles C. Thomas.

Smart, C., & Vertinsky, I. (1977). Decisions for crisis decision units. *Administrative Science Quarterly, 22*(4), 640–659.

Speedy and consequential new laws and policies on SARS and information flow. (2003). *Chinese Law and Government, 36*(4), 76–98.

Toronto's Economy Could Be Next Victim of SARS Outbreak. (2003, April 19, 2003). *Kingston Whig-Standard,* p. 22.

World Health Organization. (2005a). *WHO outbreak communication guidelines.* Geneva, Switzerland: Author.

World Health Organization. (2005b). *Outbreak communication: Best practices for communicating with the public during an outbreak.* Geneva, Switzerland: Author.

World Health Organization. (2006). *SARS: How a global epidemic was stopped.* Geneva, Switzerland: Author.

Yardley, J. (2004, April 27). China expands qurantine in aggressive effort to contain SARS. *New York Times,* p. A5.

CHAPTER 10

CONSTRAINTS ON THE U.S. RESPONSE TO THE 9/11 ATTACKS

Alasdair Roberts

The American government's response to terrorist threats has had three features: a reluctance to restrict the civil liberties of American citizens; an unwillingness to invest heavily or exercise regulatory authority to ensure domestic security; and a preference for a militarized response to perceived threats, evidenced in U.S. campaigns in Afghanistan and Iraq. Four features of the American political system explain this response: the increased complexity of the policy network interested in civil liberties; the persistence of populist antistatism; the militarization of the American polity; and the susceptibility of the American political system to corporate influence. The consequence is a policy response that fails to take adequate measures to assure domestic security. This recent experience in responding to terror threats also suggests larger lessons about the political system's capacity to respond to policy shocks.

INTRODUCTION

The September 11 attacks traumatized the American public. It was precisely the sort of shock that students of the policy process argue creates a

Communicable Crises: Prevention, Response, and Recovery in the Global Arena, pp. 301–321

"window of opportunity" for dramatic shifts in policy that would otherwise be impracticable. Furthermore the shock was *recognized* as such an opportunity by President Bush and his senior advisors, who were ready to execute a program of radical change. The administration's frustration with the controls that had been layered on the presidency over the preceding 3 decades was a matter of public record. The administration believed that the executive branch should have a larger degree of autonomy and a sharper focus on security matters. It was prepared to "spend political capital" on its priorities (Executive Office of the President, 2004b). And it insisted, in what might be regarded as an effort to effect change through pure power of assertion, that everything *had* changed after September 11. "History starts today," said Deputy Secretary of State Richard Armitage immediately after the attacks (Smith, 2001). There is a "new normalcy," said Vice President Dick Cheney in October 2001 (Woodward, 2001).

Cortell and Peterson (1999) have recently suggested that substantial reform occurs when there is a coincidence of a window of opportunity, the presence of state actors predisposed to reforms, and institutional conditions that facilitate reform. Such a coincidence seemed to arise after 9/11—but how substantial were the policy changes that followed? Four years after the attacks, it is now possible to say something definitive about the character of the American government's response to them. The response had three main features. First, the threat posed to the civil liberties of Americans, although much discussed, was not substantial—when compared to the damage done during comparable earlier crises. To an unprecedented degree the damage to human rights was concentrated on noncitizens. Second, the federal government's effort to deter or prepare for further terror attacks on U.S. soil was halting and incomplete. The government balked at funding essential security measures and at exercising its regulatory power to compel action by businesses or state and local governments. Third, the attacks provoked a robust and expensive military response—including military campaigns in Afghanistan and Iraq and the negotiation of new alliances with states in central and south Asia.

What considerations shaped this response to the attacks? There are four institutional and cultural factors, all of which could be marked as distinctive attributes of the American style of governance. The first was the institutionalization of the "civil liberties" policy field. By this I mean the expansion of the network of advocacy organizations and the elaboration of formal rules to regulate governmental conduct, both of which made a replication of earlier responses improbable. The second was a deeply rooted populism, typified by antistatist attitudes and an insensitivity to problems with long time horizons, that discouraged strong measures to bolster domestic security. The third was the distinctive vulnerability of the

American system to corporate influence, which again discouraged strong federal action on homeland security. The final consideration was militarism—marked by the availability of unrivalled military capacity and a popular culture that confers on the military a degree of legitimacy not ceded to other parts of the federal bureaucracy.

The American government's response to the 9/11 attacks was not extraordinary, viewed either from the point of view of the radicalism of the policy responses or the character of the forces that shaped those policy responses. The "new normal" was not qualitatively different from the "old normal." This could be taken as a sign of the robustness of the American system of governance. On the other hand, it could also be taken as a sign of the worrisome inability of the American system to respond appropriately to terror threats—because of its failure to take sensible measures to promote homeland security or its predisposition to military actions that exacerbate domestic security threats.

CONSTRUCTING THE PROBLEM

By coincidence, the 9/11 crisis confronted a presidency that was already committed to the proposition that there should be dramatic changes in the way in which the American government was run. President Bush's team of senior advisors had made an effort to cultivate a certain radical chic. During the 2000 presidential campaign, they nicknamed themselves "the Vulcans," after the Roman god of fire, the forger of arms and armor for other gods and heroes. The nickname, says James Mann, "sought to convey a sense of power, toughness, resilience and durability." The Vulcans were committed to an "epochal change" in American foreign policy, marked by the more assertive pursuit of American national interests (Mann, 2004, pp. ix–xii).

The aspiration for radical change was not limited to international affairs. At home, these same policymakers chafed at the constraints on presidential authority that had built up over the preceding 3 decades. Vice President Dick Cheney complained about the "erosion of the powers and the ability of the President of the United States to do his job ... We are weaker today as an institution because of the unwise compromises that have been made over the last thirty or thirty-five years." President Bush himself insisted that he would resist Congress' efforts to undercut a "robust" presidency. Defense Secretary Donald Rumsfeld declared the federal government to be "an institution in Chapter 11," constrained like Gulliver by a web of "debilitating" restrictions. The image of Gulliver was so frequently evoked during President Bush's first term that Senator Robert Byrd speculated that Swift's book had been made required reading for senior administration officials. All of this echoed long-standing conservative fears that the United States faced a "crisis of governability," by which was meant an inability on the part of government to manage the burgeoning number of demands that were thrust upon it (Roberts, 2006, pp. 51–81).

The 9/11 attacks were a tragedy that demanded a firm response by the American government. However, the attacks also created a "window of opportunity" for the Bush administration to pursue institutional changes to which it was already committed—which would essentially expand the executive branch's autonomy in domestic and foreign affairs. Recognizing this, the Bush administration sought to make the window as large as it could by, for example, placing heavy emphasis on the primacy of antiterrorism on the policy agenda. (The proposition that policy problems must be socially constructed is discussed by Kingdon (Kingdon, 2003, p. 179)). The Bush administration was aided in this effort by a mass media that gave constant and often sensational coverage to the 9/11 attacks and the aftermath (Kellner, 2005, pp. 25-44).) It also made clear that the appropriate response was bold executive action.

Again, this was as true in the domestic as in the foreign sphere. When Congress appeared ready to block proposed homeland security legislation in Fall 2002, President Bush publicly chastised its leaders for being "more interested in special interests in Washington and not interested in the security of the American people" (Fisher, 2003, p. 398). "At a time of national emergency," according to the president's FY2003 budget, it was critical for federal officials to be given broad discretion "to get the job done." To drive the point home, the budget included a century-old lithograph of Gulliver, tied down by the Lilliputians (Office of Management and Budget, 2002).

THE NATURE OF THE RESPONSE

An administration predisposed to radical change and preoccupied with security threats is confronted with an exceptional window of opportunity. And what follows from this? The U.S. government's response to this security crisis had three distinctive features: It did not tread heavily on the civil liberties of U.S. citizens, as it had in response to the major security crises of the twentieth century; on the contrary, rights abuses were concentrated primarily on foreign nationals. Nor did it take vigorous action to promote domestic security; rather, its response was halting and inadequate. But it *did* take bold and expensive military action overseas.

Protecting the Civil Liberties of Citizens

Every great security emergency of the twentieth century was accompanied by governmental actions that undercut the civil liberties of U.S. citizens. ("Civil liberties," in the American context, typically refers a set of protections for citizens or residents of the United States against abuse of governmental authority, which are recognized in the U.S. Constitution or federal statutes.) After the United States entered the Great War in April 1917, it passed the Espionage Act, which banned the distribution of "seditious materials" such as those which "impugned the motives of the government," and later the Sedition Act, which criminalized the utterance of "disloyal" language. Socialist presidential candidate Eugene V. Debs was stripped of his citizenship and imprisoned for violating the law; labor leaders such as Bill Haywood, a native-born American, fled the United States to avoid imprisonment following conviction. (Congress restored Debs' full rights of citizenship posthumously in 1976.) Naturalized German-Americans were harassed by government-supported vigilante groups, fired, tarred and feathered, and in one instance lynched (Brinkley, 2003, pp. 26-28).

The persecution of radicals was further fueled following the Russian revolutions of 1917, and the strikes and riots in Europe and North America that followed the end of the Great War in November 1918. In December 1919, the U.S. government deported 249 radicals, including many naturalized Americans, to the Soviet Union; a few weeks later, the Justice Department organized raids that resulted in the detention of ten thousand people. The Japanese strike against Pearl Harbor provoked another round of restrictions of Americans' civil liberties. Over 110,000 individuals of "Japanese ancestry" were removed from their homes to "war relocation camps" in remote parts of the nation's interior; over 60,000 of the detainees were U.S. citizens.

Further restrictions followed the start of the Cold War in 1947-48. Citizens whose political beliefs or sexual orientation made them seem to be "loyalty risks" were purged from the federal bureaucracy (Johnson, 2004); a ban on employment in the federal government for such individuals was effectively codified in directives issued by President Truman in 1947 and President Eisenhower in 1953 (Joelson, 1963). Comparable "blacklists" were maintained in the private sector for citizens who refused to collaborate in investigations of suspected subversion. (For a recent discussion of Harvard University's treatment of individuals who refused to collaborate, see Bellah, 2005.) Many citizens were also denied passports that would allow them to travel abroad.

Even in the 1960s and early 1970s, security concerns led to infringements of citizens' rights. The FBI's response to domestic protests was

COINTELPRO, a program aimed at infiltrating and disrupting civil rights and antiwar protest movements. The Church Committee later characterized COINTELPRO as "a sophisticated vigilante operation aimed squarely at preventing the exercise of First Amendment rights of speech and association, on the theory that preventing the growth of dangerous groups and the propagation of dangerous ideas would protect the national security and deter violence" (Select Senate Committee to Study Government Operations, 1976, Book III). (W. Mark Felt, the senior FBI official who recently acknowledged he was "Deep Throat," was convicted in 1980 for authorizing break-ins against suspected domestic terrorist groups 8 years earlier. Felt justified the actions by arguing that the FBI had a duty to "prevent violence ... rather than wait until the bomb had exploded" (Woodward, 2005, pp. 126-127).)

That the United States should have reacted to security crises in this way is often regarded as unfortunate but understandable. A terrorized public, it is generally acknowledged, is not in the best frame of mind to make nuanced decisions about the balance to be struck between public order and civil liberties. If this is the case, however, we might expect that pressure for strong counter-terror measures would be stronger at the end of the century than at its beginning. In the early decades of the century, communications were slow and principally text-based; by the end of the decade communications were instantaneous and highly graphic. The American public did not "witness" Pearl Harbor; but it might reasonably be said to have witnessed the 9/11 attacks. "Live television broadcasting," says Douglas Kellner, "brought a 'you are there' drama to the September 11 spectacle" (Kellner, 2005, p. 28).

Even so, the government's response to the 9/11 attacks differed qualitatively from the response to earlier emergencies. There were no mass arrests of U.S. citizens; and no systematic efforts to disenfranchise and deport citizens. There were, to the best of our knowledge, no systematic efforts at illegal surveillance of Muslim-American groups; no reports of "black-bag" jobs to uncover domestic plots; no efforts to blacklist Muslim-Americans; and no federal infringements of First Amendment rights. (The ACLU did express concern about the infiltration and monitoring of nonviolent protest groups by the FBI and local police through their Joint Terrorism Task Forces. However, there is a qualitative difference between the "chilling effect" that is alleged to follow from federal surveillance and the more severe infringements on the right of free expression that characterized earlier security crises.)

This is not to say that there were not substantial abuses of governmental authority following the 9/11 attacks. Several thousand people—foreign nationals, rather than citizens—*were* taken into preventative detention after the attacks. This emphasis on foreign nationals was driven, in part, by the state of the law. Because the United States lacks a general law authorizing preventative detention, federal officials relied on immigration laws that allow broad discretion to detain individuals who violate immigration rules. Federal investigators later found that the conditions under which these detainees were held were often harsh. Only one of an estimated 5,000 detainees was convicted on a terrorism-related offence. Hundreds, however, were deported for technical violations of immigration requirements. Critics complained that the federal response unfairly targeted Arab immigrants and was disproportionate to the perceived threat (Bernstein, 2004; Cole, 2003, pp. 25-35; Lawyers Committee for Human Rights, 2003, pp. 37-40).

There were more severe violations of rights as the federal government waged its "Global War on Terror." Perhaps 700 foreign nationals were held in detention by the U.S. Army at Guantanamo; more are held by the CIA at other facilities worldwide. Federal officials adopted narrow interpretations of their obligations under domestic and international law, to allow interrogation techniques that many critics said constituted abuse or torture. The CIA also expanded its "extraordinary rendition" program, under which foreign nationals were abducted while abroad, and delivered for interrogation by the intelligence services of countries allied with the United States in the war on terror. In this way, the business of abusing rights was outsourced: U.S. agencies delivered a Canadian national to Syrian intelligence, and Swedish residents to Egyptian intelligence; the U.S. trained Iraqi paramilitary forces to interrogate Iraqi insurgents; and finally began turning over its Guantanamo detainees for indefinite detention by the Afghan and other governments (Greenberg & Dratel, 2005; McCoy, 2006).

In every emergency there has been a tendency to ostracize perceived outsiders. But the response to 9/11 has been marked by the degree to which the harm, in terms of human rights, has been concentrated on noncitizens, and particularly on noncitizens outside the United States. By contrast, the federal government encountered stiff resistance when it attempted to restrict the civil liberties of citizens. David Cole notes Congress' swift action to bar the Justice Department's "Operation TIPS" and its response to the Defense Department's "Total Information Awareness" project—which was to block its implementation *as applied to U.S. citizens* (Cole, 2003, p. 6). Privacy advocates also resisted efforts to establish databases that would improve security screening of airline passengers; other databases that would permit law enforcement agencies to check the background of suspicious persons; efforts to standardize procedures for the issuance of driver's licenses; and technologies such as closed-circuit television (CCTV) that would improve monitoring of public spaces. ("Have you caught any terrorists?" a skeptical Jeffrey Rosen asked the City of London Police press officer while visiting its CCTV monitoring center in 2002 (Rosen, 2004, pp. 33-61).)

The heated debate over changes made by the PATRIOT Act in October 2001 illustrated the American public's sensitivity to policy shifts that appeared to jeopardize citizen rights. Amendments that expanded the FBI's capacity to collect evidence for antiterrorism investigations became a lightning rod for protests of civil liberties groups. Although the new authority was still subject to several restrictions—a requirement that there be a connection to antiterrorism investigations, a requirement of review by the Foreign Intelligence Surveillance Court, a bar on investigations based solely on activities protected by the First Amendment—it was nevertheless criticized as a license for "snooping" against innocent citizens by "curious" federal agents (Schulhofer, 2002, p. 51).

Critics dwelt specifically on the threat that the PATRIOT Act was thought to pose to the integrity of public libraries and "reader privacy," and by 2005 there was an emerging bipartisan consensus to restrict the provision to eliminate this threat, even though there was no evidence that the authority had ever been used for this purpose ("Patriot Misfire," 2005). That there were legitimate questions surrounding the drafting of the PATRIOT Act could not be disputed; but the problem of "reader privacy" differed by an order of magnitude from the predicament of foreign nationals detained indefinitely at Guantanamo or flown covertly to Damascus or Diego Garcia.

Neglect of Homeland Security

At the same time the United States has taken only limited steps to protect itself against further terrorist attacks. Before 9/11, says analyst Stephen Flynn, it was "the consensus view … that it would take a catastrophic terrorist attack on U.S. soil to get the federal government to embrace real change." But the attack has occurred—and the United States, rather than meeting the new threat, "has fallen back asleep" (Flynn, 2005, pp. 1, 178).

The failure to prepare adequately has, in Flynn's view, two broad elements. The first is the unwillingness to fund homeland security initiatives adequately. The $49.9 billion that the Bush administration requested for homeland security purposes in FY 2006 is inadequate for the job, Flynn concludes; and yet he notes stiff resistance from influential Republican members of Congress to more generous funding (Flynn, 2005, pp. 171-172).

Flynn cites several areas in which funding shortfalls have compromised security. The Coast Guard, he says, still relies on a pre-9/11 plan for fleet modernization that will not be completed for another quarter-century. (The House version of the FY2006 Homeland Security spending bill proposes a half-billion dollar cut to the modernization program.) The Department of Homeland Security's Bureau of Customs and Border Protection has been denied the funding needed to properly administer its initiative to improve shipping container security. The public health system, including federal agencies such as the Centers for Disease Control and Prevention, lacks the ability to manage the consequences of a bioterror attack. Federal agencies responsible for overseeing the security of radioactive materials used by the private and nonprofit sectors have actually experienced budget cuts since 2001. There is inadequate funding for the training of first responders; not enough money for better information technology for the law enforcement community; and a shortfall in resources for U.S. attorneys charged with prosecuting terrorism cases (Flynn, 2005, pp. 42, 44, 108, and 122-129).

Congress' recent debate over the formula for allocation of funds in grant programs established by the PATRIOT Act provides further depressing evidence of its inattention to security needs. The initial formula guaranteed an equal base amount for each state, with a top-up based on population; in other words, assessment of actual risk played no role in allocating funds. This addressed equity concerns but did little for security. An effort to overhaul the formula in the FY2006 Homeland Security spending bill before the summer recess failed.

The federal government's failure on homeland security is not rooted exclusively in its unwillingness to invest in security measures. As Flynn again notes, it has declined to exercise its regulatory authority as well. Its approach to the protection of "critical infrastructure" in private hands— gas, electricity and water systems, telecommunications and computer systems—relies heavily on the voluntary efforts of the owners of that infrastructure. The government has taken extraordinary measures to allay industry fears about sharing information on vulnerabilities with federal officials. (These included the "critical infrastructure information" provisions of the Homeland Security Act of 2002, as well as separate measures on "critical energy infrastructure information" adopted by the Federal Energy Regulatory Commission.) Nonetheless, these voluntary efforts have been compromised by the unwillingness of businesses to participate in critical infrastructure protection efforts or share information about security risks (General Accounting Office, 2004). Relying on "industry self-policing," says Flynn, is "simply inadequate in the post-9/11 security world" (Flynn, 2005, pp. 54, 130). The reluctance to exercise federal authority is evident elsewhere: in the unwillingness to impose security standards for chemical plants and research labs that handle dangerous pathogens, and to establish minimum standards on capabilities for emergency responders (Flynn, 2005, 119, 123 and 129).

The federal government has undertaken two large efforts at bureaucratic reorganization since the 9/11 attacks. Following the passage of the Homeland Security Act of 2002, many agencies with homeland security responsibilities were combined to form the new Department of Homeland Security. And after the 2004 report of the 9/11 Commission, Congress created a new post of Director of National Intelligence and took other steps to encourage cooperation between components of the intelligence community through the Intelligence Reform and Terrorism Prevention Act of 2004. The need for reorganization in the homeland security and intelligence fields has been generally recognized. On the other hand, reorganization alone cannot compensate for the failure to commit funds or exercise regulatory authority. To think that it can is to repeat the error of Clinton-era reformers: that management reform, if done cleverly, can overcome the damage to administrative capabilities that follows from expenditure constraints and the refusal to regulate.

The Global War on Terrorism

The federal government's hesitancy on homeland security is sharply contrasted by the vigor with which it has pursued military action overseas. The Bush administration has waged campaigns in Afghanistan and Iraq, and deployed forces elsewhere in central and south Asia (including new force deployments in Kyrgyzstan, Tajikistan, and Uzbekistan) as part of a campaign that it calls the Global War on Terrorism, or GWOT ("News release," 2003).

GWOT has been expensive, in both human and financial terms. By August 2005, over 2,000 soldiers had died in the Afghan and Iraqi campaigns, while over 7,000 had been wounded in action and not returned to duty ("U.S. Casualty Status," 2005). Between FY2001 and FY2005, the defense budget has increased by 42% in real terms. It now exceeds the defense budget in the last year of the Cold War, 1989, again in real terms. Congress' willingness to tolerate this substantial build-up in defense spending has particularly galled advocates for tighter homeland security. The *increase alone* in defense spending in nominal terms between FY2001 and FY2005, $160 billion, is more than triple the entire homeland security budget requested by President Bush for FY2006.

There are by now many questions about the extent to which these military operations can reasonably be described as an *antiterror* campaign. The connection between military action in Afghanistan and domestic terror attacks seemed unambiguous; but this was not true of the larger military effort in Iraq. Critics have observed that the United States has a critical strategic interest in securing oil supplies in the Middle East and had been reorienting its military forces to that region for this reason for at least 2 decades before 9/11 (Bacevich, 2005, pp. 193–201). Administration claims regarding a connection between the Iraqi regime and the 9/11 attackers, or more generally to the global network of Islamist radicals, or about Iraq's capacity to employ weapons of mass destruction, have now been discredited (Cirincione, Mathews, & Perkovich, 2004; Commission on Intelligence Capabilities of the United States Regarding Weapons of Mass Destruction, 2005; Prados, 2004; Senate Intelligence Committee, 2004). There is also evidence that the Administration contorted available intelligence on these points in order to make a case for war against Iraq. After meeting with CIA chief George Tenet and others in Washington in July 2002, the head of British intelligence reported to Prime Minister Blair that "intelligence and facts were being fixed around the policy" of removing Saddam through military action (Danner & Kinsley, 2005).

On the other hand, there is an important distinction between distortion of evidence and outright fraud. The 9/11 Commission found that senior policymakers were motivated by a real, if misguided, apprehension about the threat posed by Iraq (National Commission On Terrorist Attacks Upon the United States, 2004, pp. 334–338). The assertion that the invasion of Iraq is part of "Global War on Terrorism" continues today. The United States is "fighting the terrorists in Afghanistan and Iraq," President Bush said in July 2005, "so we do not have to face them here at home" (Executive Office of the President, 2005).

CONSTRAINTS ON POLICY RESPONSE

The United States' distinctive response to the 9/11 shock may be explained by four considerations:

Institutionalization of the "Civil Liberties" Field

The first constraint on policy response is the institutionalization of the "civil liberties" policy field. This has at least four components: first, the growth in number and capacity of nongovernmental organizations with the ability to protest possible violations of citizen rights; second, the growth in the number of formal rules intended to deter violations of civil liberties; third, the increased predisposition of key actors, such as the judiciary, to acknowledge rights violations; and finally, a broader public sensitivity to rights violations, which is also connected to decreased trust in state authority.

The institutionalization of the civil liberties field is described by Alan Brinkley, who observes that the preoccupation with this subject is a distinctive feature of twentieth century American politics. Brinkley suggests that the current "civil liberties regime" is the product of a reaction against the abuses of power that marked the major security crises of that century. The American Civil Liberties Union, for example, was established following the Palmer Raids of 1919; the Supreme Court as well became more attentive to civil liberties. (Although slowly: it affirmed convictions under the Sedition Act during the first Red Scare and also the detention of Japanese Americans during the Second World War.) Following the second Red Scare, says Brinkley (2003), there was

> an aggressive effort to create bulwarks against a repetition of the harrowing events of the 1950s ... [which] contributed to the dramatic growth in the protection of political, cultural and religious dissent in the 1960s and the expansion of protections available to those accused of crimes. (p. 43)

Other factors—such as the increased wealth and education of U.S. voters, and changes in media structure—have likely contributed to heightened consciousness of civil liberties as well. Whatever the cause, there has undoubtedly been a "rights revolution" in the latter part of the twentieth century (Friedman, 2002, pp. 598–607); accompanied by an increased capacity on the part of citizens to act upon their tetchiness about rights violations. This may have been evidenced in the aftermath of the July 2005 London bombings, when the New York Police Department—seeking to avoid ACLU complaints about racial profiling—initiated the practice of randomly searching subway passengers. The ACLU promptly sued, alleging that random searches violated the Fourth Amendment (American Civil Liberties Union, 2005).

Populism

A second constraint arises from the populist tendency in U.S. politics. Populism, says Bernard Crick, is "a style of politics and rhetoric that seeks to arouse a majority ... who are, have been, or think themselves to be outside the polity, scorned and despised by an educated establishment" (Crick, 2002, p. 77). In the United States it is evidenced in political culture and in an array of institutional rules that check the authority of policymakers in the executive and legislative branches.

The populist tendency is evident in the close regard that is paid to the protection of civil liberties. But there is also an antistatist tendency that looks with skepticism on federal power even when it does not clearly trench on civil liberties. There has been a corrosion of trust in government in many of the advanced democracies over the past 3 decades. But the United States is likely a distinctive case—both because initial levels of trust were lower and the subsequent downtrend was, as Pharr and Putnam note, "longest and clearest" (Pharr, Putnam, & Dalton, 2000, p. 9). Trust in the federal government increased for a brief period immediately following the 9/11 attacks, but then reverted to more familiar levels (Deane, 2002). The predisposition against expansion of federal power is still deeply entrenched (See Tables 10.1 and 10.2).

Populist systems of government are also prone to policy myopia: the inability to attend properly to the long-term implications of collective decisions. This is evidenced in the inability (or unwillingness) of American policymakers to take actions that would control the long-term cost of

Table 10.1.   Do You Think The Federal Government Today Has Too Much Power, Has About The Right Amount Of Power, Or Has Too Little Power?

Date	Too Much	About Right	Too Little	No Opinion
Do you think the federal government today has too much power, has about the right amount of power, or has too little power?				
Sep-04	42	49	7	1
Oct-03	43	49	7	1
Sep-02	39	52	7	2
Aug-95	58	32	8	3
Jun-87	46	37	8	10

Source: Gallup Polls.

Table 10.2.   Satisfaction With the Size and Power of the Federal Government

Date	VS	SS	SD	VD	DK/NA
Please say whether you are—Very satisfied, Somewhat satisfied, Somewhat dissatisfied, or Very dissatisfied [about] the size and power of the federal government?					
Jan-04	11	38	31	20	1
Jan-03	10	41	29	18	2
Jan-02	13	48	26	13	1

Source: Gallup Polls.

federal programs such as Social Security, Medicare, and Medicaid, which will rise substantially as the American population ages. Other anglophone democracies have handled this issue more decisively, taking steps to curb long-term obligations (Roberts, 2003); in the United States, the reform debate has centered on proposals (such as prescription drug coverage under Medicare Part D or private retirement accounts) that actually exacerbate long-term costs. (After 2006, outlays for Medicare Part D will substantially exceed total homeland security spending, according to Congressional Budget Office projections (Congressional Budget Office, 2005).)

At the same time, the American public has resisted tax increases (or reversals of earlier tax cuts) to pay for increased spending. In a 2003 Pew poll, for example, 59% of respondents preferred to fund increased military and homeland security spending through borrowing or cuts to other programs ("War viewed," 2003). As a result, the long-term fiscal position of the federal government is not favorable. In May 2005, the United States was faulted by the International Monetary Fund (IMF) for its failure to take the task of fiscal consolidation more seriously (International Monetary Fund, 2005). Entitlement spending and tax resistance create a powerful pair of fiscal pincers that make it difficult to fund homeland security initiatives properly. Indeed, the IMF has noted that the Bush administration's plan for fiscal consolidation hinges on the assumption that tight controls on discretionary spending will be maintained for at least the next 5 years. (Flynn, incidentally, favors an approach to funding homeland security deployed in other areas caught in these fiscal pincers (Roberts, 2002): an independent and self-financed "Federal Security Reserve System," modeled on the existing Federal Reserve System, the independent body that regulates monetary policy.

Susceptibility to Corporate Influence

The preceding two points suggest an inability on the part of the federal government to impose costs (comprising both pecuniary costs or rights infringements) on the American public, even in a moment of crisis and in the name of collective security. Combined with this is a comparable inability to impose costs on corporate actors, likely as a consequence of the distinctive susceptibility of the American system to corporate influence. (Or, as Beetham and others would put it, the relative lack of autonomy of the American state from the corporate sector (Beetham, 2005, pp. 45-51).) This is the result of several institutional features: the fragmentation of political authority, and therefore the increased number of access points for influence; the relative weakness of controls on political funding; and the lack of a government-wide career civil service at the highest level of the executive branch.

Whatever the cause, the effect has been to make it very difficult to impose burdens on the private sector in the name of security. Shortly before the 9/11 attacks, opposition from the airline industry blocked efforts to improve passenger-screening practices at U.S. airports (General Accounting Office, 2000). The controversy over the extraordinary measures taken to protect "critical infrastructure information" that is provided to federal agencies (Roberts, 2004) arises largely because the federal government has been unwilling to *mandate* the provision of such information, and must therefore offer strong assurances to prod voluntary action. In specific sectors, there is equal reluctance to deal firmly with private owners of infrastructure. The Nuclear Regulatory Commission, for example, has been criticized for its unwillingness to require the tightening of security requirements at nuclear plants; the GAO recently suggested that the NRC's efforts have been compromised by its close relationships with plant owners (Davidson, 2004).

The federal government is also said to have "bowed to pressure from the chemical industry" against legislation that would mandate plant security standards (OMBWatch, 2005). The *New York Times* editorialized in May 2005:

> Chalmette Refining, a joint venture of Exxon Mobil, is one of more than 15,000 potentially deadly chemical plants and refineries nationwide. More than 100 of them put a million or more people at risk. These time bombs are everywhere.... The worst possible outcomes [from a terrorist attack] are chilling. A successful terrorist attack on a chlorine tank could produce, according to a Department of Homeland Security report, 17,500 deaths, 10,000 severe injuries and 100,000 hospitalization.... Nuclear power plants are required by federal law to have physical barriers and trained security forces, and to hold simulated terrorist attack exercises. Chemical plants should be subject to the same sort of requirements. But common-sense safety measures are being blocked by special interest politics. Chemical companies do not want to pay for reasonable security, and the industry, a major contributor to presidential and Congressional campaigns, has succeeded in preventing Congress from acting. ("Inside the Kill Zone," 2005)

Industry lobbying is also said to have blocked initiatives for tighter security for shipping of hazardous material by rail and truck. The World Shipping Council, one of several lobby groups that have pushed for a voluntary approach to container security, has spent $1.2 million lobbying federal officials in the 2 years following 9/11 (Public Citizen, 2004, pp. 13, 63–73). The Air Transport Association has resisted proposals for enhanced security, such as improved baggage screening systems, that would "saddl[e] U.S. airlines and their customers with unfunded security mandates" (Milligan, 2004).

Militarism

Another tendency, again consisting of cultural predispositions and institutional arrangements that express and reinforce those predispositions, is militarism. By this I mean (following the definition proposed by Bacevich) a popular attachment to military ideals and deference to military institutions; a tendency to define the nation's well-being in terms of its military preparedness; and a tendency to prefer military action as a tool for addressing policy problems (Bacevich, 2005, p. 2).

To say that the American polity is militaristic may seem offensive. For much of its history the United States might reasonably have been described as antimilitarist: slow to enter the Great War, for example, and quick to disband its forces afterward; poorly armed on the eve of the Second World War (Ambrose & Brinkley, 1997, pp. ix, 2), and again quick to demobilize afterward. Even after the advent of the Cold War, the United States was often described as a "reluctant" superpower (Bacevich, 2002, pp. 7-31). Still, the country has now sustained a high level of military preparedness for many years. For more than a half-century it has maintained a standing force of (on average) 2.3 million active duty military personnel. In 2000, the nation had 28 million veterans; this meant that at least one out of every eight adult Americans was on active duty or a veteran of military service.

Although the capabilities and reputation of the military flagged after Vietnam, these effects proved to be transient. By the end of the millennium, the U.S. military had impressive and unrivalled capabilities. Furthermore, it had largely escaped the crises of legitimacy that had beset other parts of government. The military had much higher confidence ratings than the executive, legislative, or judicial branches; indeed, trust in the military *increased* over the last quarter-century, so that, by 2001, roughly two-thirds of Americans professed to put a "great deal" or "quite a lot" of trust in the military (Gronke & Feaver, 2001; King & Karabell, 2003, pp. 4-5) (A 1995 Gallup survey found that only 18% of Americans thought the military had "too much power," contrasted with 58% who thought this of "the Federal government in Washington.") The image of the military as a technologically sophisticated and powerful force, and as an "enclave of virtue" (the phrase is Bacevich's) was reinforced in movies and other popular media, often produced with the aid of the military itself (King & Karabell, 2003, pp. 70-79). Not only was the defense sector advantaged in terms of capability and legitimacy: it was also true that the executive enjoyed greater freedom of movement in this area than in other policy fields. Policymakers were able to operate with greater secrecy, and courts and legislators were less likely to second-guess policy decisions. The defense sector, in other words, was the field in which the Lillliputians' grip was least firm.

In the post-Vietnam era, the military's leadership had attempted to craft a policy of restraint in the use of military capacities—a policy expressed in the Weinberger Doctrine and later the Powell Doctrine. But this position proved untenable: faced with pressing problems, and the relative weakness of other components of the federal administrative apparatus, heavy reliance on the military became inevitable. "What's the point of having this superb military that you're always talking about if we can't use it?" Secretary of State Madeleine Albright asked Colin Powell, Chairman of the Joint Chiefs of Staff, in 1993.

Throughout the Clinton years, the military engaged in a series of interventions at odds with the Weinberger and Powell Doctrines (Murphey, 2000). It also assumed "a slew of odd jobs" that might have been undertaken by civilian agencies: international diplomacy, antidrug trafficking, disaster relief, antiterrorism, disarmament, and public health (Priest, 2003, p. 45). The Bush administration, says Stephen Flynn, adopted the "escapist" view after 9/11 that "the terrorist threat can be contained by taking the battle to the enemy, in overseas efforts to isolate and topple rogue states" (Flynn, 2005, pp. 11, 38). Its decision to take this path may not be wholly sui generis: the practice of militarizing policy problems was, by 2001, a familiar one.

A NEW NORMAL, OR THE OLD?

September 11 "changed everything," White House Press Secretary Scott McClellan told reporters shortly before the 2004 election (Executive Office of the President, 2004a). But this is not the case, when considered either from the point of view of policy processes or policy outcomes. The harm to fundamental rights was concentrated mainly on foreign nationals, while U.S. citizens were protected by a robust set of rules on civil rights. The set of agencies now located within the field of "homeland security" continued to suffer from constraints that were familiar in the Clinton era. The militarization of antiterrorism policy was a similarly familiar phenomenon.

The American response to the policy shock of 9/11 was driven heavily by institutional and cultural constraints peculiar to the American polity. The relevance of the ideological predispositions of key decision makers, while often emphasized in popular literature as well as scholarly work

(Cortell & Peterson, 1999, p. 189), can be overstressed. A Democratic president would have faced a comparable demand for action and comparable constraints on his response, which likely would have caused that response to share the same substantive features.

Nevertheless, the "Vulcans" *were* in power, and the fact that a set of policymakers committed to radical change largely failed to effect such change ought to tell us something. But what? One view might be that the reaction to 9/11 gives us assurance about the robustness of the American way of governance—about its capacity, for example, to deter substantial violations of civil liberties at home, or constrain tendencies to bureaucratic growth.

But this assumes that the status quo is largely benign. And it may well be that it is not. Improved security may actually require that law information agencies have greater power to collect information, and better capabilities in sharing and interpreting data. Improved security may also require better funding of agencies with homeland security functions and more active regulation of private actors. A consequence of the militarization of antiterrorism policy may be to aggravate, rather than moderate, the terrorist threat. And if all this is true, then the conclusion is more depressing: The rigidities of the American system make it less capable of defending against further terror attacks.

REFERENCES

Ambrose, S. E., & Brinkley, D. (1997). *Rise to globalism: American foreign policy since 1938.* New York: Penguin Books.

American Civil Liberties Union. (2005). NYCLU sues New York City over subway bag search policy. *American Civil Liberties Union.*
Retrieved August 9, 2005, from http://www.aclu.org//police/searchseizure/20054prs20050804.html. Accessed.

Bacevich, A. (2002). *American empire.* Cambridge, MA: Harvard University Press.

Bacevich, A. (2005). *The new American militarism.* New York: Oxford University Press.

Beetham, D. (2005). *Democracy: A beginner's guide.* Oxford: OneWorld.

Bellah, R. (2005). McCarthyism at Harvard. *New York Review of Books, 52*(2), 42-43.

Bernstein, N. (2004, October 11). Post-9/11, Even evading subway fares can raise the prospect of deportation. *New York Times,* p. B2.

Brinkley, A. (2003). A familiar story: Lessons from past assaults on freedoms. In R. C. Leone (Ed.), *The war on our freedoms* (pp. 23-46). New York: Public Affairs.

Cirincione, J., Mathews, J., & Perkovich, G. (2004). *WMD in Iraq: Evidence and implications.* Washington, DC: Carnegie Endowment for International Peace.

Cole, D. (2003). *Enemy aliens: Double standards and constitutional freedoms in the war on terrorism.* New York: The New Press.

Commission on Intelligence Capabilities of the United States Regarding Weapons of Mass Destruction. (2005). *Report to the president.* Washington, DC. Author.

Congressional Budget Office. (2005). Updated estimates of spending for the medicare prescription drug program. *Congressional Budget Office.* Retrieved August 8, 2005, from http://www.cbo.gov/ showdoc.cfm?index=6139&sequence=0

Cortell, A. & Peterson, S. (1999). Altered states: Explaining domestic institutional change. *British Journal of Political Science, 29*(1), 177-203.

Crick, B. R. (2002). Democracy: A very short introduction. New York: Oxford University Press.

Danner, M., & Kinsley, M. (2005, August 11). The memo, the press, and the war: An exchange. *New York Review of Books, 53*(13), 60–63.

Davidson, K. (2004, September 15). Security faulted at nuclear reactors. *San Francisco Chronicle,* p. A10.

Deane, C. (2002, May 31). Trust in government declines. *Washington Post,* p. A29.

Executive office of the president. (2004a, October 1). *Press gaggle with Scott McClellan.* Retrieved July 15, 2005, from http://www.whitehouse.gov/news/releases/ 2004/10/20041001-8.html.

Executive office of the president. (2004b, November 4). *Presidential press conference.t.* Retrieved August 3, 2005, from http://www.whitehouse.gov/news/ releases/2004/11/20041104-5.html

Executive office of the president. (2005). *President discusses war on terror at FBI academy.* Retrieved August 9, 2005, from http://www.whitehouse.gov/news/releases/ 2005/07/20050711-1.html

Fisher, L. (2003). Deciding on war against Iraq: Institutional failures. *Political Science Quarterly, 118*(3), 389–410.

Flynn, S. (2005). *America the vulnerable.* New York: Harper Perennial.

Friedman, L. M. (2002). *American law in the 20th century.* New Haven, CT: Yale University Press.

General Accounting Office (2000). *Aviation security: Long-standing problems impair airport screeners' performance* (GAO/RCED-00-75). Washington, DC: Author.

General Accounting Office. (2004). *Critical infrastructure protection: Establishing effective information sharing with infrastructure sectors* (GAO-04-699T). Washington, DC: Author.

Greenberg, K. J., & Dratel, J. L. (2005). *The torture papers: The road to Abu Ghraib.* New York: Cambridge University Press.

Gronke, P., & Feaver, P. (2001). *The foundations of institutional trust: Reexamining public confidence in the U.S. military from a civil-military perspective. Soldier and civilians: The gap between the military and american society and what it means for national security.* Cambridge, MA: MIT Press.

Inside the kill zone (2005, May 22). *New York Times,* p. 11.

International Monetary Fund. (2005). *2005 Article IV consultation with the United States of America: Concluding statement of the IMF Mission.* Retrieved June 30, 2005, from http://www.imf.org/external/np/ms/2005/052505a.htm

Joelson, M. R. (1963). The dismissal of civil servants in the interests of national security. *Public Law,* 51–75.

Johnson, D. K. (2004). *The lavender scare.* Chicago: University of Chicago Press.

Kellner, D. (2005). *Media spectacle and the crisis of democracy.* Boulder, CO: Paradigm.

King, D. C., & Karabell, Z. (2003). *The generation of trust: Public confidence in the U.S. military since Vietnam.* Washington, DC: AEI Press.

Kingdon, J. W. (2003). *Agendas, alternatives, and public policies.* New York: Longman.

Lawyers Committee for Human Rights (2003). *Assessing the new normal: Liberty and security for the post-September 11 United States.* New York: Authors.

Mann, J. (2004). *Rise of the Vulcans.* New York: Viking.

McCoy, A. W. (2006). *A question of torture: CIA interrogation, from the Cold War to the War on Terror.* New York: Metropolitan Books/Henry Holt.

Milligan, M. (2004, August 3). Travel industry contemplates 9/11 report findings. *Travel Weekly.* Retrieved July 15, 2005, from http://www.travelweekly.com/articles.aspx?articleid=42541

Murphey, D. (2000). The post-Cold War American interventions into Haiti, Somalia, Bosnia and Kosovo. *Journal of Social, Political and Economic Studies 25*(4), 489–510.

National Commission On Terrorist Attacks Upon the United States. (2004). *Final Report.* New York: W.W. Norton.

News release: President authorizes two medals. (2003, March 15). *Department of Defense.* Retrieved August 9, 2005, from http://www.defenselink.mil/releases/2003/b03152003_bt121-03.html

Office of Management and Budget. (2002). *Budget of the U.S. government, fiscal year 2003.* Washington, DC: Author.

OMBWatch. (2005, June 1). Journalists find chemical plants insecure. *The OMB-Watcher, 6*(11). Retrieved July 15, 2005, from http://www.ombwatch.org/article/articleview/2855/1/344?TopicID=2

Patriot misfire. (2005, July 2). *Washington Post,* p. A28.

Pharr, S, Putnam, R., Dalton, R. (2000). A quarter-century of declining confidence. *Journal of Democracy, 11*(2), 5–25.

Prados, J. (2004). *Hoodwinked.* New York: The New Press.

Priest, D. (2003). *The mission: Waging war and keeping peace with america's military.* New York: W.W. Norton.

Public Citizen. (2004). *Homeland unsecured.* Washington, DC: Author.

Roberts, A. (2002). Lockbox government: Segmented funding strategies and the erosion of governmental flexibility. *Governance, 15*(2), 105–134.

Roberts, A. (2003). In the eye of the storm? Societal aging and the future of public service reform. *Public Administration Review, 63*(6), 720–733.

Roberts, A. (2004). ORCON Creep: Networked governance, Information sharing, and the threat to government accountability. *Government Information Quarterly, 21*(3), 249–267.

Roberts, A. (2006). *Blacked out: Government secrecy in the information age.* New York: Cambridge University Press.

Rosen, J. (2004). *The naked crowd: Reclaiming security and freedom in an anxious age.* New York: Random House.

Schulhofer, S. J. (2002). *The enemy within: Intelligence gathering, law enforcement, and civil liberties in the wake of September 11.* New York: Century Foundation Press.

Select Senate Committee to Study Government Operations. (1976). *Final report with respect to intelligence activities.* Washington, DC: U.S. Senate.

Senate Intelligence Committee. (2004). *Report on the U.S. intelligence community's prewar intelligence assessments on Iraq.* Washington, DC: Author.

Smith, P. (2001, September 29). Looking over Powell's shoulder with unease. *Irish Times,* p. 12.

U.S. casualty status. (2005). *Department of Defense.* Retrieved August 8, 2005, from http://www.defenselink.mil/news/casualty.pdf

War viewed as top national problem. (2003). *Pew Research Center for the People and the Press.* Retrieved July 17, 2005, from http://people-press.org/reports/display.php3?PageID=677

Woodward, B. (2001, October 21). CIA told to do "whatever necessary" to kill Bin Laden. *Washington Post,* p. A1.

Woodward, B. (2005). *The secret man.* New York: Simon & Schuster.

CHAPTER 11

SUPPORT FOR CRISIS MANAGEMENT IN ASIA–PACIFIC

Lessons From ADB in the Past Decade1

Clay Wescott

The chapter analyzes three crisis events to which the Asian Development Bank (ADB) has been closely involved in responding: the financial contagion in Southeast (SE) Asia in 1997, the SARS crisis of 2003, and the Tsunami of 2004. These rather different types of events demonstrate that a combination of factors has been at work in shaping the response to and outcome of each crisis, including globalization, corresponding technology advances, and structures and business process of national and international organizations. In each of the three events to which ADB has responded, the chapter explores ADB's role as an international organization working with numerous national governments in Asia and elsewhere to address crisis situations. The chapter concludes with lessons learned and future directions for action.

Communicable Crises: Prevention, Response, and Recovery in the Global Arena, pp. 323–351
Copyright © 2007 by Information Age Publishing

INTRODUCTION

Crisis response management is of great interest in the Asia–Pacific region in view of recent natural disasters and the threats posed by potential rapid spread of communicable diseases such as avian flu. The chapter analyzes three crisis events to which the Asian Development Bank (ADB) has been closely involved in responding: the financial contagion in SE Asia in 1997, the SARS crisis of 2003, and the Tsunami of 2004. Theoretical and case study research help to explain how the crises arose, how and why various entities responded to them, and facilitated effective recognition and response patterns to reduce crisis impacts and to facilitate recovery.

Theoretical Framework

Case studies of financial contagion, SARS, and Tsunami will be analyzed by applying insights from several theoretical frameworks. One perspective looks at how best to manage unexpected, high-consequence crisis events requiring urgent responses (Drabek & McEntire, 2003; McEntire, 2001; Ursacki-Bryant, Vertinsky, & Smart, 2005). Some argue that national governments are ill-equipped to deal with globalization[2] induced, regional crises, and their contagion effects. The outcome is an ineffective system of weakly coordinated national and international action to muddle through, with results much less than desired.

Remedies proposed (Australian Government, 2005) to strengthen country responses to crisis management include:

- Advance planning and training in crisis management, and updating protocols in response to emerging threats;
- Political will and authority to lead crisis response;
- Clear understanding of roles of all players;
- Effective coordination through interdepartmental committees and other mechanisms;
- Use of existing rules and chains of command;
- Effective and integrated public relations;
- Strategic use of partnerships with other international, regional and national organizations, including nongovernmental organizations (NGOs) and private sector.

Carrying out such an agenda may be difficult for governments and international organizations using traditional institutional arrangements, with their attendant hierarchical, compliance-oriented bureaucracies.

Institutional changes may be needed to develop abilities to effectively draw on technology and knowledge to carry out a range of tasks, and allowing for collaboration between government and communities for timely information sharing, rapid deployment, and follow-up. Missing knowledge or weak knowledge coordination sharply reduces the chance of success. Knowledge-based organizations need to draw on highly trained specialists who manage their performance through disciplined feedback from colleagues, customers, and other stakeholders (Drucker, 1998; Gingrich & Egge, 2005; Root, 2006; and Jones, 2006).

Such knowledge management practices are evident in the private sector. Firms boost productivity by linking across borders to integrate design and production networks that develop and share ideas, raise venture capital, design and test prototypes, assemble finished goods, and move them through regional and global distribution chains to consumers (Saxenian, 2006). Similarly, some countries are taking knowledge-based, systemic approaches in addressing environmental challenges such as protecting natural habitats, fisheries, biodiversity, soils, energy, photosynthetic capacity, and freshwater, while minimizing pollution, global warming, and population impact on scarce resources. Systemic approaches require well-coordinated, knowledge-based organizations and techniques (Diamond, 2005, pp. 486–525). Effective knowledge and coordination practices are equally essential to effective management of regional and international crises.

A related body of theory looks at how to best motivate high performance among public officials. Bertelli (2006) provides evidence that public officials respond to both intrinsic motivation and tangible incentives. The former includes the pleasure derived from performing tasks well and the feeling of accomplishment of achieving public-spirited objectives, while the latter includes financial incentives such as pay-for-performance and avoiding negative sanctions. There are cases where the latter crowds out the former, with the effect of reducing performance (see also Behn, 2004; Klitgaard & Light, 2005, pp. 23, 29, 309ff; O'Donnell, 2000). On the other hand, officials in compliance-driven bureaucracies may respond well to the intrinsic motivation of working in novel organizational settings to help people in crisis situations, and these officials may thereby work at a much higher than normal performance level.

Another approach to understanding the three cases focuses on promoting regional public goods (RPGs) and preventing regional public bads or costs. RPGs are public goods where the challenges can best be addressed by two or more countries working together, where the benefits to one country do not take away from the benefits to others, and where no country in the regional group can be prevented from benefiting. Because of the "free rider" problem, RPGs are difficult to fund, as explained further in the next section. ADB support in promoting RPGs requires deliberate, effective cooperation between or among countries. Examples include trade, maritime safety, prevention of infectious diseases, air pollution and financial contagion, and combating terrorism, money laundering, trafficking, and other crimes. Some of these can also be considered global public goods when cooperation is needed among countries in different regions. In the case of trade, for example, when considered by WTO it is a global public good, but when considered by Association of Southeast Asian Nations (ASEAN) Free Trade Area (AFTA) it is an RPG. The difference has to do with the number of countries involved in a trade agreement and their location. In some cases, it is easier to reach agreement at the global level because of the multidimensional tradeoffs possible. In other cases, regional agreements are more feasible due to the smaller number of countries, and historical and cultural similarities among them.[3] Regional agreements can then be a bridge to subsequent global agreements.[4]

Theories of contagion address that category of regional public bads that cross borders due to migration, trade links, information flows, and natural causes. Institutional theory is important in highlighting why each jurisdiction is organized rather differently to crisis, promoting public goods (and preventing public bads), and combating contagion.

Finally, separate bodies of theory address the specific issues that come up in each case study. The financial crisis was largely a banking crisis in each of the affected countries, and can be partially understood through theories explaining financial bubbles (Allen & Gale, 2000; Wilson & Zurbruegg, 2004). The SARS crisis was a medical and health event, and can be understood in part through theories of incubation, adaptation, transmission, surveillance and control of infectious disease, and also using research findings on political incentives for problem avoidance and networks.

This chapter draws from this wide range of theory in understanding the financial contagion in SE Asia in 1997, the SARS crisis of 2003, and the Tsunami of 2004, with respect to how national governments responded, and how ADB provided various types of assistance in each of the three cases.

Role of International Organizations Such as ADB

A network of intergovernmental organizations has emerged to help national governments address some of the consequences of globalization, including regulating cross-border movements of people and goods, promoting international standards (e.g., intellectual property protection, fiscal and monetary transparency, surveillance of infectious disease), addressing challenges of unequal economic development, and providing support in coordinated responses to a variety of crises. ADB is a multilateral development finance institution that engages in mostly public sector lending for development purposes in its developing member countries. ADB's clients are its member governments, who are also its shareholders. It works with partner international organizations such as the World Bank and United Nations, and also increasingly with international NGOs, including diaspora organizations (Wescott & Brinkerhoff, 2006; ADB, in press), and international media. In both its internal and external operations, ADB functions as a hierarchical, compliance-driven organization.

ADB provides financial and technical support to national governments to support both national and regional programs. Yet, for many reasons, the latter of these are underfunded. Since there is stronger political support in most countries for country-based health clinics, environmental protection, and so forth, they tend to be given priority for public funding. Global and regional investments to address, for example, cross-border health surveillance and environmental management, have much less political support. There are also coordination problems in designing and implementing regional investments, since common agreements are needed from governments and other stakeholders in two or more countries. In addition, multilateral donors such as ADB lack suitable financing instruments; loans require coordinated allocation of responsibility among countries, which is very difficult, and grant funds are often too small. Bilateral donors have grant funds, but recipients prefer to use them in country-based programs. There are no good methodologies for measuring higher returns of cross-border vis a vis country-based investments. Regional rather than global approaches to address cross-border challenges face additional challenges. Donors normally lack the self interest to finance regional investments since they are outside the region and do not directly benefit; they prefer to finance global public goods from which they directly benefit, and to prevent global public costs to which they stand at risk. There is the additional problem of "pariah" countries reducing the effectiveness of regional schemes, such as Cuba in the Caribbean, Iran in West Asia and Burma in Southeast Asia (Birdsall & Rojas-Suarez, 2004; Sandler, 2004). Thus, increased connectivity across national borders may be increasing the risks of environmental or economic contagions crossing borders, while public investments financed by the ADB and other bodies to address the risks are underfunded.

The underfunding of global and regional public goods is an issue for other intergovernmental organizations such as the World Health Organization (WHO). The WHO has an annual, worldwide budget that is less than the annual budget for a single hospital in New York City. However, this chapter will focus mainly on the challenges faced by the ADB and the role it played in helping national governments respond to three crises: the financial contagion in Southeast Asia in 1997, the SARS crisis of 2003, and the Tsunami of 2004.

THE 1997 EAST ASIAN FINANCIAL CRISIS

The 1997 East Asian financial crisis issued a wake-up call that exposed vulnerabilities across Southeast Asian economies. These included weak supervision and standards of companies and heavy reliance on the banking system based on directed lending tied to personal relationships, a mismatch between bank assets (domestic real estate and corporate operations) and liabilities (short-term foreign debt), excessive debt-equity ratios, unsustainable exchange rate policies, and inadequate supplies of foreign exchange reserves. It forced governments and international organizations to recognize the high level of interdependence among countries in the region, and the need for putting in place intergovernmental risk mitigating mechanisms such as the Chiang Mai Initiative, Association of Southeast Asian Nations (ASEAN) +3 surveillance,[5] and Asia Bond Fund 1 and 2.[6] However, even more important in explaining the rapid recovery from the crisis has been the growing importance of production sharing networks noted above. These private sector networks helped to increasingly link crisis countries' economies with the booming People's Republic of China (PRC), and facilitate their recovery much more rapidly than initially expected.

The 1997 crisis mainly involved Japan and eight emerging market countries: five members of ASEAN (Singapore, Thailand, Malaysia, Indonesia and the Philippines), the Special Administrative Region of Hong Kong, China, the Republic of Korea, and Taipei, China.[7] The specific causes were different in each country but included macroeconomic and exchange rate policies, weak financial systems dominated by banks, and open capital accounts.

The crisis was triggered by events in Thailand. Its fixed exchange rate, pegged to the U.S. dollar for 13 years, was causing competitive problems as the U.S. dollar appreciated against the Japanese Yen, starting in 1996. In combination with increased export competition from neighboring countries and a cyclical downturn in the semiconductor industry, the current account deficit had reached 8% of GDP in 1996. In 1997, many Thai businesses had large, short-term, unhedged foreign debt, about half with Japanese banks that offered very low interest rates. High domestic savings and foreign debt also fueled property market speculation. Under attack by currency speculators, authorities were reluctant to defend the currency by raising interest rates, since this might lead to bank failures. On July 2, 1997, Thailand allowed the Thai Baht to float, and it dropped like a stone (Dobson, 2000).

Contagion effects led investors to reevaluate their positions in neighboring "Asia miracle" countries.[8] Some countries were able to control the damage through an ongoing International Monetary Fund (IMF) program (e.g., the Philippines), huge reserves (e.g., Hong Kong) and curbs on international financial transactions (e.g., Malaysia). Others were not so successful. Indonesia was forced to float its currency, and emergency hedging operations on short-term foreign debt exacerbated the rapid fall of the Rupiah, along with political uncertainty and high liquidity creation by the Central Bank. The South Korean *Won* plummeted due to some high-profile corporate failures and uncertainty over the December 1997 elections. Nonperforming loans grew in both Indonesia and South Korea as interest rates rose (Dobson, 2000). In 1998, after average per capita growth rates of 6% since the early 1980s in East Asia, there was negative growth ranging from 13.2% in Indonesia to 0.5% in the Philippines. There were also severe social costs including increasing unemployment and poverty, and a weakening of funding for public services including education and health. Only two of the affected countries, Singapore and Taipei, China, had positive growth in 1998 (ADB, 2000, p. 242).

Yet, toward the end of 1998, positive signs began to emerge, including a rebound in equity and currency markets. By 1999, all affected countries had positive rates of growth again, led by the Republic of Korea (10.7%) and Malaysia (5.4%) (ADB, 2000, p. 242). Since then, growth rates in excess of 4 percent have been common in Asia—except in Japan where they have been lower and China where the average rate of increase has been around 9% annually.

Many factors explain the containment of the crisis and the return to positive growth. These include rapid policy and regulatory reforms by governments and fast financial support from international donors. How these and other factors played out, whether the recovery from the crisis could have been faster and social costs reduced, and whether future such crises are likely, is a contentious subject (see Birdsall & Haggard, 2000; Collyns & Senhadji, 2002; Fischer, 1998; Rogoff, 2002; Stiglitz, 2002). This chapter focuses on only a small part of this debate: the role of the ADB.

ADB's role in addressing the 1997 East Asian Crisis was summed up by an ADB official at the time as follows, "East Asia reeled. The world paused. The Bank acted." (ADB, 1999). In the months following the fall of the Thai Baht, the ADB mounted an unprecedented effort to provide financial support to three of the worst affected countries. Small teams were urgently assembled to put together financial packages in each.

Although the planning and approval cycle for a project normally takes a minimum of 18 months, ADB, in less than 1 month, approved and made its first disbursement in December 1997, from a $4 billion Financial Sector Program loan (FSPL) to the Republic of Korea, as part of a $58 billion IMF-led assistance package. The FSPL contributed to the initiation of reform measures designed to address four issues: (i) restructuring financial institutions, (ii) recapitalizing financial institutions, (iii) strengthening prudential regulation and supervision, and (iv) capital market liberalization and development. The ADB goal was to establish transparent and arms-length relationships among the government, the banks, and the conglomerates, and thus restore investor confidence in the economy of the Republic of Korea (ADB, 2000, p. 242).

ADB support to Indonesia comprised five largely quickly disbursed loans, totaling $2.8 billion, during 1998–1999. These loans formed a part of the initial crisis assistance package of $18 billion put together by the IMF in November 1997. For example, in June 1998, ADB approved a total of $1.5 billion in aid to Indonesia in the form of the Financial Governance Reforms: Sector Development Program. The overall objective of the program was to improve the governance of financial and public sector resource allocation through (i) adoption of good practices in financial governance, (ii) increased disclosure and transparency of financial information, and (iii) strengthened legal and regulatory frameworks in the financial sector. The goal was to build up credible financial institutions and prudent regulation to help restore investment flows.

A $500 million Social Sector Program loan in Thailand was part of the ADB's $1.2 billion contribution to the $17.2 billion IMF-led rescue package. The loan and the related $2.1 million technical assistance grant took a dual approach to (i) mitigate the short-term social impact of the crisis and (ii) implement structural reforms to increase economic competitiveness in Thailand, and (iii) to bring governance systems in line with the country's 1997 Constitution. To mitigate the social impact of the crisis, creative partnerships were built between the government and civil society to maintain access to health, education, and nutrition. Since the ADB didn't have an office in Thailand, one of the members of the Thai program design team stayed on a 4-year extended mission in Thailand to help ensure sound implementation.

In addition to these country-based financing operations, ADB took a number of steps to support new regional mechanisms intended to prevent future contagions, especially under the Association of Southeast Asian Nations (ASEAN) +3 Finance Ministers' Process established in November 1999. Within this process, cooperation has proceeded in four main areas: economic review and policy dialogue, the Chiang Mai Initiative (CMI), the Asian Bond Market Initiative (ABMI), and the ASEAN+3 Research Group (ADB, 2005, 60–61).

The ASEAN+3 Finance Ministers meet annually and their ministry of finance and central bank deputies meet semiannually for economic review and policy dialogue on major economic policy challenges facing the region and to conduct peer reviews of each other's policies. Under the Chiang Mai Initiative launched during the ADB annual meeting in May 2000, 16 bilateral swap agreements have been signed for a total of $36 billion. A more recent initiative of the ASEAN+3 Finance Ministers is the ABMI of December 2002. The ABMI Focal Group and six ABMI working groups have been established. The ASEAN+3 Research Group is a networking arrangement among some 30 think tanks in the region that conduct research to support the various components of the ASEAN+3 Finance Ministers' Process.

The Regional Economic Monitoring Unit (now Office of Regional Economic Integration—OREI) was established by the ADB (2004) in early 1999 for closer regional economic monitoring in the wake of the 1997 Asian financial crisis. It supports all of these components in various ways. OREI prepares the semiannual Asia Economic Monitor and the Asia Bond Monitor reports. It provides technical assistance to build DMCs regional economic policy making and associated institutional capacities, and supports the activities of various ABMI Working Groups. OREI also conducts research on regional cooperation and integration, and recently has started extending support for ongoing efforts to promote Asian economic integration by helping to build bridges between various Asian regions. OREI develops and maintains the Asia Regional Information Center and the *AsianBondsOnline* Web sites.

To what extent did ADB's country-based and/or regional support help affected countries to mitigate the 1997 financial crisis, and to put in place national and regional mechanisms to help prevent future such crises? It is difficult to prove cause-and-effect relationships linking the interventions of an aid agency to country outcomes because of problems of multiple attribution, lack of baseline data, lack of robust experimental designs, absence of agreed conceptual frameworks and language for reform, and methodological difficulties in comparing reform outcomes with counterfactuals. ADB's financial contributions to reform efforts in three crisis countries were of major scope to ADB, but only small portions of the overall IMF-led assistance packages.

An evaluation of ADB crisis support to Indonesia found that a common purpose was to provide liquidity and budgetary support to the government through quick-disbursing policy loans. This was only partially achieved as delays occurred in compliance with ADB conditions related to release of subsequent funding. The crisis was also seen as an opportunity to initiate difficult and challenging reforms, including a move toward multibuyer, multiseller electricity markets. While government leaders gave full support to this and other proposed reform measures, efforts at building ownership at the level of implementing entities and personnel were not always fruitful. In its eagerness to obtain quick-disbursing funds, the government may have made commitments without fully weighing either the underlying implications or the difficulties of reform implementation in a compressed time frame. Political instability in the country and the increase in the price of crude oil, a significant revenue source for Indonesia, also appear to have dampened the government's enthusiasm to push ahead with major reforms (ADB, 2001).

The flexibility and vigor displayed during the processing of the projects was part of the much larger IMF-led program to restore investor confidence by injecting quick-disbursing funds and supporting the reforms needed to prevent future crises. However, initial success was not sustained by ADB and the government during post-approval phases. Expeditious and pragmatic support for solving routine implementation problems, such as recruitment of consultants, was inadequate. Similarly, ADB support to the government on policy matters and its involvement in policy dialogue between the government and multilateral financial institutions (MFIs) could have been stronger.

This difference between high and lower performance at initial and subsequent stages of the crisis may stem from at least two factors. On the one hand, strong intrinsic motivation comes from the desire to help people in distress, and from the novelty of working in special purpose teams. In the subsequent phase, officials went back to their normal bureaucratic roles, and motivation and performance suffered. A second factor is that achievements at the early stage (e.g., agreement on strategic and borrowing plans) are easier to reach because small groups of decision makers are involved. However, at later stages, many stakeholders need to work together to implement the plans and loans. Outputs are harder to measure, and interagency coordination and accountability more difficult to achieve (Fukuyama, 2004).

To be more effective in responding to future crises, an ADB evaluation of the response to the 1997 financial crisis recommended more flexible application of standard procedures, better internal coordination, and more delegation of authority and responsibility to field staff. Also, it was recommended that ADB consider offering new financial products to catalyze private investment in crisis situations, possibly including an enhanced guarantee mechanism (ADB, 2001).

ADB support to regional efforts to contain future contagion also was part of a much larger effort, one that is particularly difficult to assess since the preventative measures have not yet been tested by a succeeding crisis.

ADB had not supported such measures prior to the crisis partly because of the lack of funding for supporting regional public goods, as explained above. In addition, cooperation in finance and monetary matters was considered too sensitive for regional approaches and not a "traditional type" of regional cooperation compared to trade liberalization. When the crisis initially struck, some badly affected countries acted in an uncoordinated manner, desperately seeking to address the particular issues facing their economies. As countries began to stabilize and then recover in 1999, they began to consider financial and monetary cooperation to prevent such region-wide financial contagions from occurring again. ADB facilitation at that time and since was much appreciated, and was one of many factors contributing to restabilization achievements to date.

To what extent was the 1997 crisis exacerbated by globalization processes, and to what extent do the same risks of future financial crises remain with us today? Without getting into the details of each country situation and response, the floating of the Thai Baht was clearly the catalyst that triggered financial crises in the other nations, and the speed of the effects was no doubt pushed by media coverage, information technology, and the close trading links that had emerged among countries in the region. The global contagion effects of the East Asian crisis (e.g., 1998 financial crises in Russia and Brazil, collapse of U.S. hedge fund–Long Term Capital Management) also were catalyzed through the same processes. Yet in retrospect, the crisis in each affected country stemming from banking and competitiveness challenges was waiting to happen, and similar in many ways to single-country financial crises such as the one that faced Mexico in December 1994. Indeed, a comparison between Mexico and the Republic of Korea shows similar movements of exchange rates, trade balances, manufacturing production and unemployment rates for the period before and after the respective crises (Frankel, 2000, pp. 26–28). Furthermore, while globalization processes helped to catalyze the East Asian crises, the same processes also helped to ensure a rapid and coordinated response among international financial institutions and donors to assist countries in recovery. Similar processes are helping to support regional mechanisms to prevent future crises. On balance, this case seems to show that the possible higher level of risk of contagion due to increased trade and technological development may be offset by mitigating processes—the same technologies enable better aid coordination, standard setting, and sharing best practice.

Although risk mitigating measures have been put in place and are being strengthened, financial risks have not gone away. Corrupt and fraudulent practices in the People's Republic of China's (PRC) SOEs listed in Hong Kong or other external markets could lead to trouble along the lines of Guangdong Enterprises or China Aviation Oil.[9] The membership commitment of the PRC to the World Trade Organization (WTO)—to open up trade in 2006 in its financial sector to international competition—could put pressure on major domestic banks. New and retaliatory tariffs could reduce U.S. and European imports of PRC products. A combination of these and other possible factors could have contagion effects that might cripple global production sharing arrangements and prompt another 1997-style financial crisis in the region, which would severely test newly established risk mitigating measures.

THE 2003 SARS CRISIS

As a second example of crisis management, the severe acute respiratory syndrome (SARS) disease first occurred in the southern People's Republic of China in late November 2002. To date, there is no vaccine and no effective treatment against SARS, which has an overall fatality rate of 6–15 percent and many unexplained features. SARS was recognized as a global threat on March 12 by World Health Organization (WHO). The outbreak spread rapidly, and within a month about 3,000 cases and more than 100 deaths were recorded on all continents. During the peak of the global outbreak, in early May, more than 200 new cases were being reported each day. Although the disease spread fast and globally for a while, the forceful response of national governments, combined with international agency supported travel warnings and other coordinated actions, stopped the spread of the disease by June. Hundreds of people died, notably less than the millions lost in prior global pandemics. The details of the case have been examined by Ursacki-Bryant et al. (2005), Ling (2005), and deLisle (2004).[10] This section will focus on the role of the ADB in working with governments and others in the region to control the disease.

ADB's role in SARS was unforeseen, as ADB's capacity in the health sector is limited. Only a small fraction of loans and grant-funded technical assistance fell into the health category. Going along with this, only a handful of ADB staff had any expertise in the health field, including only two medical doctors, one of whom worked full time supervising the ADB medical clinic serving ADB Manila-based staff.

ADB's role in SARS had four important features: the use of special purpose groups, emphasis on external and media relations, technical partnerships, and support from regional donors. The following section draws on ADB reports and other materials cited (ADB, 2003; "Perspective," 2003, pp. 20–21).

Special Purpose Groups

ADB work started in April, 2003 when some ADB staff agreed during lunch that SARS had become the most significant event in the region and that ADB should take a leading role in fighting SARS. The staff members started lobbying, and within a week the president set up three groups to focus emergency planning and support, all reporting to a special advisor to the president. These small, cross-functional groups turned out to be an effective means of quickly building consensus and preparing documentation.

The first was formation of an emergency management team (EMT), set up under ADB Emergency Management System Procedures. Under these procedures, the EMT reported to the Crisis Management Committee chaired by the vice president of finance and administration, with the ADB's other two vice presidents as members of the committee. The EMT ensured that medical information on the SARS outbreak was distributed to staff. Travel restrictions and advisories were implemented, guidelines on regional meetings were provided, staff returning from mission to affected locations were screened, and procedures for household isolation of staff, if necessary, were put in place. SARS awareness stations were set up at ADB reception areas. They also worked to address the unreasonable fears of staff when a colleague would return from overseas, perhaps transiting the airport in Singapore.

The second group advised ADB management on the potential impact of SARS on ADB's operations. The team comprised representatives from the Strategy and Policy department and regional departments, and examined the potential impact of SARS and the consequent travel restrictions on ADB's ability to undertake operations, and on lending, technical assistance, and portfolio management activities. For example, what would happen if SARS in PRC were not contained before the end of 2003, so that headquarters missions could not visit China to complete loan design and negotiations? PRC staff were allowed to continue to live and work there, but not to visit Manila. Or, what would happen if the Philippines became an infected country, and for this reason ADB staff were not allowed to enter other countries in the region to carry out essential work? Could business that is normally carried out face-to-face be done effectively using telephone or video conferencing?

A third group, the SARS Crisis Response Team, comprised representatives from operations and knowledge departments with specialized expertise.[11] It met full time from April 25 to May 2, 2003, and developed a comprehensive proposal (ADB, 2003a). Although emergency responses of this type are not normally financed by ADB,[12] on May 7, 2003, the president approved an action plan to meet the immediate needs of developing member countries (DMCs) affected or potentially affected by SARS (ADB, 2003a). The proposal included rapid assessments, placing SARS features on the ADB's Web site, two emergency technical assistance (TA) projects (ADB, 2003b, 2003c) that enabled ADB to assist its DMCs, and a memorandum of understanding (MOU) with WHO.

The first step in implementing ADB's SARS action plan was to prepare a rapid assessment of the likely direct and indirect impacts of SARS, based on the most recent data. The 2003 Asia Development Outlook (ADB, 2003d), released on May 5, had initial estimates for the region as a whole. These estimates were expanded and refined in two economic reports focusing on SARS (ADB, 2003e; Fan, 2003). The Economics and Research Department report estimated that if SARS were contained by the end of the second quarter, the cost to East and Southeast Asia in reduced growth would be around $28 billion. Although this estimate was much less than those of many other economic forecasters at the time, it turned out to be correct.

The SARS action plan also provided for borrowing countries to reallocate loan funds for SARS work. The first country to do so was Viet Nam, agreeing on June 2 to reallocate $6.17 million from a health sector loan to help strengthen the country's fight against SARS. These funds were reallocated from a $70 million primary and preventative health care project (ADB, 2000). However, these funds were not disbursed because of competing administrative priorities and cumbersome official procedures. Similar reallocations were considered in several other DMCs, but in the end were not done because the disease came under control by the end of June.

By 10 June 10, ADB had fully allocated its regional emergency grant support to fight the outbreak. In response to proposals received to enhance surveillance and infection control, ADB allocated funds to support programs in 14 countries: Afghanistan, Bangladesh, Cambodia, Fiji Islands, Indonesia, Kyrgyz Republic, Lao PDR, Mongolia, Nepal, Pakistan, Philippines, Sri Lanka, Tajikistan, and Viet Nam. In addition, ADB agreed to support a regional proposal for Pacific Island countries from the Secretariat of the Pacific Community.

Under a separate technical assistance project, ADB responded to a request from the PRC for containing and coping with the spread of SARS in its western region. The western region was vulnerable to SARS' spread for many reasons, including economic migration and cross-border traffic with the Mekong and Central Asian regions. The western region area faces a substantial risk due to weaknesses in local health systems' capacities for surveillance, information dissemination, prevention, and treatment, as well as broader constraints on financial resources and higher levels of poverty.

ADB supported four PRC provinces: Ningxia, Qinghai, Xinjiang, and Yunnan. A rapid assessment in Xinjiang and Yunnan in July 2003 preceded an informal roundtable bringing together ADB, WHO, World Bank, UNDP, UNICEF, JBIC, Medecins Sans Frontieres). The recommended approach called for a seminar series on provincial planning for SARS and other infectious diseases, combined with pilot testing new approaches for capacity building for local hospitals and county-level centers for disease control (CDCs). A Beijing seminar on SARS and Other Infectious Disease Prevention and Control in November 2003 brought together representatives from the four ADB target provinces and the eight World Bank-supported provinces, including Guangxi, Inner Mongolia, Beijing and Guangdong among others. All affected provinces agreed to expand capacity building of frontline staff in county-level CDCs and local hospitals.

External and Media Relations

The second feature of the ADB crisis response to SARS was an emphasis on external and media relations. Both the action plan and economic report generated extensive media attention, with ADB officials spotlighted in high profile, international television, radio, and newspaper coverage. This coverage received a boost from ADB sponsorship of the Bo'ao Forum's conference, "SARS and Asia's Economy: Impacts and Policy Recommendations," held on May 13–14 in Beijing. The president and the chief economist gave keynote addresses by video, since ADB Manila staff were not allowed to travel to the PRC. ADB also gave extensive publicity to its project approvals, and other support to combat SARS.

At the time, there was considerable uncertainty in the region on how best to protect staff and community. ADB worked in close coordination with its partners to ensure that key messages were widely disseminated as soon as facts became clear. For example, one important message is that the PRC government had become much more forthcoming about what was going on in the nation—in researching the causes of SARS and methods for containing and treating the disease. Problems were caused in the initial spread of SARS because people did not have access to adequate information; they did not know what was going on and thus could not take the appropriate preventative measures they might have otherwise. The absence of adequate information tended to breed fear and stress in the PRC and elsewhere. As it turned out, such fear and stress had significant medium-term consequences of all kinds for the region.

Technical Partnerships

The third feature of the ADB crisis response to SARS was an emphasis on technical partnerships. ADB's core areas of expertise in its response were economic analysis, financial engineering, and project management. ADB had only limited in-house expertise in health. To rectify this gap, on June 18, 2003, the ADB president signed a memorandum of understanding (MOU) with WHO to cooperate in the fight against SARS and other emerging diseases. The MOU, earlier signed by Gro Harlem Brundtland, Director-General of Geneva-based WHO, formalized a partnership envisioned in ADB's SARS action plan, with ADB providing funding and WHO contributing additional technical expertise. The partnership helped to guide the short-term response of DMCs to SARS and, equally important, longer term preparedness for potential next waves of emerging infectious diseases.

A key activity under this partnership was the appointment and funding by ADB of a WHO-based "regional response team" consisting of four specialists (an epidemiologist, a public health specialist, a laboratory specialist, and an infection control specialist) based at the WHO-WPRO offices to function as a regional team to respond to new outbreaks and develop long-term regional capacity for newly emerging disease outbreaks. These professionals were active in the isolated outbreaks of SARS in the PRC after its containment in June, and have focused in the past year on containing the Avian Flu disease.

Another important partnership was with ASEAN. An important achievement of this regional organization was to help reach agreement among all its member countries on common standards for the surveillance and control of travelers. As a result, all airports started taking travelers' temperatures, and required forms to be filled in with information on symptoms, countries visited, and contact addresses.

Support From Regional Donors

The fourth feature of the ADB crisis response to SARS was support from regional donors. To ensure that adequate financing was in place for DMCs to carry out essential surveillance and control, ADB sought additional funds from donor capitals. The first positive response was received from the government of Japan, which agreed to provide $3 million through the Japan Special Fund on 27 May 2003. These funds became the principal source of financing for the WHO Regional Response Team. Then, in the latter part of 2003, the International Cooperation and Development Fund (ICDF) in Taipei, China, approached ADB with an interest in providing additional funds ($500,000) for SARS-related activity. After extended discussions/negotiations on how such funds would be utilized (and in particular in which countries) agreement was reached and an MOU was signed at the end of December. Funds were provided for capacity-building activities (e.g., conferences, training) by officials and other relevant personnel from DMCs.

As noted, one of the reasons countries are under-protected against cross-border risks such as SARS is the difficulty in raising funds to promote regional public goods. One of these difficulties is that most donors are outside of the region and are not affected, and thus have less incentive to provide support. Yet in the case of SARS, regional donors were at risk and thus highly motivated to provide support.

2004 TSUNAMI CRISIS RESPONSE

Unlike the first two crises that were of human origin, the 2004 tsunami was a natural event. An earthquake off the cost of Sumatra, Indonesia, on 26 December 2004, triggered tsunami waves that devastated communities in many countries. Nearly 300,000 lives were lost and several million people were put at risk in a number of ways, especially of sliding further into poverty.

Recovery from the 2004 tsunami is still in progress as of this writing, and many results are uncertain. Three important dimensions are emerging. First, the importance of rapid response by affected governments, donor governments, and international organizations in providing relief and fundraising for reconstruction. The close proximity and logistical capacity of U.S. military forces facilitated the delivery of relief supplies and medical personnel to treat the injured. Second, formal and informal networks linking these governments and organizations with NGOs and the private sector to provide a coordinated response were important. And third, the promise that an effective tsunami early warning system (early detection and damage projection high-tech hardware combined with low-tech community awareness raising) can sharply reduce the death toll from such catastrophic events in the future

Since the Asia-Pacific region accounts for 90 percent of people worldwide affected by natural disasters (ADB, 2004; ADB, 2005a), ADB had significant prior experience in providing disaster assistance to its DMCs in response to flooding, typhoons, earthquakes, and for post-conflict rehabilitation. A common finding in evaluations of ADB disaster assistance is that too much time is needed for loan processing and implementation, both because of ADB and government procedures. Another finding is that ADB response to disasters tends to be ad hoc, without attention to best or smart practices. Few ADB staff have relevant training, and there are no focal points for disaster assistance (ADB, 2004; ADB, 2005a).

In response to these findings, a new policy went into effect in May 2004, advocating a systematic approach to disaster management, strengthening partnerships, more efficient and effective use of resources, and improved organizational arrangements within ADB. The emphasis now is on prevention of disasters. Other types of intervention include emergency response to disasters, and support to recovery efforts. Post-conflict situations are approached in a similar manner (ADB, 2004).

To address reported shortcomings, ADB has and continues to stream-line its business processes, including reducing processing time (to under 12 weeks), flexible interpretation of procedures, special audit procedures for emergency assistance, relaxed procurement requirements, rapid dis-bursement, retroactive and supplementary financing, and relaxed con-sultant recruitment requirements. In addition, ADB is committed to recruiting a disaster focal point, to encourage secondment to support the focal point, focal points in regional departments and resident missions, participatory processes, and partnerships. The new policy states that additional resources, when needed, will be met by reallocating available resources to the extent possible. No new resources were budgeted when the policy was approved. To what extent did this new policy make a differ-ence in ADB response to the tsunami? The following section answers this question by focusing on ADB's role with respect to three aspects of post-tsunami support.

Rapid Response

Although the new disaster policy had been in effect for over 1½ years, many of the planned institutional arrangements were not in place. The focal point position had not been filled, so a director in the concerned department was appointed to lead ADB's special-purpose Tsunami team. Focal points from regional departments had to be identified, and partner-ships forged with other agencies. Adjustments to ADB's business pro-cesses were also made, or are being quickly made, to ensure necessary flexibility, and to streamline procurement and consultant recruitments. Although most of these arrangements are being made, most had not been done before the tsunami struck.

A major success area for ADB in tsunami response was to quickly mobi-lize financial resources. The $600 million of new money for the Asian Tsu-nami Fund (ATF) and $175 million in reallocated funds, for a total of $775 million, established ADB as the third largest source of relief funds. The first project (for the Maldives) was approved on March 31, 2005, and the remaining projects were approved on April 7 (Indonesia) and April 14 (India and Sri Lanka). By April, ADB had committed $570.3 million of ATF funds to tsunami projects. In addition, $80 million in loan reallocations had been approved for Indonesia, Maldives, and Sri Lanka, and $2.15 million in grant-funded technical assistance projects were approved for these countries, along with Thailand and India, as of June 2005.

Agency Coordination

Because of the extent of devastation in affected areas, coordination has been essential between ADB and other development agencies, governments, and NGOs. Indeed, the most immediately useful assistance provided in Aceh was undoubtedly the logistical support provided by the U.S. Navy. More than 15,000 U.S. military personnel took part in the immediate effort to deliver over 1 million kilograms of relief supplies, supported by 25 ships and 94 aircraft (U.S. Department of State, 2005). Private businesses and NGOs have raised far more than ADB or other official donors. Such organizations in the USA alone raised $1.6 billion in cash and in-kind donations (Indiana University, 2005). Thus, to ensure effective tsunami relief, ADB has no choice but to coordinate closely with its partners.

There is evidence that extensive coordination has taken place. The ADB assessment mission in Indonesia was timed to feed initial findings to the January meeting of the Consultative Group on Indonesia, chaired by the World Bank, to ensure coordinated aid flows. A joint ADB-World Bank mission carried out a damage assessment in the Maldives. In Sri Lanka, it was agreed that ADB would focus on roads, railways, and livelihoods; the World Bank on education, health, and housing; JBIC on power, water supply, and telecommunication; and the UN system on linking emergency relief to long-term reconstruction (ADB, 2005b). A joint ADB-World Bank United Nations assessment was carried out in India, and a coordinated financing agreement signed by ADB, the World Bank, and the government in May. Coordination was also facilitated by MOUs with affected governments, such as the MOU signed between ADB and the government of Indonesia. The MOU, as well as clarifying expectations between the two signatories, also signaled the importance of donor coordination: "ADB will coordinate with the World Bank to harmonize the procurement procedures to facilitate emergency support" (ADB, 2005c) To ensure attention remained focused on tsunami support, and that donor support for and confidence in the affected countries remained high, ADB hosted a high-level meeting for government officials and donors in March (ADB, 2005d). Given the risks associated with shortcutting usual procedures and safeguards, ADB organized a regional Expert

Meeting on Corruption Prevention in Tsunami Relief jointly with Organisation for Economic Co-operation and Development (OECD), and Transparency International (TI), in cooperation with the government of Indonesia (ADB, 2005e).

Given the enormity and complexity of the challenges, some coordination problems are inevitable, particularly at the field level. For example, at one point there were reportedly 72 coordination meetings per week in Banda Aceh, most attended by 10–40 agencies. Yet most of the 400 international NGOs present could not attend. Such meetings were wide-ranging in quality, some without clear objectives and failing to clarify roles of participants. Some felt that the chairs of such meetings used them to push their own narrow personal or institutional agendas, rather than to build consensus and clarify roles for the best interest of the relief effort. Some senior staff spent more time on coordination than implementation, without clear results to show for either. UN-led coordination groups were working on the same issues in Jakarta, Medan, Banda Aceh, and Meulaboh without communicating with each other. The fact that the Indonesian military coordinated foreign military assets went against normal practice that they should be under civilian control. This sometimes led to unexplained restrictions (e.g., NGOs not allowed access to transport) and sometimes to duplication between military and civilian aid efforts (Völz, 2005). Some communities were flooded with relief that did not match their needs. Some relief supplies sat for months waiting for customs clearance. Some governments' entry procedures delayed arrival of essential specialists; other governments restricted use of satellite systems. Yet coordination in Aceh has reportedly improved since May 2005, when the government set up a reconstruction coordinating authority (Sipress, 2005)

A final coordination issue to consider is disaster response capability and resources as a global public good, and to examine whether the tsunami has diverted funds from other worthy causes in, for example, Central African Republic, Chad, Chechnya, Eritrea, Guinea, Somalia, Sudan and Niger. Key donors involved in humanitarian assistance (not including the ADB) agreed in 2003 to the Principles and Good Practice of Humanitarian Donorship, calling for better coordination and consistency in accord with agreed standards. One such standard is: "Strive to ensure that funding of humanitarian action in new crises does not adversely affect the meeting of needs in ongoing crises" (International Meeting on Good Humanitarian Donorship, 2003).

In the case of tsunami aid, the evidence is mixed. As of June 2005, there was more humanitarian financing available than in the past, even without considering tsunami funding: $847 million, compared to the $697 available at the same time in 2004. However, since over half of the funds this year are going for Sudan, other countries facing emergencies are worse off than last year; for example, as of October 2005, the UN was $150 million short of funds needed to assist drought-affected populations in Southern Africa, and $440 million short of funds needed "at once" to assist earthquake victims in Pakistan. This is in part because donors have lacked experienced staff to attend to these emergencies, so that funding contracts are being issued more slowly than would normally be the case. It is also the case that although some donors committed new funds for the tsunami, these funds have not yet been appropriated by legislatures, so donor agencies are diverting funds intended for other emergencies as a temporary measure (Lanzer, 2005).

Tsunami Early Warning System

One of the reasons for the high loss of life was the lack of a tsunami early warning system in the Indian Ocean. Such systems are in place throughout the Pacific, and could potentially save lives, although there have also been major costs because of false alarms. Another concern is that the 2004 tsunami was the worst in over 100 years, may not be repeated for another 100 years, and thus the considerable funds needed for setting up such a system could be put to better use.

In an effort to weigh the tradeoffs and feasibility of such a system, ADB's president offered at the ASEAN Leaders' Special Meeting 6 January to lead and fund a $1 million study to develop a tsunami early warning system for the Indian Ocean. However, this idea had many supporters, and ADB's study was not needed. In a coincidence of timing, the World Conference on Disaster Reduction took place in January 2005 in Kobe, Japan. At the conference, the UN launched plans for a global warning system of natural disaster—including droughts, wildfires, floods, typhoons, hurricanes, landslides, volcanoes and tsunamis—by using a combination of information technology and training populations at risk from such natural hazards.

There have been many meetings and conferences since, including one in Perth 3–5 August 2005. Delegates at that meeting were informed that 23 sea-level stations will be set up in Indian Ocean countries by the end of the year. Six stations are already operational in the region. Facilitated by UNESCO (United Nations Educational, Scientific and Cultural Organization), the meeting underlined that countries cannot rely solely on this international system, but need "to develop their own national detection networks, their own risk-assessment and preparedness plans, and their own national educational or awareness plans" (UNESCO, 2005)

CONCLUSIONS

These three rather different case studies show that a combination of factors have been at work in shaping ADB's response to each crises. In all three cases, a major success area for ADB was to quickly mobilize financial resources in close partnership with other funding agents. ADB's lending to Indonesia, the Republic of Korea, and Thailand in response to the 1997 crisis was part of IMF-led rescue packages that included many mainly public sector funding entities. ADB's mainly grant support to combat SARS contributed to an overall effort coordinated by WHO. ADB is the third largest official financier of the tsunami relief effort.

Additionally, in all of these cases, special purpose teams were assembled to fast-track the design and approval of ADB support. In responding to the 1997 crisis, small teams were urgently assembled to put together financial packages in each of the worst affected countries. In responding to SARS, three cross-functional, headquarters-based teams led the effort, reporting to a special advisor to the president. In responding to the tsunami, an ADB director was appointed to lead the ADB special-purpose tsunami team, drawing on staff from all concerned departments. The urgency of each crisis motivated the team members to work long hours. The team structure avoided departmental, procedural and personal issues that tend to slow down normal workflow, thus helping ADB in all cases to deliver rapid funding responses.

In all three cases, the immediate crisis response was led by governments and intergovernmental agencies like ADB. The three worst affected countries in 1997 all agreed to stringent IMF-led reform programs, and the concerned governments were able to mainly adhere to the conditions agreed to. In the SARS crisis, the two main players were WHO, that coordinated the international relief effort, and the government of the PRC that drastically improved its infectious disease control, surveillance, and reporting regime. In the case of the tsunami, the affected governments, donor governments, and intergovernmental agencies led the relief effort. Although governments took the lead, the tsunami case was unlike the other two in that private businesses and NGOs contributed more resources than ADB or other official donors. Such organizations in the U.S. alone raised $1.6 billion in cash and in-kind donations. This contributed to reported coordination problems where NGOs and private donors believed they were not linking up effectively with government-led and, in some cases, military-led assistance efforts.

Despite ADB's pragmatic approach to the three crises, some features of its traditional, compliance-driven bureaucracy created challenges. Disbursement delays resulted from both ADB and government procedures. Similar delays are reported by other international agencies, and result in part from understandable concern to minimize risks from working in corruption prone settings such as Aceh, Indonesia. Other challenges, such as delayed implementation of ADB's crisis management policy and lack of sufficient delegation to field offices, are mainly the responsibility of ADB.

Some progress in addressing these challenges has been made. To address the organizational and business process issues arising from crisis management and other aspects of ADB's work, ADB's Board approved a series of reforms in 2005 (Jin, 2005) including: (i) improving strategic clarity and results-orientation of country strategies, (ii) streamlining business processes related to the efficient conversion of project pipeline into investment and noninvestment operations, (iii) streamlining procurement, (iv) changing cost-sharing and expenditure eligibility, (v) new financial instruments and modalities, and (vi) appropriate safeguards. In addition, ADB appointed an experienced crisis management focal point in April 2006. However, it is expected that, despite these steps, ADB will continue to perform better in the initial phase of crisis response, than in the subsequent implementation phase. Reasons include greater intrinsic motivation of staff in the initial phase, and greater difficulty of work achievement in the subsequent phase.

What broader lessons and implications may be drawn from study and comparison of these cases? It is perilous to compare and analyze diverse case studies to extract accurate and reliable general conclusions. Nonetheless, such an effort is made here, as follows:

- Crisis response by ADB in these cases involved both standard operating procedures (SOPs) and innovative team-directed responsive action. As with all large and complex organizations, effective crisis response by ADB requires some deviation from SOPs through the exertion of leadership at a number of levels—from the top of the organization through to the area and other specialist staff. Innovative responses to crisis do not result automatically. Commitment to problem resolution and well-organized and coordinated initiative is required to respond to crises effectively.

- As an institution, ADB is highly capable of responding to crises situations through a variety of measures, some involving redirection of resources from previously dedicated purposes (funded projects in progress) in response to and in cooperation with the highest priority needs of DMCs.

- Effective crisis response to problems of serious national or regional impact cannot be performed unilaterally. They necessarily involve a considerable amount of networking and spontaneous international organization, enhanced by rapid advances in information technologies. Therefore, ADB should continue to strengthen its ties and relationships with DMCs and other nations, NGOs, the private sector, and additional entities so as to better prepare network members to increase crisis response capability, including clarifying the different roles and responsibilities of each party.

- A certain amount of uncertainty (often high in crisis situations where information inadequacy is evident) must be tolerated by ADB and partner entities with respect to speed of response, because effective response requires careful coordination.

Theoretical and case study research teach many things about crisis response. From theory and cases, we learn how crises are born, how various entities respond to them, and how we may facilitate effective recognition and response patterns to reduce their impact and facilitate recovery.

NOTES

1. Paper presented for discussion at the IPMN conference: "Communicable Crises: Prevention, Management and Resolution in an Era of Globalization," Vancouver, BC, Canada, August 15–17, 2005 (Thompson, 2005). This is a personal view of the author drawing on valuable contributions and insights provided by L. R. Jones.

2. For various definitions of globalization, see World Bank (undated), World Bank (2000), Economic and Social Commission for Asia and the Pacific (UNESCAP, 2004), Rivlin (1995) Prasad, Rogoff, Shang-Jin, & Kose (2003)

3. The difficulties with the Doha round of World Trade Organization (WTO) negotiations point this out. See http://www.wto.org/english/tratop_e/dda_e/dohaexplained_e.htm

4. The formulation of regional trade agreements (RTAs) has increasingly become a common trend in the world economy, especially after a number of failures of the multilateral trade system supported by the WTO. There has been a mushrooming of RTAs worldwide with the establishment of the North American Free Trade Agreement (NAFTA), the Central American Common Market, Latin American Free Trade Area, the Central African Customs and Economic Union, the East African Community, the Arab Common Market, the New Zealand–Australia Trade Area, Common Market of the Southern Cone, ASEAN Economic Community (AEC), ASEAN-China FTA, and others.

5. ASEAN+3 refers to the 10 member nations of ASEAN (Brunei Darussalam, Cambodia, Indonesia, Laos, Malaysia, Myanmar, Philippines, Singapore, Thailand, Vietnam) plus Japan, PRC, and Republic of Korea. Representatives of these countries meet on a regular basis to coordinate financial and economic policies.

6. The 11-member Executives' Meeting of East Asia Pacific Central Banks Initiative on Asian Bond Fund (EMEAP) agreed to launch in 2003 its first Asian Bond Fund (ABF1) with an initial size of around U.S.$1 billion. A second issue (ABF2) was launched in 2004.

7.   This is the official ADB designation for the country commonly known as Taiwan outside political circles.

8.   The World Bank (1993) and ADB (1997) were among those publishing extensive studies arguing in effect that emerging Asia might be immune to business cycles affecting other regions.

9.   To prevent the bankruptcy of Guangdong Enterprises in 1999, hundreds of lenders agreed to a bailout of $3.6 billion. China Aviation Oil (Singapore) Corp., after disclosing in 2004 $550 million of losses on derivatives trades, was accused by Singapore authorities of insider trading, forgery, a cover up, and other irregularities. Creditors had to agree to a restructuring plan, and the suspended CEO has been charged.

10.   Dr. Jiang Yanyong, a retired surgeon, People's Liberation Army veteran, and long-time Communist Party member was one of the heroes of the SARS epidemic. In early 2003, when SARS began to spread from its original habitat in Guandong Province to Hong Kong and beyond, through contacts in Beijing's hospitals he learned of the alarming number of SARS cases and deaths in the capital. Yet as the threat of an epidemic mounted, China's health minister announced, on April 3, SARS figures that grossly understated the facts. Jiang wrote and signed a letter to the Beijing TV station and *Time Magazine* telling the truth about the magnitude of the SARS epidemic in Beijing. Other doctors and the World Health Organization corroborated his revelations and the news spread around the world. Consequently, the Chinese authorities acted quickly; they fired the health minister and, on April 21, made SARS the subject of a massive public health campaign and, by June, a comprehensive system of monitoring was in place; by July, the deadly virus was contained (Ling, 2005, pp. 61-62.).

11.   C. Wescott (Team Leader), J. M. Hunt (Alternate Team Leader), P. Abeygunawardena, E. Araneta, E. Bloom, B. Edes, K. Horton, J. Jeugmans, N. Rao, P. Safran, C. Spohr, A. Sweetser, E. Valmores, J. Zhuang, J. Aquino (Consultant), and C. Molina (consultant).

12.   The ADB normally finances infrastructure repairs in responding to emergencies; see *ADB Operation Manual Section 25*, issued December 12, 1995.

REFERENCES

Asian Development Bank. (1997). *Emerging Asia: Changes and challenges.* Manila, Philippines: ADB.

Asian Development Bank. (1999). *Governance in Asia: From crisis to opportunity in annual report 1998.* Manila, Philippines: Author.

Asian Development Bank. (2000). *Asia development outlook.* Manila, Philippines: Author.

Asian Development Bank. (2001). *Special evaluation study of the Asian development bank's crisis management interventions in Indonesia.* Manila, Philippines: Author. Retrieved September 17, 2006, from http://adb.org/Documents/PERs/sst_ino200109.pdf

Asian Development Bank. (2003). *ADB'S crisis response to severe acute respiratory syndrom (SARS).* Manila, Philippines: Author. Retrieved September 17, 2006, from www.adb.org/sars

Asian Development Bank. (2003a). *Action plan to address outbreak of severe acute respiratory syndrome (SARS) in Asia and the pacific, May 2003.* Manila, Philippines: Author.

Asian Development Bank. (2003b). *TA-4118-PRC, Combating Severe Acute Respiratory Syndrome in the Western region, approved on 22 May for $2,000,000.* Manila, Philippines: Author.

Asian Development Bank. (2003c). *TA-6108, emergency regional support to address the outbreak of severe acute respiratory syndrome (SARS), approved on 23 May for $2,000,000.* Manila, Philippines: Author.

Asian Development Bank. (2003d). *2003 Asia development outlook.* Manila, Philippines: Author.

Asian Development Bank. (2003e). *SARS: Economic impacts and implications.* Manila, Philippines: Author. Retrieved September, 17, 2006, from http://www.adb.org/Documents/EDRC/Policy_Briefs/PB015.pdf

Asian Development Bank. (2004). *Disaster and emergency assistance policy.* Manila, Philippines: Author. Retrieved September 17, 2006, from http://www.adb.org/Documents/Policies/Disaster_Emergency/default.asp

Asian Development Bank. (2005). *Annual report 2004.* Manila, Philippines: Author.

Asian Development Bank. (2005a). *ADB's response to emergencies: Were we prepared for the tsunamis?* Manila, Philippines: ADB Operations Evaluation Department. Retrieved September, 17, 2006, from http://adb.org/Documents/OED/Articles/mar01-oed-article05.pdf

Asian Development Bank. (2005b). *ADB, partners to begin needs assessment surveys in tsunami afflicted zones.* Manila, Philippines: Author. Retrieved September, 17, 2006, from http://www.adb.org/media/Articles/2005/6649_tsunami_disaster_tsunami_relief/default.asp?registrationID=guest

Asian Development Bank. (2005c). *ADB signs MOU with Indonesia for framework on disaster support.* Manila, Philippines: Author. Retrieved on September 17, 2006, from http://www.adb.org/Media/Articles/2005/6621_Indonesia_MOU/default.asp?registrationID=guest

Asian Development Bank. (2005d). *High-level coordination meeting on rehabilitation and reconstruction assistance to tsunami-affected countries.* Manila, Philippines: Author. Retrieved September, 17, 2006, from http://www.adb.org/Documents/Events/2005/Rehabilitation-Reconstruction/default.asp

Asian Development Bank. (2005e). *Expert meeting on corruption prevention in tsunami relief.* Manila, Philippines: Author. Retrieved September, 17, 2006, from http://www.adb.org/Documents/Events/2005/Tsunami-Relief/default.asp

Allen, F., & Gale, D., (2000). Financial contagion. *The Journal of Political Economy. 108*(1), 1–33.

Australian Government. (2005). *Chapter 7: Managing crises and their consequences in Australian government, connecting government: Whole of government responses to Australia's priority challenges.* Australia: Author.

Behn, R. (2004, January 2004). *The Behn report.* Retrieved 17 September 17, 2006, from http://www.ksg.harvard.edu/TheBehnReport/January2004.pdf

Bertelli, A. M. (2006). Motivation crowding and the federal civil servant: Evidence from the U.S. Internal Revenue Service. *International Public Management Journal, 9*(1), 3–24.

Birdsall, N., & Haggard, S. (2000). *After the crisis: The social contract and the middle class in east Asia.* Washington, DC: Carnegie Endowment for International Peace.

Birdsall, N., & Rojas-Suarez, L. (Eds.). (2004). *Financing development: The power of regionalism.* Washington, DC: Center for Global Development.

Collyns, C., & Senhadji, A. (2002). *Lending booms, real estate bubbles and the Asian Crisis.* IMF Working Paper 02/20.

delisle, J. (2004). Atypical pneumonia and ambivalent law and politics: SARS and the response to SARS in China, *Temple Law Review 77,* 193–246.

Diamond, J. (2005). *Collapse.* London: Penguin.

Dobson, W. (2000). Financial reform in East Asia Post-crisis. In P. Petri, (ed.), *Regional cooperation and Asian recovery* (pp. 51-81). Singapore: Institute of Southeast Asian Studies.

Drabek, T. E., & McEntire, D. A. (2003). Emergent phenomena and the sociology of disaster: Lessons, trends and opportunities from the research literature. *Disaster Prevention and Management, 12*(2), 97–112.

Drucker, P. (1998). *The coming of the new organization, in Harvard Business Review on knowledge management.* Cambridge, MA: Harvard Business School Press.

Economic and Social Commission for Asia and the Pacific. (2004b). *Meeting the challenges in an era of globalization by strengthening regional development cooperation* New York: United Nations.

Fan, E. (2003). SARS: Economic *Impacts and implic*ations (ERD Policy Brief No. 15). Manila, Phillipines: Author.

Fischer, S. (1998, October 3–9) Lessons from a crisis, *The Economist.* Retrieved September 17, 2006, from http://www.imfsite.org/recentfin/lessons.html

Frankel, J. A. (2000). The Asian financial crisis in perspective. In P. Petri (Ed.), *Regional Cooperation and Asian Recovery* (pp. 20–35). Singapore: Institute of Southeast Asian Studies.

Fukuyama, F. (2004). Why there is no science of public administration. *Journal of International Affairs, 58*(1),189–201.

Gingrich, N., & Egge, R. (2005, November 6). To fight the flu, change how government works. *New York Times.* Retrieved December 12, 2006, from http://www.nytimes.com/2005/11/06/opinion/06gingrich.html?ex=1166072400&en=753b5b99f3141a30&ei=5070

Indiana University. (2005). *Tsunami relief giving.* Bloomington, IN: Center on Philanthropy. Retrieved September 17, 2006, from http://www.philanthropy.iupui.edu/tsunami_relief_giving_1-18-05.html

International Meeting on Good Humanitarian Donorship. (2003). *Principles and good practice of humanitarian donorship.* Stockholm, 16–17 June. Retrieved September, 17, 2006, from http://www.reliefweb.int/ghd/Stockholm%20-%20GHD%20Principles%20and%20IP.doc

Jin, L. (2005). *ADB: Its new visions, strategies and modalities for development financing.* Retrieved September 17, 2006, from http://www.adb.org/Documents/Speeches/2005/ms2005089.asp

Jones, C. I. (2006). *Knowledge and the theory of economic development.* Draft paper, University of California, Berkeley. Retrieved September 17, 2006, from http://elsa.berkeley.edu/~chad/know025.pdf

Klitgaard, R., & Light, P. C. (2005). *High performance government: Structure, leadership, incentives.* Santa Monica, CA: Rand Corporation.

Lanzer, T. (2005, July). Has the tsunami affected funding for other crises? *Forced Migration Review,* 17. Retrieved December 12, 2006 from http://www.fmreview.org/FMRpdfs/Tsunami/full.pdf

Ling L. (2005). Open government and transparent policy: China's Experience with SARS. *International Public Management Review, 6*(1), 60–74.

McEntire, D. A. (2001). Triggering agents, vulnerabilities and disaster reduction: towards a holistic paradigm. *Disaster Prevention and Management, 10*(3), 189–196.

O'Donnell, M. (2000). Creating a performance culture? Performance-based pay in the Australian public service. *Australian Journal of Public Administration, 57*(3), 28–40.

Perspective: the Coordinator, (2003). *Business Management Asia,* BMA10.

Prasad, E., Rogoff, K., Shang-Jin, W., & Kose, M. A. (2003). *Effects of financial globalization on developing countries: Some empirical evidence.* Retrieved September 17, 2006, from http://www.imf.org/external/np/res/docs/2003/031703.htm

Rivlin, B. (1995, November). *The United Nations and regionalism in an era of globalization: Envisioning the United Nations in the twenty-first century.* Proceedings of the Inaugural Symposium on the United Nations System in the Twenty-first Century, Tokyo.

Rogoff, K. (2002). *An open letter to Joseph Stiglitz.* Washington, DC: IMF. Retrieved from September 17, 2006, at http://www.imf.org/external/np/vc/2002/070202.htm

Root, H. (2006). Opening the doors of invention: Institutions, technology and developing nations. *International Public Management Review, 7*(1), 14–29. Retrieved September 17, 2006. from http://www.ipmr.net

Sandler, T. (2004). *Demand and institutions for regional public goods in IADB and ADB. Regional public goods and regional development assistance.* Washington, DC: IADB. Retrieved 17 September 17, 2006, from http://www.adb.org/Documents/Books/Regional-Public-Goods/default.asp

Saxenian, A. (2006). *The new argonauts: Regional advantage in a global economy.* Cambridge, MA: Harvard University Press.

Sipress, A. (2005, August 15). Sumatra battles shifting shore. *The Asian Wall Street Journal,* p. A2.

Stiglitz, J. E. (2002). *Globalization and Its discontents.* New York: Norton.

Thompson, F. (2005, August). *Call for papers, communicable crises: Prevention, management and resolution in an era of globalization.* International Public Management Network Workshop, Green College, University of British Columbia, Vancouver, BC, Canada.

United Nations Educational, Scientific and Cultural Organization. (2005, August). *Results of the meeting: First session of the intergovernmental coordination group for the Indian Ocean tsunami warning and mitigation system* (ICG/IOTWS-I), Perth, Australia. Retrieved September 17, 2006 from http://ioc.unesco.org/indotsunami/perth05/perth05_results.htm

Ursacki-Bryant, T. J., Vertinsky, I., & Smart, C. (2005, August). *Contagion in International Crises: A Case Study of SARS.* Prepared for the International Public

Management Network Workshop, Communicable Crises, Prevention, Management and Resolution, Vancouver, BC.

U.S. Department of State. (2005). *Going the distance: The US tsunami relief effort.* Washington, DC: Author

Völz, C. (2005, July). Humanitarian coordination in Indonesia: An NGO viewpoint. *Forced Migration Review*, 26-7. Retrieved December 12, 2006, from http://www.fmreview.org/FMRpdfs/Tsunami/full.pdf

Wescott, C. (2006). Harnessing knowledge exchange among overseas professionals. *International Public Management Review*, 7(1), 30–69. Retrieved September 17, 2006, from http://www.ipmr.net

Wescott, C., & Brinkerhoff, J. (2006). *Converting migration drains into gains: Harnessing the resources of overseas professionals.* Manila, Philippines: Asian Development ment Bank.

Wilson, P., & Zurbruegg, R. (2004). Contagion or interdependence? Evidence from co-movements in Asia-Pacific securitised real estate markets during the 1997 crisis. *Journal of Property Investment & Finance*, 22(5), 401–413.

World Bank, (n.d.) *Assessing globalization.* Retrieved September 17, 2006, from http://www1.worldbank.org/economicpolicy/globalization/documents/AssessingGlobalizationP1.pdf

World Bank. (1993). *The East Asia miracle: Economic growth and public policy. World bank policy research report.* Oxford, England: University Press.

World Bank. (2000). *Poverty in an age of globalization.* Washington, DC: Author.

CHAPTER 12

SYNTHESIZING PERSPECTIVES ON RESPONSE TO COMMUNICABLE CRISES

Deborah E. Gibbons

This chapter merges insights from several authors whose work appears in this volume. By integrating these perspectives, we obtain an overview of the issues that must be addressed to prepare for crisis. Careful analysis of prior successes and failures, combined with realistic assessment of structural and governmental limitations, reveals principles that enhance capacity to mitigate or manage the consequences of a disaster. These principles can and should be applied at the policy level and within operational guidelines that are likely to be invoked during an emergency. Through proactive preparation and design, we may improve the ability of government, businesses, nonprofit organizations, and communities to response successfully to future crises.

INTRODUCTION

Despite a plethora of emergency plans within organizations and governments, few if any interorganizational systems are fully prepared for communicable crises that might spread across local, national, or international

Communicable Crises: Prevention, Response, and Recovery in the Global Arena, pp. 353–374

regions. This lack of response capability may reflect strategic and operational goals of leaders that limit contingency thinking. It may result from a practical focus on day to day concerns. It is exacerbated by inability or unwillingness of member entities to share information, resources, and solutions. Lack of experience with crises, and the corollary improbability of ever having to face one, may reduce crisis preparations to token efforts that are more useful for public relations than for public safety.

With the exception of the *Katrina Lessons Learned* report (The White House, 2006), state and national governments have invested surprisingly little effort to systematically assess and develop guidelines for improving their crisis response capacities. Documents such as the National Incident Management System (NIMS) (U.S. Department of Homeland Security, 2004) outline organizing principles that could be effective, but conditions in many regions and nations preclude functional implementation of even the most basic recommendations. More detailed examination of structural and procedural factors that influence crisis response could lead to better preparation that will improve response and decrease costs following potentially communicable crises. Several issues arise as we attempt to build foundations for successful response and recovery.

From the analytical perspective, we are constrained by existing politics, practices, and even limitations on language that might enable creative and productive investigation of crisis response issues (LaPorte, in this volume). Our natural tendency to categorize new information in terms of what we already know can blind us to novel threats in crisis emergencies, and our learned responses to normal emergencies may supersede detailed, rational analysis of new or changing situations (Leonard & Howitt, in this volume). Patterned behaviors that help during normal operations can hinder crisis handling. Patterned thinking, if based on irrelevant or incorrect information, forms a poor base for subsequent analysis. As people recognize an emerging crisis and begin to mobilize their response, they build mental models that influence subsequent problem-solving, often in unproductive ways (Ansell & Gingrich, in this volume).

From a response perspective, we may be constrained by institutional limitations, inflexible structures within and between organizations, and lack of planning for situations in which normal resources are not available. Cultural expectations demand particular actions by leaders while forbidding other actions that might be more useful (Roberts, in this volume). The nature of a government further influences its members' willingness and ability to cooperate, potentiating very different actions and outcomes in response to similar initial circumstances (Bryant, Vertinsky, & Smart, in this volume). Distinct aspects of various governments with regard to information sharing and containment can then affect response capability outside their borders. Because crises that cross jurisdictional borders invoke coordination problems and potential cost sharing, they require collaboration among government agencies and other stakeholders that may not normally work together.

Finally, interwoven throughout the analysis and response processes, communication, coordination, and asset tracking become vital supports for joint intervention by community groups, organizations, and governments. Compatible technologies that enable lateral communication and centralized data processing in the absence of normal infrastructure provide the foundation for effective response (Braunbeck & Mastria, in this volume; Comfort, in this volume; Gibbons, in this volume). Although government actions often drive large-scale interventions, the majority of first responders are members of the affected community (Seifert, in this volume) and volunteers from nearby regions (Gibbons, in this volume). To the extent that community members are prepared to manage themselves and coordinate with others in an emergency, they become assets rather than liabilities when professional responders enter the situation. Rapid distribution of accurate information is crucial. Without the situational awareness that results from strong communication networks, coordination among nonprofit organizations, government agencies, and local responders becomes nearly impossible.

Although interconnectedness among municipalities, regional governments, and states increases the availability of help for local disasters from outside sources, it also increases the potential for crisis contagion across borders. Contagion may occur in many realms, including economy and environment (Wescott, in this volume), health threats (Ansell & Gingrich, in this volume; Bryant, Vertinsky, & Smart, in this volume), and terrorism (Roberts, in this volume). Given that a large-scale crisis necessarily introduces unexpected and overwhelming circumstances, preparations that improve the ability of interorganizational systems to cope with uncertainty under conditions of impaired infrastructure and interrupted resource flows seem most likely to succeed. Such preparations require that we understand relationships between organizational attributes and crisis response. Armed with this understanding, we may be able to develop the structures and processes that are needed to optimize crisis management capabilities.

COMMUNICABLE CRISES AND BOUNDARIES FOR RESPONSE

Leonard and Howitt (in this volume) identify crisis emergencies by their unusually large scale, previously unknown causes, and atypical combinations of disaster sources. These conditions introduce "significantly new circumstances and different kinds of intellectual challenges." LaPorte (in this volume) argues that crises exceed emergencies in uncertainty, scope, and potential for irreparable damage. He equates a crisis with a "rude surprise" that overwhelms institutional capacity. In many cases, the source of the crisis interferes with or destroys infrastructure and other resources that are needed for adequate response. Further, a crisis situation introduces uncertainties, needs, or challenges that available responders have neither seen nor considered before. Standard operating procedures and coordination channels are likely to be unsuitable or unusable, so responders need to plan and coordinate their actions in the midst of unfolding emergencies. In a crisis, people face uncertainty regarding high stakes outcomes, and they have limited time to respond (Bryant, Vertinsky, & Smart, in this volume).

Sources of crisis may be as diverse as storms, germs, monetary shifts, and terrorists. A communicable crisis begins when adverse initial occurrences build toward a critical juncture that will determine future, potentially devastating, outcomes. Communicable crises not only require rapid, high-quality decisions and responses to address current threats, they require advance thought about events that may follow the immediate situation. Given the breadth of potential crises, the uncertainty surrounding a crisis, and the possibility of debilitating results when initial emergencies trigger ongoing disasters, what can be done to prepare our responses?

BUREAUCRACY AND BEST PRACTICES

Best practices in public organizations generally include tight internal control, transparent punitive accountability, and limitations on slack resources (LaPorte, in this volume). None of these attributes are likely to facilitate successful responses to crises, which require adaptability, creativity, and rapid direction of resources toward problem solving. Errors in implementation can occur because of uncertainty about circumstances and effects of interventions, rapidly developing challenges and response skills, and the need to learn from doing (Leonard & Howitt, in this volume). Tolerance for errors under crisis situations may be crucial for successful response and recovery. Instead of allowing standard operating procedures or red tape to impede disaster responses, systems that hope to be ready for crises must develop the capacity to process information, allocate resources, and coordinate responses to emergency events as they unfold.

Emergency response organizations develop their own habits, routines, and bureaucratic tendencies. While some of their experiences have led to "best practices" that serve well under familiar types of emergencies, these practices may not fit every type of disaster. Dissimilar circumstances require different approaches to situational awareness, planning and decision-making, and execution of responses (Leonard & Howitt, in this volume). Organizations dealing with crisis emergencies need freedom to incorporate new ideas and remix old approaches to fit developing situations and the surprises they bring.

Crucial for crisis emergency response is the ability to set aside standard bureaucracy. This was exemplified by the University of Alabama when they allocated housing to hurricane evacuees from Louisiana and processed the transfer students into ongoing classes within a few hours (Gibbons, in this volume). Abandoning the usual paperwork sped the in-processing for students fleeing the hurricane, but once these students had been enrolled, they became subject to normal bureaucratic requirements. Wescott (in this volume) observes a similar phenomenon, saying that the desire to help distressed people and to tackle a novel project encourages responders to perform effectively at first, but over time they tend to return to standard bureaucracy that may not support ongoing performance.

Sometimes, bureaucracy has indirect negative impacts on crisis management. For example, Ansell and Gingrich (in this volume) explain how the setup of official committees to advise investigations of mad cow disease incorporated earlier biases into the process. This occurred because of representation by people who were already indoctrinated in existing beliefs and because of linkages between the committees and ongoing investigations. Overall, despite the creation of new research entities with new personnel, early ideas dominated the problem solving.

Similarly, duplication of existing processes can inhibit analytic quality and freedom to act rapidly. Selective information processing, including attention to salient issues and stakeholders at the possible expense of meaningful information, negatively influences national and organizational responses to emergencies. Along these lines, representatives of the World Health Organization missed several opportunities for early diagnosis of SARS because they were looking for other illnesses (such as avian flu) that were known to pose a health threat (Bryant, Vertinsky, & Smart, in this volume).

Hierarchical coordination authority with decentralized response management may address logistical needs while maintaining capacity for timely intervention in changing circumstances. Centralized command and control can facilitate successful coordination of unified response plans (Leonard & Howitt, in this volume). Yet rigid political control over the actions that may be taken by leaders can reduce their ability to implement logical responses to crisis. In some cases, this leads to suboptimal or even detrimental government interventions (Roberts, in this volume).

When a plethora of health experts assembled in Toronto to track and combat SARS, several aspects of bureaucracy impeded their progress. These included incompatible data systems, multiple uncoordinated voices, and lots of red tape (Bryant, Vertinsky, & Smart, in this volume)

Despite the natural tendency of bureaucracies to become rigid and formalized, steps can be taken to build readiness for crisis into the system. Training that instills analysis and decision making capacity alongside more routine skills can ready an organization or a set of organizations for surprise emergencies. Besides the obvious benefits of having better prepared people, training exercises can expose differently skilled people to each other. They learn how the others do their jobs, and they begin to forge relationships to undergird future cooperation. Positive interpersonal relations increase trust that may be crucial under stressful conditions. Formal exercises can reveal communication mismatches, bottlenecks, and potential conflicts among people who are likely to take different roles in a crisis situation. At the same time, crisis simulations build organizational memory of two valuable types. Transactive memory—knowing others and what they know—enables rapid coordination under uncertainty because the responders can predict the kinds of help they are likely to receive from each other. Institutional memory—storage of lessons learned—enables future access to learning that occurs through the crisis simulations (Seifert, in this volume). Both types of organizational memory build foundations for successful response to rude surprises in the future.

Bridging From Normal Operations to Crisis Responses

Organizations face several challenges when they must shift from normal or emergency operations into crisis management. To the extent that feared effects are devastating, abruptly delivered, and concentrated, the organization is less able to respond appropriately. Further, lower confidence in knowledge about causes and consequences, more secret information about remedies, and more disagreement about the credibility of information increase the process difficulties (LaPorte, in this volume).

Moving from normal procedures to crisis response requires new ways of thinking and active questioning or rejection of previous beliefs and standard practices. Normal emergency procedures, which rest on prior experience and specialized expertise among responders, are unlikely to fit the demands of a crisis (Leonard & Howitt, in this volume). In addition, stress under threat increases reliance on dominant cues and filtering of information. These, in turn, lead to poor decisions (Seifert, in this volume). Rather than shifting to a more adaptable stance, many organizations facing emergencies increase centralization and formalization, becoming more rigid and less likely to allow improvisation. This common response removes authority from the people who know most about what is happening and concentrates analysis and decision making in a core that may be insulated from actual developments (Seifert, in this volume). Thus, the organizations lose their ability to adapt quickly and creatively to emergent threats or novel situations.

Organizations may not support ideal norms for crisis management, but freedom to try and fail, along with a culture that values system-wide learning, can increase ability to cope with disaster (LaPorte, in this volume). As responders progress through stages of problem awareness, response design, implementation, and observation of results, they build understanding that supports ongoing response to evolving circumstances (Leonard & Howitt, in this volume). When frontline responders are allowed to make tactical choices, with the understanding that errors may occur, logjams of central processing can be avoided, and more lives may be saved (Seifert, in this volume). Fear of reprisals and adherence to formal protocols can delay sensible action and reduce crisis response to useless political bickering or bureaucratic plodding.

POLITICAL CONSTRAINTS ON CRISIS MANAGEMENT

Political activities, legislative oversight, and public relations tend to place excessive, often irrational constraints on behavior within governmental institutions. Political players tend to act more slowly than operational experts when faced with a crisis. When they do act, their decisions and responses may overlap or even conflict across jurisdictions and levels of government (Leonard & Howitt, in this volume). Lack of formal coordination among various government entities introduces further confusion into situations that are already rife with uncertainty. This lays a foundation for disorganized response by nongovernment organizations that rely on information and synchronization mechanisms maintained by government(s). Amid the interjurisdictional clashes, governments' tight control over resource allocations can result in lengthy delays while requests float through multiple layers of bureaucracy. By planning flexible accounting practices that enable immediate resource availability in crises, some of the institutional paralysis may be avoided (LaPorte, in this volume).

Planning for international collaboration also needs to be done before a disaster strikes. Cooperative response agreements between nations can support joint action, but variance in politico-economic institutions drastically affects handling of trans-border crises. Differences in culture, values, and infrastructure impact the speed and capacity for collaboration (Bryant, Vertinsky, & Smart, in this volume), complicating the need for compatibility in response approaches. Supranational organizations, such as the World Health Organization, can assist in handling cross-border crises, but they are also subject to political and cultural limitations. These limitations increase the need for negotiated solutions to shared problems, which require good communication among stakeholders.

National and organizational differences affect people's interpretations of good communication, and they can influence the nature of communications regarding a shared emergency (Bryant, Vertinsky, & Smart, in this volume). Some governments create pressure on their people that inhibits sharing of information about potential disasters (Bryant, Vertinsky, & Smart, in this volume). Without access to reliable information, problem solving is crippled. At the other extreme, a free press, while generally considered to be positive, can influence political processes in negative ways. Information releases by nongovernment organizations and news media can draw public attention toward issues that are not central to solving a crisis (Bryant, Vertinsky, & Smart, in this volume). Political action may then lead to unproductive or even inappropriate responses. For example, Roberts (in this volume) explains how increasing demands (and litigation) for civil rights in the United States have limited the government's ability to respond to terrorism within the nation.

Beyond cultural and media influences, the balance of governmental power impacts high-level decision making as well as low-level response behaviors. Bryant, Vertinsky, and Smart (in this volume) identify distinct hazards associated with hierarchical (e.g., China) versus less centralized (e.g., Canada) governments. Hierarchical control over people's day to day actions removes their sense of personal responsibility in situations where the government cannot or will not coordinate them. To foster appropriate action, then, people in high power-distance societies must be given precise instructions by accepted authorities. Without such instructions, they are unlikely to respond appropriately. In contrast, in a less controlled society, people must be convinced to cooperate with the government. In the case of communicable diseases, public education about appropriate action regarding treatment and travel could safeguard community members' health and prevent an epidemic (Bryant, Vertinsky, & Smart, in this volume).

National characteristics create predictable tendencies in the way a country responds to crisis. Cultural beliefs and values influence options for addressing a crisis (Roberts, in this volume). Under some forms of government, political expediency supersedes concern for citizens' well-being and for the spread of communicable crises to other regions (Bryant, Vertinsky, & Smart, in this volume). Some forms of government can be handicapped in their responses because of their citizens' demands for civil liberties. Roberts (in this volume) argues that public expectations in the United States regarding citizens' rights to freedom from government intervention, monitoring, or new costs associated with security have heavily limited domestic responses to terrorism. Coupled with a high need for action, this political environment pushes toward external interventions. At the same time, the political system in the United States has increasingly constrained the ability of the executive branch of government to take action, except through the military. Considering these political attributes of the United States, it is not surprising that the majority of its response to terrorism has occurred through the Department of Defense outside the boundaries of the country (Roberts, in this volume). This sort of analysis may be repeated, in different forms, for any nation in the world. Although the specific attributes and outcomes may vary widely, the general message applies universally: political, ideological, and social environments preclude some response behaviors while facilitating others. This forces crisis managers to choose among the remaining options, which may or may not be ideal.

LEADERSHIP, CRITICAL ANALYSIS, AND PROBLEM SOLVING

Leadership under crisis requires faster thinking, broader problem solving, and more constant critical analysis than are needed to address standard emergency situations. Flexible delegation that allows more qualified or fresher thinking individuals to take charge when appropriate reduces rigid thinking (Seifert, in this volume). By bringing more people into decision making and encouraging problem solving at the point of action, we may obtain better information processing and analysis than could occur among leaders whose more distant positions limit their awareness of actual circumstances (Gibbons, in this volume). While it is important to establish authority structures and logistics coordination, it is equally important to enable intelligent self-organization by responders on the ground. At every level, leaders can only function as well as the information and analysis expertise that are available to them.

Institutionalized Thinking Versus Embracing Surprise

If a crisis continues over time, new institutions arise, but they may not always provide the best avenues to address emerging problems. Sometimes, early establishment of response patterns can anchor subsequent definitions of the problem space and categories of solutions that will be considered. This, in turn, may lead to inadequate exploration of possible sources and solutions for a problem. By the time a gradually emerging crisis becomes salient, many people have been involved with analysis and interventions in earlier stages. These people may be heavily invested in the approaches that they have begun, and they may feel strong ownership of the problem. Both of these attitudes can lead them to resist help from outside sources, even when it is badly needed (Leonard & Howitt, in this volume). Further, the initial beliefs and practices applied to a potential emergency create a platform for subsequent thinking and action.

Ansell and Gingrich (in this volume) explain how protracted failure to recognize implications of mad cow disease for human health followed from early responses to unfolding events and discoveries. Initial investigators viewed the problem as a livestock issue. Because the problem was framed in terms of animals and economy, response teams and subsequent committee members did not focus on threats to people. Successful leadership under uncertainty requires broad searches for information, careful analysis of facts from disparate sources, and synthesis of multiple viewpoints (Gibbons, in this volume). If this does not occur, suboptimal solutions or even no solutions may occur.

Intervention networks often develop in ways that continue to support the ideas held by existing members, particularly when subsequent teams and committees include or build on the ideas of prior investigators (Ansell & Gingrich, in this volume). When a single approach to problem solving takes over a disaster response system, such that information search and analysis are dampened, good solutions are likely to be missed. In contrast, when responding organizations "embrace surprise," (LaPorte, in this volume), they are better equipped to deal with the unexpected because they are less likely to become paralyzed by the magnitude of the events.

Flexibility and Stress Reduction

Decision making under crisis may have large effects on important outcomes, and it tends to induce stress (Leonard & Howitt, in this volume). Faced with major crises, our stress levels are likely to skyrocket. Small amounts of stress can improve performance, but excessive or sustained stress reduces decision makers' effectiveness. This is particularly true for unfamiliar emergencies because increasing stress decreases responders' ability to recognize novel circumstances and rationally evaluate alternatives (Leonard & Howitt, in this volume).

Perceptions of control reduce stress levels, enabling more effective problem solving and response. Flexible organization and communication structures, proactive development of potential responders' skills and relationships, and integration of community members and resources can increase perceived control and actual response quality. These three factors—perceived control over the situation, stress reduction, and prior response success—reinforce each other as the crisis unfolds (Seifert, in this volume).

Good emergency leadership requires ability to process information rapidly and to change one's strategy to fit the newest updates. Leonard and Howitt (in this volume) refer to this analytical, exploratory approach as "adaptive leadership," and they argue that it is crucial for effective response to crisis emergencies.

ONGOING EFFECTS OF RESPONDERS' STRUCTURES

Ansell and Gingrich (in this volume) address the process through which an emergent problem causes a response network to emerge. As new aspects of the problem are recognized, the network forms around the unique demands for resources, expertise, and authorization to move forward. At each phase, the interpretation of the problem influences the development of the response network, and the nature of the response network subsequently influences ongoing interpretations of the problem. According to Ansell and Gingrich, ways of thinking about and addressing the problem become institutionalized within the network, leading participants to ignore contrary possibilities. As a result, delays and dead-ends encountered in the investigation of an emergent problem arise from the nature of the problem, its prior interpretations, and the dynamics of the response network, independent of actors' intent.

Centralized decision making can delay response and increase costs associated with recovery efforts. At the same time, centralized control of functions that are common to all aspects of the organization or system streamlines operations and avoids noncompatibility issues. Standardized coordination procedures, logistics support, and communications channels should operate at the system level. These can then support self-organization and decision-making within subgroups at the local level. This combination facilitates rapid, effective, and efficient responses to natural disasters (Gibbons, in this volume). Wescott (in this volume) reaches a similar conclusion for financial responders, stating that "more flexible application of standard procedures, better internal coordination, and more delegation of authority and responsibility to field staff" could improve financial recovery efforts.

The ability to be surprised without freezing (LaPorte, in this volume) may be cultivated within an organization's culture, supported by frequently-freshened norms, and joined with adaptable preparedness to enable rapid decision making under crisis. Appropriate organizational designs for crisis response allow "ad hoc authority patterns," access to supplemental resources, and freedom to seek unique solutions without fear of subsequent reprisal (LaPorte, in this volume).

INTERORGANIZATIONAL COORDINATION

Interorganizational Communications and Use of Media

Continuous communication among responders in a crisis undergirds everyone's capacity for success, so an integrated communication network is necessary at all stages of and levels of response. An incident command system can only function if information from all aspects of the system travels reliably in every direction. To accomplish this, we need asset tracking with information relays throughout the supply chain. We need linkage to centralized databases that cannot be corrupted by emergency events, and we need mechanisms that build a common operational picture for all responders (Braunbeck & Mastria, in this volume). A good emergency communication system provides centralized sources of information alongside decentralized communication media to support self-organization by people who are acting in the midst of crisis. Reciprocal interdependence among responders demands continuous ability for lateral communication within the framework of systemic goals and events. To adjust their actions to new situations and needs, the responders require system-level information as well as the ability to coordinate among themselves (Comfort, in this volume; Gibbons, in this volume).

We cannot overemphasize the importance of centralized information processing and distribution to all relevant parties; however, we must also recognize the importance of decentralized information sharing among people in the field. Because communication infrastructure is likely to be damaged in a major disaster, sensible preparation requires that we build overarching communication networks that do not depend on local resources. Redundancy in media types and communication channels increases the likelihood that official responders will be able to coordinate their own and others' actions. At the same time, it is crucial for local organizations to develop their own communication systems that will operate under extreme circumstances (Gibbons, in this volume).

Resource databases and application software that enable system-level, real-time analysis of incoming data support a competent crisis response and reduce the likelihood of ongoing disasters. Comfort (in this volume) emphasizes the need to obtain information from dispersed groups of responders and to inform them of system-wide developments. She advocates "bowtie" information technology architecture that simultaneously brings information from key sources to a central processing unit (at the middle of the bowtie) that can analyze the data from a system perspective. Results are then distributed to responders who can incorporate the higher-level information into their own operational plans (Csete & Doyle, 2004).

Adaptable, multipurpose crisis communication systems will only arise through adherence to universal standards and specifications for databases, software, and communication technology. Current satellite systems operate with a variety of communication devices, enabling several different methods of data transfer (Braunbeck & Mastria, in this volume). Similar compatibility among land-based communications and databases is needed for system-level coordination of responding organizations. Communication speed and quality influence ability to route resources sensibly, to inform the public of necessary actions, and to enable timely professional interventions. For example, initial lack of information caused problems in responding to SARS, including fear, stress, and failure to take preventative measures (Wescott, in this volume). Active routing of information to easily accessible outlets may help governments, individuals and businesses make informed decisions under crisis without overtaxing responders' time and resources with noncritical questions. Zolin and Kropp (in this volume) suggest that government could support business survival by providing a Web site with information about survivor locations, business recovery tips, and current conditions in a disaster area. By distributing clear information about local business opportunities, government agencies may help business owners build their own recovery strategies.

A potential challenge for international crisis management stems from differences in willingness or capacity to communicate between countries. A logistics system that is flexible and modular provides scalable support for emergencies of varying scope and complexity (Braunbeck & Mastria, in this volume). Modularity may also provide capability to rapidly set up a control center in locations that lack native infrastructure. Hastily constructed networks that rely only on portable equipment operated by trained technicians can become centers for communication and coordination in otherwise isolated regions (Gibbons, in this volume). By maintaining portable communication capacity, governments and nonprofit organizations can dramatically improve responders' awareness of needs, resources, and potential partners. This communication and logistics support improves the ability to coordinate resource flows, human services, and other life-saving interventions following a disaster. Because many local and faith-based groups are too small to maintain their own communication and logistics support systems, these become crucial roles for government and other large responders.

Technology Choice and Implementation

Compatible, accessible, functional communication technology can facilitate coordinated action in what would otherwise be isolated pockets of chaos. When multiple agencies, community groups, and nonprofit organizations are trying to respond to crises, they must be able to integrate their efforts, share information, and distribute resources sensibly. Telephones may not work, cellular phone systems may overload, and internet resources may be unavailable due to power failure. In these situations, amateur radio may provide reliable communication among respondents, and hastily formed networks may be assembled by rescue teams to enable crucial information flows (Gibbons, in this volume). Technological designs that build continuous feedback loops between responders and the environment enable informed decision making (Comfort, in this volume).

How can we effectively combine centralized information processing—the necessary system overview—with rapid information sharing at the local level? The goal is to gather information from all parts of the system, synthesize and analyze it, and report to operatives as rapidly as possible in a continuous loop (Comfort, in this volume). This center-to-periphery loop adds an overview of the system to information that is shared directly among responders. When both are in place, the likelihood of successful decision making and coordination increases.

Braunbeck and Mastria (in this volume) identify several aspects of technology that support a common operational picture, or shared understanding of the situation. To be useful in disasters, standardized tracking and communication technology must be able to operate reliably when normal infrastructure is not functioning. We need a system that can operate in conjunction with various existing telecommunications infrastructures but can also operate independent of them. Radio frequency identification (RFID) chips, coupled with universal product code (UPC) stickers, already support logistics for many large businesses. Implemented by military or other large government organizations, integrated logistics systems can provide enormous benefits at all levels of disaster response. By labeling all resources at the warehouse, the routing of each shipment can be easily monitored, and the information can be fed into centralized databases. From there, information can be distributed to people in the field, keeping them apprised of current and expected resource arrivals. Integration of asset tracking with satellite communications throughout the supply chain could streamline resource coordination and delivery that are vital when preparing or responding to a disaster.

Logistics tracking is a crucial element of any crisis response system (Gibbons, in this volume), with potential to support success or precipitate failure. Braunbeck and Mastria (in this volume) explain how and why a properly designed logistical framework increases the effectiveness of a crisis response system. To be successful, a logistics support system should be "built on the concepts of open architecture, reliable asset visibility, and operational security," and modeled on existing systems employed by technologically advanced military organizations (Braunbeck & Mastria, in this volume). Along these lines, Wescott identifies logistics support from the U.S. Navy as the "most immediately useful assistance provided in Aceh" following the 2004 tsunami. He argues that complete, coordinated knowledge among responders builds the likelihood of success.

Integrating Nonprofit Organizations, Volunteers, and Businesses Into Disaster Response and Recovery Systems

Collaboration between government and communities is crucial for rapid deployment of help and for timely information sharing that enables disaster response and follow-up (Comfort, in this volume; Wescott, in this volume). Community involvement and resource management increases the number of positive interventions, reduces negative behaviors, and supports the quality of response following a disaster (Seifert, in this volume). While large nonprofit organizations and external rescue forces often bring resources and expertise into a disaster area, they may be dependent on local groups for knowledge of the context and language (Comfort, in this volume). This interdependence creates a demand for communication and coordination among very different organizations that may have largely incompatible structures, values, and practices. Comfort (in this volume) emphasizes the importance of establishing inclusive communication networks, and she argues that the time to do this is before a disaster strikes.

Although many government agencies and some nonprofit organizations overlook the value of volunteers, the majority of rescues that occur in disaster situations are accomplished by community members who are not affiliated with a formal response organization (Seifert, in this volume). By integrating as many local organizations and qualified individuals as possible into disaster planning, we can increase the likelihood of effective response to a major emergency. At the individual level, this means issuing practical information, encouraging appropriate precautions, and training volunteers so they will be able to serve under disaster circumstances. At the organization level, it means planning coordination and support mechanisms that will include all potential contributors to the response and recovery efforts.

Preexisting ties, compatible training, effective communication channels, and ability to obtain a broad view of needs and resources underlie the success of multiparty disaster responses (Gibbons, in this volume). Relationships among first responders support organizational memory and facilitate decision making under extreme emergencies (Seifert, in this volume). They build transactive memory that supports task coordination, and they build positive attitudes that enable resource sharing and cooperative action (Gibbons, in this volume). Networks of relationships among responders carry information, support joint efforts, and sustain members that may be cut off from more formal information and resource transfer mechanisms. To be ready for disaster, these networks should be established before a disaster occurs, and they should include both front line workers and administrative/coordinating people (Gibbons, in this volume).

Training for disaster management yields the triple benefits of improved skills, stronger relationships, and greater confidence when disaster strikes (Seifert, in this volume). As organizational memory builds, the shared understandings of responders increase the likelihood of clear communication and successful problem solving under uncertain, unstable, or threatening circumstances.

Sometimes multiple entities attacking the same problem are restrained from cooperative interventions or subjected to increased danger because of communication problems. Radios that are not compatible, isolated groups that lack communication equipment, or interorganizational barriers can drastically reduce the overall effectiveness of response efforts. In contrast, pooling of communication and social network resources can increase efficiency and insure identification and response to high-priority needs. Seifert (in this volume) reports the story of New Zealand fire fighters and New Zealand's Civil Defence tackling six concurrent fires in a rural region. Dispatched by different organizations and lacking communication, they couldn't locate one another. Although both groups had radios, the fire fighters' radios were not working. Recognizing the possibility for increasing danger or disaster, the Civil Defence implemented emergency coordination measures as outlined in the Coordinated Incident Management System (CIMS). By assembling a team of representatives from the various organizations, pooling their communication resources, and transferring information through the network of responders, they were able to locate all of the firefighters and redistribute workers to better meet the demands of the situation. This ability to receive and distribute information from an overview position to people in the midst of the chaos greatly enhances performance at all levels of the response effort.

Economic Crises and Business Recovery

Crises are not restricted to storms, sicknesses, and terrorist attacks. Financial disasters can affect millions of people, decreasing quality of life, reducing access to food or medicine, and inciting criminal behavior. A financial crisis may be triggered by natural phenomena, such as drought or insect infestations. It may follow war, corruption in government, or ethnic feuding. When economic crisis affects a country or region, action may be warranted from local organizations, large banks, and the government. Even in a small-scale disaster, businesses, banks, and government may be able to work together to reestablish the local economy.

Business survival following a natural or man-made disaster may be aided by attributes of the business leaders and their organizational designs. Proactive behavior, risk-taking, creativity and innovation, autonomy, and competitive aggressiveness can influence new businesses' success (Lumpkin & Dess, 1996). Zolin and Kropp (in this volume) argue that many of these same attributes enable a business to survive and prosper during and after a disaster. Because disaster situations create new circumstances, resource shortages, and unanticipated demands, the entrepreneurial orientation provides a survival advantage. Proactive planning establishes a foundation for success in environments that suddenly become hostile. Creativity, innovation, and autonomy support rapid adjustment to changing circumstances. Finally, reasonable risk-taking and competitive aggressiveness enable leaders to take advantage of opportunities that arise as a result of the crisis (Zolin & Kropp, in this volume).

Economic crises can easily spread from one triggering point to many related industries or geographic regions. For example, in Southeast Asia during the late 1990s, financial crisis followed the Thai bhat's sudden drop in value. According to Wescott (in this volume), the crisis rapidly spread to other Asian countries, which responded with varying levels of success. Of particular interest for our purposes is the way in which successful responses were achieved. Wescott identifies several steps taken by the Asian Development Bank to stabilize economies in hard-hit nations. These included improving governance practices, increasing disclosure and transparency of information, and strengthening legal and regulatory frameworks in the financial sector. The goal for turning around a failing regional economy was to build (or rebuild) credible financial institutions and implement prudent regulation. These steps help restore investment flows and enhance the overall governance of resource allocation. In the short term, the goal was to combat shortages in access to health, education, and nutrition by creating partnerships between the government and voluntary organizations. For long-term recovery, new financial products that include an enhanced guarantee mechanism may be needed to catalyze private investment in crisis situations. Although globalization processes can exacerbate and spread regional financial crises, they can also support unified responses and proactive efforts to prevent future disasters (Wescott, in this volume).

RESPONSE SYSTEM DEVELOPMENT AND DESIGN

What can governmental entities, nonprofit organizations, community groups, businesses, and volunteers do to prepare for crisis emergencies? Based on the principles that we've discussed, several recommendations emerge. These are summarized in Figure 12.1.

Intraorganizational Design and Local Response Organizations

Flexibility, novelty-seeking, and freedom to deviate from standard operating procedures are necessary for successful crisis response. Within any organization, preparation for crisis should include rehearsals of a variety of emergency scenarios with a focus on readiness to adapt, not on memorization of specific routines. Organizational members should be informed about emergency communication procedures. Leaders should be encouraged to consider possible extreme situations when assessing their readiness to cope with a crisis. Over time, institutions and their leaders have the opportunity to improve early crisis management strategies by learning from their own and others' experiences. LaPorte (in this volume) argues that a focus on long-term, consistent, and reliable crisis response capacity must accompany any short-term disaster plan.

Response Partnerships and Interorganizational Design

Coordination and creative use of resources can be more important than the actual value of resources invested in crisis response. By planning for collaboration among organizations of different types and jurisdictions, we can build platforms for success. Development of appropriate technology for logistics and communication is fundamental preparation for a large-scale crisis. Explicit attention to benchmarking and technological compatibility among government agencies and major nonprofit organizations

Responder Factors ⟶	Quality of Response ⟶	Outcomes

Intraorganizational Design
Freedom to deviate from standard
  operating procedures
Internal coordination
Delegation of authority
Specialized teams that practice jointly
Norms that embrace uncertainty
Entrepreneurial orientation
Unconstrained observation and
  analysis process
Novelty-seeking by leaders

Local Response Organizations
Preparedness/training
Integration of local volunteers
Self-coordination mechanisms

Problem Diagnosis and Analysis
Broad search for facts, joint
  analysis by appropriate experts
Information transfer
Objective assessment by multiple
  unbiased parties
Creative problem solving

Short term Relief
Curtailment of disaster spread
  or acceleration
Preservation of life and
  property
Food
Shelter
Health care
Rebuilding

Response Partnerships
Readiness for collaboration (civil
  society, government, and business)
Learning, benchmarking
Volunteer coordination
Bridging political and administrative
  differences
Community involvement
Information sharing

Immediate Response
Situational awareness
Responder coordination
Efficient use of available resources
Capacity of local responders to act
  in isolation

Impact Reduction
Speed of intervention
Limitation of scope
Timely containment of losses

Inter-organizational Design
Cross-functional teams
Independent lateral communication
Common operating picture
Inclusive networks
Flexible, modular logistics
Crisis simulations to aid preparations

Financial Intervention
Disclosure
Regulation
Teach good practices
Support private investment

Long term Recovery
Resource Governance
  Credible financial institutions
  Prudent regulation
  Positive investment flows
Healthier Economy
Business reestablishment

Government/Military Response
Institutionalized flexibility in crisis
Rapid deployment of standing military
Logistics tracking and control
Broad participation in problem solving
Support for nonprofit organizations
  and businesses
Collaborative analysis and planning
Hierarchical control over execution
Inter-jurisdictional agreements

Recovery Management
Planning/preparation
Collaboration
Sustainability

Ongoing Crisis Readiness
Capacity for response to
  uncertain future events
Institutional policies that
  support rapid problem solving
Effective communication and
  coordination channels
Transactive memory
Institutional memory
Infrastructure for cross-border
  communication and
  coordination

Technology Use
Early warning systems
RFID asset tracking
Satellite coordination
Decentralized, redundant responder
  communication channels
Systemwide, centralized
  communication infrastructure

Figure 12.1.   Proactive preparation and design to improve response quality and
outcomes.

then assures that collaboration will be possible under extreme circumstances. Growth of responder networks that hold regular meetings to update communication channels, simulate crisis scenarios, and share new ideas can build social structures to undergird joint response. These networks should include organizations that have disparate competencies and resources. An ideal network includes uncertainty- and disaster-competent (often nonprofit or military) organizations as well as organizations (often business, government, and community) that can provide infrastructure and other resources (Gibbons, in this volume). Finally, at the community level, volunteer registration, organization, and education can transform potential victims into potential responders.

Government/Military Response

Measures of governmental effectiveness should include capacity to address communicable crises. Emergency protocols and bureaucratic shortcuts need to be developed as part of governmental design to enable rapid switching from standard operations to flexible response. Clear interjurisdictional agreements and authorizations to take action in an emergency need to be developed. These should include a distinct role for military organizations, which often have superior skills and resources for dealing with uncertain, hostile environments. Finally, channels for cooperation with nonprofit organizations, businesses, and communities must be developed. These changes will require ongoing support from political and functional stakeholders.

LaPorte (in this volume) recommends that strategic planners incorporate provisions for crisis preparation and response, including maintenance of uncommitted leadership time, financial resources, and backups for core technical and operational systems. When planning for events that may arise from "social or political predators," he argues that institutions must go beyond fail safe designs to produce "predatory confounding systems." Although overseers of organizations and systems may be unable to anticipate and prepare for specific events, they can embed defenses against predator-instigated disasters within broader crisis management planning.

Technology Use

Integrated technology serves several purposes in crisis response. First, good warning systems can prevent losses. Second, satellite coordination remains feasible even when local power and communication lines are disrupted. Third, improved asset tracking and logistics maximize the use of available resources. Finally, adaptable communication networks can be designed to support centralized processing and broad distribution of information. By improving accuracy and dissemination of relevant information, appropriate use of technology increases capacity for large-scale interventions.

CONCLUSION

Successful crisis management planning depends on flexibility. When we prepare for crisis, we must develop the ability to adapt, to analyze, and to maintain rationality in circumstances that do not lend themselves to clear thinking and coordinated action. Preparation on the part of governments and organizations dedicated to disaster relief must include both internal and interorganizational coordination plans.

A systemic view of crisis management includes all stakeholders and draws them into the solution process. Adequate communication structures, cooperative agreements, logistics systems, and resource allocation processes create the foundation for effective response to a communicable crisis. A culture of readiness to accept change and think freely under environmental challenge increases the likelihood that individuals, organizations, and global coalitions will rise to that challenge.

REFERENCES

Ansell, C., & Gingrich, J. (2007). Emergent institutionalism: The UK's response to the BSE epidemic. In D. E. Gibbons (Ed.), *Communicable crises: Prevention, response and recovery in the global arena* (pp. 167-200). Charlotte, NC: Information Age.

Braunbeck, R. A., III, & Mastria, M. F. (2007). Technological transformation of logistics in support of crisis management. In D. E. Gibbons (Ed.), *Communicable crises: Prevention, response and recovery in the global arena* (pp. 45-80). Charlotte, NC: Information Age.

Bryant, T. J., Vertinsky, I., & Smart, C. (2007). Globalization and international communicable crises: A case study of SARS. In D. E. Gibbons (Ed.), *Communicable crises: Prevention, response and recovery in the global arena* (pp. 263-297). Charlotte, NC: Information Age.

Comfort, L. K. (2007). Asymmetric information processes in extreme events: The 26 December 2004 Sumatran earthquake and tsunami. In D. E. Gibbons (Ed.), *Communicable crises: Prevention, Response and Recovery in the global arena* (pp. 135-166). Charlotte, NC: Information Age.

Csete, M., & J.Doyle. (2004). *Bowties, metabolism, and disease.* Pasadena: California Institute of Technology. Preprint.

Gibbons, D. E. (2007). Maximizing the impact of disaster response by nonprofit organizations and volunteers. In D. E. Gibbons (Ed.), *Communicable crises: Prevention, response and recovery in the global arena* (pp. 201-238). Charlotte, NC: Information Age.

LaPorte, T. R. (2007). Anticipating rude surprises: Reflections on "Crisis Management" without end. In D. E. Gibbons (Ed.) *Communicable crises: Prevention, response and recovery in the global arena* (pp. 25-44). Charlotte, NC: Information Age.

Leonard, H. B., & Howitt, A. M. (2007). Governmental preparation for, and response to, major emergencies. In D. E. Gibbons (Ed.) *Communicable crises: Prevention, response and recovery in the global arena* (pp. 1-23). Charlotte, NC: Information Age.

Lumpkin, G. T., & Dess, G.G. (1996). Clarifying the entrepreneurial orientation construct and linking it to performance. *Academy of Management Review, 21,* 135-172.

U.S. Department of Homeland Security. (2004, March 1). *National incident management system.* Washington, DC: Author.

Roberts, A. (2007). Constraints on the U.S. Response to the 9/11 Attacks. In D. E. Gibbons (Ed.) *Communicable crises: Prevention, response and recovery in the global arena* (pp. 299-319). Charlotte, NC: Information Age.

Seifert, C. (2007). Improving disaster management through structured flexibility among frontline responders. In D. E. Gibbons (Ed.) *Communicable crises: Prevention, response and recovery in the global arena* (pp. 81-134). Charlotte, NC: Information Age.

Wescott, C. (2007). Support for crisis management in Asia-Pacific: Lessons from ADB in the past decade. In D. E. Gibbons (Ed.), *Communicable crises: Prevention, response and recovery in the global arena* (pp. 321-349). Charlotte, NC: Information Age.

The White House. (2006). *The federal response to Hurricane Katrina: Lessons learned, chapter 2.* Retrieved May 25, 2006, from http://www.whitehouse.gov/reports/katrina-lessons-learned

Zolin, R., & Kropp, F. (2007). Assisting business survival: How governments can help businesses weather a cataclysmic disaster. In D. E. Gibbons (Ed.), *Communicable crises: Prevention, response and recovery in the global arena* (pp. 239-262). Charlotte, NC: Information Age.

ABOUT THE AUTHORS

Christopher Ansell is an associate professor of political science at the University of California, Berkeley, where he teaches organization theory and public administration. Most recently, he is coeditor with David Vogel of *What's the Beef? The Contested Governance of European Food Safety* (MIT Press) and is currently at work on a book that develops a Pragmatist perspective on political institutions. He can be contacted at cansell@berkeley.edu.

Richard A. Braunbeck III, Lieutenant Commander, USN, received his BS in mechanical engineering from Old Dominion University (1995) and an MBA in logistics management from the Naval Postgraduate School in Monterey, CA (2006). He is currently assigned to the aircraft carrier USS Theodore Roosevelt, CVN 71 as the assistant maintenance officer. He can be contacted at rbraunbeck@sbcglobal.net.

Teri Jane Bryant received her MBA and doctorate from the University of British Columbia in Vancouver, Canada. Her research has focused on executive management and public policy issues in the Asia-Pacific, especially Japan, China, and Korea. A past president of the Japan Studies Association of Canada, she currently teaches at the Haskayne School of Business of the University of Calgary. She can be contacted at teri.bryant@haskayne.ucalgary.ca.

Louise K. Comfort is a professor of public and international affairs at the University of Pittsburgh. She teaches in the field of public policy analysis, information policy, organizational theory, and policy design and implementation. She holds degrees in political science from Macalester College (BA); University of California, Berkeley (MA), and Yale University (PhD). She is principal investigator, Interactive, Intelligent, Spatial Information System (IISIS) Project, 1994-present: (http://www.iisis.pitt.edu). She has served as principal investigator/project coordinator on 21 funded research projects; coinvestigator on seven funded research projects; team leader on two field research teams and team member on six field research teams. She has conducted field research on information processes in disaster operations following earthquakes in Mexico City, 1985; San Salvador, 1986; Ecuador, 1987; Whittier Narrows, California, 1987; Armenia, 1988; Loma Prieta, 1989; Costa Rica, 1991; Erzincan, Turkey, 1992, Killari, India, 1993; Northridge, California, 1994, Hanshin, Japan, 1995, Izmit, Turkey, 1999, Nantou County, Taiwan, 1999, Gujarat, India, 2001, and Sumatra and Thailand, 2005.

Recent publications related to disaster management include: "Risk, Security and Disaster Management," 2005 for *Annual Review of Political Science*; "Coordination in Rapidly Evolving Systems: The Role of Information," 2004, with Kilkon Ko and Adam Zagorecki for *American Behavioral Scientist*; "Coordination in Complex Systems: Increasing Efficiency in Disaster Mitigation and Response" 2004, with Mark Dunn, David Johnson, Adam Zagorecki, and Robert Skertich for *International Journal of Emergency Management*; and "Fragility in Disaster Response: Hurricane Katrina," 2005, published by Berkeley Electronic Press (http://www.bepress.com/cgi). She can be contacted at comfort@gspia.pitt.edu.

Deborah E. Gibbons is an assistant professor at the Graduate School of Business and Public Policy in the Naval Postgraduate School. She received her PhD in organizational behavior and theory from Carnegie Mellon University. Her research addresses antecedents, attributes, and outcomes of social networks at levels ranging from individual relationships through inter-organizational systems. Deborah has partnered with several public and private institutions to study effects of social relations and networks on cooperation, innovation, attitudes, and knowledge dissemination. Recently, she has expanded this work to assessment and development of community-based networks. She can be reached at deborah .gibbons@gmail.com.

Jane Gingrich is an assistant professor in political science at the University of Minnesota. She received her PhD from the University of California, Berkeley, in 2006. Her research interests focus primarily on reforms to social services in advanced industrial countries, particularly market-oriented reforms. She has previously authored work on the politics of decentralization and participatory governance (with Christopher Ansell). She can be contacted at jgingrich@berkeley.edu.

Arnold M. Howitt, a faculty member at the John F. Kennedy School of Government, Harvard University, is executive director of the Taubman Center for State and Local Government and codirects its research program on emergency preparedness and crisis management. From 1999-2003, he directed the Executive Session on Domestic Preparedness, sponsored by the U.S. Department of Justice, which conducted research on preparedness and worked closely with local, state, and federal officials in emergency management, public safety, law enforcement, and public health. He currently serves on a study panel of the Transportation Research Board/National Academies of Science on the role of transit in disaster evacuation and was a member of an Institute of Medicine/ National Academies panel on assessing the federal Metropolitan Medical Response System program. In the wake of the anthrax attacks in the United States, he served on the governor's bioterrorism coordinating council in Massachusetts (2002). Dr. Howitt speaks widely on related topics and has written a number of articles on emergency preparedness. He is coauthor and coeditor of *Countering Terrorism: Dimensions of Preparedness* (MIT Press, 2003) and a contributor to *Preparing for Terrorism: Tools for Evaluating the Metropolitan Medical Response System Program* (National Academies Press, 2002). He can be contacted at arnold_howitt@harvard.edu.

Fredric Kropp is an associate professor of marketing and entrepreneurship at the Fisher Graduate School of International Business, in the Monterey Institute of International Studies. He received his PhD in marketing from the University of Oregon, an MBA from the IBEAR Program at the University of Southern California, a master's degree in economics from Northeastern University, and a bachelor's degree in social science from Pratt Institute. Fredric has taught at Bond University, in Australia, the University of Oregon, and several other universities. In addition to extensive research in entrepreneurship, Fredric also conducts research in cross-cultural consumer behavior and marketing. He is working on a book that explores long-term changes in values. Prior to joining academia, Fredric was a consultant for Fortune 500 companies, such as General Electric and Hewlett-Packard, for government agencies, such as the Federal Aviation Administration and the Department of Energy, and numerous smaller start-up firms. He also was an executive vice-president for Texcom, an international specialty product placement company. He can be contacted at fredric.kropp@miis.edu.

Todd R. LaPorte is professor of political science at the University of California, Berkeley (1965-to present), where he was also associate director of the Institute of Governmental Studies (1973-88.) He received his BA from the University of Dubuque (IA) (1953); his MA and PhD from Stanford University (1962), and held faculty posts at the University of Southern California, and Stanford University as well as UCB. He teaches and publishes in the areas of organization theory, technology and politics and the organizational and decision-making dynamics of large, complex, technologically intensive organizations, as well as public attitudes toward advanced technologies, and the challenges of governance in a technological society. He was a principal of the Berkeley High Reliability Organization Project, a multidisciplinary team that studied the organizational aspects of safety-critical systems such as nuclear power, air traffic control, and nuclear aircraft carriers. His research concerns the evolution of large-scale organizations operating technologies demanding very high level of operating reliable (nearly failure-free) performance across a number of management generations, and the relationship of large-scale technical systems to political legitimacy. This took him to Los Alamos National Laboratory (1998-2003) examining the institutional challenges of multi-generation nuclear missions. Most recently, he has taken up questions of crisis management in the face of new types of threats emerging from our sustained engagement with radical Islam. In a parallel effort, he is examining the institutional evolution of a critical element in the nation's meteorological monitoring environment, the development of the National Polar-Orbiter Operational Environmental Satellite System.

He was a Fellow, Woodrow Wilson International Center for Scholars, Smithsonian Institution, and Research Fellow, Wissenschaftszentrum (Sciences Center)—Berlin and the Max Planck Institute for Social Research, Cologne. In 1985, he was elected to the National Academy of Public Administration. Service on editorial boards includes *Policy Sciences, Public Administration Review, Technology Studies, Journal of Contingencies and Crisis Management,* and the Steering Committee, Large Technical Systems International Study Group. He has been a member of the Board on Radioactive Waste Management, and served on panels of the Committee on Human Factors, and Transportation Research Board, National Academy of Sciences. He served on the Secretary of Energy Advisory Board, Department of Energy, and chaired its Task Force on Radioactive Waste Management, examining questions of institutional trustworthiness, and was on the Technical Review Committee, Nuclear Materials Technology Division, Los Alamos National Laboratory. He has also served as a member of: the Committee on Long Term Institutional Management of DOE Legacy Waste Sites: Phase Two; and the Committee on Principles and Operational Strategies for Staged Repository Systems, both of the Board on Radioactive Waste Management, The National Academies of Science (2001-2003). He has consulted with DOE's, Defense Nuclear Facilities Safety Board, and currently is a Faculty Affiliate, Decision Sciences Division, Los Alamos National Laboratory. He can be contacted at tlaporte@socrates.berkeley.edu.

Herman B. ("Dutch") Leonard is the George F. Baker, Jr. professor of public sector management at Harvard University's John F. Kennedy School of Government and the Eliot I. Snider and family professor of business administration at the Harvard Business School, where he also serves as the faculty cochair of the HBS Social Enterprise Initiative. He teaches extensively in executive programs at the Business School and the Kennedy School and around the world in the areas of crisis management and leadership. His work on leadership in crisis and in noncrisis situations encompasses general organizational strategy, advocacy and persuasion, innovation, creativity, and effective decision making. His work also includes nonprofit and social enterprise management, governance, performance management, corporate social responsibility, and strategic management, and he also works on issues in public and nonprofit sector finance. He is the author of *Checks Unbalanced: The Quiet Side of Public Spending* (1984), of *By Choice or By Chance: Tracking the Values in Massachusetts Public Spending* (1992), and (annually from 1994 through 1999) of *The Federal Budget and the States* (an annual report on the geographic distribution of federal spending and taxation). Professor Leonard is a member of the Board of Directors of Harvard Pilgrim Health Care, a 900,000-member Massachusetts HMO. He was for a decade a member of the board of directors of the Massachusetts Health and Educational Facilities Authority, was a member of the Board Of Directors of Civic Investments, and was a member of the U.S. Comptroller General's Research and Education Advisory Panel and of the Massachusetts Commission on Performance Enhancement. He has been a financial advisor to the Connecticut Governor's Office of Policy and Management, to the Massachusetts Turnpike Authority, and to the Central Artery-Third Harbor Tunnel Project. Professor Leonard was a member of the Governor's Council on Economic Policy for the State of Alaska, of the Governor's Advisory Council on Infrastructure in Massachusetts, and of the U.S. Senate Budget Committee's Private Sector Advisory Committee on Infrastructure. He served as chairman of the Massachusetts Governor's Task Force on Tuition Prepayment Plans, on the National Academy of Sciences Committees on National Urban Policy and on the Superconducting Supercollider, and on the New York City Comptroller's Debt Management Advisory Committee. In addition to his academic studies and teaching, he has been chief financial officer and chief executive officer of a human services agency and has served as a director of public, non-profit, and private sector organizations. He can be contacted at dutch_leonard@harvard.edu.

Michael F. Mastria, Captain, USMC, received his BS in marketing from the University of Maryland at College Park (1991) and a BS in accounting from the University of Maryland University College (2004). He holds an MBA in defense systems analysis from the Naval Postgraduate School in Monterey, CA (2006). He is currently assigned to the Economic Analysis Team, Marine Corps Systems Command, Headquarters Marine Corps, Quantico, VA. He can be contacted at mastriamf2004@yahoo.com.

Alasdair Roberts is an associate professor of public administration at the Maxwell School of Syracuse University. He is also an honorary senior research fellow of the School of Public Policy, University College London. He received his JD from the University of Toronto and his PhD from Harvard University. Professor Roberts' book, *Blacked Out: Government Secrecy in the Information Age*, was published in 2006. His Web site is http://www.aroberts.us.

Claudia Seifert earned her doctorate from the Department of Management, University of Otago, New Zealand. Her interests include research on organizational crises with a focus on theory building approaches to crisis-causal processes. She holds a master's of science in business management and administration from the Leipzig Graduate School of Management, Germany. She can be contacted at claudia.seifert@hhl.de.

Carolyne Smart is dean of the faculty of business administration at Simon Fraser University in Vancouver, British Columbia, Canada. A long-time professor with SFU Business, Carolyne has held a number of executive positions within the faculty. She is a professor of Strategy and her research in recent years has focused on women's entrepreneurship issues. She also has a long-standing interest in crisis management. Her most recent work examines the management of major public health crises and the significant strategic issues involved. Carolyne earned her PhD from the University of British Columbia. She may be contacted at smart@sfu.ca.

Fred Thompson was the founding editor of *International Public Management Journal*. He is the author of "Responsibility Budgeting at the Air Force Materiel Command," *Public Administration Review* (Jan/Feb 2006, with Michael Barzelay), *Reinventing the Pentagon* (1994, with LR Jones), *Digital State at the Leading Edge* (2007, with Sandy Borins, Ken Kernaghan, David Brown, Nick Bontis, and Perri 6) and over a hundred other books and articles in journals such as the *Academy of Management Review, Journal* *of Policy Analysis and Management, Public Choice,* and the *American Political Science Review.* He also recently edited the *Handbook of Public Finance and Public Ethics and Governance* (with Denis Saint Martin).

Fred has served as a contributing editor to *Policy Sciences* and *Journal of Comparative Policy Analysis,* and on more than a dozen other editorial boards, currently including, *Journal of Public Administration Research and Theory* and *Public Budgeting & Finance.* He is the recipient of PAR's Mosher Award, the NASPAA-ASPA Distinguished Research Award, and ABFM's Aaron B. Wildavsky Award for lifetime contributions to the field of public budgeting and finance. He recently served on the NRC-NIM's Committee on Accelerating the Research, Development, and Acquisition of Medical Countermeasures against Biological Warfare Agents and as a member of the United Nations Development Program's Blue Ribbon Commission on Macedonia. He has consulted on Treasury practice and policy in Ukraine, Georgia, and Armenia.

Fred is the Grace and Elmer Goudy Professor of Public Management and Policy, Geo. M. Atkinson Graduate School of Management, Willamette University, Salem OR.

Ilan Vertinsky is the Vinod Sood professor and the director of the Center of International Business Studies at the Sauder School of Business at the University of British Columbia. He has published more than 250 journal papers, book chapters, books, and monographs. He is interested in crisis management and prevention. His Web site is http://strategy.sauder.ubc.ca/vertinsky.

Clay G. Wescott is director of the Asia-Pacific Governance Institute. Previously, he was principal regional cooperation specialist for the Asian Development Bank, deputy director for the Management Development and Governance Division of the United Nations Development Program, and director of the finance, management, and economics division of Development Alternatives, Inc. in Washington, DC. He has degrees in government from Harvard College (AB, 1968, Magna cum Laude), and Boston University (PhD, 1980), and is an editorial board member of the *International Public Management Journal,* the *International Public Management Review,* and *Comparative Technology Transfer and Society.* He can be contacted at clay.wescott@gmail.com.

Roxanne Zolin is an assistant professor in the Graduate School of Business and Public Policy at the Naval Postgraduate School, Monterey, California. She received her PhD and a master's degree in sociology from Stanford University, an MBA from Monash University, Melbourne, and a bachelor of business (management) from Queensland Institute of Technology, Australia. Roxanne operated her own businesses for over 15 years in software development and enterprise development, helping start over 500 new businesses. Previously Roxanne was national marketing manager for Myer's Stores, Australia. Her promotions won national awards from the Sales Promotion Association of Australia. Roxanne's research focuses on issues of organizational design and trust at the intersection of entrepreneurship and government. Current projects include evaluation of government programs designed to facilitate entrepreneurship, organizational design to minimize the risk of forward forces, and facilitation of business disaster survival. She can be contacted at rvzolin@nps.edu.